MW01622949

Bringing War Back In

Bringing War Back In provides a new theory connecting war and state formation that incorporates the contingency of warfare and the effects of war outcomes in the long run. The book demonstrates that international wars in nineteenth-century Latin America triggered state-building, that the outcomes of those wars affected the legitimacy and continuity of such efforts, and that the relative capacity of states in this region today continues to reflect those distant processes. Combining comparative historical analysis with cutting edge social science methods, the book provides a comprehensive picture of state formation in nineteenth-century Latin America that is compelling for readers across disciplines, breathes new life into bellicist approaches to state formation, and offers a novel framework to explain variation in state capacity across the world.

LUIS L. SCHENONI is Lecturer (Assistant Professor) and Director of the Security Studies Programme at the Department of Political Science, University College London. His work on war and the state has been published, by the *American Journal of Political Science* and International Security, among others.

Bringing War Back In

Victory, Defeat, and the State in Nineteenth-Century Latin America

LUIS L. SCHENONI
University College London

Shaftesbury Road, Cambridge CB2 8EA, United Kingdom

One Liberty Plaza, 20th Floor, New York, NY 10006, USA

477 Williamstown Road, Port Melbourne, VIC 3207, Australia

314–321, 3rd Floor, Plot 3, Splendor Forum, Jasola District Centre, New Delhi – 110025, India

103 Penang Road, #05–06/07, Visioncrest Commercial, Singapore 238467

Cambridge University Press is part of Cambridge University Press & Assessment, a department of the University of Cambridge.

We share the University's mission to contribute to society through the pursuit of education, learning and research at the highest international levels of excellence.

www.cambridge.org
Information on this title: www.cambridge.org/9781009442138

DOI: 10.1017/9781009442145

When citing this work, please include a reference to the DOI 10.1017/9781009442145

First published 2024

A catalogue record for this publication is available from the British Library.

Library of Congress Cataloging-in-Publication Data
NAMES: Schenoni, Luis L., author.
TITLE: Bringing war back in : victory, defeat, and the state in nineteenth-century Latin America / Luis L. Schenoni.
OTHER TITLES: Victory, defeat, and the state in nineteenth-century Latin America
DESCRIPTION: [New York] : Cambridge University Press, [2024] | Includes bibliographical references and index.
IDENTIFIERS: LCCN 2023053962 (print) | LCCN 2023053963 (ebook) | ISBN 9781009442138 (hardback) | ISBN 9781009442152 (paperback) | ISBN 9781009442145 (ebook)
SUBJECTS: LCSH: Latin America–Politics and government–1830-1948. | Politics and war–Latin America–History–19th century. | Nation-building–Latin America–History–19th century. | Latin America–History, Military–19th century.
CLASSIFICATION: LCC F1413 .S345 2024 (print) | LCC F1413 (ebook) | DDC 980.03/4–dc23/eng/20240215
LC record available at https://lccn.loc.gov/2023053962
LC ebook record available at https://lccn.loc.gov/2023053963

ISBN 978-1-009-44213-8 Hardback

War is father of all, and king of all. He renders some gods, others men; he makes some slaves, others free.

Heraclitus

Contents

Figures

Tables

Preface

As a Latin American with a penchant for history, I always wanted to write a book that could summarize the conclusions of my considerable pondering about the region's past in a few brushstrokes. As a political scientist with Weberian influences, I tried to do so while contributing to our understanding of how war affects political development from the unique perspective that Latin America provides. *Bringing War Back In* is the result of these converging ambitions.

Although every attempt to synthesize the political history of entire regions in a single theoretical narrative is bound to fail, such simplifications are both inevitable and necessary. Paraphrasing my compatriot Jorge Luis Borges, it would be useless to draw a map of Latin America that reproduced the region in its exact size and shape. The key to social scientific knowledge is our ability to draw abstract yet informative conceptual maps that encapsulate the most important features of history, allowing others to navigate its vastness.

Bringing War Back In intends to draw such a simplified map of Latin American history. In doing so it unveils a pattern neglected by most: a pattern that shows that war made the Latin American state as we know it.

The goal of this book is illustrated by the cover. Wassily Kandinsky's *Sea Battle*, like history, is difficult to decipher even after a long examination. Only when the observer is pointed to the masts, the sails, and the cannon blasts, does the image fall into place. I hope this work will have a similar effect on my readers, most of whom have already been exposed to Latin American history: that once the role played by war is revealed, they will be unable to unsee it.

The handful of social science methods I use in *Bringing War Back In* uncover only a few patterns and colors of history. Overall I paint a rather abstract picture of how war made the state in Latin America. A lot is missing. A lot is only sketched out. The merits of this fragmentary picture are to be decided, ultimately, by its capacity to provide a new framework and new ways of thinking about the problem of the state, both in Latin America and beyond.

Acknowledgments

As most other books, *Bringing War Back In* is the product of a long and exciting intellectual journey, which I started as a doctoral student at the University of Notre Dame, continued as a postdoctoral researcher at the University of Konstanz, and finished as a faculty member at University College London. Along the way, countless people offered their support, guidance, and encouragement, and I could easily devote as many words as this book contains to thank them.

Leading to a book there is always a serendipitous discovery. In my case it took place during a superb graduate course on the state taught by Victoria Tin-bor Hui. A student of Charles Tilly herself, and having shown how war made the state in historical China, Victoria challenged me to apply this theory to my own region back in the spring of 2017. The main ideas in this book emerged back then – albeit in very raw form – and benefited from three workshops at Notre Dame's Political Science Department, as well as two generous grants by the Kellogg Institute. Among my esteemed colleagues on the Ph.D. program, Juan Albarracín, Omar Coronel, Laura Gamboa, Benjamín Garcia Holgado, Camilo Nieto-Matiz, Ana Petrova, Natan Skigin, Lucía Tiscornia, and Jake Turner offered outstanding support. Ted Beatty, Michael Coppedge, Eugene Gholz, Jeffrey Harden, Scott Mainwaring, Virginia Oliveros, Victoria Paniagua, Joe Parent, Luis Schiumerini, Jazmin Sierra, and Guillermo Trejo are among the faculty members and visiting scholars who generously offered constructive criticism.

Eventually the project became my dissertation, and my committee members played a prominent role in its development. Michael Desch, the most bellicist of them all, was a great source of encouragement and wisdom. James Mahoney provided many of the intellectual foundations on which this book rests and a very high bar to measure my work against. Aníbal Pérez Liñán played a critical role in integrating the conceptual and methodological components of this book and offered the valuable view of someone who, like myself, was born into Latin America and its history. To Victoria – who ended up on my committee as well – I owe the initial intellectual spark and the intuitions that guided my research. It is fitting that she carries the name of the state-making goddess inspiring this book. Finally, to my Ph.D. advisor, Gary Goertz, I owe a most special debt of gratitude for his dedicated mentorship and earnest friendship and for challenging me to produce an ambitious multi-method dissertation.

At some point the ideas in this book grew legs and ventured beyond the confines of the Notre Dame campus. I presented the argument at the Comparative Historical Social Science Conference at Northwestern University and the Institute for Qualitative and Multi-Method Research at Syracuse University in 2018, where Andrés Mejía Acosta, Nicolás Albertoni, Rodrigo Barrenechea, Robert Braun, Laura García, and Emilio Lehouq provided feedback that helped me prepare a first round of fieldwork at the National Archives in College Park. In early 2019 I continued the archival work at the British National Archives at Kew Gardens, thanks to Raúl Aldaz's hospitality.

In parallel, I started a series of travels to archives in Latin America. In a 2018 visit to the Catholic University of Chile, I was kindly hosted by Francisco Urdinez and benefited from conversations with him and Joaquín Fermandois, María Huidobro, Nicole Jenne, Sabine Kurtenbach, Detlef Nolte, José Frank Ragas, Carsten-Andreas Schulz, Elvira Lopez Taverne, and Pablo Whipple. In a 2019 visit to the University of São Paulo and the Getúlio Vargas Foundation, I was welcomed by Matias Spektor and Pedro Feliú and received valuable insights from them and from Eduardo Mello, Umberto Mignozzetti, Amancio Oliveira, Janina Onuki, Oliver Stuenkel, and Paula Vedoveli. Later in that same year, I gave talks at the Monterrey Institute of Technology and the Center for Research and Teaching in Economics (CIDE), where Gabriel Aguilera López, Juan Carlos Cobián, Ignacio Irazuzta, Pablo Kalamanovitz, Gerardo Maldonado, and Lorena Ruano provided encouraging comments.

Argentina was a frequent destination throughout the project. I visited my hometown, Buenos Aires, every year from 2019 to 2022, and each year I presented a different chapter at either Torcuato Di Tella University or the University of San Andrés. There I received insightful comments from Victoria Baratta, Juan Battaleme, Ariel Coremberg, Jennifer Cyr, Sebastián Etchemendy, Germán Feierherd, Carlos Freytes, Jorge Garzón, Carlos Gervasoni, Marcelo Leiras, Ignacio Mamone, Oscar Oszlak, Francisco Santibañez, Andrés Schipani, Hayley Stevenson, and Javier Zelaznik, among many others.

Clearly, being in frequent contact with Latin American scholars was key to ponder on their views, and spending time in libraries across the region was necessary to properly represent the rich historiography of these countries. Yet a series of presentations at the Wissenschaftszentrum Berlin für Sozialforschung, the University of Oxford, and Salamanca University provided opportunities to cross the pond as well. In those occasions great feedback from David Doyle, Agustín Ferraro, Ezequiel González Ocantos, Macartan Humphreys, Naomi

Ichino, Frederike Louise Kelle, Francisco Sánchez, Mariano Torcal, and Michael Zürn convinced me that *Bringing War Back In* had to engage with the European conversation as well.

The postdoc I started in 2020 at the University of Konstanz provided just this opportunity and a unique chance to reengage the scholarship of Otto Hintze, Max Weber, and their contemporaries. There I received support from a Young Scholar grant for the development of this book. Lorenz Ade, Carsten Heine, Camila Montero, Gabriel Schroeder, and Hannes Zehnle helped greatly with data collection during those years, and Leslie Fischer was essential for a review of the scholarship of those classical bellicist theorists.

As I worked on classical bellicist theory, I also presented my work at the German Institute for Global and Area Studies – where I received valuable feedback from Belén Gonzalez, Felix Haass, Desiree Reder, Adam Scharpf, Christian von Soest, and Eric Stollenwerk – and the London School of Economics, the University of Oxford, and Cambridge University. My gratitude goes to Chris Alden, Toby Dodge, Mette Eilstrup-Sangiovanni, Anna Getmansky, Francesca Lessa, Giovanni Mantilla, Eduardo Posada Carbó, Diego Sanchez Ancochea, Jason Sharman, Karen Smith, and Peter Trubowitz for their insights.

Eventually I joined the Department of Political Science at University College London (UCL), where my colleagues Rod Abouharb, Kristin Bakke, Inken von Borzyskowski, Zeynep Bulutgil, Nils Metternich, Neil Mitchell, Katerina Tertytchnaya, and Manuel Vogt saved this book from intellectual fatigue with their fresh insights and camaraderie. They were the third stroke of luck that I needed to wrap up the project. At UCL I also benefited from a British Academy grant, two departmental grants, and the work of my research assistants, Pablo Torres and Carolina Zacatto. In this final phase I presented these ideas at the Institut Barcelona d'Estudis Internacionals, Université Laval, the University of California in San Diego, and Radboud University. Among others, Andrea Bianculli, Erik Gartzke, Matthew Singer, Matthias Vom Hau, and Nina Wiesehomeier offered valuable feedback on those occasions.

Several chapters and analyses that now form part of the book were presented at multiple meetings, including those of the American Political Science Association (APSA) and the Latin American Studies Association (LASA) between 2019 and 2023, as well as at the 2021 Midwest Political Science Association (MPSA) meeting. Juan Pablo Balán, Lars-Erik Cederman, Rafael Ch, Sebastián Mazzuca, Karl Müller-Crepon, Victoria Murillo, Oriol Sabaté, Juan Pablo Scarfi, Jan Teorell, and Alex Weisiger offered valuable feedback. Esteban Alfaro Salas, Nicolas Beckmann, Manuel Cabal, Miguel Centeno, Paul Diehl, Douglas Lemke, Tom Long, Camilo López Burian, Andrés Malamud, Victor Mijares, Andrew Owsiak, Hillel Soifer, Nicolás Somma, and Arturo Valenzuela, among others, also contributed significantly to the development of the book through email exchanges and conversations. In this regard, I would like to thank Raúl Madrid especially. After many conversations throughout the years, Raúl and I have collaborated in building a Latin American Revolts Dataset (LARD), which we are now expanding with Guillermo Kreiman and Paola Galano Toro and could be partly incorporated into the empirics of this final manuscript. At the last stages the book also benefited greatly from the input of my commissioning editor, Rachel Blaifeder, and the copyediting of Catherine Dunn.

To conclude, I would like to thank my family. My parents, Graciela and Luis Eduardo, always encouraged me to pursue my vocation and provided unwavering support throughout this journey. Together with my younger brother and best friend, Mariano, they were a sturdy anchor in the midst of raging storms. Although they would have preferred to have me around for the Sunday *asado*, they selflessly encouraged my adventures and dreams every step of the way. This book is dedicated to them.

PART I

PUZZLE AND ARGUMENT

1

Overview

According to a family story, in 1859 two Italian brothers arrived in Argentina escaping poverty and conflict. One travel-weary brother stayed in Buenos Aires, while the other decided to make a last effort and continue upriver to Asunción, Paraguay. This neighboring country had been politically stable for decades, was known for its superior security forces and public education system, and flourished economically. In Argentina, on the other hand, the rulers of Buenos Aires refused to accept the constitution and the authority of the capital, Paraná. Tellingly, after the defeat of Buenos Aires in the Battle of Cepeda, the son of the Paraguayan president had arrived to mediate the Argentine conflict. Considering the relative ability of these governments to enforce rules and deliver services – their *state capacity*, in short – it would have seemed the second brother had made a smarter choice by continuing his travels.

By the end of that century, however, Argentina had consolidated a strong state that could exert authority across its expansive territory and population. Buenos Aires, now its capital, received more immigrants than any other port in the Americas besides New York and was the hub of a dense railway network transporting agricultural produce sufficient to generate a per capita product comparable to that of the United Kingdom. Literacy rates in Argentina were now the highest in Latin America and twice as high as in Paraguay, where the state had become weak, plunging the country into poverty and conflict. Because the gap between Argentina and Paraguay persisted, my great-great-grandfather who stayed in Buenos Aires proved lucky, but why?

State capacity is fundamental for development and peace. Capable states able to enforce the rule of law and provide public goods and services can set countries on a stable path toward economic growth and social development. Yet, as the preceding paragraphs illustrate, state capacity varies widely across countries, even within the same world region. What causes these disparities in state capacity? And why do countries – sometimes even neighbors such as Paraguay and Argentina – switch places, change trajectories, and find themselves on opposing state-building paths?

According to the existing literature, one factor stands out as the most powerful explanation for state building: war (Tilly, 1990). To mobilize armies, states had to concentrate authority, collect tribute, suppress dissidents, and develop efficient administrations. Even public roads, education, and healthcare seem to have originated primarily for the fulfillment of military needs. In the process of fighting wars, states became stronger, and those states that failed to keep up disappeared. This logic is quite compelling, and, indeed, it does not take an encyclopedic knowledge of history to see the pattern. Normative concerns aside, it must be admitted that, intuitively, if violence is not the mother of the state, it must have been at least its midwife. Those who fail to see this should be considered, as Max Weber (1994, 362) put it, political infants.

Yet history is not so linear. Wars are full of examples of aborted mobilization, weaker states resulting victorious, and losers that fail to disappear. In the War of the Triple Alliance (1864–1870), for example, notwithstanding its superior state capacity and greater wartime mobilization, and having almost forced Argentina, Brazil, and Uruguay to surrender after the Battle of Curupaití, Paraguay was finally defeated. However, despite having lost what was arguably the deadliest international war in the entire world from 1815 to 1914, the Paraguayan state did not disappear. What is more, the divergence in state capacity between the contenders did not develop during the war, nor immediately after Paraguay's demographic collapse and occupation, but during the several decades that followed. In short, the most capable state lost the war, the state that lost the war survived, and most of the effects of warfare on the state capacity of both the losers and the winners manifested long after the war. These three observations do not fit our current understanding of how wars make states and require a new theory that emphasizes the contingency of war outcomes and how they affect the state in a postwar period.

In this book, I advance a more complete understanding of how wars make states, which allows me to make sense of cases that seemed hitherto unexplained. I argue that states facing the threat of international war are forced to mobilize large armies and strengthen their bureaucracy to support them, but this is only an initial phase of a longer and more complex process triggered by war. Wartime state building develops in a state of exception, its long-term stability being therefore contingent on the unforeseeable outcome of the war. Winners will typically consolidate and enlarge their wartime political coalitions and see their states strengthen in the postwar era. Losers, on the other hand, will usually see their statist politicians, bureaucrats, and military officers fall into disgrace and, with those actors excluded from power, will experience protracted declines in state capacity.

This logic provides a better explanation for the relative capacity of states across the world today, the rigidity of state-building trajectories, and why historical turns happened when they did. It also illuminates why (re)building states after military defeat has been difficult, why defeated states can only be rebuilt in the presence of new external threats, and why the wars of today – where both winners and losers survive – have contradictory effects on state building. Most importantly, however, this book brings war back into our discussions about the state in a world where war itself is back.

The idea that "war made the state and the state made war" (Tilly, 1975, 42), on which I elaborate, has been largely validated by research in fields ranging from anthropology to economic theory. Variations of this approach have been used to explain state formation from prehistory (Carneiro, 1970; Boix, 2015) to modern Europe (Downing, 1993; Ertman, 1997), including the oldest state alive, China, which was born out of a period of "warring states" in the third century BC (Hui, 2005; see also Fukuyama, 2011; Dincecco and Wang, 2018). In regions like Africa (Bates, 2014; Herbst, 2014; Sharman, 2023), Latin America (Centeno, 2002; Thies, 2005), and parts of the Middle East (Lustick, 1997; Jung, 2006) less stringent interstate warfare seems to account for the existence of relatively less capable states (Migdal, 1988, 273; Desch, 1996, 242). No competing explanation of state formation comes even close in empirical breadth and explanatory power.

Nonetheless, this *bellicist theory* of state formation has faced considerable criticism as of late. These objections have been normative, logical, and empirical. Normatively, bellicism has been called into question by scholars who see it as a Trojan horse for social Darwinism and fascist ideas.[1] Logically, it has been criticized for extrapolating from the history of successful states in a functionalistic manner and without paying much attention to agency and contingency.[2] Perhaps, more importantly, many have convincingly argued that the theory can no longer account for empirical trends in a world where conquest has virtually disappeared (Tir et al., 1998; Zacher, 2001, 218; Atzili, 2011, 24), states rarely die (Lake and O'Mahony, 2004, 703; Fazal, 2011, 29), wars cannot be won anymore (Chowdhury, 2018), and warfare has become infrequent (Taylor and Botea, 2008, 33; Goertz et al., 2016, 92; Lee, 2020, 6–8).

Put together, these normative, logical, and empirical concerns have operated as a strong argument against the theory, facilitating its portrayal

[1] The normative critique often focuses on the political and propagandistic tergiversations of this so-called German school of state formation (Mann, 1988, 2; Hui, 2017, 268). Pieces that seem to suggest the virtues of letting states fight (Herbst, 2004, 316; see also Cohen et al., 1981) continue to give bellicists a bad name.

[2] Some versions of the paradigm asking "Why did the European states eventually converge on different variants of the national states?" (Tilly, 1990, 5) are arguably guilty of extrapolating back into the past based on the end result of the process. This is exacerbated when the paradigm takes the form of a natural selection argument (Spruyt, 2001) whereby only the states that developed large armies, efficient bureaucracies, and extractive capacities were able to survive. When (unobservable) "dead" states are assumed to have lacked the attributes of the survivors, bellicists incur an *ad hoc ergo propter hoc* fallacy (Spruyt, 2017, 86), which craves to be amended by (re)incorporating contingency – in particular that of the outcomes of war – into the theory.

as "Eurocentric and inapplicable to non-European contexts" (Hui, 2017, 268). For most social scientists nowadays, wars might have formed states in modern Europe, but "state formation and warfare did not go hand in hand in other regions" (Grzymala-Busse, 2023, 1). Such a situation urgently calls for a serious reevaluation of bellicist theory.

In this book I go back to the classics of bellicist theory and extract two main lessons from them, which will hopefully breathe new life into the paradigm: These scholars did not endorse an evolutionary understanding of bellicist theory that requires states to fight to the death (Sharman, 2015, 201) and were mainly concerned with the lingering effects of the outcomes of war in a postwar period. Their more holistic version of the theory integrated pre and postwar dynamics in a way that resolves all three issues highlighted earlier and explains patterns of state formation even in what is considered to be the hardest case for the theory: Latin America.

1.1 THE STATE OF BELLICIST THEORY IN LATIN AMERICA

Latin America has become the poster child of the "antibellicist" camp in the state formation literature. Paradoxically born out of pioneering works exploring the nuances of the European-inspired bellicist paradigm in the region (Centeno, 1997, 2002; López-Alves, 2000; Thies, 2005), more recent studies of Latin America have taken a strong stance against the paradigm, arguing that war could be financed by external substitutes for domestic taxation (Queralt, 2022) and was not frequent or severe enough to have produced state capacity (Kurtz, 2013; Saylor, 2014; Soifer, 2015; Mazzuca, 2021).

In his celebrated work *Latin American State Building in Comparative Perspective*, Marcus Kurtz (2013, 35) set up the foundations of this new anti-bellicist consensus, discarding the "conflict-centric" approach to Latin America on the basis that the region features only "some interstate conflict of a severe character." Instead he proposes that state building in the nineteenth century depended on the existence of free labor and the elites' disposition to delegate political authority.

In *State Building in Boom Times*, Ryan Saylor (2014, 52) also argues that "outside of Europe the relative lack of warfare has severed a chief pathway to new state capacity." He observes that Latin America "features little warfare" and did not develop extractive capacity because states "could generally fund their activities with foreign aid and loans" and "depended on customs duties for revenue." He alternatively suggests that states are born out of commodity booms and specific patterns of elite competition.

Hillel Soifer also dismisses the "bellic approach" in *State Building in Latin America*, concluding that "in trying to understand variation among Latin American states in the nineteenth century the overall absence of war in the region cannot be helpful" (Soifer, 2015, 18). Since "war did not make states in Latin America" (Soifer, 2015, 202) and "is better seen as a crucible that *tests* the state rather than as a forge that *makes* the state" (Soifer, 2015, 235),[3] he proposes that liberal elites in countries with a single urban hub consolidated states when the deployment of central bureaucrats to the peripheries was possible.

In his groundbreaking work *Latecomer State Formation*, Sebastián Mazzuca (2021, 38) writes that "Kurtz, Saylor, and Soifer rightly dismiss the war-led path." For him, while "western European leaders of state formation were war-makers, their Latin American counterparts should be considered market-makers" (Mazzuca, 2021, 8). Since the *Pax Britannica* eliminated international anarchy, a key scope condition of bellicist theory, to understand "trade-led" state building, Mazzuca points instead to the preferences and strategies of commercial elites, *caudillos*, and political parties.

Finally, in *Pawned States*, Didac Queralt (2022) builds strongly on evidence from nineteenth-century Latin America to conclude that war did not make states in world peripheries during the nineteenth century. Although he differentiates himself by admitting that "war in the nineteenth century in the global periphery was bigger, longer, and more frequent than usually understood" (Queralt, 2022, 2), he reproduces the antibellicist argument according to which "it did not translate into stronger states because it was disproportionally financed with external capital" (Queralt, 2022, 13).

These authors illustrate a new consensus (Thies, 2022) that has been highly influential on those who discard the value of bellicist theory beyond Europe (Hui, 2017; Grzymala-Busse, 2023) but does little justice to studies of Latin America, the findings of which align with the theory (Thies, 2005; Cardenas, 2010) and suggest that we should give war a chance.

One problem of the current antibellicist consensus is that it builds strongly on the *argumentum ab auctoritate*, according to which "[Miguel] Centeno has shown that this [bellicist] argument does not apply to Latin America" (Soifer, 2015, 204; see also Kurtz, 2013, 22; Saylor, 2014, 52; Mazzuca, 2021, 36; Queralt, 2022, 5). Indeed, Centeno (2002) popularized the idea that the current relative weakness of Latin American states can be explained by the absence of total warfare in the region and the use of custom tariffs and external financial assistance – instead of income taxes – to fight limited wars (see also Rouquié, 1987, 61; Centeno, 1997). Yet his reference to total warfare and income taxes suggests Centeno wrote mostly with the twentieth century in mind. In fact, he explicitly recognizes the importance of war in explaining intraregional variation in state capacity during the nineteenth century.[4] Put differently, Centeno focused on a broad regional comparison with Europe across two centuries, but he never discarded war as an important factor

3 Emphases present in the original.

4 For example, he admits that "war did have some of the expected results in Latin America. As in Europe, it often led to the destruction of the losing side. At least in three cases (Peru in the 1880s, Mexico in the 1850s, and Paraguay after 1870) war led to the practical elimination of the state as an entity. Among winners (Argentina and Brazil in the 1870s) war led to an increase in the

driving differences *within* Latin America, particularly during the nineteenth century.

This observation gains greater significance when considering that the entire body of academic literature on state formation in Latin America uniformly identifies the late nineteenth century as the pivotal period for the emergence and consolidation of national states in this region (Oszlak, 1981, 19). This historical turn was pioneered by James Mahoney (2003, 2010), who noted that the ranking of social and economic development in Latin America changed notably in the late nineteenth century and rigidified afterward. Indeed, the authors of the recent Latin American antibellicist consensus start with the observation that "the hierarchies of political development" in the region have "remained strikingly stable over long periods of time" (Kurtz, 2013, 16–17) and refer to the nineteenth century as a critical juncture that set states onto path-dependent trajectories (see also Soifer, 2015, 15; Mazzuca, 2021, 40).

Current scholarship has missed three important implications of this historical insight, all of which point to war as a key variable explaining state formation. First, the weaker states of today might be the result of the conspicuous absence of international wars during the twentieth century (Mares, 2001; Kacowicz, 2005; Schenoni et al., 2023), a period when the regional state capacity ranking effectively froze. Second, state formation took place precisely during the nineteenth century – in particular its second half – when we know the most severe wars were waged.[5] Third, this scholarship fails to explain the fundamental inversion of the state capacity ranking that sent colonial centers to the bottom and peripheries to the top. Mahoney (2010, 190) himself suggested that to completely resolve this puzzle, "attention in the search for causes must gravitate toward interstate warfare." Following this advice, one cannot help but notice that the victorious and defeated states of nineteenth-century wars are those at the top and bottom of the current state capacity ranking, respectively.

These macroscopic observations indicate that war may have played a crucial role in the emergence of the Latin American state.

size of government" (Centeno, 1997, 1571). Centeno then adds Chile in the 1880s as another example of victory leading to state formation.

5 Some scholars seem to consider that "Latin American wars were more frequent in the first decades after independence than in the second half of the nineteenth century, which was the key period of state formation in the region" (Mazzuca, 2021, 37), but this is wrong. Two-thirds of the wars and militarized interstate disputes in the region concentrate on the second half of the century. Then "one sees patterns of peace and war, intervention, territorial predation, alliances, arms-racing, and power-balancing quite similar to those found in eighteenth-century Europe" (Holsti, 1996, 153). Severe episodes like the Franco-Mexican War (1862–1867), the Paraguayan War (1864–1870), and the War of the Pacific (1879–1884) demonstrate the collapse of the *Pax Britannica* precisely during the key period of state formation in the region.

1.2 BELLICIST THEORY REDUX

Many authors have noted that the reason why the bellicist approach seems unfit to explain Latin America and most of the world beyond modern Europe has to stem from an underspecification of its causal mechanisms (Spruyt, 2017, 89) and scope conditions (Vu, 2010, 153; Hui, 2017, 272).

In the social sciences, two distinct interpretations of bellicist theory are prevalent. The first one suggests that international wars lead to the expansion of armies and bureaucracies. In this view, "*preparation for war* has been the great state building activity" (Tilly, 1975, 42).[6] The second interpretation proposes that "the mechanism of state formation resides solely in the selection of the weaker actor" (Kurtz, 2013, 32; Saylor, 2014, 200; Soifer, 2015, 233; Spruyt, 2017, 78), suggesting an evolutionist interpretation of state formation.

In short, current understandings of the theory focus on a *prewar phase* and see the outcomes of war as mere selection mechanisms. This has naturally narrowed the scope of the theory to very competitive international environments characterized by mass mobilization and frequent state death. It has also concealed how defeat and victory might have lingering effects well into the *postwar phase* by virtue of mechanisms other than selection – for example, mechanisms of adaptation and reproduction. In other words, both interpretations miss the importance of the long-term, enduring effects of the outcomes of international war. This has become a significant blind spot in the literature.

Moreover, scholars who see international war as a mechanism for killing weak states assume that war outcomes are determined by previous state capacity. This belief is wrong. Not only do major theories of war agree that "in the whole range of human activities, war most closely resembles a game of cards" (Clausewitz, 1984, 86; see Waltz, 1979, 61; Fearon, 1995, 387) but in light of empirical evidence it seems clear that state capacity does not define the outcomes of international wars (see Reiter and Stam, 2002, 58–83; Arreguin-Toft, 2005, 1–18; Biddle, 2006, 20–25; Henderson and Bayer, 2013). The fact that weak states frequently win wars simultaneously deals a fatal blow to the evolutionary understanding of bellicist theory and hints at a possible solution to the infinite regress in Tilly's famous aphorism, "Which came first, states or wars?" (Centeno, 2002, 106). While the "War made the state and the state made war" dictum is explicitly circular, the exogeneity of war outcomes is an aspect of warfare that can be leveraged in research design.

Incorporating this insight, I propose that international wars have a compound effect on state formation. In a prewar phase and when hostilities are taking place, mobilization boosts state building by triggering the extraction–coercion cycle and the development of some wartime institutions – in particular

[6] The emphasis is mine. Note that bellicist theory is about international wars and not civil wars (Slater, 2010, 37; Schwartz, 2023, 10). This distinction is fundamentally about the type and range of mobilization they produce and is elaborated on further in Section 2.2.

those necessary to support a standing army – but the institutionalization of state building does not take place during such a state of exception, in which the law is put on hold and institutionalization remains rather thin.

Only the contingent outcomes of war can determine whether those temporary policies become institutionalized after the critical juncture and reverberate in the postwar phase. While victory consolidates the wartime political coalitions and allows these actors to continue building the state, defeat delegitimizes them, leading to the demise of wartime institutions and setting losers on a path of state weakening.

Victorious states will no doubt demilitarize once the war is over. The size of their armies is likely to shrink, and rulers will find it difficult to impose new taxes now the foreign threat has receded. However, having demonstrated their capacity to protect their citizens and property, winning states will quickly consolidate their treasuries, establish the authority of their armed forces, and widen the ranks of the state-building party, which will have overwhelming popular support. Such states will thus continue on a trajectory characterized by the provision of new services, bureaucratic expansion, and centralization.

Defeated states, on the other hand, will be severely impaired and weakened. Immediately after a war, defeated states that survive can suffer from destruction, pillaging, territorial loss, and foreign occupation. Yet once they have reached rock bottom and the storm has cleared, their capacity to enforce rules and deliver services could be restored if it was not for the collapse of state authority and the mechanisms that reproduce it. Citizens will distrust the inefficient state that could not protect them and make the military and bureaucracy responsible for their misfortune, siding instead with those who opposed the war effort and state building in the first place. Unless a new threat arises, making the state an absolute necessity again, defeated states will thus shrink and decentralize.

Notably, this story should hold in environments where states systematically survive and in those where they are more likely to die, explaining the divergent evolution of Latin American states while continuing to fit the modern European experience.

My understanding of these mechanisms is very much aligned with the process that the forefathers of bellicist theory had in mind. Pioneers of this paradigm such as Max Weber (1978) and Otto Hintze (1975) hardly mention selection mechanisms while putting a strong emphasis on military success and how victory made the state. Although the emphasis on the outcomes of war declined in his later works, Charles Tilly (1975, 42) himself ended the paragraph featuring his famous dictum by mentioning "*success* in war" as an important mechanism of state formation (see also Lemke and Carter, 2016, 501). Because the focus on postwar dynamics is particularly prominent in these classical works, I refer to my interpretation of the theory as *classical bellicist theory*.

Intuitive as it is, classical bellicist theory – in particular the idea that states lose capacity after defeat – faced the challenge of two apparent outliers in the postwar era: Germany and Japan. However, under the magnifying glass it is clear that such historical anomalies – and a few others such as Prussia after Jena–Auerstedt – can be explained by the effects of subsequent mobilization. Like Prussia in 1806, the German and Japanese states collapsed in 1945 and only regenerated years later with the support of the victor, because a new conflict found them on the frontline. Most states, however, rarely have the opportunity to rise from the ashes of devastating defeats via immediate postwar mobilization and are more commonly set onto declining, state-weakening trajectories – if they survive at all.

The long-term institutional effects of war outcomes that classical bellicists were interested in are far more consequential for the state than the short-term, material consequences of war. While defeat can be immediately devastating for a country, Germany and Japan illustrate how the rapid regeneration of a pro-state coalition can prevent the dismantling of key state institutions and set a country back onto a trajectory of state building and development. Yet when defeat not only entails human and material loss but the discrediting of the state as an ideal, together with the dissolution of the political coalition that supports it, the dismantling of state institutions is likely to take place, leading to a rigid trajectory of state weakening and the development problems associated with this.

When understood in this holistic form, the theory sheds new light on how international wars of the past can explain path-dependent state-building trajectories now, affecting economic development, democracy, and other relevant outcomes (Mahoney, 2010). Because wars can both strengthen and weaken the state depending on their highly contingent outcomes, this interpretation of the theory provides a solid response to normative and functionalist critiques. Normatively, it sees war as a double-edged sword, both creating and destroying states. Logically, it does not assume that states strengthened because they performed a specific function (Spruyt, 2017) and points to agency and contingency as key forces determining both the shape of state institutions and their success. As Michael Mann (1993, 55) puts it, classical bellicist theory provides "an institutional, not a functional definition of the state," which is very much in line with historical institutionalism.

Moreover, the incorporation of postwar trends *can* "explain the development of states in a world in which war to the death is not the state of nature" (Kurtz, 2013, 35) by focusing on the effect of minor shocks such as those produced by militarized interstate disputes short of war, or providing some insights into the marginal mutations that take place when competitive pressure is milder, as in the case of rivalries (Thies, 2005). When such nuances are incorporated, classical bellicist theory improves our understanding of state formation in nineteenth-century Latin America in at least three ways.

To begin with, the focus on the outcomes of war easily satisfies the "Occam's razor" criterion, as it offers the most parsimonious explanation for the diversity in state capacity trajectories. In contrast, other competing explanations rely on complex and convoluted sequences, which often involve the interplay of two or more factors. Moreover, while previous authors need to differentiate between state formation and state building (Mazzuca, 2021, 6) and state-building emergence from state-building consolidation (Soifer, 2015, 3) – each requiring specific explanations – I show how the outcomes of war can account for all these (largely endogenous) processes simultaneously.

Second, this explanation is more broadly applicable than any other alternative. While the current antibellicist consensus builds upon small comparisons, providing idiosyncratic stories that are modest in scope, my version of classical bellicist theory should generalize to all of Latin America and, ultimately, all other states as well, both contemporarily and historically.

Third, the outcomes of war not only outperform but also precede and ostensibly cause some prominent factors in the literature, such as the effective exploitation of economic booms (Saylor, 2014), the pro-state ideology and the policies of governing elites (Mahoney, 2010; Kurtz, 2013), the consolidation of ports, lords, and parties (Mazzuca, 2021), and even the preeminence of one city over others (Soifer, 2015). Once we take into account the structural shocks that wars brought about in Latin American societies, it becomes apparent that victory in war could plausibly account for all of these outcomes.[7]

1.3 CASE SELECTION AND CHAPTER LAYOUT

A specter has been haunting bellicism: the specter of Europe. A curious feature of the theory that posits a connection between war and state formation is that it has been primarily developed and refined by analyzing a region where most defeated states were effectively winnowed out by war – sometimes along with their historical records. Although reconstructing the history of defeated states is not impossible (Ziblatt, 2008; see also Davies, 2011), the postwar trajectory of

7 The Chilean nitrate boom and the Argentine wool boom, to name two examples, were admittedly key to the formation of those states, yet victory in a previous war played a large role in allowing those states to capture and control those resources. Paraguay was similarly blessed with a yerba mate, timber, and cotton boom and Peru enjoyed both a guano and a nitrate boom, yet they lost their window of opportunity due to their inability to exploit those resources after military defeat. In a similar fashion, the consolidation of state-building elites supporting *paz y administración* in Argentina and *ordem e progresso* in Brazil, similarly to the Mexican *científicos*, can also be understood as a product of victory in war. The *civilistas* in Peru illustrate the fate of state-building elites who were defeated in war. The liberal parties in Mexico and Colombia, as well as the Uruguayan *doctores* – an alliance of urban elites from the traditional *blanco* and *colorado* parties – were all admittedly central to state formation, but they were also strengthened by international victories against France, Ecuador, and Argentina, respectively. Even apparently structural factors like the preeminence of one urban hub over others were often a consequence of war. While the deadlock between Alajuela, Heredia, and San José in Costa Rica, for example, was definitively brought to an end by a war, the struggle between Leon and Managua continued to feature prominently in defeated Nicaragua and in countries that did not feature significant international warfare, such as Colombia. These points are all further discussed in Part III of this book.

states that died in war can only be pictured counterfactually. This has resulted in a skewed European sample, which overrepresents victorious states while severely underrepresenting losers. Tilly (1975, 38) himself was aware that in Europe, "the disproportionate distribution of success and failure puts us in the unpleasant situation of dealing with an experience in which most of the cases are negative, while only the positive cases are well documented."[8]

Although this is an unresolvable problem for Europe, the postwar trajectories of defeated states can be systematically studied in regions or historical periods where both losers and winners tended to survive. Nineteenth-century Latin America is an ideal setting in which to examine this phenomenon.

On the one hand, nineteenth-century Latin America looked much like Europe in many respects. First, because the norms that regulate interstate conflict were still in their infancy at the time, borders were changing and contested, and great power intervention acted as a destabilizing rather than a pacifying factor, the nineteenth century provides many examples of severe and enduring warfare. Second, since other parts of the world were either colonized or organized as suzerain systems involving a mix of states and prestate polities, Latin America was probably the only region with a European-like system of sovereign states at the time.[9] Third, initial conditions for state-making in Latin America – for example, certain levels of cultural homogeneity amongst elites and a relatively uniform institutional background inherited from the collapse of previous empires (Tilly, 1975, 18–21) – were akin to those in Europe, not least because Latin American states were built on the ruins of European colonial institutions. In all these ways, Latin America can be seen as a useful mirror of Europe (Centeno and López-Alves, 2001).

On the other hand, nineteenth-century Latin America presents one key difference: While Europe had around 200 sovereign entities at the end of the Napoleonic Wars, and this number was reduced tenfold by the end of the century, the eight sovereign entities in Latin America that were born after

8 Early Tilly seems to be especially preoccupied with the problem of looking only at victorious states: "The tension appears in the very selection of a small number of West European states still existing in the nineteenth and twentieth centuries for comparison. For England, France, and even Spain are survivors of a ruthless competition in which most contenders lost. The Europe of 1500 included some five hundred more or less independent political units, the Europe of 1900 about twenty-five. The German state did not exist in 1500, or even in 1800. Comparing the histories of France, Germany, Spain, Belgium, and England (or, for that matter, any other set of Western European countries) for illumination of the process of state-making weights the whole inquiry toward a certain kind of outcome which was, in fact, quite rare. Having chosen to deal comparatively with those large historical experiences, we never quite escaped the difficulty" (Tilly, 1975, 15). In previous pages, he had already highlighted the fact that "as seen from 1600 or so, the development of the state in Europe was very contingent; many aspiring states crumpled and fell along the way" (Tilly, 1975, 7).

9 Recent studies that try to generalize to the Global South in the nineteenth century include states – for example, China, Ethiopia, Japan, and Siam (Queralt, 2022) – that were surrounded by European colonies and did not conform to a clustered Westphalian subsystem in the way Europe and the Americas did.

the Wars of Independence expanded into more than twenty during the same period.[10] Although leaders feared their states would be taken over by colonial powers and neighbors, the absorption of smaller states rarely took place, even after military defeat.[11] The systematic survival of defeated states means that, contrary to the European case, we can observe and compare postwar phases in both winners and losers of all Latin American wars. Moreover, the fact that virtually no international war has taken place in Latin America since the Chaco War (1932–1935) – and even this war was anomalous in the twentieth century (Butt, 2013) – means that we can look at the very long-term effects of wars in the distant past, with these effects remaining uninfluenced by subsequent competition in the region.[12]

Latin America should be considered a puzzle for bellicist theory, given the evolutionary understanding of the theory that prevails in the current literature (Rapport, 2015). If this amended theory proves to be a good fit for Latin America while continuing to work for other regions and eras, the impact of this study should prove critical for the paradigm (Gerring and Cojocaru, 2016).

This book is divided into three parts. This part lays the conceptual and theoretical groundwork for the rest of the study. After this introductory chapter, Chapter 2 discusses the mechanisms by which war makes states before, during, and after war, according to classical bellicist theory. First, I introduce the theory in the abstract and by reference to how Max Weber, Otto Hintze, and other forefathers of the bellicist approach pictured the formation of the first states. Second, I use the more recent tools and insights of historical institutionalism and the comparative historical approach to lay out the main concepts and stages in the theory, situating it historically in the modern context, and with reference to the national state. Third, I offer a detailed description of the actors, processes, and institutions that would have been relevant in nineteenth-century Latin America, discussing the validity of state capacity indicators and providing concrete observational expectations to test the theory against.

Although the purpose of this book is to explain variation in state capacity *within* Latin America, in Chapter 3 I provide some comparisons between

[10] The proliferation of national states was mostly due to secessions like those of Uruguay (1828) and the Dominican Republic (1848) and to the breakup of federations like Great Colombia (1831) and Central America (1841).

[11] The few exceptions seem to be quasi-states often lacking international recognition, for example, the Confederation of the Equator (1824–1825), Los Altos (1838–1840), the Miskito Kingdom (1844–1860), the Argentine Confederation (1853–1861), the Republic of Piratini (1836–1845), the Republic of the Rio Grande (1840), and the Republic of Yucatán (1841–1848); see Mazzuca (2021) for a deeper discussion. It is likely that many other cases of de facto sovereignty are retrospectively overlooked, but in general these short-lived experiences would be better conceptualized as having died in secessionist civil war rather than in international war due to the comparatively limited dimensions of state mobilization to suppress them.

[12] As we will see, the sequencing of wars and intense rivalries confounds the effects of previous warfare, rendering cases such as Germany – and previously Prussia – particularly difficult to interpret.

Latin America and Europe, which are necessary to give context. The purpose of this chapter is fourfold. First, I aim to show that although comparisons between Europe and Latin America are impossible before the independence of the Iberian colonies gave birth to Latin American states, the evolution of Latin American colonial institutions was shaped by warfare both in Europe and on the peripheries of European empires. Second, I review basic descriptive statistics that challenge the idea of Latin America as a pacific international environment in the nineteenth century and help me identify a subset of cases of severe warfare that will be the focus of an in-depth historical analysis of the mechanisms behind classical bellicist theory in Part III of the book. Third, I document the fact that despite the formation of a norm of territorial integrity in Latin America, territorial conquest was prevalent until the end of the nineteenth century. Fourth, this chapter compares Europe and Latin America with regard to the modes of war financing and tax structures in the nineteenth century, showing that the state capacity gap between the two regions was small before World War I and that states financed war in roughly similar ways.

The rest of the book tests the observational expectations of classical bellicist theory using a multimethod inference strategy that combines different forms of cross-case and within-case analysis (Goertz, 2017, 5). Given the interdisciplinary nature of studies on state formation, I employ a diverse range of methodologies to make my argument more compelling and persuasive for a broad range of audiences and cultures (Goertz and Mahoney, 2012) within the social sciences.

Part II looks at variation in state building within Latin America. Because states "appear in clusters, and usually form systems" (Tilly, 1990, 4), this part looks at the entirety of the Latin American interstate system,[13] combining a traditional comparative historical approach with statistical approaches that are relatively new to the literature (Thies, 2022).[14]

In Chapter 4 I explore whether preparation for war in Latin America triggered bellicist dynamics. One of the key tenets of the antibellicist consensus is that wartime mobilization in Latin America was financed through external sources – customs revenue and foreign loans – allowing rulers to avoid domestic taxation and confrontation with entrenched patrimonial interests. However, a systematic analysis of historical statistical data ranging from 1830 to 1913 and covering the entirety of the region demonstrates that, in the wake of a foreign threat, access to external resources actually decreased – ostensibly due

13 Like Mazzuca (2021) and Centeno (2002), I believe in the necessity of discussing the region as a whole, given the selection issues that arise when one focuses on a small subset of cases, as do Kurtz (2013), Saylor (2014), and Soifer (2015).

14 Cameron Thies (2005) tests the bellicist argument statistically in Latin America but does so for the twentieth century. Didac Queralt (2022) does apply regression-type analyses to nineteenth-century data but does so comparing very different regions and excluding some Latin American cases. The statistical approach in this book is more precise in terms of regional scope – exploring more meaningful variation – and focuses on a time-frame of especial interest for bellicist theory.

to blockades and sovereign defaults – while the likelihood of domestic taxation and internal conflict increased, just as bellicist theory would expect.

In Chapter 5 I turn from preparation for war to the long-term effects of the outcomes of war in the postwar period. To do so, I apply a different set of statistical techniques to a similar cross-national time-series dataset covering all of Latin America and zooming in to the period of state building when the big Latin American wars took place (1865–1913). The results of these analyses show that the state capacity trajectories of winners and losers diverged when the outcomes of war were revealed, and the gap between them grew with time, just as classical bellicist theory predicts.

In Chapter 6 I replicate previous comparative historical analyses that try to explain the Latin American ranking of state capacity by the year 1900. Since state building relatively froze in the twentieth century, authors agree that explaining the cross-national variation at that point amounts to explaining the similar variation we see now (see Mahoney, 2003; Soifer, 2015, 205). By replicating these analyses and introducing my variable of interest, I show that a state's martial record at that point in time predicts the Latin American hierarchy better than any other alternative explanations, even when we use the methodological approaches and designs of previous scholarship. In this chapter I also discuss how international wars coincide with shifts in trajectories of state capacity and better explain their precise timing. This sets the stage for some longitudinal analyses in my case study chapters.

After examining the entire region through various statistical and Boolean methods, Part III analyzes individual cases by looking at three different subregions. While previous analyses uncover broad trends and provide a strong basis for generalization, the case studies in this part confirm that the mechanisms outlined in the theory are present in virtually all the cases when they are considered separately and in greater historical detail.

The selected cases represent the most intense and enduring examples of warfare in the nineteenth century. Thus the mechanisms of classical bellicist theory should be clearly evident in them. This allows me to conduct within-case analyses, observing how warfare affected individual countries, as well as small-n cross-case comparisons that contrast winners and losers. Historical sources quoted in this part of the book test expectations at the level of concrete causal processes that are difficult to incorporate into statistical analyses and allow me to discard theories that, unlike bellicist theory, clearly do not fit certain cases.

My detailed examination of the historiographies of these wars reveals that secondary sources are often biased and tainted by nationalism.[15] For this

[15] Just to give an example, Argentine historiography tends to misrepresent embarrassing events like an outright invasion of Uruguay and a defeat against the army of Brazil as a civil war, denying the very international dimension of these processes. Another common tendency is that of victorious states to downplay the historical importance of a military victory and represent it retrospectively as a predictable outcome, while defeated states tend to put considerable weight

reason I rely on a critical comparative understanding of secondary sources that considers the historiography of every country involved in the conflict. I then complement this with primary sources, leveraging months of original archival work at the American and British National Archives. For all major wars I analyze, my interpretation of events is fundamentally based on my reading of first-hand accounts by American and British diplomats deployed to these countries at the time, which provide a more impartial representation of the events as they were seen by contemporaries. It is against this nuanced understanding that I evaluate the accuracy of key expectations of classical bellicist theory, such as the preferences of central and peripheral elites or the contingency of battles and their domestic effects.

Part III is divided into three chapters. In Chapter 7 a detailed analysis is presented of the River Plate basin, comprising Argentina, Brazil, Paraguay, and Uruguay, with a specific focus on the Paraguayan War and a brief detour to cover the Great Siege of Montevideo. Similarly, in Chapter 8 an in-depth examination is undertaken of countries in the South Pacific, including Bolivia, Chile, and Peru, with a particular emphasis on the War of the Pacific. Finally Chapter 9 concentrates mainly on Mexican history, with a focus on the Mexican–American War and the Second Franco-Mexican War, along with a brief digression to discuss William Walker's attempted invasion of Central America.

The chapter structure allows me to illustrate, albeit summarily, how the systematically positive outcomes of war can explain all cases of high state capacity in Latin America: Chile, Costa Rica, and Uruguay. Analytical historical narratives are offered for cases that experienced a mix of victory and defeat, such as Argentina, Brazil, and Mexico, and three cases of losers that experienced an abrupt decline in state capacity: Bolivia, Paraguay, and Peru. Although it is quite clear how these nine countries fit the expectations of the theory in a correlational sense, the case studies will make a much more compelling case for a causal association.

The downside of a case selection strategy based on wars is that countries that did not experience major international warfare – Colombia, Ecuador, Venezuela, and most of Central America – are not dealt with individually or in any detail. To compensate for their absence in the case study chapters, I refer to these countries in several examples throughout the book. When possible, I also document that these countries did not experience a sudden expansion of their armies and bureaucracies, nor the drastic partisan or financial consequences related to war outcomes, and therefore followed a relatively flat and stable state capacity trend, remaining roughly in the middle of the Latin American ranking throughout the century – just as classical bellicist theory would predict.

on those events as detrimental to their development and blame the defeat – by no means predictable – for their misfortunes.

My case studies systematically demonstrate how the rise of external threats triggered a coercion–extraction cycle. They also illustrate the fragile domestic equilibria during wartime and how the thick fog that covers all wars made the outcome of these conflagrations essentially unpredictable for contemporary observers. Finally, they show how defeat and victory affected state capacity by weakening or strengthening, respectively, nationalist parties and the military. By identifying critical actors and institutions and offering a detailed account of causal processes, these amount to a thorough evaluation of the theory almost case by case. Because "national states always appear in competition with each other" (Tilly, 1990, 23), directly comparing contenders during wars also proves effective in illustrating concomitant mobilization and the contrasting fates of losers and winners after wars by mirroring their histories.

In relation to other potential explanations, these case studies allow me to focus on concrete, temporally bounded causal processes (Collier et al., 2004) and show that other factors are either epiphenomenal to war dynamics – for example, how elite cohesion, economic booms, party consolidation, and so on happen after victory – or are simply nonconcurrent with temporal changes in state-building trajectories. In other words, the case studies in this book are not mere illustrations of causal mechanisms. These small-n cross-case comparisons and within-case process-tracing exercises analyze alternative hypotheses as well.

The richness of the cross-national analyses and case studies is boosted by the level of detail of the theory itself, which renders multiple observational expectations ranging from long-term state capacity trends in victors and losers to changes in the preferences of actors immediately after a battle is won or lost. Let us then delve into what classical bellicist theory is and how it can enhance our understanding of war-making as state-making.

2

Classical Bellicist Theory

Assuming our intuitions are correct and variation in state capacity across Latin America can be explained by war, why have scholars missed this so far? The reason seems to be a lack of fit between the dynamics of state formation in Latin America and two partial representations of bellicist theory. One of them focuses on war outcomes as a selection mechanism. The other looks at preparation for war but neglects war outcomes. It is worth reviewing them briefly.

Some scholars represent bellicist theory as working only in stringent environments where states that fail to win wars are out-selected by them (Elias, 2000, 269; Sharman, 2015; Spruyt, 2017). The well-known high survival rate of Latin American states automatically renders this representation of the theory inapplicable. Latin Americanists have applied this knowledge retrospectively to argue that "threats to the *survival* of the state" (Soifer, 2015, 233) were not pressing, and thus "*survival* has demanded neither the erection of probing fiscal institutions nor the supply of plentiful public goods" (Saylor, 2014, 200).[1] These conclusions are controversial because, unlike us, rulers in nineteenth-century Latin America were fairly concerned about the survival of their incipient independent projects and developed a strong norm of nonintervention to protect their sovereignty against European powers trying to reconquer the region, as well as against invasions of the United States and Latin American neighbors (Schenoni et al., 2023). Yet while these actors might have feared state death, it continues to be factually true that a "selection mechanism" (Kurtz, 2013, 32–34) was not present in Latin America.

Figure 2.1 shows the understanding of bellicist theory based purely on a selection or evolutionary logic. The y-axis represents levels of state capacity. Time is represented on the x-axis and illustrates a continuum ranging from

[1] The emphases are mine.

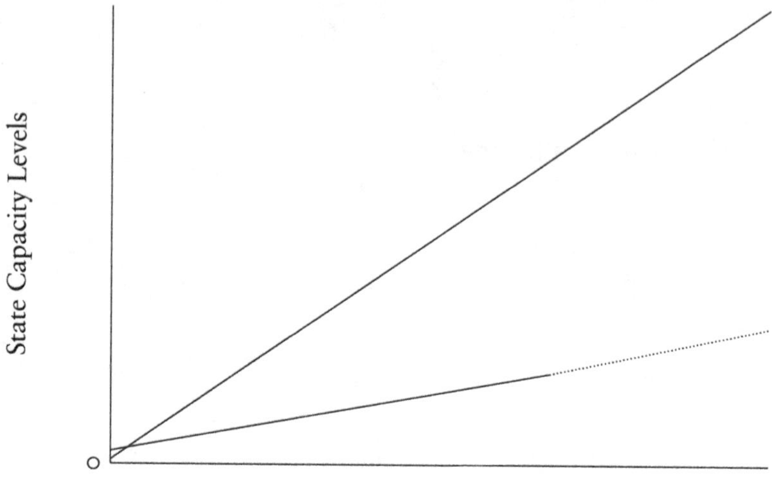

FIGURE 2.1 Selection logic

peace or no threat through a prewar/war context to a postwar phase. The death of the losing state is represented by a dotted line showing the postwar trend it would have followed. Note that war here is a simple mechanism of out-selection and has no effect on state capacity trends.

This Darwinian interpretation of bellicist theory incorrectly assumes strong states win wars (Arreguin-Toft, 2005) and does not work in places like Latin America, where defeated states tend to survive wars. Even recent analyses of European state formation have come to discard this interpretation (Abramson, 2017; Cederman et al., 2023; Grzymala-Busse, 2023).

Instead, most bellicist scholars today propose that foreign threats justify the mobilization of societal resources, prompting the expansion – sometimes territorial but also bureaucratic (Figueroa, 2023) – of the state. The elimination of weak states does not play any role here. The focus shifts to a prewar phase, where preparation for war makes the state (Desch, 1996, 243). According to this understanding, preparation for war generates a swell in public expenditure via a "displacement effect" but when foreign threats recede, society has no need to support further state expansion, and levels of state capacity stabilize by virtue of a "ratchet effect" (Peacock and Wiseman, 1967; Porter, 1994; Kiser and Linton, 2001; Scheve and Stasavage, 2012).

Figure 2.2 represents the "preparation for war" logic. According to this alternative understanding, contenders produce state capacity as they prepare to fight, but both winners and losers halt the process once the struggle is over. Since it is the threat of war that causes state capacity to increase, the end of the war eliminates this causal force independently of its outcome.

This understanding of bellicist theory paints a particularly rosy picture for defeated states. Even if defeated states survive wars most of the time, it is

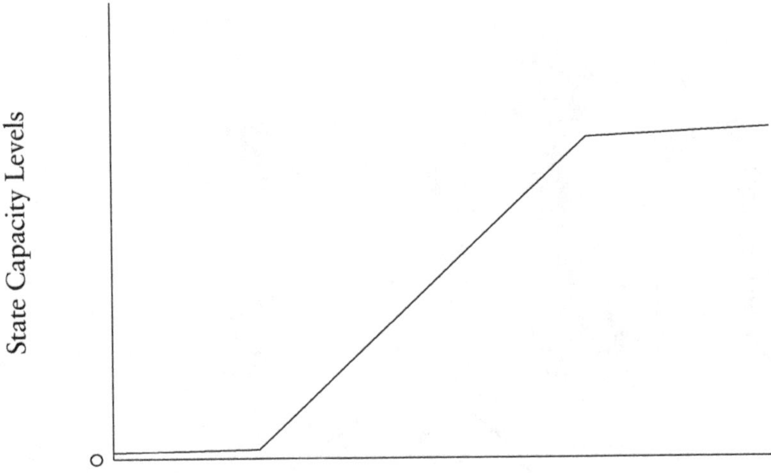

FIGURE 2.2 Preparation for war logic

unlikely that they will stabilize at the same state capacity levels as victors. Furthermore, because the expectation is that all contenders will be affected equally and during a delimited period of time, the preparation for war logic struggles to account for the kind of intraregional variation we see in Latin America and elsewhere in the world, and it fails to explain variation in state capacity levels that takes place during peaceful periods.

To solve this puzzle, I return to the classics of bellicist theory, which propose a more holistic approach combining both prewar and postwar phases into a single overarching theory. In a nutshell, state building is triggered by war, but the outcomes of war determine whether those dynamics are reproduced or dismantled in the longer term. This explains why surviving losers in Latin America subsequently lost state capacity while winners accumulated it.

The importance of the postwar phase is implicit in the literature. For example, an early work by Tilly (1975, 42) mentions "success in war" as the mechanism of war-led state formation but does not expand on it. A later book by Tilly (1990, 14) then shifts more clearly to a view of "preparation for war" as instrumental in state formation, but he still recognizes that "states that lost wars commonly contracted" (Tilly, 1990, 28). In this way, the importance of victory and defeat is always hinted at but never fully fleshed out.[2]

Figure 2.3 presents the basic predictions of classical bellicist theory. This original understanding of the theory accepts the existence of prewar mechanisms that boost state capacity but changes the observational

2 More recently studies on civil war (Walter, 1997; Wallensteen, 2015) and regime survival (de Mesquita et al., 1992; Lachapelle et al., 2020; Levitsky and Way, 2022), and their intersection (Lyons, 2016; Martin, 2022) have elaborated on a link between military victory and postwar stability along the lines of the classical bellicist argument.

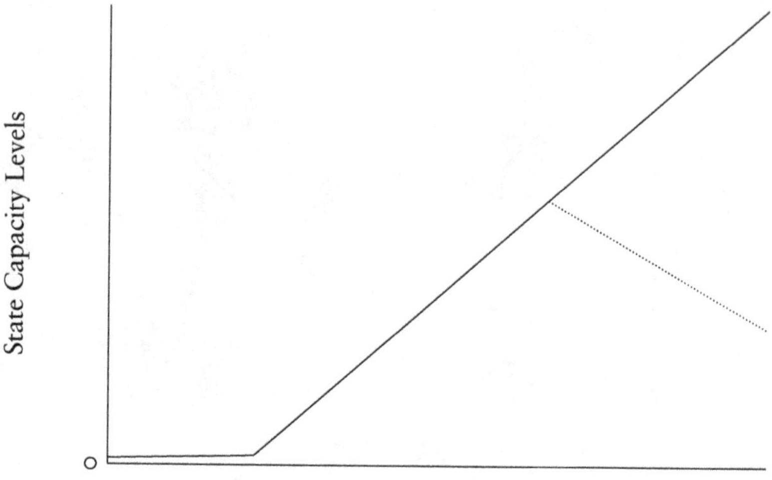

FIGURE 2.3 Classical bellicist logic

expectations in the postwar phase by proposing that the outcomes of war will affect the trajectories of victors and losers differently.

The rest of this chapter reflects on the specific mechanisms underpinning a theory that combines prewar and postwar effects. The building blocks of such a theory can be found in the classics of bellicist theory (Mann, 1988, 2). In Section 2.1 I look at how these insights played out in the work of Otto Hintze, Franz Oppenheimer, Alexander Rüstow, and Max Weber. Then I develop a schematic account of the theory and mechanisms implied in their work, using the conceptual and theoretical tools of historical institutionalism to generate some clear predictions in Section 2.2. Finally, in Section 2.3 I bring the theory down one level of abstraction to think about its concrete implications for the nineteenth century and the Latin American context in particular.

2.1 BELLICIST THEORY: BACK TO THE CLASSICS

Analogies to stationary bandits (Olson, 1993, 567) and protection rackets (Tilly, 1985, 169) have been useful points of departure for theorists of the state. Max Weber famously compared the state to a robber (Weber, 1978, 902) to illustrate that before states developed into complex legal orders and impersonal bureaucracies, they must have looked like small brotherhoods or mafia-like organizations that "lived on war booty and the contributions they levied on non-members" (Weber, 1978, 906).[3]

[3] The term *Gemeinschaft*, often translated as "community" in Weber's definition, denotes such a personal face-to-face relationship naturally bonded by emotions and sentiment (Tönnies, 1957).

This understanding of the state as a community trying to dominate others is difficult to wrap our heads around, but it is essential to grasp what states are at their core and their relation to warfare. All the forefathers of bellicist theory shared this view. Franz Oppenheimer, for example, agreed that "war at primitive stages can be equated to robbery" and "the first stage of state formation consists of nothing more than a predatory war on its borders" (Oppenheimer, 1964, 563), while Otto Hintze proposed that "all state organization was originally a military organization, organization for war" (Hintze, 1975, 178) where "the state and the army were virtually identical units" (Hintze, 1975, 188).

The question of when and how these aggressive fellowships placed themselves at the crest of newly stratified societies – therefore creating the first states – was a matter of speculation for all of these scholars.[4] Nonetheless, they agreed on their best guess: Fear of an external threat must have boosted cohesion between marauders and sedentary populations, prompting stable relations where the former offered permanent protection to the latter in exchange for tribute.

Weber (1978, 905), for example, pictured the inception of the state as being more likely "where a territorial association is attacked by an external enemy in its traditional domain, and arms are taken up by the members in the manner of a home guard." In such conditions, "increasing rational precautions against such eventualities might engender a political organization regarded as enjoying particular legitimacy." Initially the accepted internally oriented violence would have been related to the very purpose of war-fighting and "directed against members of the fraternity who have acted treasonably or who have harmed it by disobedience or cowardice." This distinction between out-group violence and in-group violence directed against warriors and society permitted the legitimization of the latter (Oppenheimer, 1975, 88). In this way, "out of this martial organization, there first developed a more severe government with coercive power over individuals" (Hintze, 1975, 181).[5]

4 Looking at the very inception of the state can help scholars get rid of many layers of confounding factors that affected the makeup of states throughout history as a product of interaction with their environment. The literature on "pristine state formation" (Wright, 1977; Spencer, 2010) still revolves very much around the theses discussed by classical bellicist scholars in the early twentieth century. The notion of the state as a fusion of elite groups in violent contexts has been largely corroborated by anthropology and archeology (Blanton and Fargher, 2007; Bouchard, 2011). Contemporary social science has provided some tentative answers to the question of why these marauders might have chosen to settle and tax others instead of plundering them (Levi, 1988; Olson, 1993; North et al., 2009; Acemoglu, 2012; Boix, 2015), but classical bellicist theorists rejected the idea that these two primary groups chose to enter into a contract. They all agreed that this was fundamentally "a compulsory association" (Weber, 1958, 82). The puzzle they faced was not how it formed but why a purely coercive relation suddenly acquired legitimacy, and Hintze (1982b, 239–270), Oppenheimer (1975, 82–88), Rüstow (1980, 19–21), and Weber (1978, 905–911) all saw integration or amalgamation as a product of the emotions triggered by war.

5 In this story, instinctive reactions like fear, vengeance, and pride play a far more central role than rationality. In other words, classical bellicists did not see the state as the product of a bargain struck between two distinct groups. Warriors and peasants have almost no agency in

The notion that state-making wars are fundamentally defensive deserves special consideration. Classical bellicist theorists reasoned that the psychological mechanisms that could justify the conferral of the power of life and death upon the state should be akin to those activated in the "kinship group in the fulfilment of the obligation of blood vengeance." They underscored that "this connection is weak, on the other hand, with regard to organizational action of a military type, directed against an external enemy" (Weber, 1978, 905). The emphasis on warriors as "avengers" (Oppenheimer, 1975, 85) and the focus "not only on wars of aggression but especially on wars of defense" (Hintze, 1982b, 292) sets classical bellicist theory apart from *Realpolitik* approaches, which see offensive war as a rational strategy for state building (Sambanis et al., 2015).[6] The decision to go to war must have been based on "sentiments of prestige" and "irrational elements" (Weber, 1978, 911). For the same reasons, classical bellicist theorists saw the results of these wars as highly contingent and dependent on the "accidental" results of battles (Weber, 1949, 172).[7]

Most importantly, classical bellicist theorists considered the *outcomes* of these wars as a fundamental piece in the puzzle. Military victory was in the very definition of the state for many of them. For Hintze (1982b, 239), "the state is a legal order imposed on the vanquished by the victors." For Oppenheimer (1926, 58), "the state is the legal institution, imposed on a subjugated group by a victorious group, with the purpose of taxing the defeated as high and as permanently as possible in favor of the victors." Yet for these classics, victory not only imposes a relation of domination with the vanquished but also acts as a powerful bonding mechanism that legitimizes internal relations of domination as well:

this narrative. They are melted and forged into a single grouping by the exogenous shock of war. In sociology, the idea that external threats produce instinctive in-group cohesion has a long tradition (Sumner, 1940; Simmel, 1955). This has been called a "general law" and a "ubiquitous principle" (Stein, 1976, 145) and found to work systematically under basic conditions (Gould, 2003). Realistic group theory proposes that competing interests between groups are a *sufficient condition* (Sherif, 1966, 85) for an increase in cohesion, a finding that has been shown to be very robust in different experimental settings (Jackson, 1993; Bornstein, 2003). These experiments show not only that groups become more cohesive while facing such threats but also that members perceive the *oughtness* of cohesion, leading them to enforce the behavior upon others as a social norm (Benard, 2012). Social identity theory also arrives at the conclusion that external competition boosts identification with the group (Tajfel and Turner, 1986).

6 Besides making heroic assumptions about cognitive and decision-making processes in the primitive societies we are discussing, approaches that propose that wars of aggression were purposely sought as a way to enlarge the state face a logical problem. Since we know tribes and chiefdoms waged war before the existence of the first states, we can deduce that war was exogenous to the first state.

7 This understanding of war should be regarded as the conventional wisdom in international relations. Authors who have scrutinized rationalist explanations for war have come to the conclusion that "a better understanding of what the assumption of rationality really implies may actually raise our estimate of the importance of particular irrational ... factors" (Fearon, 1995, 409).

Still another tendency knots yet more closely these psychic relations. The peasants become accustomed, when danger threatens, to call on the herdsmen, whom they no longer regard as robbers and murderers, but as protectors and saviors. Imagine the joy of the peasants when the returning band of avengers brings back to the village the looted women and children, and the enemies' heads or scalps. These ties are no longer threads, but strong and knotted bonds. (Oppenheimer, 1975, 85)

It is also implicit in Weber (1978, 905) that the imaginary pact between protectors and protected could only be legitimized by martial victory. Overall, these authors considered victory as a key mechanism for not only imposing but also legitimizing the state as a form of authority (see also Rüstow, 1980, 30), including its territorial and legal dimensions:

The origin of the state is violence, but with victory, the winning party also secures the legal system and the border, which guarantees the exploitation of the labor of these subjects by the victors and, on the other hand, is supposed to preserve the subject's ability to operate[.] [T]he protection of the border of course, is against any other hordes of robbers who might seek the same source of income ... and thereby elements of a *community* are introduced into this newly established relationship of violence, which soften it, and transform it into what is called *power* and *rule*. (Hintze, 1982b, 274)[8]

For Weber, victory in combat legitimized domination when "members [of the state] may pretend to a special prestige" (Weber, 1978, 910). "The prestige of power," Weber (1978, 911) argued, "means in practice the glory of power over other communities." After victory, "every highly privileged group develops the myth of its natural, especially its blood, superiority" (Weber, 1978, 953). Conversely, upon defeat, "that very myth of the highly privileged about everyone having deserved his particular lot has often become one of the most passionately hated objects of attack" (Weber, 1978, 953). In the Weberian rendition, victory has the particular effect of consolidating charismatic leadership and allowing for its routinization (Weber, 1978, 246–251), a process that he describes as follows:

It is arbitrary to derive kingship and state, in adaptation of Nietzschean concepts, from the subjection of one tribe by another, which then creates a permanent apparatus in order to maintain its ascendancy and extract tribute, for the same differentiation between arms-bearing and tax-exempt warriors and unarmed, service-rendering non-combatants can easily develop within any tribe that is chronically threatened with war.... The conquest theory is correct to the extent that kingship [i.e., early forms of statehood] is normally charismatic war leadership that has become permanent and has developed a repressive apparatus for the domestication of the unarmed subjects. This apparatus naturally became strongest in conquered territories because of the continuous threat to the ruling stratum. (Weber, 1978, 1135)

In the charismatic authority account, "risen to be a prince, the victorious military leader then gets legitimized" (Oppenheimer, 1926, 18), but "this stage

8 Emphases are in the original.

[i.e., war] is transcended gradually, and this *ad hoc* consociation develops into a permanent structure" (Weber, 1978, 905). Eventually, "through the cultivation of military prowess and war as a vocation such structure develops into a coercive apparatus able to lay effective and comprehensive claims to obedience" (Weber, 1978, 906).

It is abundantly clear that classical bellicist theorists put a large emphasis on the outcomes of war and theorized the legitimizing effects of victory in ways that have been largely validated by anthropological, archeological, and historical research thereafter.[9]

2.2 A NEW HISTORICAL–INSTITUTIONALIST RENDITION

As Michael Mann (1993, 55) noted, "Weber was a theorist of the historical development of social institutions," and thus both he and his contemporaries made conscientious efforts to apply their theories about the origins of the state in order to understand the evolution of national states in modern Europe as well. In this section I build on such insights and the conceptual toolkit provided by historical institutionalism (Thelen, 1999; Mahoney and Rueschemeyer, 2003; Mahoney and Thelen, 2010) to formulate a concrete, falsifiable version of classical bellicist theory that could be tested in nineteenth-century Latin America and other modern settings.[10]

To understand why the outcomes of war can have such an important effect on the fate of states it is essential to understand that war – in a broad sense that includes preparation for war[11] – has contradictory effects on state institutions (Mann, 1993, 62). Geopolitical pressures structure and corrode political orders at the same time and, ultimately, can either strengthen the state or lead to its demise (Skocpol, 1979). In this sense, war is a permissive condition (Soifer, 2012) – that is, a necessary but insufficient condition – for state formation.

9 In a recent review of this scholarly enterprise, James Scott (2017, 130) agrees with this point. He even risks the hypothesis "no slavery, no state" when discussing the capture of prisoners of war as a virtually necessary condition for the development of early states. In his own review of the field, Francis Fukuyama (2011, 85) similarly arrives at the conclusion that states originated as a compulsory association between tribal segments where "the victor would establish a relation of dominance."

10 This is also in line with the recent literature about state formation in Latin America, which has built on a strong Latin American tradition (Collier and Collier, 1991) of thinking about critical junctures and rigid institutional paths. To be as much in line with this literature as possible in terms of methodological language, I will build strongly upon the rendition of key comparative historical concepts proposed by these authors (Soifer, 2012).

11 To understand the bellicist process as a whole, it is useful to think of war like Hugo Grotius (1901, 131) did, as "a state of affairs which may exist even while its operations are not continued," or like Thomas Hobbes (1914, 104), who opined that "the nature of war consisteth not of actual fighting but in the known disposition thereto." To make the distinction between actual warfare and the disposition to conduct future operations, I will often refer to the latter as preparation for war or a prewar phase.

Although war will lead to the creation of certain wartime institutions, it will also erode prewar institutional arrangements. The most fundamental effect of war is probably to suspend permanent understandings about state institutions, now subordinated to the needs of the military campaign, given the state of exception (Agamben, 2005). This window of opportunity in which the sovereign can transcend the rule of law in order to preserve the public good will then remain open until peace defines a new political landscape and institutional order.[12]

The "preparation for war" logic often misses how mobilization and centralization corrode political orders (see Garfias and Sellars, 2022). Instead it often takes the form of a linear story in which foreign threats lead to the expansion of the military and the bureaucracies needed to support the war effort financially and logistically. In this view, "war, state apparatus, taxation, and borrowing advanced in tight cadence" (Tilly, 1985, 180, cited in Thies, 2004, 55).

The process, however, is more dialectical and involves an interaction between "war, state building, and contentious politics" (Tarrow, 2015, 12). As Tilly (1990, 83) puts it, "With the nation in arms, the state's extractive power rose enormously as did the claims of citizens on their state. Although a call to defend the fatherland stimulated extraordinary support for the efforts of war, reliance on mass conscription, confiscatory taxation, and conversion of production to the ends of war made any state vulnerable to popular resistance, and answerable to popular demands, as never before" (see also Besley and Persson, 2009; Stasavage, 2011; Feinstein and Wimmer, 2023).

Classical bellicists were fully aware of these contradictions. On the one hand they agreed that "as the product of constant warlike tension," states in Europe "had to hold standing armies and arrange their entire internal constitution and administration in such a way that they could achieve a maximum of military and financial efficiency" (Hintze, 1961f, 407), but they saw preparation for war as a highly contingent and contested process whereby "military discipline unified these honorable associations [*ehrbare Mannschaft*] before socio-economic and fiscal interest *consolidated* their union" (Hintze, 1961e, 205).

The consolidation of the state beyond its military core required overcoming resistance from elites and society.[13] This is indeed the most important insight in

12 Curiously, our understanding of wartime domestic institutions is rather limited when it comes to international wars. Recently political scientists have made important progress in the understanding of wartime institutions in the context of civil wars, both on the side of the state (Schwartz, 2023) and the rebels (Mampilly, 2011; Arjona, 2014; Stewart, 2018).

13 For example, considering the Thirty Years' War, Hintze (1961g, 429) notes that "Richelieu enforced the tighter consolidation of the previously loosely connected provinces of France through violent internal struggles"; had to deploy "dreaded, bloody commissioners" to this effect; and even then, "the country often resisted these officials" until long after the end of the conflict.

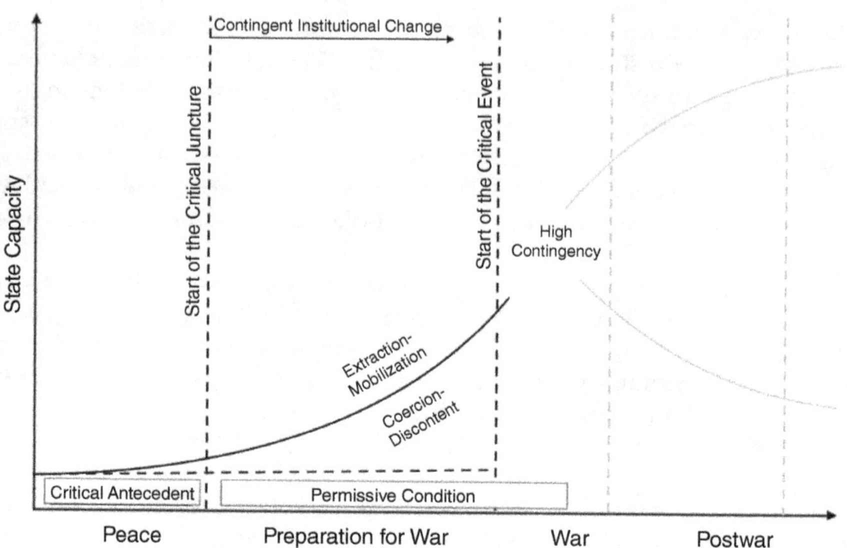

FIGURE 2.4 The prewar phase

the literature that has explored the bellicist argument in the modern European context (Downing, 1993; Ertman, 1997; Stasavage, 2010; Cox et al., 2023). This literature, however, moves too fast toward analyzing variation in regime type, a different outcome that confounds the analysis of the state intended here.

Whichever regime institutions are in place – that is, those that determine how officials are elected and regulate how they rule – state building depends on certain levels of contingent consent by societal actors (Levi, 1997). This consent to wartime institutions will be determined by the balance between the perceived benefits of war and perceived costs in terms of extraction – taxation, conscription, and so on – and subjection to more or less arbitrary rule. Because societal actors have reasons to fear a mighty state perhaps even as much as an invader, they will favor the devil they know while trying to limit this support to the sacrifices that are strictly needed for the success of the military campaign (see Levi, 1998; Rosenthal, 1998; Besley and Torsten, 2011; Feinstein and Wimmer, 2023).

This is a key difference between the prewar bellicist approach and the classical bellicist approach. While the former assumes that "the general resistance to social and political change, in any event, is more likely to be either weakened or even overwhelmed by the need to respond to the demands of the war effort" (Rasler and Thompson, 1985, 494), the latter considers how citizens can oppose the war effort, take flight together with their mobile assets (Paine, 2023), or even rebel against the state, their consent being contingent on the belief that the campaign will succeed.

Figure 2.4 is the first of three figures I will use to flesh out the mechanisms underpinning my theory. The focus is on the part of the figure in black, which is concerned with the beginning of the critical juncture or prewar phase – the right-hand side in gray will be expanded and explained in more detail later. Note that during a period of peace – understood as the absence of an external threat – state capacity stays flat in accordance with state institutions that define a certain level of authority of the state vis-à-vis society. These laws and informal understandings regulating governmental expenditure, tax levels, debt acquisitions, and so on constrain the *Machtinteresse* (power interest) of the rulers – but also the military and state bureaucracy, which have a permanent appetite for "right and peace, security and [their own] power" (Hintze, 1981, 25). These tensions between the state and other sociopolitical groups precede the emergence of an external threat, but such an event – which determines the start of our critical juncture (Soifer, 2012) – will bring them to the surface.

External threats – for example, episodes of militarization still short of war – will already upset the prewar equilibria, giving the state an excuse to extract and mobilize, develop wartime institutions, and produce a contingent increase in state capacity. However, while societal actors will acquiesce in the first instance, they will expect a return to peacetime levels, depicted by a dashed horizontal line. Discontent is therefore destined to increase as an inverse function of extraction. This gap prevents the consolidation of the state-building project and leads to an extraction–coercion cycle if societal actors resist violently (Centeno, 1997, 1569). Preparation for war thus acts fundamentally as a permissive condition for wartime mobilization by eroding the institutional understandings in place during peacetime, but it cannot by itself consolidate a new institutional equilibrium, given the gap between the expectations of state and societal actors.

The second moment of theoretical interest is when violent confrontations effectively begin to take place and the state, although "fundamentally Janus-faced" (Skocpol, 1979, 32), turns its full attention to the international front.

It is important to underscore that the wars classical (and modern) bellicists refer to are, strictly speaking, international wars. Scholars who have pondered over civil wars agree that "the consensus is that extractive capacity grows in response to international rather than domestic conflict" (Slater, 2010, 37; see also Rich and Stubbs, 1997), that civil war is the "wrong kind" of war for building states, or, as Rachel Schwartz (2023, 10) puts it, that "civil war instead often builds the *wrong kind* of state institutions."

This does not mean that civil wars cannot show state-building effects under certain circumstances (see Rodríguez-Franco, 2016; Sanchez Talanquer, 2017; Flores Macías, 2018; Garfias, 2018; Arias and de la Calle, 2021; Paglayan, 2022), but they will almost always lack the intensity of international warfare.[14]

14 The American Civil War is a notable exception to this general rule, which can be also distinguished by its unusual state-building effects. It is likely that the state-building effects of civil wars are somewhat dependent on the type of warfare, with more conventional civil wars resembling international wars more closely (Kalyvas and Balcells, 2010). A somewhat similar

Because civil wars pitch the state and the societal actors it is supposed to rule against each other, they divide rather than unite the nation. Because of this they are likely to negatively affect state capacity on average (Thies, 2005; Besley and Persson, 2009; Herbst, 2014) and are better pictured as a loss of the monopoly on legitimate violence. Episodes of international militarization, on the contrary, consistently bring state and societal actors together against an external threat regarded as existential, which both requires and facilitates much more impressive levels of mobilization.

Due to their dramatic dimensions, when international wars break out, the domestic bargain has to be put on hold. Facing an immediate and present existential threat from an external peer, the sovereign state can suspend all institutional arrangements and implement a full range of wartime institutions. This state of exception (Agamben, 2005; Schmitt, 2005; see also Buzan et al., 1998) allows the government to take all necessary action vis-à-vis other groups in society in order to secure its capacity to fight. As Cicero put it, *silent leges inter arma* – among arms, the laws are silent. At this stage institutionalization of state–society relations becomes rather thin and the fortunes of war can, to paraphrase Napoleon, either strengthen the state or break it like a glass.

I use the term "critical event" (Garcia and Mahoney, 2023) to underscore the specific nature of the process that opens up when two states effectively engage in organized physical violence against each other. During this clearly delimited period of time, mobilization is at its greatest extent, and small events fundamentally subject to chance can become veritable turning points of great causal importance (see also Capoccia and Kelemen, 2007, 348).

Perhaps the clearest example is how individual battles can radically affect the domestic legitimacy of the state and the entire war effort. The Ancient Greeks called the major turning points in the history of their city-states *trope*. The *trope* was a specific time and place during a battle where some whimsical god intervened in favor of the victorious contender. After the war ended, a shrine or *tropaion* – the origin of our word *trophy* – was built in that precise location and worshiped (Schivelbusch, 2004, 6). The Romans commemorated these moments with triumphal arches, and it only takes a little attention to the monuments and the street names around us – no matter where in the world we are – to see how common the enshrinement of battles and heroes continues to be and the role that these events play in the legitimization of national states.

The main reason why these battles have such a strong emotional appeal, besides the sacrifice of lives, is that they defined history in a context of high uncertainty for both contenders. This understanding of battles as events of utmost contingency (Clausewitz, 1984, 66; see Bendor and Shapiro, 2019)

logic might apply to asymmetric international wars, which might not lead to high levels of mobilization on the stronger side. The state-building effects of the Afghanistan, Iraq, or Vietnam wars in the United States, for example, are probably not comparable to those of the World Wars.

clearly influenced the thought of classical bellicist theorists as well.[15] In his methodological annotations on the work of comparative historians like Karl Hampe (1894) and Eduard Meyer (1989), Weber (1949, 172) describes battles as fortuitously assigning a treatment and allowing us to assess the causal impact of the war's outcome "on the basis of weighing the various *possibilities*, the *decision* between which was made by the battle's entirely *accidental* outcome – *accidental* meaning here determined by quite individual tactical events,"[16] a methodological insight I exploit in Chapter 5.

Figure 2.5 concentrates on the phase of war – now understood as the moment when actual physical violence takes place. It highlights the contingency that determines the outcomes of individual battles, as well as their immediate impact on domestic dynamics. In this hypothetical war, four battles take place, and one could look into each of these battles to test the implications of the classical bellicist argument.

Battles are events of key importance because they directly affect the domestic balance between the state and societal actors. If the state is defeated on the battlefield, discontent will be bolstered. Conversely, a victorious battle will reinforce support for the war, granting more leverage to the state-makers in this underlying domestic bargain.

15 Hintze (1961f, 403) – and scholars like him – scolded his militaristic contemporaries, reminding them that "successes like those from 1864 to 1871 cannot be repeated in every generation" and that Germany "does well to accustom the world to the quiet existence of its saturated and fortified power, instead of pursuing efforts to expand with restless ambition that are not necessarily required by his vital interests." After World War I, Hintze (1982a, 215) continued to promote the healing of a "militaristic war psychosis that still prevents a real internal pacification of Europe." In other words, the forefathers of this theory were far from bellicist in a prescriptive sense (see Sambanis et al., 2015).

16 Analyzing the logic behind Eduard Meyer's work on the Persian Wars and the causal importance of the battle of Marathon, Weber explains this further: "How does this happen, logically speaking? It takes place essentially in the following way. It is argued that a *decision* was made between two *possibilities*. The first of these possibilities was the development of theocratic-religious culture, the beginnings of which lay in the mysteries and oracles, under the aegis of the Persian protectorate, which wherever possible utilized, as for example, among the Jews, the national religion as an instrument of domination. The other possibility was represented by the triumph of the free Hellenic circle of ideas oriented towards this world, which gave us those cultural values from which we still draw our sustenance. The *decision* was made by a contest of the meager dimension of the battle of Marathon. This in its turn was the indispensable precondition of the development of the Attic fleet and thus of the further development of the war of liberation, the salvation of the independence of Hellenic culture, the positive stimulus of the beginnings of the specifically western historiography, the full development of the drama and all that unique life of the mind which took place in this – by purely quantitative standards – miniature theater of world history" (Weber, 1949, 171, emphasis mine). Hintze (1961g, 427) noted: "[Leopold von] Ranke in particular shared such perceptions; but again he was not theoretician enough to grasp and formulate the relationship [between battle outcomes and institutional outcomes] in its general meaning."

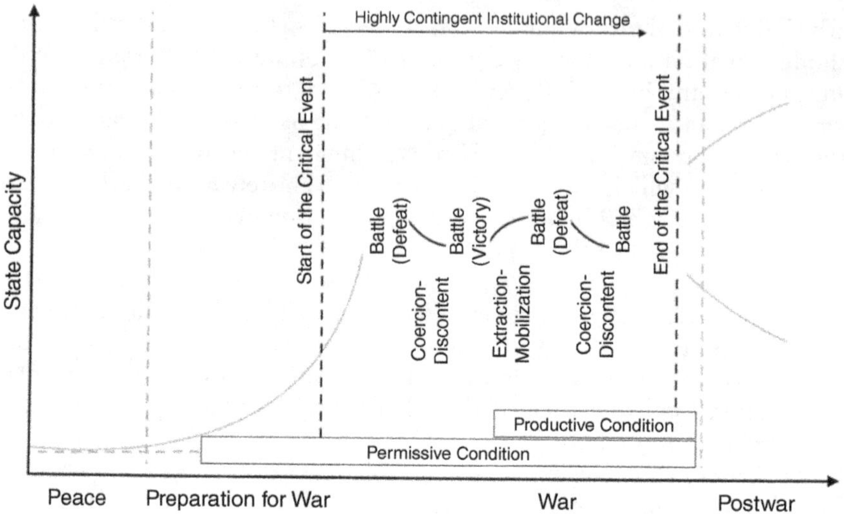

FIGURE 2.5 The war phase

The final revelation of the war outcome, which can be due to a decisive battle or some other reason,[17] is the productive condition that, in interaction with the institutional reshuffling generated by the war effort – that is, the erosion of old arrangements and the rise of wartime institutions – sets states onto different postwar institutional paths.

Although Jean-Paul Sartre was probably right in *Le Diable et le Bon Dieu* when he wrote that "if a victory is told in detail, one can no longer distinguish it from a defeat," the final outcome of a war seems to lead to a sort of general amnesia, an almost complete rewrite of history from the perspective of the victor, and a blanket justification – or condemnation – of every wartime sacrifice. Either by fear or by love, after victory everyone thinks that the price paid to strengthen the state was justified. Societal actors will continue under the charismatic spell cast by state authorities, now anointed by martial glory and the commandeering of material spoils. Wartime state institutions will be accepted swiftly under these circumstances (Oppenheimer, 1964, 444).

Defeat, on the other hand, will make society realize that the emperor has no clothes. Classical bellicists saw such a process unfold before their eyes in the aftermath of World War I (Weber, 1978, 953). Otto Hintze brings this all together most eloquently:

[17] Consequential battles that defined wars have obsessed military historians through the ages, but they are far from the only contingent event that, like a *trope* at a strategic level, can define wars – one could also think of switching alliances or the discovery of a new technology as similarly defining events. However, due to their contingency, war-defining events almost invariably make it possible to think counterfactually of an alternative outcome (Tetlock and Belkin, 1996; Goertz and Levy, 2007; see Lewis, 1986).

> [S]harp minds with predominantly legal training replaced the ideal-aesthetic analogy of the [state as a] *work of art* with the sober legal category of an *institution*, which then through sociological processing in the hands of a master like Max Weber gained a lively content in the dynamic view as a *company*, distinguished from other establishments by its exclusive power to exercise lawful coercion. The resemblance of the state to an economic enterprise is obvious, though the moral-political collapse at the end of the Great War was needed in order to destroy the old nimbus of the state, and lower its dignity and sovereignty to make such a comparison appear permissible. Since the glory of our empire has passed, since the old state ideology and the old constitution have been overturned, since our people have been deprived of the honor of arms and the pride of independence and yet there still exists a state whose primary purpose, besides maintaining internal order, has been to raise an unaffordable contribution to the syndicate of the victorious powers, since this state, comparable to a collapsed company, has to secure the tribute payments, has been placed under the business supervision of the creditors' syndicate, with all these changes, there is no longer any reason to ideologically conceal the bare fact that the state for us is basically nothing more than an institution with coercive force with the purpose of maintaining the possibility of existence internally and externally and, insofar as the narrow scope allows, to provide for a very modest amount of welfare and culture. While the victorious powers drape their successful state, which is productive for the vital interests of its members, with all sorts of ideological emblems in the exuberance of nationalistic exhilaration, we have no reason to let this cloud the light of the new objectivity that has fallen upon us. At its core, the state (which should be distinguished from the people more than it usually happens) is an establishment, that is, an organized system of institutions for the control of the people who form the state and for the protection of their common interests. (Hintze, 1982a, 206–207)

Importantly, and perhaps surprisingly, classical bellicist theorists never refer to the out-selection of weak states as a mechanism connecting the outcomes of war with the formation of European states (Hintze, 1961g, 425). Aware that defeat only rarely out-selected states, even in Europe, classical bellicist theorists interpreted the aftermath of wars as a theoretically relevant moment when losers and victors were set onto diverging institutional trajectories.[18]

[18] In the case of Oppenheimer (1964, 454–461), this is nicely illustrated with reference to the rise and decline of medieval kingdoms, such as the rise of the Carolingian empire after the Battle of Tetry of 687 AD and the subsequent victory of Charles Martel in the Battle of Tours of 732 AD, contrasting with the decline of the Visigoth empire after the Battle of Guadalete in 711 AD. In a study of municipal institutions across Europe, Otto Hintze (1961d, 229) noted that "[i]n southern Italy, over the past centuries, one emperor displaced the other and even in the cities, the spirit of municipality was suppressed or stunned." If defeat decreases trust in a polity and its institutions (Grosjean, 2014), this should be considered a valid alternative to explain social capital in Italy (Putnam, 1994), for example. In Poland as well, due to repeated defeats, "conditions of medieval state life have not been eliminated here in recent centuries but were driven to extremes and became rigid" (Hintze, 1961a, 517). "The constitution of Poland made the state powerless, and external powerlessness perpetuated anarchy within" (Hintze, 1961a, 562). Of course, these rigid trajectories could have been reversed by subsequent victories. Hintze (1961h, 343, 348) illustrates this with the case of Austria. He notes that the military success of the Habsburgs allowed "the Austrian and Bohemian group to merge into a real unitary state"

Thomas Ertman (2017, 56) already noted the key importance that the "organizational residue" (Tilly, 1985, 181) of war had for classical bellicist theory in the long term. I refer to the "political structures" that "become rigid" after war (Hintze, 1961a, 517) as *state institutions*, understood as the "set of administrative, policing, and military organizations headed and more or less well co-ordinated by an executive authority" (Skocpol, 1979, 29). During the nineteenth century, this set of state institutions arguably expanded to encompass other bureaucracies. Michael Mann (1993, 62), for example, identified six state institutions of relevance in this period: supreme executives, the judiciary and police, civil administration, the diplomacy, parties and assemblies, and the military. Importantly, we are concerned with these as state institutions and not as regime institutions.[19]

The immediate causal link connecting the outcomes of war with postwar trajectories in state institutions and capacity is nicely summarized by the saying, attributed to Tacitus, that victory has many fathers, while defeat is an orphan. After victory, even those who opposed the war will identify with the state-building project. Conversely, upon defeat, almost everyone will abandon the political coalition that supported the war effort and blame state authorities for the blunder.[20] Yet war outcomes do not only transfer stocks of power toward

after the Second Silesian War (1748), while "after the end of the Seven Years' War [i.e., the Third Silesian War ending in 1763] the Bohemian Estates made one last push against the system," encouraged by Vienna's defeat. In the nineteenth century the creation of Austro-Hungary as a double monarchy after a new, crushing defeat by Prussia in 1867 provides yet another example. These ebbs and flows of military success and state capacity get confusing in regions where wars were all too frequent, but this insight becomes clearer when I analyze Latin America. Hintze's Bohemian example also illustrates that in regions where the war effort was higher, the effects of victory and defeat on the state-building process tend to be stronger – something we will also see in Latin America when paying attention to subnational dynamics.

19 Historian Margaret MacMillan (2020, 25) writes: "War has often opened the way to massive political and social changes when it weakens government and undermines its legitimacy, while victory can entrench a regime in power." This observation is probably correct (de Mesquita et al., 1992). Yet most historical–sociological studies on the institutions resulting from war tend to confound state institutions with regime type. Following a line pioneered by John Robert Seeley (1922) and picked up in some of the writings of Otto Hintze (1975) as well, most scholars of European state building (Tilly, 1990; Downing, 1993; Ertman, 1997; Stasavage, 2010; Mann, 2012; Cox et al., 2023) tend to focus on postwar regimes and states at the same time. Dan Slater (2010) does the same in his seminal study of southeast Asia, and Fernando López-Alves (2000) provides a good example for Latin America. By departing from this tradition I do not mean to say that there is not a thread connecting war, state formation, and regime change. However, I am convinced that states and regimes are sufficiently distinct outcomes to require separate treatment.

20 Sociologists have noted that after almost every war, those who opposed the effort scapegoat the authorities and celebrate the victory of the foreign attackers as a liberation. This cleansing moment when the guilt is transferred to the deposed tyrant is called a "dreamland" moment by Wolfgang Schivelbusch (2004). This author recorded massive demonstrations of joy and the exaltation of former traitors following the American Civil War, the Franco-Prussian War, and World War I.

the state or away from it: They also determine flows in the future (Pierson, 2015).

Defeat not only delegitimizes state officials and results in immediate material destruction but also results in the long-term discrediting of state institutions and state-building policies, generating what Norbert Elias (2000, 295) called "centrifugal tendencies." After defeat, new elites who opposed the war effort – even those who collaborated with the enemy – will reach power and roll back all pro-state institutional change (Hoffman, 2015). In the terms of historical institutionalism, subversives – that is, actors that secretly undermined wartime institutions while acquiescing to them during the war – will now actively eliminate state institutions (Mahoney and Thelen, 2010, 23). This can lead to what Michael Bernhard (2015) has called chronic instability – that is, a sheer lack of institutionalization characterized by multiple, frequent, and connected episodes of change – or even the consolidating state-weakening institutions (Hui, 2005)[21] aimed at perpetuating the decentralization of power into the hands of nonstate political actors.

Some will argue that there were instances in history where defeat bolstered state formation. For example, this is the conventional interpretation of the institutional reforms that took place in Prussia after its initial defeats during the Napoleonic Wars. But even those stories align with classical bellicist theory when closely examined. Before its rebirth, "the Prussian state collapsed quickly and completely after the Battle of Jena in 1806 because it ... failed in the clash with France" (Hintze, 1961g, 446). Prussia incurred institutional reforms that were antiabsolutist and antistatist for many years after the defeat. Hintze (1970, 130) notes that state-strengthening reforms started only in late 1812, during the War of the Sixth Coalition, and compulsory military service – the most important of these reforms – was implemented only in 1814, when Napoleon was already in Elba. These state-strengthening institutions consolidated after Waterloo and subsequent victories. It was while riding with Victoria in her quadriga that Prussia regained its former strength. In the subsequent decades, "Germany, which had fallen into political degeneration and weakness, rose to new power and greatness through his example and powerful leadership" (Hintze, 1961f, 407). Germany continued to be an odd case of regeneration after defeat in the World Wars, but under the magnifying glass, the process here was similar, with the expected state collapse after defeat – think of the weak Weimar Republic and the Morgenthau Plan – being countered by a process of subsequent mobilization during the Cold War that locked in institutions only after 1949 (Bernhard, 2015).

21 I borrow the concepts of state-strengthening and state-weakening arrangements from Victoria Hui (2005, 42–51), who distinguishes between self-strengthening reforms and self-weakening expedients. In the context of my theory, however, these alternative strategies are linked to the preferences of specific actors, and the prevalence of one over the other is exogenously determined by the outcomes of war.

Conversely, victory not only results in material gains immediately legitimizing state authorities but also allows them to consolidate and lock in wartime state-strengthening institutions (see Feinstein and Wimmer, 2023, 198), which will evolve in a self-reinforcing, path-dependent manner, setting countries onto long-term state-building trajectories (Mahoney and Thelen, 2010, 16). This interpretation emphasizes a sort of incrementalism and institutional spillover that is radically different from the "ratchet effect" understanding of postwar effects – a notion that might apply to the size of armies, certain forms of taxation, and public spending (Peacock and Wiseman, 1967; Scheve and Stasavage, 2012) but does not generalize to most other dimensions of state building. The process of state consolidation after victory is sequential and cannot be captured by looking at one indicator – for example, income taxes – alone.

The sequential logic of state building after victory also requires us to look at several indicators within a single dimension. Take, for example, the military as a state institution. Logically, some demobilization must follow right after a war ends – conscription and military expenditure, for example, will be relaxed even after victory (see Simmel, 1955, 98, cited in Desch, 1996, 243) – but this does not mean that the military necessarily loses power after wars. In the case of victory, we should see the charismatic legitimacy of war heroes and military commanders being at its highest, granting the military enough leverage to institutionalize and preserve its acquired political and social status.[22] Similarly, while peace eliminates a compelling excuse for implementing new taxes and contracting new loans (Campbell, 1993, 165), victory will reassure societal actors of the capacity of the state to protect private property and repay its debts, attracting investments that will expand the tax base and securing cheaper credit in the future. Bureaucracies initially created for the purpose of financing and administering the war effort will thus continue to grow, legitimized by victory and benefiting from its fiscal and financial spoils.

Empirically, this means that the reproduction of state institutions in the long term is a moving target. Conceptually, this requires the researcher to hone in on key state institutions. Because the "infrastructural power [of the state] is a two-way street" (Mann, 1993, 59), classical bellicist theorists tended to focus on institutions that allow the power of the state to radiate outward – the bureaucracy and military – and inward from society – that is, political parties that seek to control the state, rather than factions aiming for its demise (Mann, 2008, 356).

[22] The exaltation of victorious soldiers is ubiquitous in history. In Rome, war veterans were granted citizenship and victorious generals were often elected into high office, and one would not struggle to find similar examples in almost every modern war. The effects on nationalism are perhaps more contemporary *stricto sensu*. Prussia's victory in the Seven Years' War and the implementation of the *Generallandschulreglement* of 1763, a landmark in the history of education as state and nation formation, provides a good example of these dynamics in a paradigmatic case (Paglayan, 2022, 8).

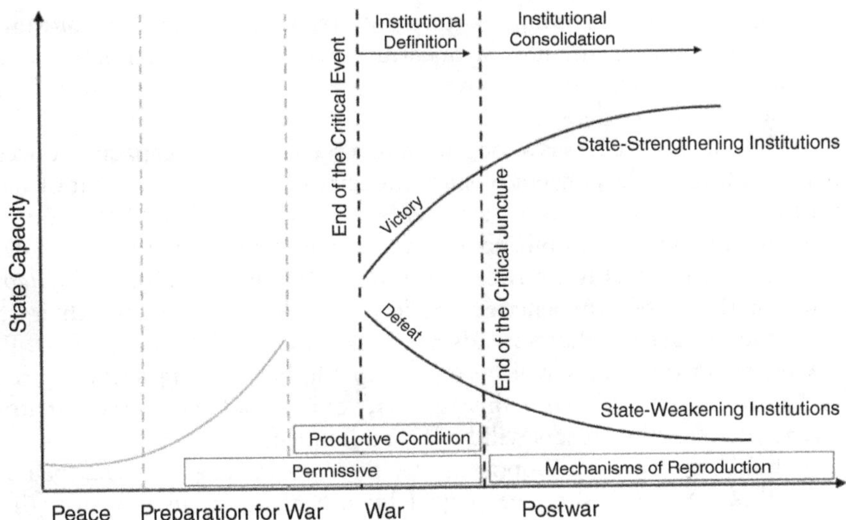

FIGURE 2.6 The postwar phase

Victory will empower those who have politics as a profession (*Beruf*) or live "from" politics (Weber, 1994, 316) and depend on the state for the success of their corporate interests: the military and the bureaucracy. Naturally, after victory "this class becomes the actual commanding factor [*der eigentliche herrschende Faktor*] in the state" (Hintze, 1981, 92). These actors will try to safeguard organizational survival and growth via expansion of the state (Schumpeter, 1991), leading a self-reinforcing process by which more resources lead to further institutional reform and spill over to new areas (Levi, 1988, 2; Slater, 2010, 19).

Victory will also unite those who pursue the vocation (*Betrieb*) of politics or live "for" it (Weber, 1994, 312): politicians (Weber, 1994, 309). Given the legitimacy of the state-building project, it is to be expected that even those who opposed the war effort will see it as a major political price. Victory will usually consolidate a party of the state, born strong as every party forged on in "struggle and violence" (Huntington, 1970, 13–14, cited in Levitsky and Way, 2022, 11), and strengthened even more due to the overwhelming popular support and the collapse of the treacherous opposition. Most importantly, however, the opposition to this party will not struggle against the state but for access to it, restructuring partisan competition along state-building lines.

Figure 2.6 illustrates mechanisms in the postwar phase, differentiating the end of the critical event – actual war – from the critical juncture – potential war. As Soifer (2012, 1585) has noted, critical junctures end when permissive conditions disappear. Thus for the critical juncture to end, foreign threats need to be overcome. Logically, there might be cases where a subsequent threat arises, suspending the emerging institutional arrangements and putting state–society relations once again into the uncertain terrain of preparation for war.[23] However, in most cases the window of opportunity will close and postwar institutions will consolidate.[24]

The result of this process is a long-term divergence in state capacity between winners and losers. The concept of state capacity is different from that of state institutions. We should think of state capacity as the ability of the state to enforce rules and provide public goods and services, which is in turn dependent on the actual infrastructural power of the state (Mann, 1988, 5), or the *depth* with which the state can penetrate society and the extent to which it can *reach* all the population that spreads across its realm (O'Donnell, 1993). Put otherwise, victorious states will be more capable of *asserting* authority over societal actors and *broadcasting* this authority over broad expanses of territory (Slater, 2010, 36), while losers will be less so (Hintze, 1961c).[25]

As a final remark, it is important to underscore how classical bellicist theorists thought about the role played by other factors in this story. The most important of these are economic factors or what we might vaguely refer to as capitalism. The view that capitalism played a central role in the state formation process gained much prominence in twentieth-century sociology and features prominently in the work of Tilly (1990), among others. These ideas are also particularly strong in Latin America, where Marxism has exerted great influence on the humanities and social sciences.

Classical bellicist scholars conceived state formation and capitalism as broadly separate phenomena and were inclined to believe that states provided the "fundamental conditions for its development and the possibility of its success" (Hintze, 1970, 131) by protecting private property rights and allowing

[23] One such example we have discussed is Prussia after the battle of Jena-Auerstedt of 1806. Hintze (1961b, 506) also mentions how "the terror of 1793, a consequence of the enemy invasion, brought into being the general conscription" as external pressure continued, and it consolidates after birthing many French victories. Germany and Japan after World War II provide similar examples. It was initially the will of the Allies, and in particular the United States, to consolidate weak states during occupation (the so-called Morgenthau Plan), but with the rise of the Soviet threat, both indigenous elites and the United States were prompted to change their preferences and favor a surge in state capacity. State-strengthening reforms were therefore implemented during the Cold War and consolidated in both Germany and Japan after it.

[24] Of course, "[t]he longer the duration of the conflict, the greater the political opportunity for the bureaucratic mechanisms associated with war mobilization to become institutionalized into the political arena." The applies to the severity of the conflict. "Both dimensions of warfare could be posited as having direct implications for postwar state growth" (Jaggers, 1992, 34).

[25] State capacity is not the only state attributed affected by warfare. There are reasons to believe that war enhances the *autonomy* of the state vis-à-vis other groups in society (Skocpol, 1985, 19) and also by notably expanding its *scope* (Fukuyama, 2004), that is, the range of activities that the state regulates and undertakes. Although powerful conceptual tools for the analysis of the twentieth century, these dimensions of the state are less relevant to understand capacity further back in time when states were in general thinner in scope and lacking clear autonomy vis-à-vis elites.

for capital accumulation. According to Hintze (1970, 157), "Max Weber once said that it is the closed national state that guarantees capitalism the chance of survival." He himself opined that "[the] state creates a large market for capitalism: the army and its needs provide a powerful stimulus for capitalist production, while it ensures order and discipline also in the economy" (Hintze, 1970, 132).

This of course does not mean that economic variables cannot interact with warfare to generate different types of state formation trajectories – a line of thought that prevails in the literature, to explain divergence in both regime and state institutions. It is also clear that victory and defeat will have economic effects by signaling the (in)capacity of the state to protect and enforce property rights, repay its debts, and control resources, among other things. However, this book adopts the classical bellicist view that political factors are independent of and take precedence over economic factors.

2.3 IMPLICATIONS FOR NINETEENTH-CENTURY LATIN AMERICA

Any theory of state formation should, at least in principle, account for the evolution of states in the long run, avoiding the use of analytical categories that can only describe later stages in their development (Oszlak, 1981, 4). However, because the observable process leading to state building always takes place in a bounded time and place, the empirical grounding of theory requires some historical contextualization of the actors and institutions affected by war, as well as the meaning of state capacity itself. In this sense, any theory of state formation should be specified on two levels, one abstract and general and another concrete and particular (Goertz, 2020). This section lays out the more concrete observational implications of the theory for nineteenth-century Latin America.

Authors working on nineteenth-century Latin America have identified the pro-state and anti-state constituencies referred to above with state officials and local elites – sometimes called agrarian, provincial, rural, or patrimonial (Kurtz, 2013, 22; Soifer, 2015, 22; Mazzuca, 2021, 34). Yet because states in Latin America were far from autonomous organizations at the time (Skocpol, 1979, 29; see also Giraudi, 2012), we should picture pro-state constituencies as a much broader elite group reaching beyond state officials (Mann, 1988, 4; Tilly, 1988, 53; see also Vu, 2010). I therefore call these two groups *central elites* and *peripheral elites*.[26]

26 Other authors have often adopted what Michael Mann (1993, 48) calls a "statist" theory of the state. Soifer (2015, 19), for example, asserts that "state building was a *state* project, not a class or sectoral project," therefore picturing the state as an organization with motives and strategies or, to put it differently, with agency. Classical bellicist theorists define the state more loosely, as a community, which is the approach I adopt by referring to central elites.

Both central and peripheral elites in nineteenth-century Latin America were sufficiently cohesive and small in size to enact collective action (Olson, 1965), and they routinely built upon relationships – informal ties with officials, partisan linkages, and so on – and resources – newspapers, money, and so on – to influence the outcome of state formation (Fairfield, 2015, 29).

Central elites do not necessarily mean rulers or central bureaucrats. This category includes all those individuals of political relevance with a vested interest in the expansion of the state. Such elite groups tended to include educated urban elites, usually based in the capital city and internationally connected, the officers of the national armed forces, and the commercial and financial bourgeoisie. Yet one can find examples of pro-state elites that were strong at the local or provincial level and only loosely connected to the national government, bureaucracy, and military. What ultimately distinguished central elites was their preference for increasing the capacity of the state vis-à-vis the societal political groupings they were also part of.

Conversely, peripheral elites were usually based in second-tier cities, small townships, and the countryside. Typically, they supported *caudillos* or warlords in command of local militias and included conservative actors[27] such as the Church and landed elites, who would lose autonomy and privileges to a more centralized bureaucracy and military. Yet one can also find notable exceptions. Peripheral elites were also strong in the capital cities and many times governed the national state in times of peace and decentralization. Many military officers pursued a personal political career opposing the interest of the national armed forces. Antimonarchical and federalist elements of the urban petty bourgeoisie – early liberals akin to the *Girondins* – could also fall into this category. Therefore the distinctive feature of this group was not the class or geographic origin of individual members but their shared preference for a small and weak state that would devolve functions to subnational orders.

The division between central and peripheral elites was always politically salient. The question of state building was invariably at the forefront of the political debate since the Wars of Independence and was one of the main political cleavages around which factions first and then political parties were formed. Naturally, partisan strife included other agendas – for example, free trade, religion, federalism, regime type, etc. – and politicians used ideological banners – for example, conservatism and liberalism – sometimes transversal to state formation. Yet central and peripheral elites usually sat on opposite sides of the political aisle.

[27] The liberal–conservative distinction, although usually salient in nineteenth-century Latin America, should be taken with a grain of salt, since it does not identify with the distinction between central and peripheral elites perfectly. Although during the last half of the century, liberal elites in the colonial peripheries tended to support state building, liberals were also usually federalists and opposed the centralization of power in the national state. Conversely, during the first half of the century, conservative elites in the colonial centers of yore were usually monarchical and staunch supporters of the national army, which sometimes puts conservative parties in the state-building camp.

The struggle between these two forces resulted in a center–periphery equilibrium that was always in tension (Mazzuca, 2021; Cabal, 2022). Although Latin American states presented all the attributes of a modern state shortly after independence, the expanse of their territories, their young bureaucracies and armies, and their weak national identities all meant that they often struggled to effectively monopolize violence. The disputes between central and peripheral elites, therefore, were not always resolved within the rules of the political game and often led to coups and rebellions. Yet these revolts – even severe civil wars – produced only marginal changes to institutional arrangements and state capacity trajectories. Only the rise of a foreign threat broke the deadlock, invariably requiring the strengthening of the national army, which opened a window of opportunity for central elites to strengthen the state.

Preparation for war tightened the bond among the central elites and had the effect of converting a fraction of moderate peripheral elites that were initially disinclined to invest in their project, as long as they had some stakes in the survival of the national state. When members of the peripheral elite were governing, for example, they quickly converted to the pro-state camp if facing an external threat.[28]

However, the main effect of a looming international threat was to reveal the opposing preferences of pro- and anti-state actors, leading to polarization between the wartime coalition and an antiwar opposition. The latter, having agreed to a limited level of centralization and mobilization against their will, became increasingly dissatisfied with the sacrifices required. Of course, given this opposition, central elites would have had an incentive to resort to foreign sources to finance war and thus avoid confrontation with peripheral elites, but international resources were rarely available – due to sovereign debt defaults, blockades, and so on – and almost never sufficient. Extraction in the form of domestic taxation and conscription was therefore almost always unavoidable.

The reaction of peripheral elites to these processes varied along a spectrum from mild to strong opposition. Some accepted the growth of the state in return for some representation or the promise that the status quo ante would be restored after the conflict. Others denied their collaboration, resisting non-

[28] A notable example is that of Juan Manuel de Rosas, an Argentine *estanciero* who opposed an ill-fated war against Brazil (1825–1828) and subsequently rose to lead the peripheral elites or *federales*. While he was president of the Argentine Confederation (1835–1852), a series of external threats prompted him to enact a swift process of centralization resented by his former allies in the provinces. A similar case is that of Nicolás de Piérola in Peru, who opposed state formation and the War of the Pacific, but once he became president by virtue of a coup, he turned even more intransigent and bellicose than his predecessors, increasing taxes and conscripting all able men for the defense of Lima. Piérola continued to promote war as leader of the resistance for months after Lima had fallen. The changes in the policy preferences of General José Joaquín Herrera provide yet another example on the eve of the Mexican–American War.

violently or fleeing into exile. Still others rebelled against the state, provoking coups and civil wars and triggering the extraction–coercion cycle – leading to state repression and the development of inward-looking security forces. A minority even defected to actively support the enemy.[29] Across the board, extraction–coercion had the effect of bringing peripheral elites opposed to conscription and taxation together into more cohesive forms of organization as well (Carter, 2023).

When wars effectively broke out, state capacity was pursued relentlessly as a matter of life or death. Those for and against state building were forced to pick sides and openly declare their allegiances. In the context of war, those openly against the state were promptly portrayed as traitors. Domestic disagreements regarding acceptable levels of state strength would be therefore suspended and dealt with after the existential threat receded.

In nineteenth-century Latin America, rudimentary technology and small forces meant that it was very difficult, if not impossible, to determine who would win or lose a battle, much less a war (Visoni-Alonzo and Jacob, 2017). Factors affecting logistics, such as the roughness of the terrain and long distances, usually leveled the playing field when the fate of a war came down to a single hours-long confrontation of regular forces on a delimited battlefield.

Their contingency notwithstanding, battles were thought to reveal information about the capacity of governments to win a war and led to immediate domestic reactions. The cohesion of central elites and their resolve to continue the fight, for example, were negatively impacted by momentous defeats. News of a defeat almost immediately emboldened peripheral elites on the verge of rebellion to start a civil war or plot a coup. Conversely, central elites strengthened after victorious battles, which also rallied former skeptics and dissidents.

A romantic view of these wars suggests that the genius and mistakes of military commanders often decided the results of decisive battles. Yet a less rose-tinted look reveals that strokes of luck that defined the outcomes of wars could take place both on and off the battlefield. Fortuitous, exogenous changes in the international environment, such as sudden credit stoppages or changes in the composition of international alliances, were in many cases more decisive than military performance.[30]

[29] Latin American history is full of rebel *caudillos* who took their militias to fight alongside the enemy. In Argentina, Justo José de Urquiza, anointed the new leader of the *federales*, defeated Rosas with the help of Brazilian troops in 1852. One prominent story is that of Agustín Gamarra, a Peruvian soldier and two-time president who fought alongside Chilean troops, playing an important role in defeating his former commander Andrés de Santa Cruz in the Battle of Yungay on January 20, 1839.

[30] Think of how Benito Juárez's campaign against Emperor Maximilian was changed by the end of the American Civil War and the support that he received from the Union thereafter. This fortuitous and clearly exogenous event led to a turnabout in the Mexican struggle and eventually to Juárez's victory.

Nonetheless, this romantic view inevitably took hold when wars ended. For the winners, the effort was immediately justified. For the losers, the war became the worst of mistakes. In the blame game that ensued, individuals were attributed direct responsibility for the outcome. On the winning side, victorious commanders became the charismatic leaders of the nation. Leaders on the defeated side were usually chastised and ostracized.

Postwar effects remained observable in both victorious and defeated states, since the latter always survived (Child, 1985, 9). In such a context we can think schematically of two types of postwar mechanisms available in Latin America. For simplicity's sake we might call them external and internal (Tilly, 1990, 207). The former refers to the impact of territorial transfers, the physical destruction of war, and the constructive impact of occupations, the latter to the impact of the war outcomes on the domestic political arena.

External postwar mechanisms were arguably secondary in Latin American history. Although, as in Europe, "conquest entailed administration" (Tilly, 1990, 20), the occupation of a defeated state was rare and was usually too short for major long-term consequences to be attributed to it.[31] Similarly, territorial transfers were constrained by the principle of *uti possidetis* and similar norms enshrining territorial integrity, limiting them to relatively peripheral and uninhabited territories.[32] Finally the destruction that took place as a consequence of the war was never so extensive that it would have impeded the resurgence of the defeated states. With the possible exception of the War of the Pacific and the Paraguayan War – which in the cases of Argentina and Chile were closely followed by the "conquest" of Patagonia – the Latin American experience differs in this sense from that of Europe and the United States.[33]

Internal postwar mechanisms, in comparison, are ubiquitous after Latin American wars and invariably consequential. Each and every war seems to have transformed the domestic political scene, cursing or blessing the state formation project depending on its outcome.

31 The only three episodes are the occupation of Lima (1881–1883) after the War of the Pacific, the occupation of Asunción (1870–1876) after the Paraguayan War, and the occupation of Mexico City (1847–1848) after the Mexican–American War. All of these entailed extended mobilization of the winners and forced disarmament of the losers, but only for a short period of time. These states were very quickly given back their full sovereignty and, like Prussia after the Napoleonic occupations, could have restored their state formation project.

32 One clear exception is the transfer of strategic and resource-abundant territories that took place after the War of the Pacific. This arguably fueled Chilean state expansion and severely harmed Bolivian and Peruvian capacity to fund state building in the future.

33 The American case is not explored in this book, but the relative weight of external postwar mechanisms might explain to some extent the divergence in state capacity from the rest of the Americas. The United States followed a European-like pattern, which combined large territorial incorporations after the Mexican–American War and the occupation of Mexico for a year. Expansion to the west and the occupation of those acquired territories also fostered state building, and a similar dynamic was triggered by the permanent occupation of the South after the Civil War. One could easily see this dynamic replicating after the Spanish–American War, World War I, and World War II, although territorial expansion was then more limited.

On the losing side, a defeat usually shattered the coalition backing the war effort and transferred political power almost immediately from central to peripheral elites. Some observational implications of this are straightforward. First, the party or coalition in power during the war – which invariably favored centralization, extraction, and the development of state capacity – was typically ousted. Second, the new parties in power – comprised of those who had opposed the war and even those who had sided with the enemy – disbanded the military, transferred its functions to local militias, and defunded the central government. Third, parties representing the interests of the peripheral elites proliferated, and competition between them became fierce as they struggled to maintain both the autonomy of their local feuds and their influence over a rachitic state unable to impose order.

Winning a war, on the other hand, strengthened the central elites in power and weakened the peripheral elites that opposed the war. This took place by virtue of several concurrent mechanisms. First, the party or coalition in power during the war generally consolidated its grip on the state, prompting important factions of the peripheral elites that had joined the war effort – now socialized into the bureaucracy and the military – to remain in government.[34] Second, victory strengthened the armed forces, leading to the disarmament of local militias and resulting in the permanent ostracism of those sectors of the peripheral elite that betrayed the nation during the war. Third, victory legitimized the state formation project, forcing peripheral elites still in the opposition to change strategy. While the main goal of the peripheral elites was usually to prevent the expansion of the national state, after victory they accepted this expansion and focused on protecting their rights and influencing decision-making instead. This hints at a potential mechanism connecting military victory, state formation, and democratization, which is not explored in this book.

All in all, victories were far from a political panacea. New issues continued to divide elites, some leading to virulent conflict. Yet the political struggles of the postwar period were fundamentally reshaped by victory. For example, the rebellions against state building in victorious states usually ended with the ousting of a certain leader seen as a tyrant, but these sacrificial lambs were generally replaced by new state builders that doubled down on the strengthening of the armed forces and centralization of power.[35]

To summarize, the postwar effects of the outcomes of war are fundamentally mediated by the institutions that prevail, which differ greatly between winners and losers. Following Fernando López-Alves (2000), I consider the armed forces and political parties to be the key state institutions in this regard.

34 Mazzuca (2021) already offers evidence that war might be connected to the strengthening of state-making parties in Colombia, Mexico, and Uruguay.

35 This is the case of Porfirio Díaz, who opposed Benito Juárez's centralization only to outdo him later on. The opponents of Bartolomé Mitre, José Manuel Balmaceda, Emperor Pedro II, and Juan Rafael Mora Porras, to mention a few, followed the same logic.

Because of their direct link to armed conflict, we should first and foremost consider how the outcomes of war affected the national army as a state institution. Due to the glory vested upon its members – which often resulted in both social prestige and their incorporation into elite circles – the necessary reduction of the standing army after a war was compensated for by the incorporation of officers into parties and bureaucracies and by investment in the professionalization of the armed forces. This was not always a linear process, and sometimes the national army had to take it into its own hands to acquire this status – for example, by way of uprisings and coups. Either way, the armed forces in victorious states were strengthened as a result, in terms of their budget, ministerial control, and legal prerogatives. This could be seen particularly clearly in their relationship with local militias, which, once ubiquitous in Latin America (Sabato, 2018, 88), tended to disappear in victorious states. Besides the legitimacy and political power of the national armies, militias were usually absorbed into them during the war effort. Moreover, the national army was usually empowered by purchases of updated military technology needed for external wars, which created a huge gap with militias and other rebels, who often used arrows, *boleadoras*, lances, pikes, and swords (Arraíz, 1991; Rabinovich and Sobrevilla Perea, 2019).[36] With time, the institutionalization of the armed forces in victorious states ensured that they would play a praetorian role in protecting the state-building project that was their very *raison d'être* (López-Alves, 2000).[37]

A second, parallel dynamic was the transformation of political parties. Once defectors were outcast and the wartime coalition strengthened, political parties in victorious states tended to converge on the necessity of higher state capacity. Because of the overwhelming power of the victorious armies, peripheral elites still in the opposition camp considered violent opposition impossible and acquiesced to state building in exchange for participation (Madrid, 2019). Eventually the barrier between anti-state and pro-state elites was overcome, and the discussion started to revolve around the basic rules for gaining access to the state – that is, the regime instead of the state itself. As Hilda Sabato (2018) puts it, "Wars brought about both a renewal and enlargement of leadership: new and more men were attracted to politics." But victory in war also consolidated

36 This centralization of violence in the armed forces and a subordinate police also led to the restriction of arms imports by non-governmental entities, and arms registries. These measures were also driven in part by international competition, which put pressure on military organizations to become more centralized and cohesive in order to prevent local forces from being coopted by foreign foes and used as fifth columns.

37 Latin Americanists have long pointed to the importance of the armed forces as an institution (Rouquié, 1987). In the words of Fernando López-Alves (2001, 172), "It is useful, however, to look at Latin America through Tillean lenses. The contrasts pointed to questions not fully explored in the literature about the Latin American state and forced a revision of commonly assumed notions. For example, the poorly studied subject of the formation of the armed forces and the evolution of civil-military relations stand as two major priorities within the research agenda after this Tillean tour of Latin America."

(nationalist) parties that basically led the war effort, were transformed by it, and had now come to identify with the state. What Mazzuca (2021) identifies as "party led" state formation can therefore be subsumed into our bellicist logic.[38]

The consolidation of the military and "nationalist parties" (Mann, 1993, 74) naturally led to the reproduction of state-strengthening institutions as the legislatures passed laws expanding a whole array of reforms – for example, justice, policing, civil administration, education, and transport. This ever-growing process brought larger portions of society under the umbrella of the state as the accumulation of knowledge and resources in each of these bureaucracies fostered a self-reinforcing process of expansion.

Of course, the inverse happened in losing states, where central elites and state-building policies were associated with the defeat. In those cases peripheral elites secured the autonomy of their feuds in the long term by weakening national parties, the armed forces, and other state institutions. Societal actors who had supported the national state project during the war shifted their allegiances toward other organizations – for example, local militias and factions – and once these were strengthened, positive feedback consolidated them.

The end result of these military events and subsequent institutional developments was to affect long-term trends in state capacity.[39] The current debate on Latin American state formation has agreed in defining state capacity as infrastructural power (Mann, 1988, 5; Soifer and Vom Hau, 2008; Kurtz, 2013, 56; Saylor, 2014, 15), focusing on the conditions that allowed the state to implement policy throughout its territory. Soifer (2015, 10) proposes narrowing down the focus even more to three key empirical dimensions of infrastructural power: the administration of basic services, the mobilization of manpower, and the extraction of revenue. I will adopt this view, since these observables fit the kinds of processes classical bellicist theorists had in mind.[40] Evaluating these in nineteenth-century Latin America requires acute historical awareness. It is necessary to understand which technologies were available in order to choose whether to focus on income taxes vis-à-vis more aggregated measures of state revenue, or transport services vis-à-vis other services.

[38] This story of a pro-state party becoming hegemonic after victory is quite ubiquitous. Just to name a few, this seems to apply to the victory of the liberals of Benito Juárez against the Second French Intervention, to the liberal party of Mosquera after he defeated Ecuador, and to the hegemonic Partido Autonomista Nacional, which ruled Argentina for decades after the Paraguayan War. As I will show, this story extends to all victors in nineteenth-century Latin America in one way or another. One could apply a similar framework to interpret the role of the Republican Party in the formation of the American state after the Civil War (Bensel, 1991).

[39] It might be argued that some of the effects of international conflict will vary subnationally as well (Arias and de la Calle, 2021).

[40] I do this at the expense of analyzing the implications of the argument for other long-term outcomes such as linguistic commonality and nationalism – for example, the effect of wars on school textbooks and rituals (Vom Hau, 2012). I do recognize, however, that similar dynamics might apply to those outcomes (Darden and Mylonas, 2016) and discuss schooling as a dimension of state infrastructural power.

The mechanisms described in this chapter are an ideal type (Weber, 1949, 40–43). More intense wars will approximate the constellation of elements described, while states that faced less stringent warfare should show some of these elements and not others, being in a sort of gray zone (Goertz, 2020, 188).

Overall, this account of bellicist mechanisms builds strongly upon a recent consensus that situates Latin American state formation squarely in the nineteenth century and uniformly assigns a central role to elite preferences in determining long-term outcomes in state infrastructural power (Kurtz, 2013, 20; Saylor, 2014, 12; Soifer, 2015, 15; Mazzuca, 2021, 11; see also Urteaga Quisme, 2017). Yet by introducing the element of war, my theory better explains variation in elite preferences. So far the literature either leaves elite decisions unexplained or fails to explain why elites change their minds at different moments in time and in certain countries but not in others.[41] In my theory, the political balance of power between central and peripheral elites is affected by country and time-variant structural shocks: the outcomes of war.

My theoretical focus on central elites – instead of state leaders and officials – also allows me to see bureaucrats as an element of state capacity. Max Weber (1978, 989) tells us about Bismarck's surprise on seeing that, upon the resignation of the many statesmen he had vanquished from territories conquered by Prussia, the bureaucrats continued to administer their offices unconcerned and undismayed. Of course, these bureaucrats were core members of the defeated group or state elite and, in this sense, they were central elites. Yet these professionals were also part of a machinery for policy implementation, and in this other sense they *were* the state. This intrinsic duality of the bureaucracy – which Weber (1994, 316) tries to capture with his distinction between politics as a profession and politics as a vocation – has not been properly addressed by scholars of Latin America, who have interpreted bureaucrats as actors and bureaucratization as a strategy conducive to state building (Soifer, 2015, 61). Yet, as Ryan Saylor (2014, 21) correctly points out, to "implant state employees at the local level" *is* state capacity. My concept of central elites is intended to underscore this distinction and allow us to see bureaucracies not solely as an actor in this story but also a state institution (Mann, 1993, 62) or an outcome.[42]

41 Soifer (2015, 68–82), for example, identifies the strategic decision of state leaders to deploy government officials to the peripheries as a cause of state formation but fails to provide an explanation for such a decision. Similarly, Mazzuca (2021, 34) attributes state building to the strength of lords, parties, and ports but does not explain why they become strong. This led more structuralist scholars like Kurtz (2013, 29) to make the point that this choice must be epiphenomenal (see also Saylor, 2014, 21) and turn to time-invariant characteristics – such as the type of labor prevailing in a country (Kurtz, 2013, 36) – and country-invariant factors – such as commodity booms (Saylor, 2014, 52), a point that Soifer (2015, 19) criticizes in turn.

42 In the context of my theory, bureaucratic offices are to be thought of as state-strengthening institutions. Bureaucracies are characterized by the delimitation of the jurisdictional areas that compose the duties of each official, a clear hierarchy, the existence of a bureau – a physical

This theory is also very much in line with the current Latin American consensus on highlighting critical junctures and long-term trends. Yet it also perfects this approach by narrowing these junctures down to small critical events – occurrences that are short in duration and clearly bounded in space. Some of the critical junctures identified in this literature are simply too long (Kurtz, 2013) or affect too broad an array of countries (Saylor, 2014) to produce falsifiable implications. Moreover, while contingency is not a factor in other theories, it is central to my conceptualization of battles as critical events. If minimal historical rewrites are sufficient to change the history of war outcomes, then this theory should prove to be more persuasive than its predecessors.

To summarize, this section lays out a series of concrete observational expectations that I corroborate by looking at the entirety of Latin America before 1914 in Part II:

- External threats triggered the coercion–extraction cycle (Chapter 4).
- War outcomes caused state capacity trajectories to diverge (Chapter 5).
- The rank of state capacity c. 1900 reflects their long-term effect (Chapter 6).

This theoretical section also generates expectations about specific contexts, processes, events, relevant actors, and their preferences and behavior – in short, about mechanisms – that are difficult to summarize statistically. Part III of this book analyzes whether the type of actors and processes fleshed out here are actually representative of what happened in major Latin American wars. This section also looks with more detail at the state institutions and intermediate outcomes in the causal chain connecting war outcomes and state capacity. Among many other things, my case studies look at whether:

- the rise of external threats is preceded by a central–peripheral elite deadlock,
- external threats strengthen central elites and lead to contingent mobilization,
- peripheral elite leaders mobilize when they are themselves in power,
- during the war there are always peripheral elites opposed to mobilization,
- battle outcomes immediately affect the central–peripheral elites' bargain,
- lost battles encourage peripheral elites to come to light and even revolt,
- battle and war outcomes are fundamentally unforeseeable and contingent,
- after victory, peripheral elites flock toward the ruling coalition,
- victorious states experience an expansion of nationalist parties,
- the military becomes a powerful political actor in victorious states, and
- after defeats, peripheral elites dismantle key wartime state institutions.

This list is nonexhaustive. Many other implications of the argument are explored in Part III. Because this part of the book is written as an analytical

edifice – where documents are registered and everyday work takes place, the specialized training of officials in their fields, the full-time permanent employment of officials, and the development of internal codes (Weber, 1978, 958).

historical narrative covering nine countries and six major wars, referencing back to the theory would be too cumbersome and it might not always be apparent which implications are being tested at what point. The index of the book should help navigate this complexity by pointing to the specific pages on which evidence is offered for key elements of the theory.

3

Blood and Debt in Europe and Latin America

Were wars intense and frequent enough in Latin America to produce state formation? It is undoubtedly true that peace has reigned in this region during the twentieth century. After the Chaco War (1932–1935), no single episode of interstate warfare seems to have produced, strictly speaking, the more than 1,000 battle deaths required by the definition of war (Schenoni et al., 2023). Therefore, while frequent militarization (Mares, 2001) and international rivalry might have prompted some state building (Thies, 2005), it can be conceded that the twentieth century has been (in line with bellicist expectations) less conducive to it. Was Latin America always like this?

The historiographical debates and descriptive statistics I survey in this chapter paint a comparative picture of war and state formation from colonial times until the turn of the twentieth century in both Latin America and Europe. This historical contextualization provides some insight into the concepts of war and state capacity that is necessary before exploring how wars affected intra-regional variation in state capacity across Latin America in Part II. While doing so, this chapter will also provide a list of the most severe nineteenth-century wars in the region, which are fleshed out as case studies in Part III.

The chapter is divided into three sections. In Section 3.1 I argue that wars in Europe and geopolitical friction on the peripheries of European empires prompted investments in state capacity in the *Indias*. In Section 3.2 I show that the newborn Latin American states faced relatively frequent and severe warfare throughout the nineteenth century. In Section 3.3 I focus on how war affected the territorial configuration of the region, perhaps even more than in Europe. Finally, in Section 3.4, I demonstrate that Latin American states were not substantively more reliant on debt and indirect taxes for revenue than their European counterparts were. Put together, these sections indicate that the idea that war was either absent or financed differently in Latin America (Centeno, 2002) should not be expected to hold before 1914.

3.1 BLOOD AND EMPIRE BEFORE INDEPENDENCE

If this book were to provide a comprehensive history of the state in Latin America, it would start by showing how the formation of the original precolonial states in Mexico and the Andes resembled the speculations of Oppenheimer, Rostow, and Weber (Carneiro, 1970; Spencer and Redmond, 2004; Feltham et al., 2009). However, these debates now belong to the distant fields of anthropology and archeology. Since very little is now left of the Aztec, Incan, and Mayan institutions, European colonization marks a better starting point for a summary historical account of the institutions inherited by Latin American national states in the nineteenth century.

The institutions that the Iberian kingdoms transferred to the Americas were the product of eight centuries of struggle on one of the most contentious borders of Europe. From the Battle of Covadonga of 718 to the defeat of the Emirate of Granada in 1492 – only months before Columbus's arrival in the Indias – the Iberian kingdoms, and Castile in particular, had been forged through constant fighting. As Douglas North (1989, 1328) puts it, "In contrast [to other European kingdoms], Castile was continuously engaged in warfare, either against the Moors or in internal strife ... the result was a centralized monarchy in Castile, and it was Castile that defined the institutional evolution of both Spain and Latin America." The *Conquista* of America, a prolongation of the *Reconquista* – the reconquest of Iberia from the Muslims – replicated the severe institutions and state–society relations imposed upon the occupied territories of Al-Andaluz, which undoubtedly fit the narrative of Tilly (1990).

Institutional history has lost prominence in contemporary historiographic debates about the Spanish and Portuguese empires (Adelman, 1998), but what we know from this once-prominent field suggests metropolitan institutions were transposed to the Americas with little input from either locals or settlers. Of course, distance made monitoring more difficult, and compromises had to be struck with local strongmen, but this did not develop into alternatives to the metropolitan state institutions (Lynch, 1992). Rather, informal institutions developed in the colonies (Helmke and Levitsky, 2004).

Wars in Europe thus transformed state–society relations in both Iberia and the Americas, and many times it was the colonies that were more severely burdened. During the reign of Charles V, for example, the mobilization of Spanish *tercios* across the Old World was primarily financed by taxes imposed on the New World (Espinosa, 2006) to the extent that "lands producing enough silver to revolutionize the markets of Europe should themselves suffer chronic shortages of coin" (Halperín Donghi, 1993, 2). Such dynamics naturally triggered the extraction–coercion cycle. Populations around the sites of the largest pre-Columbian civilizations – now turned into the seats of Spanish power – were the most heavily taxed and the first to rebel. The Incas did so intermittently from 1536 to 1572 (D'Altroy, 2002, 319) and the Aztecs too in 1528 and 1548 (Hamnett, 1999, 72). The Spanish coercive apparatus thus tended to concentrate in central Mexico and the South American highlands (Jones, 2013, 122).

Extraction not only affected indigenous peoples but *criollos* – white people born in the Americas – as well. Besides implementing the *alcabala* – a form of sales tax first imposed in Mexico in 1574 – and other forms of direct and indirect taxation on local elites, including the Church, the selling of bureaucratic positions that were initially reserved for *peninsulares* to *criollos* became increasingly common. European wars were a major factor behind the expansion of the colonial bureaucracy (Rodríguez, 1998).[1]

Competition between Europeans in the Americas also shaped the colonial state by determining the strategic importance of certain sections of the empire. Privateering against shipments of precious metals and attacks on the Spanish positions in the Caribbean by the French, British, and Dutch – epitomized by Sir Francis Drake's siege of Cartagena in 1586 – eventually led to the creation of an entirely new Viceroyalty of New Granada in 1717. The new administrative unit helped to consolidate Spanish power and deterred piracy and smuggling but would require continuous investment in military and infrastructural capacity. When Cartagena was besieged in 1741 by a British fleet commanded by Admiral Edward Vernon – the episode was part of a large-scale amphibious raid during the War of Austrian Succession (1739–1748) that also targeted Cuba and Panama – the Spanish redoubled their investment in troops, fortifications, and cannons. The attack foreshadowed the occupation of Havana during the Seven Years' War (1756–1763), an episode that caused major shock in Madrid and furthered even more reforms (Archer, 2000, 5).

Portuguese colonies in the Americas were similarly harassed. French forces, led by Nicolas Durand de Villegaignon, established a colony in Guanabara Bay in 1555 and had to be driven out by the Lusitanians in 1560. The English, under the command of James Lancaster, similarly attacked the port of Santos in 1595. The Dutch captured Salvador in 1624 and Recife in 1630 – at a time when Spain and Portugal were under a single crown – and controlled the Brazilian northeast until 1654. In the next hundred years, the Portuguese forged a stable alliance with England, which reduced their vulnerability to the enemies of Spain but forced Lisbon to strengthen itself against its mighty neighbor in Europe and the Americas. Led by Prime Minister Sebastião José de Carvalho e Melo (1750–1777), also known as the Marquis of Pombal, the public works projects and tax reform that followed the 1755 Lisbon earthquake developed into a full-blown security-driven reform program after the Spanish invasion attempt of 1762.

1 For example, "The financial demands of the European wars led to the increased sale of *oidor* (*audiencia* judge) positions," although due to strategic considerations, "the Monarchy sold most *audiencia* judgeships in less threatened regions, such as Guadalajara, Quito, Lima, Charcas, and Santiago de Chile, and sold the fewest *oidor* positions in those *audiencias* subject to British attack, like Santo Domingo, Santa Fé de Bogotá, and Mexico" (Rodríguez, 1998, 21). War, in this way, shaped the geography of the colonial bureaucracies and laws that independent Latin American states would inherit.

In the colonies, this Seven Years' War resulted in the brief loss of *Colonia del Sacramento* – now Uruguay – to Spain. To strengthen Portuguese positions in Brazil, Pombal encouraged the establishment of new industries, such as textiles and mining, introduced a new system of tax collection, and reorganized the military, the judiciary, and higher education.

The concurrent Bourbonic Reforms – the usual name for the fiscal and administrative reforms that took place under the reign of Charles III (1759–1788) in Spain – were also "a case in which international threats promoted state building" (Soifer, 2015, 89). Right after the Seven Years' War, "shocked by Britain's capture of Havana in 1762, and dismayed by the trading boom that resulted, the Spanish Crown moved to initiate changes upon the cessation of hostilities ... the war clearly demonstrated that the Spanish Monarchy needed to control its American possessions if it were to reclaim its place as a major world power" (Rodríguez, 1998). Spain had also lost Florida and received Louisiana from the French, making its position more vulnerable in the northernmost section of the empire. The reform therefore started with an experiment in political centralization and trade liberalization in Cuba, which was then extended to the rest of the Hispanic colonies by the initiative of minister José de Galvez.[2] Since the Portuguese were now reinforcing Colonia del Sacramento, vulnerabilities in the south were pressing as well. The establishment of Buenos Aires as the capital of the new *Virreynato del Río de la Plata* (1777) was a direct consequence of this. Although the city was a little outpost at the time, its bureaucracy and military developed fast to control smuggling and defend the city from attacks.

Overall, the Iberian reforms tripled tax revenues for the metropoles during the late eighteenth century (Halperín Donghi, 1993, 26), but *criollos* and other local populations started to resent these pressures. Beyond taxation, extraction took the form of the increased conscription of locals into the army and militias. The proportion of soldiers born in Spain diminished, and the number of *criollo* officials rose considerably. The military career became a possible source of status for *criollo* families that could not easily bribe officials and buy bureaucratic positions anymore, but the situation also generated constraints. During the War of American Independence (1776–1783), despite Spain's desire to avenge the defeats of Cuba and Florida, the concern that *criollo* soldiers

[2] The Bourbonic Reforms aimed to modernize and centralize the colonial administration, which until then had been characterized by a decentralized and often inefficient system of government. The reforms introduced new administrative and legal institutions, such as the intendancy system, which was designed to increase royal control over colonial finances and reduce corruption. Among the most significant reforms were the establishment of free trade between Spanish colonies and the rest of the empire – as a way of extracting more revenue and increasing metropolitan exports – and the expulsion of the Jesuits, which granted the crown more centralized control of education. A new Ministry of the Indies replaced a lethargic Council of the Indies and kept a fluid connection with the *superintendentes* in charge of limiting collusion at the local level. Their subalterns, called *subdelegados*, were also deployed centrally to every corner of the empire, completing this new, tightly knit, continent-wide network of bureaucrats.

would spread revolutionary ideas to other parts of the Spanish Empire acted as a constraint on military involvement (Archer, 2000, 6).[3]

The need to police the empire beyond those cities was not great up until the late eighteenth century (McFarlane, 1995, 313), when the region registered important revolts in Quito (1765), Cuzco (1780–1782), and parts of Colombia (1781). There are records of other riots and rebellions – most notably in Paraguay (1730–1735) and Venezuela (1749–1752) – yet these cross-class rebellions directed against the metropolis were comparatively massive in size (Pérez, 1977). During the *comuneros* revolt against the levy of new taxes in New Granada, rebels gathered a force of 20,000 men and organized a march against the capital, Santa Fé de Bogotá. To give some context, this was about half the size of the entire Spanish army in the Iberian Peninsula by the mid-eighteenth century. These revolts often resisted taxation, but other aspects also caused important grievances. The Great Rebellion of the Aymara and Quechua peoples of southern Peru, led by Tupac Amaru – which involved a 60,000-strong rebel army – for instance, was a response to the changes in social status between caciques and creoles that the Bourbonic Reforms imposed (McFarlane, 1995, 321). The power of the Spanish colonial state was so strong in the central and upper highlands of Peru that it prevented the spread of the revolts in the direction of Lima (Stern, 1987, 63–71), but historians estimate that there were 100,000 deaths within a population of 2 million in the region, which amounts to 5 percent of the population – as a point of comparison. This is the same proportion of people that died during the French Revolution – at the time, France had ten times this population (Cornblit, 1978, 60).

Something similar happened in New Spain (nowadays Mexico). Although the Napoleonic Wars would change the equation, Mexico remained rather stable throughout the Bourbonic Reforms period, probably because of its incredible wealth. By the end of the eighteenth century, Mexico had a per capita income higher than that of Spain, yet it retained only 5 percent of the silver it produced and accounted for two-thirds of the revenue that the metropole extracted from all its colonies. This level of extraction, however, was a ticking time bomb and would become one of the main triggers of the Wars of Independence (Halperín Donghi, 1993, 9).

3 "The army, in contrast to the Church, gained new power and influence in America. After the Seven Years' War, Britain and Spain became the principal competitors for control of the New World. Both militarized the continent by establishing standing armies. The Crown decided to defend America with an army built around a core of regular Spanish troops and a trained local militia as a reserve. Americans would pay for the new armed forces with an increase in the alcabala tax from 2 to 6 percent. The process, which began in Cuba in 1763, later spread to New Spain, New Granada, Quito, and Peru. The army of America rapidly became an American army; by the end of the century, Americans constituted 60 percent of the officer corps and 80 percent of the troops. The militias were almost entirely American. To encourage enlistment, the new army and the militia received *fuero militar*, a privilege extended to some degree even to castas and pardos (Afro-Indians who lived in coastal regions), which provided the protection of military courts and a degree of fiscal exemption" (Rodríguez, 1998, 29).

The French Revolutionary Wars set the stage for the final collapse of the Spanish and Portuguese empires in the Americas. The independence of the colonies, as in the case of the United States, has often been represented as a reaction to increasing taxation without representation in a context of the constant military mobilization of Iberian powers since 1793.

Already in 1796, when Spain joined forces with France against the United Kingdom, the possibility of an independentist movement led by Venezuelan exile Francisco Miranda and backed by London became a serious concern. When Trinidad fell to the British in 1797, *criollo* elites realized that the defense of the colonies was increasingly falling into their hands, which increased the demand for representation. This sentiment became even stronger after the Battle of Trafalgar (1805), when the complete demise of the Spanish fleet effectively led to the collapse of trade monopoly and left the colonies even more vulnerable. The British attempts to take the port of Buenos Aires in 1806 and 1807, for example, led to the organization of a costly 10,000-strong militia in the remote port, which in turn led to friction between the Spanish authorities and the leaders of the self-organized militias.

When Napoleon invaded Portugal (1807) and Spain (1808), starting the Peninsular War, the responsibilities of creole elites as well as their political leverage vis-à-vis the metropoles became even greater. The epicenter of Iberian power shifted to the Americas. The Portuguese court fled to Rio de Janeiro, and with Madrid subdued by Marshal Joachim Murat, Spanish power decentralized to local Juntas, who recognized the status of overseas governments as kingdoms and granted them representation in a Junta Central meeting in Zaragoza. Latin Americans, however, were grossly under-represented. While 10 million *peninsulares* got twenty-six deputies, the 17 million inhabitants of Spanish America got merely nine (Earle, 2000, 10). The situation became untenable when Zaragoza and Seville fell to the French in 1810 and the seat of government moved to Cadiz, the major trading port and gateway to the New World. As it became abundantly clear that the weight of extraction and mobilization was going to fall on Latin Americans almost completely, the *criollo* elites revolted, forming de facto sovereign Juntas claiming to govern in the name of Ferdinand VII. Revolutions of this sort took place in Caracas on April 19, Buenos Aires on May 25, Bogotá on July 20, and Santiago on September 18, to mention a few prominent examples, and triggered the continent-wide fifteen-year-long process that we now know as the Wars of Independence.

The independence struggle was clearly initiated on the peripheries of the empire and reached more conservative regions from the outside in. Despite friction with indigenous peoples and other European powers on the border, state capacity in Spanish America continued to be higher in the capitals of the first viceroyalties (Soifer, 2015, 94). Mexico City and Lima had the highest concentration of military officials, priests, merchants, and bureaucrats, which meant the conservative elites were stronger. The cost of rebellion was therefore higher in those colonial centers, which would become the great losers of the Wars of Independence.

In the peripheries, now turned revolutionary epicenters, a swift militarization of politics and society took place. In places like Buenos Aires, militias, which had increased their status since the victory against the British invaders, were now dominating the scene. Celebrated studies tracing the origins of the Latin American state to the Wars of Independence unequivocally highlight how local elites – in the case of Buenos Aires, mostly merchants and priests – paid the price of this mobilization (Halperín Donghi, 1982, 88; see also Halperín Donghi, 2002). Extraction took the form of increased tax rates, the implementation of new tributes, and extraordinary contributions such as forced credit and the confiscation or requisition of cattle and slaves. Almost all these revenues went to pay for a now-professional army of some 20,000 men. In many ways wars in the Americas were more transformative than those on the Iberian Peninsula. For example, revolutionaries often offered manumission to slaves who participated in the Wars of Independence, which resulted in a reduction of the number of slaves by half after the conflict (Blanchard, 2008; Helg and Vergnaud, 2019).

To fight the *criollo* uprisings, mobilization also took place in Spain and throughout the colonies. Peter Costeloe (1981, 232) calculates that a total of 47,079 men, including 2,390 officers, sailed to the Americas between 1810 and 1819. The vast majority of these soldiers were funded by direct taxation and forced loans imposed upon local populations. War contributions included new direct taxes proportional to individuals' income, a tax on the annual income of *parroquias*, an increase of the sales tax or *alcabala* of up to 14 percent from a prewar level of 4 percent, the *octroi* – a tax levied on goods entering or leaving cities and towns – and the creation of a tobacco monopoly to raise additional revenue, among many others.

Although elites in the main Spanish strongholds managed to pay these new contributions, suffocated by the new taxes, nonelite groups in these areas revolted as well. In New Spain, priest Miguel Hidalgo gave a speech known as the *Grito de Dolores* on September 16, 1810, in which he called for the people of Mexico to rise up against the choking levels of taxation imposed by Spain. Hidalgo led an army of some 40,000 peasants that was close to taking Mexico City, although, like many of the uprisings above, his revolt was finally subdued.

The sheer size of Hidalgo's army demonstrates that the intensity of warfare in Latin America during the Wars of Independence was in many ways comparable to that in Europe during the French Revolutionary Wars and the Napoleonic Wars.[4] Due to their size and social component, the Hidalgo revolts were more akin to the Tupac Amaru and Comuneros revolts that followed the Bourbonic Reforms. Like previous peasant revolts in Peru and New Granada, the revolt

4 In all major battles surrounding the siege of Zaragoza, the size of the Peninsular armies was between 20,000 and 40,000 troops.

in New Spain covered large swaths of the Mexican Bajío, and the death of the leader was followed by even more violence, which required a great deal of repression to put down, arguably generating long-term state capacity (Arias and de la Calle, 2021). The state monopoly of violence receded to the main cities, which were surrounded by a violent, stormy countryside (Young, 1988). Due to such dynamics – more akin to anarchy or civil war – the militarization of American societies would only increase in the next fifteen years, but the existence of a continent-wide struggle for independence was already evident in the generalization of violence.[5]

Spain, therefore, was fighting a war on three fronts: against the French around Cadiz, against the *criollos* attacking the colonial centers from now de facto independent colonial peripheries, and against the *castas* opposed to extraction and mobilization around the colonial strongholds. To win this war, concessions had to be made to *criollos* and liberals, and the Spanish Constitution of 1812 came to do just that. In the colonies, the liberal charter resulted in the organization of *ayuntamientos* with great autonomy governed by elected officials, the majority of whom were *criollos* themselves. Naturally, they quelled potential rebels and turned the tide in favor of the metropole. When Napoleon left Spain in 1814, Madrid could focus on subduing the Latin American rebels.

In 1815 alone, 12,254 men were dispatched to Venezuela under the orders of General Pablo Morillo and another 4,885 to Cartagena, Lima, Montevideo, and Panama (Costeloe, 1981, 229). Simón Bolívar, who tried to spearhead two republican governments in Venezuela, was completely defeated by the 10,000 *llaneros* of Boves plus the equivalent army that Morillo used to subdue Cartagena in 1815. Bolívar thus had to move from city to city while he escaped the wrath of the *pacificador* (the pacifier, a nickname for Morillo), leaving a trail of destruction behind him. In the end, Bolívar fled into exile in Jamaica.

Meanwhile, in Mexico, after the death of Hidalgo in 1811, José María Morelos continued with the revolution that his teacher had initiated. Morelos

5 Relatedly, the Hidalgo revolt illustrates an element of guerrilla warfare that characterized the Latin American independence wars more broadly. While history books often record regular battles between royalist and independent armies, irregular or asymmetric warfare became quite prominent early on, and much more so than in the Peninsular War – where the word *guerrilla* is supposed to have originated. Several key figures, such as José María Morelos and Vicente Guerrero in Mexico, José Tomás Boves and José Antonio Páez in Venezuela, José Gervasio Artigas in Uruguay, and Martín Miguel de Gúemes and Facundo Quiroga in Argentina, to mention a few, commanded large contingents of rather undisciplined and badly armed soldiers. These first *caudillos* or warlords pioneered a form of warfare that is difficult to trace in numbers but we know to have been incredibly widespread both during the Wars of Independence and throughout the nineteenth century (Archer, 2000). Talking about battle deaths in this context and trying to compare them with those in the Napoleonic Wars makes little sense. Yet we can look at changes in the population and get an idea of how deadly these wars were. We know that, for example, by 1817 some 80,000 people had died in Venezuela as a consequence of the war, meaning one-fifth of the 420,000 inhabitants before the conflict (Rodríguez, 1998, 122).

commanded an army of some 10,000 men in southern Mexico and fought gallantly in two dozen small battles. The Royalists were merciless to the populations that supported Morelos, besieging, displacing, and starving them. After several years of the most severe counterinsurgent warfare, the movement waned, and Morelos was finally executed by Inquisition officials in Mexico City in 1815. During the first stages of the independence wars in Mexico, the Spanish forces amounted to some 40,000 men, a number equivalent to that of the entire Spanish army in Europe (Alaman, 1985).

Similarly, while the Buenos Aires revolt would not be completely quashed, it had waned in power considerably. A failed campaign toward Upper Peru ended in defeat, forcing General Manuel Belgrano to displace half the population of the city of San Salvador de Jujuy in 1812, much like the Russians were doing in Moscow, and pursue a scorched earth tactic. In 1815 the remainder of the troops in the revolutionary *Ejército del Norte* were defeated in the Battle of Sipe Sipe. Not even the indigenous 40,000-strong rebellion of the *curaca* Mateo Pumacahua could turn the tide (Graham, 2013).

Despite this initial wave of military defeats across the continent, the independence movement would eventually benefit from a chain of exogenous and rather contingent events: the end of the Napoleonic Wars, the dissatisfaction of the liberals in Spain – disappointed by Ferdinand VII's rejection of the 1812 Constitution – and British concerns with the Holy Alliance and the restoration of a Spanish empire in the Americas. Liberal soldiers with experience on the European battlefield supported the cause of independence in this new phase. This was the case of José de San Martín, the military leader of the armies of the River Plate, who envisioned a bold plan to circumvent the Spanish stronghold in Upper Peru: cross the Andes, attack Santiago, set sail from Valparaiso, and take Lima from the sea. Thanks to the impressive mobilization of local elites in the region of Cuyo – western Argentina – he was ready to cross the Andes by 1816. In the Battle of Chacabuco (1817) and the Battle of Maipu (1818), which secured Chilean independence, the commander of the *Ejército de los Andes* fought with similar tactics and army sizes as those he had witnessed in the European battlefield, during the Battle of Bailen of 1808.[6]

While San Martín was reactivating the fight in the Southern Cone, Bolívar was reorganizing in the north of South America. By early 1817, this other *Libertador* had managed to gain control of swaths of Venezuelan territory, including the city of Angostura on the Orinoco River. In 1818, José Antonio Páez, leader of the *llaneros*, pledged allegiance to Bolívar, and a sound victory

[6] The crossing of the Andes also illustrates the feats that Latin American revolutionaries had to endure, given the orography, long distances, lack of roads, and other complications. This is to say, if we compare the sizes of Latin American armies to that of the Grande Armée and battle death counts in the Americas to those of Borodino or Leipzig, we would not be doing justice to the dimensions of a continent-wide struggle with more dispersed troops in a completely different strategic setting.

at the Battle of Boyacá on August 7, 1819, resulted in the fall of Bogotá. From this new position of strength, Bolívar redirected his troops to Venezuela and gained the final independence of his native land after the Battle of Carabobo on June 24, 1821.

In a sort of pincer movement, now Bolívar and San Martín advanced against Peru, the last stronghold of the *realistas*. After the fall of Lima, the two generals met in Guayaquil and embraced each other on July 26, 1821. The independence of South America was basically achieved, although it would take until 1824 to defeat the final resistance in Upper Peru in the Battle of Junín and the Battle of Ayacucho. The events paralleled those in New Spain, where the Army of the Three Guarantees entered Mexico City and declared independence on September 27, 1821. With the recognition of the independence of Latin American states by some great powers like Great Britain and the United States around 1824 the new Latin American states were formally born into a new interstate subsystem.

As in the European context (Tilly, 1990, 20–23), Latin American national states would eventually prove superior to empires – like Brazil and Mexico, which presented great concentration but low accumulation of coercive means, and systems of fragmented sovereignty such as loose federations – with high accumulation and low concentration of coercion, which proliferated immediately after the Wars of Independence, particularly on the peripheries of the colonial empires. Bellicist dynamics would continue to drive this process.

3.2 WARS AND LEVIATHANS IN THE NINETEENTH CENTURY

Even if bellicist dynamics preexisted Latin American states, it is only after their independence that we can see how war affected them individually and compare the Latin American interstate system with its European counterpart. This section shows that if we focus strictly on the period between the independences and 1914, three key statements in the literature (Soifer, 2015, 8, 18) do not seem to hold, at least in comparison with European standards:

- That Latin America featured "low levels of international war" (severity).
- That "wars were rare" (frequency).
- That wars were "limited in scope" (or the extent of mobilization).

In one of the most celebrated studies of war in Latin America, Kalevi Holsti (1996, 152) concluded, "Looking at [the] nineteenth-century one sees patterns of peace and war, intervention, territorial predation, alliances, arms-racing, and power-balancing quite *similar to those found in eighteenth-century Europe*." This characterization suggests that in the nineteenth century, the *Pax Britannica* was little more than a euphemism. Latin America in the nineteenth century was far from an "ordinary context" where security threats were uncommon (Kurtz, 2013, 6) and interstate warfare "limited" (Centeno, 2002, 20). Rather, Latin America was a "zone of war" (Holsti, 1996, 161).

TABLE 3.1 *Warfare in nineteenth-century Europe and Latin America*

Indicator	Europe	Latin America
Interstate wars	11	17
Average duration (months)	6	25
Total battle deaths (BDs)	558,721	400,051
BDs relative to population	0.29%	1.23%
Total fatalities (Fs)	1,136,290	1,189,355
Fs relative to population	0.56%	3.96%
Territorial changes (TCs)	70	15
TCs after interstate war	8	6
Use of force (MIDs)	30	53
Display of force (MIDs)	51	22

Notes: To be considered to have taken place in Europe or Latin America, a war has to be included in the list produced by Sarkees and Wayman (2010), take place in that region, and involve at least one preexisting sovereign state from that same region. These criteria exclude wars fought in Latin America by extra-regional powers, such as the Spanish–American War (1898), as well as European colonial wars. Total fatalities are then taken from Brecke (1999). Similarly, I only consider territorial exchanges between two states within the same region as coded by Tir et al. (1998). This excludes concessions between regions, such as those made by Mexico to the United States at Guadalupe Hidalgo (1848). In order to locate militarized interstate disputes short of war (MIDs) (Palmer et al., 2019), I only consider a MID to have taken place in Europe when two European states were involved, whereas I assume that all MIDs involving a Latin American state took place in Latin America. Population is calculated in 1850 to be 200 million in Europe and 30 million in Latin America (Bolt et al., 2018).

First of all, unless we are making extemporaneous comparisons with the World Wars of the twentieth century, the idea that levels of warfare in Latin America were low during the nineteenth century seems difficult to sustain. Every indicator of interstate warfare in Table 3.1 suggests the opposite.

To start with, the likelihood of war was 0.64 times greater in Latin America than in Europe, where scholars usually see war-driven state- and nation-building dynamics taking place. This still underestimates the frequency of warfare in Latin America if we consider that the region had 45 contiguous dyads at most during the nineteenth century, compared to 259 such dyads in Europe (Stinnett et al., 2002). Because of the sheer number of states in Europe, the baseline expectation would be for war to happen 5.5 times more frequently in Europe. This means that warfare in Latin America was extremely frequent in relative terms.

Other indicators, such as the average duration of war, total battle deaths, war-related deaths, violent territorial exchanges, and episodes of militarization, also suggest the stringency of warfare in Latin America. In some aspects – such as duration and per capita measures of fatalities – interstate warfare in Latin America was similar to seventeenth- or eighteenth-century European levels, as Holsti suggested. A population loss of 3 percent, for example, is similar to that suffered by France during the Napoleonic Wars.

The numbers displayed in Table 3.1 are more in line with a minority position in the literature arguing that "the intensity of the wars that European and American states fought during the nineteenth century was typically very similar. Therefore, contemporary differences in state capacity between these two regions can hardly be attributed to their experiences prior to World War I" (Goenaga et al., 2023, 3; see also Queralt, 2022). Militarized interstate disputes (MIDs) were roughly equivalent in both continents during the period, but those in Latin America were comparatively more severe (Palmer et al., 2022).

Looking at the budget of Latin American states in the nineteenth century also reveals the importance that war might have had for these polities. Paraphrasing Hintze, states in Latin America were originally military organizations – more so than their European contemporaries. Although the data is scattered, the percentage of the total budget of these states that is devoted to the military is almost never below 30 percent, is usually around 50 percent, and can swell to 80 percent during wars and after military victories (Garavaglia, 2003, 142–148).

The Spartan image of the Latin American state described above is incompatible with the opinion that "in trying to understand variation among Latin American states in the nineteenth century the overall absence of war in the region cannot be helpful" (Soifer, 2015, 18). The prevailing idea that "outside of Europe the relative lack of warfare has severed a chief pathway to new state capacity" and Latin America "features little warfare" (Saylor, 2014, 52) misses the incredible decline of conflict in the region that takes place in the twentieth century when compared to the nineteenth century (Schenoni et al., 2023).

Authors that highlight instead the absence of "selection" (Kurtz, 2013, 32; Saylor, 2014, 200; Soifer, 2015, 233) are factually correct – few states died in Latin America – but arrive at the wrong conclusion as well. Statesmen and elites in nineteenth-century Latin America could not take survival for granted any more than their European counterparts could. The prevalence of survival is something we can only see *a posteriori*. At the time, Latin American states had been sovereign for only a few decades, and their independence seemed always at risk from the European attempts to restore colonial order and the threats of powerful elites in Bogotá, Buenos Aires, Lima, and Mexico City.[7] Even big

7 During the Great Colombia period (1819–1831), elites in Quito and Caracas had to subordinate themselves to the authorities in Bogotá, just as elites in Lima and La Paz did to the authorities in Tacna during the Peru–Bolivian Confederation (1836–1839). Elites from all Central American cities responded to authorities in Mexico City (1821–1823) first, and then Guatemala City and

cities like Asunción, Lima, and Mexico City were effectively occupied in what are often considered cases of state "death" (Fazal, 2004, 320). In these and other cases of occupation, it was not entirely clear at the time that the occupied state would eventually regain its sovereignty.

Conversely, the extent to which war had a strong selection effect in nineteenth-century Europe is often exaggerated. Half of the states that died in nineteenth-century Europe actually disappeared for reasons unrelated to war. According to Fazal (2004, 320), of the fifteen states that died in the nineteenth century, only seven died violently. Other scholars also doubt that violent selection was very prominent in Europe in previous centuries as well (see Abramson, 2017; Cederman et al., 2023; Grzymala-Busse, 2023).

High survival rates in Latin America are probably explained by the fact that early empires and states were overly ambitious and laid claim to insurmountable distances and geographic barriers that divide the region (Child, 1985, 9). But this, if anything, only demonstrates that waging wars in the Americas required more extraction and mobilization than in Europe and would lead to territorial consequences debated in Section 3.3.

The idea that "there have been very few international wars" (Centeno, 2002, 9) in Latin America is partly due to the rigidity of certain definitions. For example, the relatively complete list of interstate wars compiled by Sarkees and Wayman (2010) tends to deflate the real number of Latin American international wars by considering some of these to be extrastate or nonstate wars. This means that some international wars – that is, involving at least two preexisting internationally recognized states and producing 1,000 battle deaths within a one-year period – are not coded as strictly interstate due to the concurrency of a civil war or the presence of a nonstate actor (see also Wimmer and Min, 2009). These coding issues do not affect European wars but reduce the effective count of Latin American interstate wars by half.[8]

One might think that comparative historians with deep knowledge of Latin America would have already produced a list that takes care of these idiosyncratic factors, but there is much work to be done on that front for both

San Salvador, successive capitals of the Federal Republic of Central America (1823–1841). Elites in Buenos Aires fought several times trying to assert their claims over Asunción, Montevideo, and Sucre.

[8] Take the Uruguayan Great War (1843–1852) – also referred to as the La Plata War or the Siege of Montevideo – as an example. This conflict is coded as an extrastate conflict – that is, a conflict between a state and a nonsovereign entity – in Sarkees and Wayman (2010). Indeed, in both Argentine and Uruguayan historiography, the role of nonstate actors is very much emphasized. In Argentina, frictions with Montevideo are pictured as an offshoot of the partisan strife between the *federales* in Buenos Aires and the *unitarios* in exile. Similarly, Uruguayans tend to consider this international war as the second phase of a civil war between the *blancos* in the countryside and the *colorados* holding Montevideo. Because of these intertwined civil wars, it would seem as if political parties, and not sovereign states, were the main actors in the conflict. Yet from the moment Buenos Aires sent troops to besiege Montevideo, this clearly became an international war by any definition.

international and civil wars (Madrid and Schenoni, 2024). The list of interstate wars provided by Centeno (2002, 44) already illustrates a variety of problems, such as the inclusion of militarized disputes short of war, and conflicts between states and nonsovereign entities.[9]

Needless to say, producing a reliable list of Latin American international wars during the nineteenth century is imperative for any comparative study of this topic and for this book in particular. Here I follow a transparent and replicable procedure to produce the list in Table 3.2. First, I take the list of wars fought between 1816 and 1900 from Sarkees and Wayman (2010). This step ensures I am listing all episodes of political violence between two organized actors that rendered at least 1,000 casualties within a twelve-month period. Second, I exclude all wars that do not involve a Latin American state. Third, I exclude all wars coded as intrastate wars by Sarkees and Wayman (2010) while including all wars coded as interstate. Fourth, I take their two remaining categories (extrastate and nonstate wars) and recode those wars that are interstate according to my definition. I consider that an international war is fought by at least two preexisting sovereign entities and produces 1,000 battle deaths within a one-year period.

The evidence presented so far suggests that both levels of warfare and the frequency of wars were comparable across the Atlantic in the nineteenth century. Yet skeptics might wonder whether this is an artifact of the accumulation of several small Latin American wars rather than large state-making wars, since five wars listed in Table 3.2 barely achieve 1,000 casualties. This indicates very low levels of mobilization, particularly for large national states. A sudden outburst of violence or even a single skirmish could generate casualties beyond that threshold without any extraction or mobilization – that is, state formation – taking place. The problem is further complicated by the fact that in wars involving several states, individual contenders might have had to do little fighting.[10]

9 For instance, Centeno includes the first French invasion of Mexico or the Pastry War (1838–1839) in his list, a conflict with an estimated 123 battle deaths according to most available sources (Clodfelter, 2017). If the intention was to lower the bar for our definition of war – to, say, 100 casualties – then a dozen other militarized interstate disputes would be unlisted (Jones et al., 1996). Centeno's list also includes the War of Cuban Independence (1895–1898) while excluding all other independence wars, the War of Texan Independence (1836) without including other secessionist wars, and the Ten Years' War (1868–1878) between Cuban patriots and Spain without including other colonial wars. Perhaps more importantly, the list does not include a set of clear-cut international wars between existing sovereign entities at the onset of hostilities that yielded more than 1,000 battle deaths, such as the Peru–Great Colombia War (1828–1829) or the Filibuster War (1856–1857).

10 Many of these alliances are replaced by asterisks in Table 3.2: Honduras, Guatemala, and El Salvador fought on the Costa Rican side during the second year of the Filibuster War; Nicaragua joined Guatemala in the First Central American War; Uruguay fought during the first years of the Paraguayan War on the side of Argentina and Brazil; Honduras joined El Salvador in the Second Central American War; finally, Costa Rica and Nicaragua also joined El Salvador during the last Central American War.

TABLE 3.2 *International wars in nineteenth-century Latin America*

War	Year	Winners	Losers	Deaths
Argentina–Brazil	1825–1828	[URU]	ARG; BRA	4,000
Peru–Great Colombia	1828–1829	COL	PER	4,000
Confederation	1837–1839	ARG; CHI	BOL; PER	2,900
Peru–Bolivia	1841	BOL	PER	1,000
La Plata	1843–1852	URU; BRA	ARG	6,300
Mexican–American	1846–1847	USA	MEX	19,283
Haiti–Dominican	1855–1856	DOM	HAI	1,000
Filibuster	1856–1857	CRI*	NIC	7,700
Franco-Mexican	1862–1867	MEX	FRA	20,000
Central American (1)	1863	SAL; HON	GUA*	1,000
Ecuador–Colombia	1863	COL	ECU	1,000
Restoration	1863–1865	DOM	SPA	1,000
Paraguayan	1864–1870	ARG; BRA*	PAR	311,000
Chincha Islands	1865–1866	CHI; PER	SPA	1,000
Central American (2)	1876	GUA	SAL*	4,000
War of the Pacific	1879–1883	CHI	BOL; PER	13,868
Central American (3)	1885	SAL*	GUA	1,000

Notes: The list includes "interstate" wars and some wars coded as "nonstate" (Peru–Great Colombia, Confederation, Haiti–Dominican, Filibuster, and First Central American) and "extrastate" (Argentina–Brazil, Peru–Bolivia, La Plata, and Restoration) that are clearly international wars by our definition. Asterisks mean another state joined this side at some point. The square brackets around Uruguay convey that this state did not exist before the war – it was created as a consequence of it.
Source: Sarkees and Wayman, 2010.

Inconsistency in battle death estimates could also compromise, albeit at its margins, the list in Table 3.2. Not every source agrees on the same numbers, and some prefer to use a plausible range instead of a precise count. One prominent example is the Ecuadorian–Colombian War of 1863. This war was decided after a single battle between the Ecuadoran and Colombian generals Juan José Flores and Tomás Cipriano de Mosquera. According to the most conservative statistical sources, the Battle of Cuaspud on December 6, 1863, produced only 148 battle deaths (Clodfelter, 2017, 316). Others claim as many as 2,500 Ecuadoran soldiers died that day (Zepeda, 2009, 95) – but this figure is surely exaggerated and might take into consideration other casualties. For the sake of consistency, I align with Sarkees and Wayman (2010), who, like Centeno (2002, 44), considered this episode to have produced 1,000 battle deaths and be a war. However, it is sometimes impossible to be certain of these numbers.

For all these reasons, it is important to consider the possibility that some of the episodes in Table 3.2 might have been too benign or too short to be wars of the state-forming kind. Table 3.3 therefore avoids lower-intensity wars and compares wars with more than 10,000 battle deaths that took place in

TABLE 3.3 *Severe wars in nineteenth-century Europe and Latin America*

Conflict	Months	Battle deaths	Population loss (%)
Paraguayan War (1864–1870)	64	310,000	2.59
Crimean War (1853–1856)	29	264,200	0.26
Franco-Prussian War (1870–1871)	6	204,313	0.25
Seven Weeks' War (1866)	2	44,100	0.11
Second Italian War (1859)	2	22,500	0.03
Franco-Mexican War (1862–1867)	65	20,000	0.26
Mexican–American War (1846–1847)	21	19,283	0.04
War of the Pacific (1879–1884)	54	13,868	0.30

Notes: This table considers all wars with more than 10,000 battle deaths taking place between the Napoleonic/Independence Wars and World War I. It excludes colonial wars and those outside Europe and Latin America. Population loss is calculated by battle deaths as a percentage of population.
Sources: Sarkees and Wayman, 2010; Maddison Data Project; Bolt et al., 2018.

either Europe or Latin America during the short nineteenth century. It shows that although half of these big wars were fought in each region, they still lasted longer and killed more people on average in Latin America (fifty-one months and 0.79 percent of the population) when compared to their European counterparts (ten months and 0.16 percent). The Paraguayan War stands out as the single deadliest conflict of the century.

Understanding battle deaths and war-related casualties in relative terms is essential. By showing only the wars that generated more than 10,000 battle deaths, Table 3.3 still fails to do justice to wars fought by small populations whose effort was disproportionally great. When scholars of Latin America argue that "no countries have suffered a large number of deaths during conventional warfare" (Centeno, 2002, 9), they are probably thinking of total instead of relative casualties, ignoring instances of impressive mobilization that might have produced lower battle deaths due to the rudimentary weaponry of the time and failing to consider civilian deaths that are directly attributable to the war effort.

Take the Filibuster War (1856–1857) as an example. Roughly 10,000 Costa Ricans died of causes related to this war at a time when the country had a population of roughly 100,000. Taking scale into account, the Costa Rican death toll during the Filibuster War is comparable to the losses of France during the entire period comprising the French Revolutionary Wars and the Napoleonic Wars: In both cases it amounted to roughly 10 percent of the population (Hornstein, 2017, 186). The *Grande Armée* consisted of 685,000 soldiers or 2.7 percent of the French population before the Russian Campaign. Costa Rica's army comprised 10,000 men, or 10 percent of the population. This Costa Rican epopee should not slip under our radar.

The La Plata War (1843–1852) – known to the Uruguayans as the *Guerra Grande* or Great War – provides a similar example (Nahum, 1999, 38). Throughout the Great Siege of Montevideo (1843–1851), some 5,000 out of the 31,000 inhabitants of Montevideo were part of the national army (Méndez Vives, 2014, 57). In other words, one out of six inhabitants living inside the walls of the city was conscripted, a level only matched by Paraguayan mobilization for their own *Guerra Grande*. Alexandre Dumas underscored the epic dimensions of the Uruguayan war effort when he compared it with one of the greatest sieges in history in his *Montevideo, or The New Troy*.

To better tease out those martial experiences that fit the scope of the bellicist account – while still capturing the reality of these small countries – I define severe international wars as those that produce at least 5,000 casualties and last at least two years. I then determine that an individual country has endured high levels of mobilization if it loses at least half of the size of its army at the outset of hostilities during the war. A country that loses half of its military in a conflict that lasts more than a year is likely to levy new soldiers and taxes to rebuild its forces, therefore triggering the bellicist dynamics we are interested in exploring. This procedure generates the shortlist of severe international wars – with the specific contenders that endured high mobilization – in Table 3.4.[11]

Table 3.4 gets rid of wars that might have produced little mobilization. It also excludes countries that participated in important wars but contributed only marginally to the war effort – for example, Bolivia in the War of the Pacific or Uruguay in the Paraguayan War. Yet this definition also captures the feats of Costa Rican and Uruguayan populations during the Filibuster War and the Uruguayan Great War, thus providing a balanced account of relative impact. The definition captures all those martial experiences that resulted in the mobilization of at least 2 percent of the adult male population, a common threshold to determine the existence of mass warfare (Queralt, 2022, 226).

The cases in Table 3.4 will be treated in depth in Chapters 7–9, for it is in these cases that I expect the mechanisms of my theory to show up more clearly. Severe wars offer a larger window of time to look at the effects of individual battles and the political dynamics during war, but they are also expected to produce larger and more noticeable effects. Highly mobilized winners will have invested greatly in the war effort and thus victory will have the effect of consolidating a much larger army and a broader coalition in support of a somewhat developed state-building program. Conversely, highly mobilized losers will have paid a tremendous price for their military defeat, dooming the national military and the project of central elites.

For now, however, it will suffice to note that experiences of high mobilization affected roughly half (8) of Latin American countries. Interestingly enough, almost no European case would make it onto this short list if we applied a

[11] Except the Filibuster War, the wars listed in Table 3.4 are the same salient wars identified by Miguel Centeno (2002, 52–61).

TABLE 3.4 *Cases of high mobilization in nineteenth-century Latin America*

War	Year	Mobilized winners	Mobilized losers
La Plata	1843–1852	Uruguay	–
Mexican–American	1846–1847	–	Mexico
Filibuster	1856–1857	Costa Rica	–
Franco-Mexican	1862–1867	Mexico	–
Paraguayan	1864–1870	Argentina–Brazil	Paraguay
War of the Pacific	1879–1883	Chile	Peru

Notes: Empty cells convey that neither a winner nor a loser mobilized to a high degree.
Source: Sarkees and Wayman, 2010.

similar definition of high mobilization,[12] demonstrating yet another time that severe warfare was comparatively far more common in Latin America than previous literature would acknowledge.

Table 3.4 also shows that countries we consider paradigms of state capacity nowadays (Chile, Costa Rica, and Uruguay) were the winners of severe wars in the nineteenth century, while some usual suspects of state weakness (Peru and Paraguay) were defeated after high mobilization (Centeno, 2002, 10–11; Mahoney, 2010, 5; Kurtz, 2013, 11–16; Soifer, 2015, 13).

3.3 WARS AND BORDERS: THE TERRITORIAL DIMENSION

It is curious that although Max Weber famously defined the state as "the human community that (successfully) lays claim to the monopoly of legitimate physical violence within a certain territory" (Weber, 1994, 310), most studies on state building in Latin America pay marginal attention to violence monopolization and territorial consolidation (see Mazzuca, 2021).

Raul Madrid and I have documented the relation between war and violence monopolization in Latin America elsewhere (Madrid and Schenoni, 2024). After producing a new and complete list of revolts short of civil war in nineteenth-century Latin America, we find that the decline in revolts – defined as instances of the use or the credible threat of violence by an identifiable

12 Russia in the Crimean War is the only case where a state lost half its military during a war. Tzar Alexander II entered the conflict with an army of roughly 900,000 and lost somewhere between 470,000 and 530,000 men depending on the source. In 1862 he implemented a draft to rebuild the army. However, most of these deaths were due to noncombat causes – just 100,000 were battle deaths, according to Sarkees and Wayman (2010). Of course, the 600,000-strong Grande Armée of Napoleon was reduced to a mere 100,000 after the Russian campaign, and a similar decimation of European armed forces took place during the Great War, but these cases fall beyond our temporal scope.

domestic political group that defies the authority of the state – correlated with the swelling of armies, increases in military professionalization, and investment in military technologies, which take place mostly by the end of the nineteenth century and in winners of wars. That the consolidation of a state monopoly of violence followed a classical bellicist logic seems straightforward.

Comparatively, the territorial dimension of state formation has remained rather unexplored in Latin America. I focus briefly on this dimension because territorial change has featured prominently in recent contributions arguing both in favor of (Cederman et al., 2023) and against (Grzymala-Busse, 2023) the applicability of bellicist theory to the European context. Since the inception of this debate (Abramson, 2017), detractors have interpreted the survival of small territorial units in Europe as evidence against it. However, as we have seen, this is only true if we adopt an evolutionary understanding of the theory. Otherwise it is clear that war accounts for a large proportion of the territory acquired by victorious European states – and lost by those that were defeated – providing evidence for the theory (Cederman et al., 2023).

Translating this debate to the Latin American context is not straightforward. To start with, the death of states in Latin America was far more uncommon than in Europe. Naturally, one could find some cases of states that died or were absorbed into larger units. Mazzuca (2021) convincingly portrays the Confederation of the Equator (1824–1825), the Republic of the Rio Grande (1840), and the Republic of Piratini (1836–1845) in Brazil, as well as Los Altos (1838–1840), the Republic of Yucatán (1841–1848), the Miskito Kingdom (1844–1860), and the Argentine Confederation (1853–1861), as cases of states that died. These de facto states did not have broad international diplomatic recognition – a key attribute of sovereignty. To the extent that they can be considered states, their demise was fundamentally linked to defeat on the battlefield or their inability to muster a force to secure their independence. However, these all look more like secessionist attempts rather than the European story of long-standing smaller units being absorbed by a larger, expanding neighbor.

One apparent reason for the systematic survival of Latin American states is that they were born much bigger than their European counterparts, comprising territories beyond the real grasp of political centers of power (see Herbst, 2014).[13] Because of this, unlike European states, Latin American units got smaller and multiplied in number. We already saw this happening first with the division of the Spanish Empire from two to four viceroyalties. Although the first independent states envisioned replicating the territorial layout of these four

13 States like Brazil singlehandedly laid claim to swaths of land equivalent to the entirety of continental Europe. In the same vein, relatively small countries in the Latin American context, such as Paraguay, matched the territorial extension of the largest western European state. If anything, Latin America suggests territorial size might not be informative for an analysis of the state without considering population density and other factors that make territories valuable for extraction.

viceroyalties, all of them broke into multiple national states in the aftermath of the Independence Wars – usually following the layout of *audiencias* and *capitanías*.

Notably, defeat in international warfare preceded almost all of those territorial breakups. The breakup of Great Colombia in 1830, for example, was clearly linked to the Peru–Great Colombia War (1828–1829). The Peruvian occupation of Guayaquil and the southern provinces was a major factor leading Simón Bolívar to assume dictatorial powers and increase the size of the army from 10,000 to 40,000 men, which, together with new taxes, put insurmountable pressure on peripheral elites in Ecuador and Venezuela. The end of the war in a stalemate demonstrated to Bolívar, who dreamed of a federated Latin America, that its capacity to project power had limits. Soon thereafter he retired from office and died, and less than one year after the war, both Ecuador and Venezuela seceded (Davis, 1983). Case studies in Part III show that the secession of Central America was also a consequence of the domestic and international military defeats of Emperor Agustín I, that the independence of Uruguay was a direct consequence of stalemate in the Argentina–Brazil War (1825–1828), and that the collapse of the Peru–Bolivia Confederation is directly attributable to its defeat in the War of the Confederation (1836–1839). In short, war outcomes could explain most cases of secession in Latin America.

Other than producing the appearance and disappearance of states, war outcomes had a tremendous impact on the fluctuation of borders in Latin America. This is a point worth making, since many scholars seem to believe that the norm of *uti possidetis* – the Latin for "as you possess you will possess" – allowed Latin American states to peacefully settle their border disputes by adopting previous colonial administrative boundaries (Schenoni et al., 2023). Although it is true that Latin American states created these norms and were ahead of Europe in the codification and use of arbitration, among other mechanisms for the peaceful settlement of territorial disputes (Kacowicz, 2005), the reality is that these norms developed as Latin American states expanded their agricultural and mineral frontiers toward remote parts of the territory or simply competed for the allegiance of remote provinces with rival neighbors, having to fight back third columns and incursions in border areas (see Atzili, 2011; Lee, 2020), for which they needed to assert their territorial claims and expand the territorial reach of the state.[14]

Table 3.1 already shows that while territorial transfers were far more frequent in Europe than in Latin America, most were unrelated to war. When one considers the frequency with which war led to changes in borders, grabbing territories by force was the norm in Latin America much more than it was in

14 The latter dynamics also explain the parallel development of the norm of territorial integrity and the norm of nonintervention in this region (Schenoni et al., 2023).

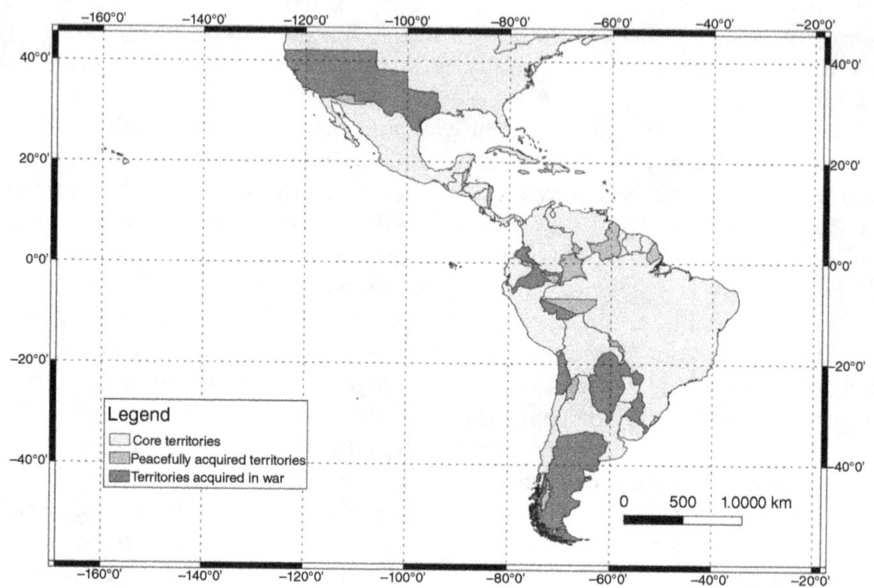

FIGURE 3.1 War-related territorial transfers in Latin America

Europe (Tir et al., 1998), which explains the haste to develop the territorial integrity norm and consolidate the principle of *uti possidetis* in the region.

In an attempt to update and geolocate the borders referred to in previous data (Tir et al., 1998), I followed a procedure similar to that applied by Cederman et al. (2023) to historical Europe (1490–1790), classifying the territories of Latin American states as historical core territories, war-related transfers, and peaceful transfers. The map in Figure 3.1 is based on transfers coded by Tir et al. (1998) with some additions and minor changes. For example, I discarded territorial changes that gave birth to countries (for example, Ecuador, Uruguay, Venezuela, and Panama) altogether and did not consider territorial transfers that were subsequently contested.[15]

To map these territories I looked at historical maps from different sources and traced the borders on which there was most agreement across the maps and with the descriptions of the boundary lines provided in treaties. Although CShapes (Schvitz et al., 2022) already maps a few territorial changes in Latin America, I had to expand coverage beyond 1886, because the main conflicts I am interested in – for example, the Mexican–American War (1846–1848), the Paraguayan War (1864–1870), the War of the Pacific (1879–1884), etc. – occurred before 1886.

[15] For example, the transfers determined in boundary treaties between Bolivia and Chile during 1866 and 1874 are not reflected in the map, since these treaties were overruled by the agreements that ended the War of the Pacific.

The resulting map provides a snapshot of Latin American territorial history up to 1945, and it improves the data by Tir et al. (1998) by producing new estimates for the size of territorial transfers based on historical maps,[16] including some new territorial transfers that, although not in the original dataset, still fit the definition (see also Hensel and Mitchell, 2017)[17] and expands the coverage of CShapes (Schvitz et al., 2022) for this region.

The map allows us to reach two important conclusions about war and territorial transfers in Latin America, which are in line with what supporters of bellicism in Europe have recently unveiled (Cederman et al., 2023).

First, the extension of territory acquired as a direct consequence of war is larger than that of the territories peacefully transferred. Although peaceful territorial transfers were more frequent than militarized ones overall (Tir et al., 1998), looking at the frequency of such transfers obscures the importance of warfare by considering settlements of different territorial sizes as equivalent and counting peaceful transfers that were later overturned by military outcomes. Overall, the area of territory transferred after an armed conflict forced a

16 Since some of these differences are substantial, they are worth reporting. A territorial transfer from Uruguay to Brazil in 1851, involving an area of 104,000 km² according to Tir et al. (1998), represents 121,317 km² on this map. Other inconsistencies include the concessions made to Brazil by Venezuela in the 1859 Treaty of Limits and Navigation (156,000 km² versus 151,600 km²); concessions made to Brazil by Bolivia in the Treaty of Ayacucho (1867) (162,500 km² versus 276,246 km²); concessions by Paraguay to Argentina (117,000 km² versus 139,242 km²) and to Brazil (65,000 km² versus 102,670 km²) after the Paraguayan War; the incorporation of Patagonia by Argentina in 1879 (669,972 km² versus 1,529,180 km²); concessions made to Chile by Peru (51,480 km² versus 58,373 km²) and Bolivia (50,215 km² versus 117,196 km²) after the War of the Pacific; the loss of Venezuelan territory in the Guyana (155,400 km² versus 141,613 km²) to Britain; the transfer of territory from Argentina to Chile (27,708 km² versus 56,178 km²) and vice versa (20,470 km² versus 67,462 km²) in the 1902 *Pactos de Mayo*; concessions made by Bolivia to Brazil in 1903 and 1907 after the Acre War (191,000 km² versus 144,323 km²); concessions made to Brazil by Ecuador (67,600 km² versus 71,777 km²) and Colombia (162,500 km² versus 215,734 km²) in 1904 and 1907, respectively; concessions from Bolivia to Peru made in the Polo-Bustamante Treaty of 1909 (26,000 km² versus 162,340 km²); transfers between Colombia and Venezuela according to a 1922 award (1 km² versus 34,952 km²); concessions in the 1934 Treaty of Friendship between Colombia and Peru that ended the Leticia War (113,882 km² versus 41,818 km²); transfers in the treaty that ended the Chaco War between Bolivia and Paraguay (233,100 km² versus 239,853 km²); transfers between Ecuador and Peru according to the 1942 Rio Protocol (190,807 km² versus 192,940 km²); transfers between the United States and Mexico by the Treaty of Guadalupe Hidalgo of 1848 (1,370,153 km² versus 2,379,455 km²) and the subsequent Gadsen purchase (76,768 km² versus 66,559 km²); and the incorporation of the Miskito territories into Honduras (33,701 km² versus 3,504 km²) and Nicaragua (21,367 km² versus 32,689 km²).

17 Namely the loss of an Ecuadoran claim after the 1863 War of the Cauca (86,656 km²); the incorporation of southern territory ruled by indigenous peoples by Chile (211,624 km²); the 1900 Swiss award that granted most of the current state of Amapá to Brazil (84,849 km²); the award that settled the Guatemala–Honduras border in 1933 (9,283 km²); the settlement of the Soconusco dispute between Mexico and Guatemala (8,947 km²); and the Costa Rican acquisition of Guanacaste (10,095 km²).

bilateral settlement is 4,549,766 km^2, compared to 1,259,552 km^2 transferred peacefully. War transferred 3.6 times more territory than diplomacy, exceeding the European ratio. These calculations do not include territories acquired via the extermination of nonstate actors in Patagonia, which appears on the map as war-related. In this case, the sum of territory transferred by war increases to 5,431,362 km^2, and the ratio of violently transferred territories to peacefully transferred ones increases to 4:3, almost duplicating the European ratio.

Second, success in war seems to precede peaceful expansion. This is most evident in the case of Brazil, the largest country in the region, which acquired territory through violent means first, in the La Plata War (1851) and the Paraguayan War (1864–1870), and expanded through a mix of diplomacy and coercion thereafter. In general, peaceful territorial transfers came after violent ones and corresponded to peripheral, largely uninhabited areas.[18]

All in all, territory being a key element of the state and the consolidation of boundaries being a fundamental aspect of state formation, it is fundamental to correctly understand how war shaped the layout of states in Latin America. This section demonstrates that nineteenth-century war outcomes played a fundamental role in determining the shape Latin American states show today.

3.4 EXTRACTION AND CAPACITY ACROSS THE ATLANTIC

Those who see war as an unlikely predictor of state capacity in Latin America also entertain the idea that extraction was timid and shallow in the region. In this section I examine whether three key statements (Centeno, 2002, 135–137) apply to nineteenth-century Latin America in particular:

- Latin American states relied on indirect taxes more than those in Europe.
- Latin American states relied on debt more than their European counterparts.
- These modes of financing did not demand state building.

Note that these descriptive questions are different from the more inferential or causal question I explore in Chapter 4 – that is, whether the rise of an external threat led Latin American states to implement trade taxes to foreign trade and acquire foreign debt. Understanding the meaning of that relation requires some historical context that can only be given by looking at Latin America in the mirror of Europe, which I do in this section.

Were direct taxes in nineteenth-century Latin America modest compared to those in Europe at the same time? Although a cornerstone of the antibellicist argument, this statement has not yet been explored in sufficient depth.

[18] There also seems to be a pattern by which peaceful settlement is more likely when it comes to territorial disputes with foreign powers. As with the pattern of peaceful conflict resolution on the peripheries of the Brazilian Empire, this suggests the importance of coercive diplomacy behind what might otherwise look like a peaceful settlement. The Gadsen Purchase of 1854 is a similar case in which the Mexican–American War (1846–1846) cannot be clearly disentangled from territorial settlement thereafter.

All we know about the extractive fiscal machinery of the Spanish and Portuguese empires suggests Latin American populations were more directly and more highly taxed than their European counterparts by the turn of the nineteenth century. In *The Wealth of Nations*, Adam Smith notes that the Spanish and Portuguese had some of the highest taxes in Europe and that tax pressure, specifically through direct taxes, was even higher in their colonies (Smith, 1976, 296, 1210). As reviewed in Section 3.1, Latin American colonies constantly provided fiscal surpluses to the metropoles. Moreover, surpluses in this region were also used in order to finance deficits in other colonial territories through the *situado* system (Marichal, 2006, 433).

Tax pressure in the Viceroyalty of New Spain (now Mexico and Central America) was therefore somewhere between 40 percent (Marichal, 1999, 92) and 70 percent (Klein, 1985, 590) higher than in Spain, one of the most highly taxed countries in Europe (de la Escosura, 2009). Direct taxes implemented in the colonies – such as the Indian tribute and the silver tax in Spanish territories or the brazilwood and slave tax in Portuguese colonies – accounted for such differences (Marichal, 2006, 426).

This fiscal order would be overturned during the Independence Wars. Mirroring the demise of the fiscal systems of the *ancien régime* during the French Revolutionary Wars, the revolutionaries of Latin America delegitimized direct taxation, which became difficult to implement due to monetary fragmentation and the collapse of the colonial bureaucracy. However, while France swiped away direct taxes like the *taille* and the *twentieth* during the revolution – much like Latin America did with the *alcabala* after the Wars of Independence – and came to rely heavily on indirect taxes, the incidence of direct taxes on rural communities continued to be high in Latin America. Miguel Centeno (2002, 126) notes direct taxation was very important in states like Bolivia and Paraguay due to the persistence of colonial taxes. The Indian tribute, in particular, was a major source of revenue for Andean countries until it was abolished in Peru (1854), Ecuador (1857), and Bolivia (1879) and replaced by new taxes still targeted toward these minorities.

Customs duties and indirect taxes were admittedly the backbone of the emerging fiscal systems of Latin America, but this was no different in Europe (Marichal, 2006, 448). While Centeno (2002, 118) is correct to point out that direct taxes in nineteenth-century Latin America usually represented less than 5 percent of revenue,[19] the main direct taxes in Britain and France – that is, the general stamp and the land tax – also represented around 5 percent of revenue before the introduction of the income tax (Schremmer, 1989, 358, 392).

Among indirect taxes, tariffs did represent a greater source of income for Brazil and Chile than they did for France and Britain (Centeno, 1997, 1577;

19 By the middle of the century, taxes on wealth and production amounted to 4 percent in Brazil; direct contributions and land taxes represented 8 percent and 3 percent in Argentina, respectively; and the tithe represented 3 percent of Chilean revenue (Centeno, 2002, 118).

Centeno, 2002, 117, 122), where the size of domestic markets allowed the sales tax to represent a higher share of total revenue, but this consumer tax was an indirect tax as well. All things considered, the ratio of direct to indirect taxation was similar across the Atlantic. "Britain derived hardly any public revenue from lands and little more from stamp duties levied in the shape of the 'general stamp,' the British fiscal system rested on two substantial pillars: government loans and taxes, especially excise and import duties" (Schremmer, 1989, 318). Like most Latin American countries, the United Kingdom "relied on custom duties as the foundation of its fiscal system, at least during the first half of the nineteenth century" (Marichal, 2006, 451).[20]

These paradigmatic European cases[21] illustrate that rates of direct taxation in Latin America during the nineteenth century were average. The direct taxes that we now associate with high state capacity, such as the income tax, were adopted by few European states during the nineteenth century – namely Great Britain (1842), Austria (1849), Italy (1864), Norway (1892), and the Netherlands (1893) – and contributed marginally to the state coffers until the Great War (Mares and Queralt, 2015). Moreover, elites effectively opposed this tax for a long time in countries like France (1911) and Germany (1920). As others have recently documented, the "great revenue divergence" between Latin America and Europe only takes place after World War I (Lee and Paine, 2023).

If modes and levels of taxation were roughly equivalent on both sides of the Atlantic during the nineteenth century, did Latin American states resort to credit more frequently than their European counterparts? Here, evidence also suggests otherwise.

In Britain, "the extraordinary military expenditures of the war years were largely met by free market means through the debt sales" (Clark, 2001, 411).[22] At the beginning of the nineteenth century, the Napoleonic Wars, which included a continental blockade of British trade, required that some direct taxation was included momentarily in the mix – Pitt's income tax is the clearest example. Yet "Britain financed the Napoleonic Wars primarily by borrowing" (Eichengreen et al., 2019, 21). At the beginning of the short nineteenth century, public indebtedness was so high that it represented 200 percent of GDP (Clark, 2001, 403), and Britain consistently held the greatest public debt in the world for the first half of the nineteenth century.

20 When the income tax was first implemented in Britain in 1842, it represented only a fourth of tariff revenues and half the excise tax (Schremmer, 1989, 318).

21 Germany also "relied on custom taxes as the key to fiscal prosperity" (Marichal, 2006, 450) after 1871. The United States, just like the Britain of the Corn Laws, had 40 percent average customs duties until the mid-nineteenth century. These were among the highest in the world and made their fiscal structure also highly reliant on this tax.

22 The figures in Clark (2001) actually suggest wars were financed by debt almost in their entirety.

France was no exception. It ran on fiscal deficits during most of the century – only in four years (1826, 1875, 1876, and 1877) did revenue exceed expenditure – and "the chronic budget deficit had to be covered by loans. They became a source of income for the expanding state, indispensable, systematically exploited" (Schremmer, 1989, 399). By the end of the century, France's public debt had surpassed Britain's and was the highest in the world in both global and per capita terms (Schremmer, 1989, 399), driven by the military adventures of Napoleon III in Crimea (1853–1856), Italy (1859), and Mexico (1861–1867). During the Second Empire, the percentage of the budget financed by debt increased from 10 to 20 percent (Dyson, 2014, 202).

These two cases illustrate that sovereign debt was instrumental to state building in Europe as much as it was in Latin America, if not more. As long as credit was available, a capital-intensive path (Tilly, 1990) was preferred on both sides of the Atlantic, as well as in other regions with flourishing nation states. Authors like David Stasavage (2011) already demonstrate that the blanket statement according to which "debt unmade the state" does not find support in European history.

In his recent book, Didac Queralt (2022) – a student of Stasavage – adds an interesting twist to the debate by arguing that a key difference exists between domestic and foreign debt and how the latter used to be repaid in the nineteenth century. According to Queralt, Latin American states had access to cheap credit in the nineteenth century due to the existence of *extreme conditionality*, a mechanism devised by investors to minimize risk, whereby they could exchange distressed debt for control over local assets. When faced with the need to service and repay their debts, Latin American rulers were thus not forced to tax and build fiscal capacity: They had an easy way out by assuming the foreclosure of those assets after a default. This argument rests on two assumptions that should be closely scrutinized.

First, as Queralt (2022, 3) himself recognizes, his book "builds on the assumption that peripheral countries had access to relatively cheap external credit during the Bond Era." However, it is not clear that this "key assumption in the argument" (Queralt, 2022, 9) holds for Latin American economies that paid higher yields than seasoned economies in Europe (Queralt, 2022, 84) and were often excluded from financial markets. As Queralt (2019) himself recognizes, credit was often unavailable for Latin American countries. Loans to the region were issued in three waves. A first short wave from 1825 to 1828 came to cover the costs of the Independence Wars and resulted in a counter-wave of defaults that was followed by more than twenty years of virtual exclusion from financial markets. The following waves – from 1850 to 1873 and from 1880 to 1890 – provided access to credit for longer periods, but outside those windows the flow of credit to Latin America was negligible (Centeno, 2002, 134; Eichengreen et al., 2019, 11; see also Marichal, 1989). The average Latin American state spent more than a third of those years in default (della Paolera and Taylor, 2013; see also Flores Zendejas, 2020, 324), which impacted access to financial markets and interest rates for the entire region.

Second, this argument assumes foreclosures were straightforward, while in reality they were most of the time enforced by gunboat diplomacy (Mitchener and Weidenmier, 2010). This renders the effects of extreme conditionality more complex in the light of the bellicist argument. To start with, handing state-owned assets to foreign creditors was not cost free for rulers. Even in cases where the state did not need to expropriate these assets from local elites, widespread nationalistic sentiment in the nineteenth century meant such policies were as politically costly as tax increases. Because rulers did not let go of these assets with ease, lenders relied on the disposition of European states to force the repayment of a debt via military occupations and naval blockades. Extreme conditionality was possible due to the legitimacy and legality of this last resort (Schenoni et al., 2023). In practice, thus, extreme conditionality often triggered new wars, required mobilization, and fostered state building through this alternative mechanism.[23]

Having explored interregional comparisons between Europe and Latin America in the fiscal and financial realms, it is worth analyzing whether nineteenth-century states heavily reliant on sovereign debt and customs duties were less susceptible to developing state capacity.

It seems fair to argue that indirect taxation – in the form of tariffs, consumer taxes, or even the inflation tax – although a weak measure of state capacity in the twentieth century, required the development of fairly sophisticated state functions, capabilities, and bureaucracies in the nineteenth century.

Tariffs were unlikely to have been collected by just "a few soldiers in the main ports," as Centeno (2002, 135) puts it. It required large numbers of personnel to account for this main source of state revenue, training a specialized bureaucracy, enhancing coastal and harbor infrastructure, erecting public buildings, policing and punishing corruption, and patrolling the border to prevent smuggling. Studies on European state building once entertained the idea that taxes on trade were easy to collect, but this notion has been abandoned at least since the work of John Brewer (1989, 66) on the formation of the British state. As one authority puts it:

[23] The argument for extreme conditionality also assumes much homogeneity across time and space both within and outside Europe. While only a few capable Latin American states could float debt in European markets, also few financial centers like London had the financial and military clout to engage in this type of overseas lending. Most of Europe – certainly Portugal and Spain, both of which defaulted on their sovereign debts – looked very much like Latin America for most of the nineteenth century. As Queralt (2022, 95) acknowledges, "Debt-equity swaps were a fairly common practice in loan negotiations in Latin America as well as in Eastern and Southern Europe."

> Far from requiring a minimum apparatus, the collection of commercial revenues in fact demanded a large number of well-trained personnel with advanced computational skills and a detailed knowledge both of numerous commodities and of an array of complex regulations. (Ertman, 1997, 16)

Even a seemingly simple tax like the inflation tax did not only require states to have minting presses. Securing seigniorage required a monopoly on the issuing of currency and control of currency circulation, which must be taken as a strong indicator of state strength in the nineteenth century (Centeno, 2002, 132).

It would be incorrect to assume that these taxes did not affect elites. Indirect taxes affected elites quite directly simply because they were the main consumers and traders. For them, trade taxes were virtually indistinguishable from consumption taxes. Furthermore, inflation hurt elites when they accumulated local currency, while customs taxes imposed a heavy burden precisely on those segments of the elites that had access to foreign currency and metal: exporters and importers. Finally, inflation affected financial elites that would lend money to the state, as it diluted public debt denominated in local currency. Therefore no elite group remained untouched by indirect taxation.

Something similar could be said of debt. The state formation literature often considers "public debt as statebuilding" (Eichengreen et al., 2019, 4), precisely because states have to secure a permanent tax base before they can issue long-term tradable debt (Stasavage, 2011, 27–28). Hui (2005, 124) notes that this type of financing should not be considered a "self-weakening expedient," for it requires concomitant administrative and fiscal reforms to boost the credibility of the sovereign borrower. For this reason, sovereign debt in nineteenth-century Latin America should be interpreted as state building (Saylor, 2014, 45–47; see also Saylor and Wheeler, 2017) even under extreme conditionality. Overall it is implausible that foreclosure clauses and debt-equity swaps would have nullified the manifold state-building effects of active participation in financial markets. Countries that could issue more debt – due to lower bond yields and smaller spreads – were able to do so precisely because they were considered to have more capable states. As Saylor (2014, 46) puts it, "It is perhaps telling that much of Argentina's and Chile's debt issues were underwritten by the Baring Brothers, the second underwriter in Latin America, while Colombia's issues were handled by the smaller London and Country Bank." The expansion of the international financial market during the bond era was accompanied by the expansion of bureaucracies dedicated to the production of economic indicators and credit ratings, as well as diplomatic missions in financial centers and even expansions of the tax base to show repayment capacity (Vedoveli, 2019).

Elites in Latin America were hardly indifferent to foreign debt issuances, which only had the effect of postponing economic costs to them. Even in the case of guaranteed debts (Queralt, 2022), assets otherwise available to these elites would be mortgaged. Because of this, every Latin American war in the short nineteenth century – even the smallest ones – provides examples of the state marginally augmenting military expenditure and peripheral elites strongly opposing indirect taxes and debt issuances. Tariffs, inflation, and loans, far from allowing "the state the luxury of not coming into conflict with those social sectors that possessed the required resources" (Centeno, 2002, 127), almost invariably supposed a political confrontation with domestic opposition. I explore this more systematically in Chapter 4.

PART II

REGION-WIDE ANALYSES

4

Preparation for War and Mobilization

In this chapter I analyze whether preparation for war in nineteenth-century Latin America led to levels of domestic taxation sufficient to generate a violent reaction of the local population that then had to be repressed – a mechanism of state formation referred to as the extraction–coercion cycle.

Conventional wisdom indicates that Latin American rulers facing international threats "could generally fund their activities with foreign aid and loans" and rely "on customs duties for revenue" (Saylor, 2014, 52). Relatedly, Latin America is portrayed as a case of trade-led – in opposition to war-led – state formation where "state-makers in the center and patrimonial rulers in the peripheries become partners" (Mazzuca, 2021, 7) and rulers were unable or unwilling to confront landed elites (Centeno, 2002, 135). Even in the event of war, friction between them would have been avoided, preventing the development of an extractive and coercive apparatus to penetrate those fiefdoms (Migdal, 1988). The regression-type analyses in this chapter are designed to test if these expectations hold or if external militarization actually led to domestic taxation and internal conflict, as predicted by classical bellicist theory.[1]

The chapter is divided into three sections. In Section 4.1 I show that blockades and defaults might have made it difficult for states to access foreign sources of finance when confronting a foreign threat. In Section 4.2 I discuss how we can measure such threats as well as economic and political outcomes proxying extraction–coercion. Finally, Section 4.3 summarizes my findings, which suggest the extraction–coercion cycle was triggered by international

1 Statistical analyses of this type have previously focused on the twentieth century (Thies, 2005). The regression-type analyses of panel data for the nineteenth century presented in this chapter and Chapter 5 remain among only a few in the literature that go back to the nineteenth century (see Dincecco and Prado, 2012; Karaman and Pamuk, 2013; Queralt, 2019, 2022; Goenaga et al., 2023) and are unique in explaining variance exclusively within Latin America.

threats and call important tenets of the existing antibellicist consensus into question.

4.1 BLOCKADES, DEFAULTS, AND EXTRACTION–COERCION

Scholars of state formation, even when they recognize the frequency and severity of war in nineteenth-century Latin America, have considered the ways in which states financed military adventures to be nonconducive to state capacity. A consolidated narrative proposes that leaders resorted to foreign loans and tariffs to foot wartime expenses, preventing the domestic taxation and confrontation with peripheral elites that was necessary for power centralization (Centeno, 2002, 135). While the literature has recently elaborated on the link between, for example, foreign debt and state capacity outcomes (Queralt, 2022), it is less clear whether international conflict was systematically financed in such ways and what the domestic political consequences of wars were.[2]

There are, however, several reasons why states in Latin America might have had a harder time accessing foreign debt and collecting foreign duties during wars, making domestic taxation during war even more likely in this region. The two most prominent were the ubiquity of naval blockades and sovereign defaults, which reinforced each other. Economic historians Sicotte and Vizcarra (2009, 249–284) note when discussing the period that "debt settlements occurred mostly during peaceful interludes" and that "in contrast, eleven of the fourteen defaults occurred during a time of war." These authors also agree that "revenues usually fell during conflict" and "blockades stand out as a key factor in the explanation of some of the most drastic reductions in revenues during wars." In such contexts, "the government financed the deficit by issuing currency, causing the value of the paper peso to plummet." Alternatively, "governments that were in default on foreign debt relied on extensive access to emergency credit that took a striking number of forms, and was often supplied by important domestic players with political and economic clout."

The prominence of blockades and defaults in nineteenth-century Latin America is summarized in Table 4.1. The last two columns show the proportion of Latin American contenders in each war that suffered a blockade of or a default on their sovereign debt during the conflict. Due to the geography of

[2] Didac Queralt (2022, 181–187) deals with this issue very briefly and finds that only Argentina and Brazil during the War of the Triple Alliance, and Chile and Peru during the Chincha Islands War, had access to foreign credit. In his models Queralt finds a slightly negative effect of war on credit flows. Although he then interprets a significant effect of a one-year lag as inflow of loans for the purposes of war preparation, the history of Latin American wars, which I cover in detail in Part III, clearly indicates that these conflicts were unforeseeable for most actors involved, making that interpretation implausible.

TABLE 4.1 *Blockades and defaults during war*

War	Year	Duration (months)	Concurrent defaults	Naval blockades
Argentina–Brazil	1825–1828	32	2/2	2/2
Peru–Great Colombia	1828–1829	7	2/2	1/2
Confederation	1837–1839	34	3/3	1/3
Peru–Bolivia	1841	7	1/2	1/2
La Plata	1843–1852	91	1/3	1/3
Mexican–American	1846–1847	17	1/1	1/1
Haiti–Dominican	1855–1856	14	1/2	1/2
Filibuster	1856–1857	22	3/4	1/4
Franco-Mexican	1862–1867	58	1/1	1/1
Central American (1)	1863	10	1/3	1/3
Ecuador–Colombia	1863	1	1/2	0/2
Restoration	1863–1865	1	1/1	1/1
Paraguayan	1864–1870	64	0/3	1/3
Chincha Islands	1865–1866	8	0/2	2/2
Central American (2)	1876	1	2/3	0/3
War of the Pacific	1879–1883	46	2/2	2/2
Central American (3)	1885	1	2/3	0/3

Note: I include all interstate conflicts in Table 3.2.

Latin America – with most foreign trade concentrated in very few ports – naval blockades were recurrent.

In the context of a blockade, states could resort to opening other ports. For example, during the Mexican–American War (1846–1848), the US Navy blockaded Veracruz and Tampico, forcing Mexico to open new ports, but to promote trade in a context of high risk, Mexico had to exempt commercial vessels from port taxes and reduce import taxes to a quarter of their former value. Despite these measures, the mere risk of capture by US raids reduced foreign trade by half its value (Bauer, 1974, 111). This case exemplifies the fact that even in the absence of a blockade, the capacity of Latin American states to raise tariffs in the context of war must have been limited due to their import needs – for example, war material – in a context of chronically high tariffs (Coatsworth and Williamson, 2002, 50). As a rule, therefore, the risk of a blockade and the concern with keeping trade flowing would have prevented the temptation to raise tariffs and reduce customs revenue during war.

Similarly, access to credit could be blocked during wars. As a rule, access to foreign credit – as with customs revenue – depended to a large extent on the situation of global markets, which could sometimes freeze access to credit for years during so-called sudden stops (Queralt, 2019, 723). Moreover, the risk of Latin American countries defaulting on their debts must have been much higher during a war, given the pressing financial requirements of the war effort itself, the probability of a blockade, and the likelihood of an eventual defeat, all of which would have impacted interest rates.

Because of the dynamics above, it is worth treating the assumption that Latin American states financed war via customs revenue and foreign loans with some initial skepticism, as hypotheses to be tested:

H1: *When facing an external threat, states collected more foreign duties.*

H2: *When facing an external threat, states raised tariffs.*

H3: *When facing an external threat, states took out more foreign loans.*

The previous discussion suggests that Latin American states might have been forced to implement some form of domestic taxation in the context of war, given the lack of alternatives. A rich historiography suggests that governments resorted to a wealth of domestic taxes and *creditos forzosos* – compulsory issuance of domestic debt – to finance war, but systematic data on taxation for the whole region and period is unfortunately unavailable.

This same historiography suggests that inflationary financing served as the standard way of taxing the local population in the context of war. Because in the nineteenth century this presupposed a conscious political decision to monetize the deficits by suspending gold convertibility and devaluing the local currency (Saiegh, 2013), we can use the depreciation rate of local currencies as a proxy for this type of indirect domestic taxation. The use of seigniorage to increase the relative value of gold reserves would have compulsorily transferred the cost of war to all those with assets valued in the local currency.[3] This leads to my following alternative hypothesis:

H4: *When facing an external threat, states devalued their currencies.*

We should think of H1, H2, and H3 as testing conventional expectations of the literature. However, H4 would be unexpected and offer strong support for bellicist theory, as inflation would have put pressure on the state to eventually strengthen and diversify tax institutions (Saylor and Wheeler, 2017, 366).

To assess whether the extraction–coercion cycle was triggered by foreign threats, one must also look at the political corollary of the antibellicist argument more closely – namely that due to the absence of domestic taxation and efforts by the state to centralize power during wars, the type of intraelite and societal contention that is often associated with state-building processes did not take place in Latin America (Centeno, 2002, 137).

Scholars in the antibellicist camp usually agree that statesmen in Latin America pursued "periphery incorporation without periphery transformation"

[3] This focus on this inflation tax might even be advantageous vis-à-vis a focus on property taxes, given the abundant evidence that elites at the time relocated or shielded their assets when threatened by taxation (Paniagua, 2022).

(Mazzuca, 2021, 27). According to this prevailing view, the unwillingness to antagonize vestigial oligarchies and *caudillos* stymied mobilization for war altogether, preserving internal peace and the domestic status quo.[4] In sum, while bellicist theory predicts that extraction for war will affect peripheral elites and the local population, therefore leading to internal violence, critics do not expect international conflicts and domestic uprisings to correlate.

Nonetheless, there are many reasons to expect that extraction–coercion dynamics might have been even more likely in Latin America than they were in Europe at the same time, perhaps even resembling those in place during seventeenth- or eighteenth-century Europe.

First, the relative strength of peripheral elites in Latin America probably meant that these groups were in a good position to put up a fight. Due to large territorial extensions and small militaries, the capacity of the state to monopolize violence vis-à-vis opposing elites – in particular when the armed forces were deployed to face an international threat – must have been rather low. If the *caudillos* were relatively strong, minimal levels of mobilization must have led to violent confrontation.

Second, the identification of elites and the general population with the national state was rather weak in Latin America for most of the nineteenth century. Young states struggled for the allegiance of their citizens in a context of continent-wide linguistic and cultural homogeneity and strong subnational identities, which should have created frictions in contexts of extraction and mobilization by the national state.

Third, presidents and armed forces could easily be called into question as well. With the exception of the Brazilian emperor, the (traditional) legitimacy of presidents in Latin America was far more questionable than that of the average European monarch, making it easier to rebel against a sitting executive. In the same vein, self-made officials from plebeian backgrounds were also of questionable social status and faced a higher rate of desertion, mutinies, and uprisings against forceful conscription.

Each of these logics points to a distinct type of domestic uprising that could have been favored by extractive policies. The aforementioned consideration about the legitimacy of presidents, for example, suggests that intraelite conflict regarding the necessity of war and how to deal with its costs would have been resolved by coups instead of by large-scale rebellions.

4 For example, Marcus Kurtz (2013, 75–76) has argued that in the months leading up to the War of the Pacific, "the threat of war was not enough to make possible the creation of an effective revenue system for the Peruvian state," that "the issue was not just the ability to collect taxes but rather the explicit unwillingness of elites in the Peruvian legislature to levy new taxes, even for the national defense," and that "elites [in Peru] were reluctant to resist the Chilean invaders, as doing so would require joining with and arming the (long-restive) local peasantry." Although I will challenge this interpretation of the Peruvian case by showing that new taxes were levied and peasants were mobilized (Basadre, 2005, 192; Contreras, 2005, 94), predictably leading to coups and rebellions in the following years, it is worth considering this point of view seriously and systematically across cases.

H5: *External threats increased the likelihood of a coup d'état.*

According to previous work in the bellicist tradition, violent regime change is more likely in situations where a state is attacked by a foreign foe or where the costs of war are increasing (de Mesquita et al., 1992). It is reasonable to expect that the increased political leverage of the military during a war (Desch, 1999, 11) could lead to a coup in such contexts.

A different type of rebellion that would provide evidence of coercion–extraction dynamics are rebellions of peripheral elites directly undermined by the state's centralization efforts (Schenoni, 2021). These elites can organize rebellions from outside the state, resisting the authority of the central state in their fiefdoms or organizing a partisan rebellion.

H6: *External threats increased the likelihood of elite rebellion.*

Finally, while bellicist dynamics usually confront pro-state and anti-state elites – for example, the monarch and local nobility – they also increase the chances of popular uprisings, as extraction from society in the form of conscription and inflation will irritate the masses. The uprising of indigenous peoples, peasants, and the urban working class indicates that mass mobilization efforts are being resisted by social groups beyond the elites.

H7: *External threats increased the likelihood of popular uprisings.*

In all of these cases – that is, the rebellion of cadres within the state in a coup, elite revolts, and popular uprisings – state authorities would have had to return violence with violence and repress the rebels to reinstate order. This would have been necessarily the case when these rebellions escalated into full-blown civil wars, which leads to the last of our hypotheses:

H8: *External threats increased the likelihood of civil war.*

By definition, a civil war exists when a state confronts a nonstate armed group, leading to more than 1,000 battle deaths. Therefore the connection between external threats and civil wars provides the ultimate evidence in support of the extraction–coercion thesis put forward by bellicist theory.

4.2 TREATMENT (MIDS), OUTCOMES, AND COVARIATES

In the analyses that follow, I will look at militarized interstate disputes (MIDs) as evidence of international conflict (Palmer et al., 2022). Militarized interstate disputes are instances of international conflict ranging from skirmishes to actual war – with wars being only the subset of MIDs that produce more than 1,000 battle deaths.

I focus on MIDs instead of wars (Sarkees and Wayman, 2010) in order to properly capture whether *the threat of war* triggered the state formation dynamics in a *preparation for war* phase. As Miguel Centeno (2002, 266) puts it, "It is not necessarily war itself, but the threat of war that often produces the positive state-building consequences" (cited in Thies, 2005, 453). Militarized interstate disputes capture episodes that could have escalated into all-out war and required preparation for such an eventuality.[5]

The list of MIDs provided by Correlates of War (Palmer et al., 2022) has been thoroughly revised throughout the years and is well-documented. In recent years, however, there has been some debate about its coverage and the interpretation of some events, leading to the development of a parallel dataset (Gibler et al., 2016). Gibler's militarized confrontations (MICs) follow the same definition, but disagreement on certain events results in a slightly different list. For nineteenth-century Latin America, the correlation between the two is high (0.922), but since there is disagreement on about thirty-six events, I include both in my analyses.

From 1830 to 1913, exactly one-fifth (310) of the total (1,550) country-year observations in Latin America show an ongoing MID (Palmer et al., 2022). Although my analyses later in the chapter will deal with concerns about zero inflation for some outcomes – for example, assuming at times a negative binomial distribution – this should provide reassurance that my main treatment of interest was far from a rare event. It is also worth mentioning that MIDs have been found to be mostly dependent on features of bilateral relations that are dyadic in nature, all of which should ease concerns about endogeneity at the monadic level.

The indicators I use for my outcomes are chosen to prioritize validity and good coverage for the period under analysis (1830–1913). To test for the impact of international conflict on the collection of foreign duties (H1), I use overall national revenue in thousands of current US dollars (Banks and Wilson, 2015). Total national revenue does not strictly capture customs duties, but more than 80 percent of the revenue of Latin American countries came from this source (Coatsworth and Williamson, 2002). This indicator is unavailable for the period before 1860, reducing my panel to 913 observations for those models specifically. For average tariff rates (H2), the sample is even more limited (Clemens and Williamson, 2004). This indicator is only available for seven countries in the post-1870 period, reducing the panel to 301 observations. To test for the impact of MIDs on foreign debt (H3), I consider whether a new loan was issued to a given country in a given year (Marichal, 1989), covering the whole period. Finally, as a proxy for domestic indirect taxation

[5] Ostensibly, this is the reason why many of these MIDs are included as relevant events in seminal studies on state formation (Centeno, 2002, 44) – for example, the Battle of Tampico (1829), the Bolivia–Peru War (1835), the Pastry War (1838), and the Chincha Islands War (1865), among others.

(H4), I consider the depreciation of Latin American currencies according to their exchange rate with the US dollar (Federico and Tena, 2019). This is not a flawless indicator of deficit monetization – for example, in some contexts states allowed the circulation of multiple currencies as an alternative to suspending the convertibility of the main local currency to gold – but should capture the states that resorted to a policy of devaluation. This indicator is also available for the entire panel.

With respect to political outcomes, testing for specific forms of contentious politics such as coups (H5), elite rebellions (H6), and popular uprisings (H7) required original data collection. The available indicator of civil war is relevant to capturing conflict that has already escalated to high levels (H8) (Sarkees and Wayman, 2010) but fails to distinguish between different categories of political violence, which are relevant to understanding how these civil wars came to be. I therefore used original data on rebellions to test these hypotheses, which expands on the list Madrid and Schenoni (2024) developed for South America. Rebellions are here defined as instances of the use or the credible threat of violence to achieve political goals by an identifiable domestic political group that defies the authority of the state. This broad definition ensured unbiased data collection before each event was categorized as a coup, an elite rebellion, or a popular uprising.

While coups are "illegal and overt attempts by the military or other elites within the state apparatus to unseat the sitting executive" (Powell and Thyne, 2011), elite rebellions consist of revolts led by elites from outside the national state that do not necessarily try to overthrow the executive. Elite rebellions typically include intraelite feuds such as opposition party revolts or secessionist uprisings. Finally, a popular uprising consists of a revolt led by members of the lower and middle classes, such as workers, peasants, indigenous peoples, or slaves. None of these definitions require a battle-death threshold, allowing us to cast the net wide and capture many instances of rebellion that did not escalate into civil war.

In my models I also control for the population and territorial extension of Latin American countries, and I include a set of variables to capture the impact of the international economic environment, considered a main determinant of trade-led state formation in the period (Mazzuca, 2021). Variables affecting international trade act as potential confounders affecting both the probability of international conflict and my economic and political outcomes of interest (Pahre, 1998). I control for three specific factors (Federico and Tena, 2019): transaction costs, commodity prices, and total exports (in current US dollars). To approximate transaction costs I use the cost of sending freight to three key ports in Latin America – Buenos Aires, Rio de Janeiro, and Valparaiso. For my commodity prices index, I use the average prices of commodities that reflect plantation (cocoa and sugar), mining (copper and silver), and ranch economies or those related to the textile industry (cotton and wool), a subset that provides a good representation of the main Latin American export profiles at the time.

Then I input freight costs and the prices of sending commodities to individual countries according to their closest port and main produce. For example, Peru is considered a mining economy with transport costs akin to those of Valparaiso.

Finally, for my models predicting rebellions and civil wars, I also control for the size of the military (Singer and Small, 1966), a variable previously found to predict their occurrence (Madrid and Schenoni, 2024).

4.3 STATISTICAL MODELS AND DISCUSSION

The models reported in Figure 4.1 test for the impact of MIDs on economic outcomes, with each column focusing on a distinct outcome. Column one, for example, reports the results of fourteen panel regressions on government revenue. Different specifications of the treatment are considered, six corresponding to a MID dummy, four to a MID count, and the last four to a one-year lag of the initial MID dummy. For each of these categories, the panel regressions include (a) a baseline model, (b) a model including international economic confounders, (c) a model including domestic political confounders, and (d) a model including all the confounders in Table 4.2. All models include country-year fixed effects. For my MID dummy treatment, results are also reported for a simple two-way fixed effects model with clustered standard errors to show the effect under the assumption of strict exogeneity (Angrist and Pischke, 2008, 236), as well as a full model including a lag of the outcome. The same procedure is replicated for each column. For the models on new loans, the dichotomous nature of the outcome requires a logistical regression complemented by a negative binomial specification in the sixth model.

Before interpreting each of the results substantively, it is worth taking a look at the general patterns in the figure. While some results are statistically significant and others are not, it is clear that all of the coefficients align with bellicist expectations and contradict antibellicist claims. Contradicting the conventional wisdom, international conflict is not associated with more duty collection, higher tariffs, and new foreign debt. On the contrary, the relation is sometimes highly significant ($p < 0.01$) in the opposite direction. Militarized interstate disputes seem to decrease average revenue, tariff levels, and the likelihood of contracting a new foreign loan. In other words, not only are the antibellicist hypotheses (H1, H2, and H3) soundly rejected but the results support the intuition that Latin American countries had a particularly hard time taxing foreign trade and accessing foreign capital in contexts of international conflict.

If Latin American states could not resort to external sources of revenue, they must have turned inward and taxed their own populations. The results on currency depreciation, although not always significant, broadly support this hypothesis as well.

The substantive interpretation of results depends partly on our beliefs about the process behind the treatment assignment. If one is persuaded that no

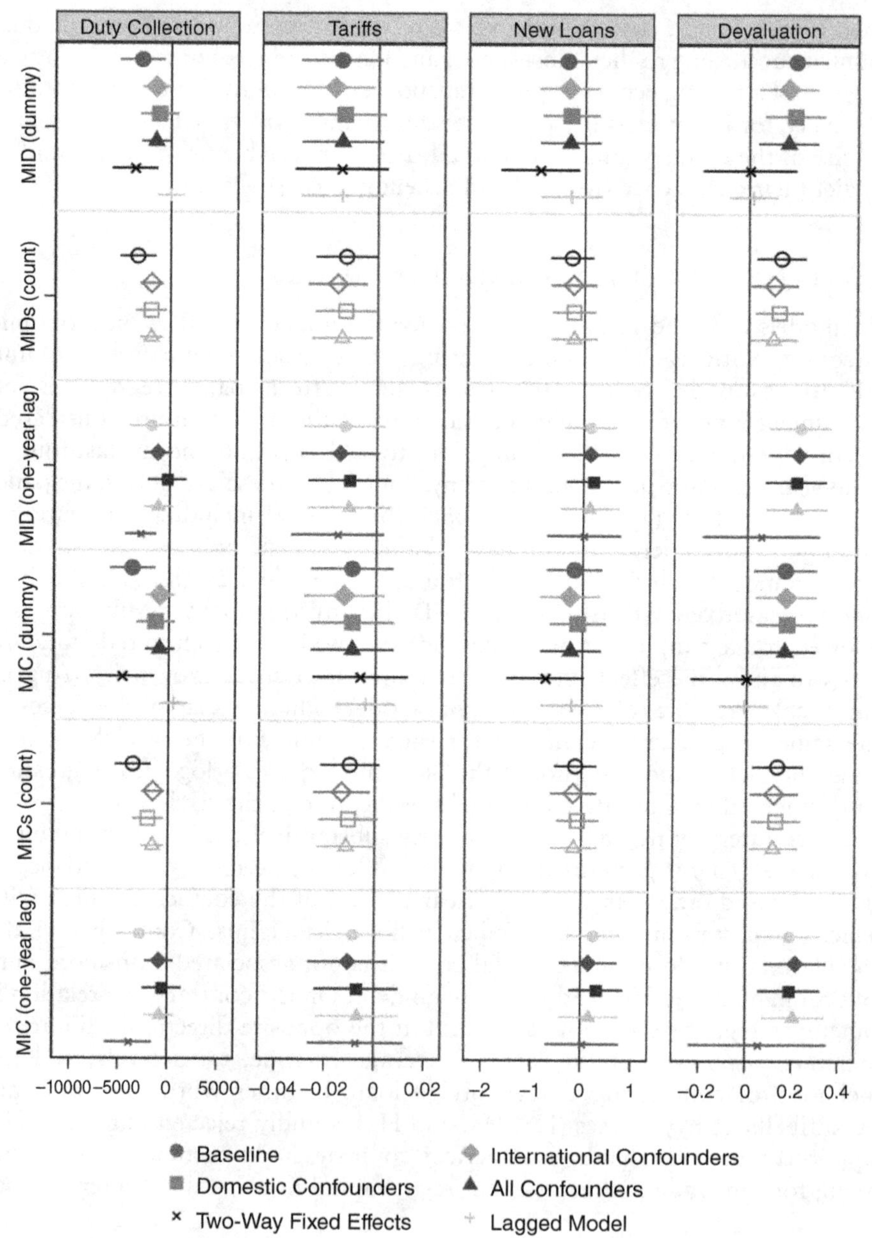

FIGURE 4.1 Economic mechanisms

time-varying factors affected both MIDs and outcomes concurrently and no feedback or carryover effects are present (Imai and Kim, 2019) – that is, a strict exogeneity assumption – then the results of the two-way fixed effects would capture the real effect. Note that if we adopt this interpretation, the

TABLE 4.2 *Summary statistics of main indicators*

Indicator	Function	Min.	Max.	Mean	Source
MID (d)	Treatment	0	1	0.2	P&al
MID (c)	Treatment	0	4	0.23	P&al
MIC (d)	Treatment	0	1	0.19	G
MIC (c)	Treatment	0	4	0.22	G
Revenue (0.001 USD)	Outcome	88	190,047	15,343	B&W
New loan (d)	Outcome	0	1	0.05	M
Tariffs (avg.)	Outcome	0.09	0.58	0.27	C&W
Exchange rate (USD)	Outcome	0	13.7	1.90	F&T
Coup (c)	Outcome	0	2	0.1	M&S
Elite rebellion (c)	Outcome	0	5	0.37	M&S
Popular uprising (c)	Outcome	0	8	0.37	M&S
Civil war (d)	Outcome	0	1	0.06	S&W
Population (0.001)	Control	59	25,255	2,293	S&S
Area (0.001 m^2)	Control	8.2	3,286	474.8	S&S
Soldiers (0.001)	Control	0	354	11.88	S&S
Freight costs (USD)	Control	41	272	12	F&T
Price index (USD)	Control	9.150	29,014.89	741.328	F&T
Exports (USD)	Control	0.061	548.32	22.42	F&T

Notes: (d) stands for dummy variables and (c) for count variables. Continuous variables are measured in thousands (0.001) and prices in current US dollars (USD). P&al = Palmer et al. (2022), G = Gibler et al. (2016), B&W = Banks and Wilson (2015), M = Marichal (1989), C&W = Clemens and Williamson (2004), F&T = Federico and Tena (2019), M&S = Madrid and Schenoni (2024), S&W = Sarkees and Wayman (2010), S&S = Singer and Small (1966).

negative effects of international conflict on customs revenue and foreign debt are usually highly significant. Because of the stability of the other models, I direct my attention to them.

Column one shows that external conflict caused a decrease of revenue collection of around 3 million current (nominal) USD, or around 1.7 million USD after controlling for other confounders, including total exports, which are good predictors of revenue.[6] The probability of acquiring foreign debt is also negatively affected by warfare, although the results in general show low statistical significance – probably due to the rarity of new loans altogether. Tariffs also decreased by around 1 percent on average in the year of the MID. Conversely, states in Latin America devalued their currency by some 20 percent vis-à-vis the US dollar whenever a MID took place. The effect remains similar one year after the treatment. In the context of the gold standard, this meant decreasing the value of assets and salaries denominated in local currency – or, in other words, increasing inflation – by a relatively large amount. Forcing citizens to lose one-fifth of their capital in a year amounts to a strong form of

6 The full tables with the results for each of the controls in my models are reported in the supplementary material, which is available upon request.

compulsory domestic taxation, very much in line with the type of extraction predicted by bellicist theory.

Note that these results are also robust when we test for a one-year lag of MIDs. In line with previous work (Queralt, 2022, 186), this specification seems to change the sign of the effect on loans, but the result is not significant. Otherwise, the one-year lag does not lead to important changes in the other outcomes.

How did scholars miss this pattern before? One possible answer regards the salience of paradigmatic examples that are not generalizable to the whole region and period. For example, foreign debt acquisition figures prominently in standard narratives of the Argentina–Brazil War (1825–1828) and the Paraguayan War (1864–1870) (Lynch, 1985). These two wars alone account for nine out of the eighteen country-years in my whole dataset in which new loans and international conflict overlap. A simple chi-squared test on a frequency table shows that the association between these two variables is far from significant ($p = 0.37$) even when calculated in a naive form.

Overall, the null findings reported earlier reject all three antibellicist hypotheses, while significant negative findings on those outcomes, together with the significant positive findings on currency depreciation, suggest that economic policy tended to focus on domestic taxation. This first set of findings already suggests that extraction might have led to political conflict, another observational implication of bellicist theory.

If Latin American states were then forced to extract from their populations to pay for wartime mobilization, did this also lead to rebellion and coercion? Figure 4.2 turns our attention to the political effects of international warfare.

The display of the results follows the logic of Figure 4.1, with three main differences. First, the outcomes considered here (except for civil war) are count variables and therefore the results reported correspond to Poisson models. Second, a variable considering the number of military personnel in Latin American countries is included as a control, given that larger security forces would have *ceteris paribus* deterred rebellion (Madrid and Schenoni, 2024). Third, I replace the two-way fixed effects models with negative binomial specifications, given that zero inflation might be regarded as a more relevant threat to inference in this particular setting.

Here as well it is worth considering the broad pattern of the results before substantively interpreting individual coefficients. A bird's-eye view of the results reported in Figure 4.2 is also surprising. While the conventional wisdom would not expect international conflict to be associated with domestic political violence, the relationship seems to be positive in general and in many cases highly significant.

Two outcomes seem to be particularly affected by the presence of a militarized interstate conflict: coups and full-blown civil wars. Transforming the results of these logarithmic regressions into odds ratios suggests that in most specifications, the presence of a MID made a coup two times more likely

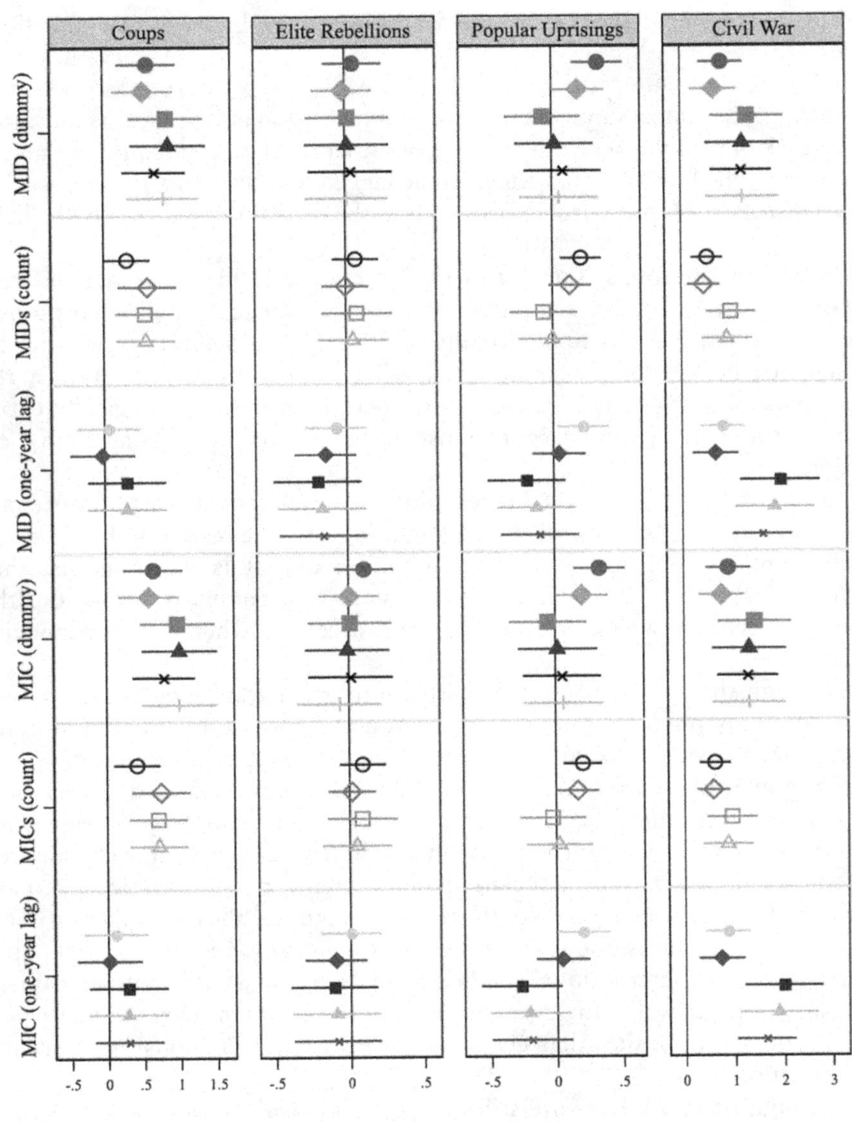

FIGURE 4.2 Political mechanisms

and increased the chances of a civil war somewhere between two and three times.

In accordance with previous research (de Mesquita et al., 1992), coups seem to be triggered almost immediately after militarization takes place, as indicated by the lack of results after a one-year lag of the treatment. Since coups are single-year events, the lack of significance on the lagged MIDs treatment is reassuring of the direction of the causal effect going in the direction predicted by bellicist theory.

The result on coups illuminates the other results in Figure 4.2 as well. Importantly, it shows that the null finding for the category of elite rebellions – which in principle seems to be broadly in line with antibellicist expectations – should not be interpreted as demonstrating intraelite concord. Rather, the significance of coups might indicate that peripheral elites strategically chose to try to topple the sitting executive instead of seceding or resisting from their fiefdoms.

The effect of MIDs on popular rebellion achieves statistical significance in a few specifications. Popular rebellions might indicate the reaction of vulnerable populations to conscription and the inflation tax. It is worth noting that both elite rebellions and popular uprisings are very common throughout the nineteenth century, which might dilute effect sizes even when they overlap with MIDs.

Although the association is not particularly strong, it seems that, together with coups, popular uprisings help explain the most impressive finding in Figure 4.2: a strong association between international conflict and civil war.

This powerful association between MIDs and civil wars is hard to overstate. Of ninety-three country-years at civil war in my sample, fifty overlap with country-years of concurrent international militarization. A simple chi-squared test shows a very strong association between the two events ($p < 0.000$). Because of this, the significance of the results in Figure 4.2 is particularly robust.

A question remains about the direction of causality. Civil wars might spill over and generate international conflict, a causal mechanism that would explain this correlation as well. However, the effect of the lagged MID treatment seems to indicate the opposite: that civil war onsets follow previous international militarization.

Although these analyses are still far from the ideal of identifying a causal effect, these results already reject the antibellicist hypothesis about the ability of rulers to avoid civil war in the context of international conflict and support the bellicist intuitions about domestic unrest and subsequent coercion.

The findings discussed in this section are surprising and potentially paradigm-shifting. The lack of significant results for foreign debt, for example, contradicts widely assumed financial practices and even puts the relevance of a research agenda that focuses narrowly on debt dynamics into question (Queralt, 2022). The results on trade variables – tariffs and revenue – are also somewhat surprising due to the prominence that previous scholarship has given to foreign trade – and in particular import taxes – as a main source of financing for military budgets – which represented most of the overall state budget – in nineteenth-century Latin America (Garavaglia, 2003).

Although it seems to be the case that military budgets were financed by external sources of revenue, those were more accessible during peacetime, which forced states to resort to domestic-oriented forms of taxation when facing extraordinary military expenditures. Indeed, authors who focus more narrowly on the very specific dynamics triggered by MIDs (Sicotte and Vizcarra, 2009) seem to suggest that blockades and similar difficulties taking place during minor military confrontations forced Latin American states toward domestic extraction and triggered the expected political unrest. This is precisely what this chapter corroborates. The implications are major. If states in Latin America were forced to prepare for war through domestic taxation, which in turn led to conflict with societal actors, then the extraction–coercion cycle was triggered in the region, and Latin America was no different from Europe in this regard (Tilly, 1990, 15).

So far, reliance on overarching historical narratives about foreign capital and trade in Latin America has taken precedence over a more thorough and detailed exploration of the dynamics that were actually taking place in the context of international conflict. However, a simple look at the wars fought in Latin America during the nineteenth century – see Table 4.1 – reveals that during most of these conflicts, access to foreign capital was virtually blocked for at least one of the contenders, and wars with no defaults or blockades tended to correspond to episodes in which the quick resolution of land battles prevented these outcomes. During severe wars, the levels of domestic direct taxation soared considerably, but since these taxes are difficult to systematize for a cross-national comparison, these will be covered more qualitatively during the case studies in Part III of the book. Those cases also systematically corroborate a fundamental truth about nineteenth-century Latin American warfare that this chapter has uncovered: that civil wars and coups were significantly more likely when states prepared for war.

5

War Outcomes and State Building

This chapter turns to war outcomes and the effect they had on postwar state capacity trajectories.[1] Unlike in Chapter 4, where I look at the immediate or short-term effect of militarized interstate disputes on preparation for war during the period 1830 to 1913, here I restrict my analysis to wars during the period 1865 to 1913 in order to leverage additional data. The late nineteenth-century focus of this chapter is thus on the "formative period" of the Latin American state (Oszlak, 1981, 19).

The chapter is divided into four sections. In Section 5.1 I look at the classical bellicist insight that underpins my research design: that war outcomes are determined by fortuitous events. After corroborating the theoretical plausibility and historical accuracy of this assumption in the subset of war outcomes under analysis, I turn to explore their impact on indicators of state capacity.

In Section 5.2 I provide a short description of the treatment, outcomes, and control variables in my models, as well as some descriptive statistics. I then turn to my first estimator, a difference-in-differences (DID) model, in Section 5.3. A standard specification of this procedure shows that defeat had a significant effect on indicators of infrastructural power of the state such as railroad mileage and per capita revenue. The effect does not take place immediately after the war but rather increases with time, as expected by our theory, and remains remarkably robust despite many changes to the initial specification of the models.

Finally, in Section 5.4 I use the synthetic control method (SCM) to estimate how state capacity in Paraguay and Peru would have evolved in a counterfactual world where these countries were spared crushing defeats.

[1] This chapter reproduces analyses previously published in "Bringing War Back In: Victory and State Formation in Latin America," *American Journal of Political Science* 65(2): 405–421, 2021. I would like to thank AJPS for the permission to use that material.

These models introduce a more in-depth discussion of the Paraguayan War and the War of the Pacific provided in Chapter 7 and Chapter 8, respectively.

5.1 IDENTIFICATION STRATEGY: WAR OUTCOMES AND CHANCE

My identification strategy in this chapter relies substantively on the idea that defeat and victory were exogenous or haphazardly assigned to states in the eight wars we will analyze.

As discussed in Chapter 2, the notion that decisive battles are critical events of high contingency is ubiquitous in the classics of bellicist theory. In his methodological annotations on the work of his contemporary German historians, Max Weber (1949, 171) concluded that major battles could be attributed great causal impact precisely because of the element of chance leading to their outcomes. This made it plausible to reason counterfactually (Tetlock and Belkin, 1996; Goertz and Levy, 2007), considering all potential outcomes (Holland, 1986), "the *decision* between which was made by the battle's entirely *accidental* outcome" (Weber, 1949, 172).

Scholarly research highlighting the inherent uncertainty arising from the stochastic elements of the war-fighting process is also ubiquitous in canonical texts in international relations (see Beyerchen, 1992; Bas and Schub, 2016, 1099). According to the most cited article in the field, "Almost all analysts of war have stressed that war is a gamble whose outcome might be determined by random or otherwise unforeseeable events" (Fearon, 1995, 387). The notion that war "is everywhere in contact with chance, and brings about effects that cannot be measured, just because they are largely due to chance," as Clausewitz (1984, 66) put it, is endorsed and further developed by virtually all major theorists of war after him.[2] This assumption has also been incorporated into

[2] For Thomas Schelling (1966, 93), "war is a confused and uncertain activity, highly unpredictable." More recently Kenneth Waltz (1979, 61) said about war that "from attributes one cannot predict outcomes if outcomes depend on the situation of the actors as well as their attributes." In another place he clarifies: "The outcome of battles and the course of campaigns are hard to foresee because so many things affect them, including the shifting allegiance and determination of alliance members" (Waltz, 1981, 6). The determination of some international relations scholars to predict war outcomes also clashes very often with the perception of the leaders involved in the process, who fake their certainty during war for obvious reasons – no matter the side they are on, they are always sure of victory – but readily admit the contingency of the result in more intimate settings or when they look back at the events in their memoirs. Suffice it to remember Winston Churchill's famous lines: "Never, never, never believe any war will be smooth and easy, or that anyone who embarks on the strange voyage can measure the tides and hurricanes he will encounter. The statesman who yields to war fever must realize that once the signal is given, he is no longer the master of policy, but the slave of unforeseeable and uncontrollable events" (Mitzen and Schweller, 2011). As noted by Margaret MacMillan (2020, 111), the metaphor of the storm is already in Shakespeare's *Henry VI*: "This battle fares like the morning's war / When dying clouds contend with growing light / What time the shepherd, blowing of his nails / Can neither call it perfect day nor night. / Now sways it this way like a mighty sea / Forced by the tide to combat with the wind; / Now sways it that way, like the

TABLE 5.1 *Winners and losers in Latin American wars 1863–1913*

War	End	Winners	Losers
Colombo-Ecuadoran	1863	Ecuador	Colombia
Restoration	1865	Dominican Republic	Spain
Chincha Islands	1866	Chile, Peru	Spain
Franco-Mexican	1867	Mexico	France
Paraguayan	1870	Argentina, Brazil*	Paraguay
Central American (2)	1876	Guatemala	El Salvador, Honduras
War of the Pacific	1883	Chile	Bolivia, Peru
Central American (3)	1885	El Salvador*	Guatemala

Notes: Countries with an asterisk were joined by other allies at some point: Uruguay fought during the first years of the Paraguayan War, and Costa Rica and Nicaragua joined El Salvador during the last Central American war listed. France and Spain are not considered in the analysis.
Source: Sarkees and Wayman, 2010.

models that formalize bellicist theory, assigning a value of 0.5 to the probability of victory (Sambanis et al., 2015, 282).

However, I do not solely base my decision on those abstract and general insights. Because we are looking at a limited number of wars, the assumption can be substantiated on a case-by-case basis. As we will see, military historians invariably highlight the role of chance in determining the outcomes of wars.

Following the definition and selection criteria established in Table 3.2, I consider the winners and losers in Table 5.1 for my analysis. I do not include countries that achieved independence during the period under analysis – Cuba (1898) and Panama (1903) – which leaves only two countries in the region unaffected by war: Haiti and Venezuela. The vast majority of Latin American countries – seventeen in total – were affected by war as defined here.

Some of the wars in Table 5.1 were decided by a stroke of luck in a single battle. In the Battle of Cuaspud on December 6, 1863, for example, the 6,000-strong Ecuadoran forces of General Juan José Flores had virtually secured victory when General Tomás Cipriano de Mosquera, leader of a Colombian force of 3,000, ordered a retreat. The Ecuadoran cavalry had started the final pursuit when, by a fateful turn of events, the disbanding army ran across a marsh. Noting that the Ecuadoran horses were getting bogged down in the mud, the Colombian forces grasped the momentum and surrounded the advancing Ecuadoran army, taking 2,000 prisoners. The result was an unexpected Ecuadoran defeat in the war (Lauderbaugh, 2012, 58). Unable to believe his bad luck, the Ecuadoran president, Gabriel García Moreno, wrote to General Flores, "God has decided to punish us" (Martinez, 1982,

selfsame sea / Forced to retire by fury of the wind; / Sometime the flood prevails, and then the wind; / Now one the better, then another best; / Both tugging to be victors, breast to breast, / Yet neither conqueror nor conquered: / So is the equal poise of this fell war."

17–18).[3] Flores and García Moreno were Catholic monarchists, a rare breed of conservatives that supported centralization and state building. The project collapsed after their defeat. Ecuador had its army reduced to only hundreds, and only by the year 1930 would its armed forces again muster a force of 6,000 soldiers (Henderson, 2008). In Colombia the confrontation strengthened the Liberal Party of Mosquera, which had heralded state formation since his victory in the War of the Supreme Captains (Mazzuca and Robinson, 2009, 322) and turned it hegemonic for more than two decades.[4]

The Central American wars in Table 5.1 were also decided by fateful battles confronting the liberal leader Justo Rufino Barrios, President of Guatemala, and his Central American neighbors. The War of 1876 was initiated when the conservative party of Honduras conspired with Guatemalan conservatives to unseat the liberal government of Barrios, who was implementing centralizing reforms. The war was decided by the Battle of Pasaquina on April 17, 1876, which lasted an entire day. The battle was a close call, with both armies running out of bullets and drawing bayonets to decide it (Bustamante, 1935, 76).

As a result of the 1876 victory, Guatemala prevented the secessionist threat from Los Altos and strengthened its armed forces. The legitimation and consolidation of Barrios as a charismatic military and political leader was such that on February 28, 1885, Barrios declared himself President of Central America and attempted to reunify the isthmus with the help of his liberal allies in Honduras. In the War of 1885 against El Salvador the element of luck was even clearer. Guatemala's army was larger and had already scored a victory on March 30 (Gibler, 2018, 79), but during the Battle of Chalchuapa on April 2, 1885, Barrios was unintentionally shot in the back by one of his own soldiers (Barrientos, 1948, 3). After the accident the army disbanded and Guatemala surrendered.

The naval Battle of Papudo on November 26, 1865, shows how similar dynamics played out on the sea. After the guano-rich Chincha Islands were occupied by the Spanish Armada in 1864, a coalition of South American states on the Pacific coast – including Chile, Bolivia, and Ecuador – formed in support

3 Mosquera himself recognizes in a letter that he was largely outnumbered and out-equipped, and his forces came close to disbanding at the sight of the enemy. In the same letter he admits that his strategy depended entirely on Flores going through the narrow valley of Cuaspud – where his inferior numbers could stand a chance – and this was very unlikely to happen (Velasco, 2018, 499).

4 Colombian liberals, like their counterparts in Brazil and Mexico, were federalists as well. This meant that the period of liberal hegemony that followed Mosquera's victory was not characterized by centralization but rather the strengthening of the state against the Catholic Church. Conversely, the conservatives of Rafael Nuñez who became hegemonic after 1885 centralize while redressing state building vis-à-vis local orders and civil society. Because of the lack of a big external war, the central–peripheral elites cleavage never quite aligned with ideological cleavages, as happened in Brazil, Chile, and Mexico, among other cases.

of Peru. The size of the Spanish Armada, however, remained superior to all those navies put together, and, trying to dissuade Chile from assisting her northern neighbor, Admiral José Manuel Pareja sent four ships to blockade Valparaiso. On November 26, the Chilean corvette *Esmeralda* approached the Spanish schooner *Covadonga* using a British flag and after a close fight was able to capture it. Although the Spanish fleet remained superior despite the loss of the *Covadonga*, the event brought such shame on Admiral Pareja that he killed himself, dooming the campaign.[5]

Other wars in Table 5.1 were not so much decided by fortuitous events during a battle as by equally unpredictable exogenous shocks. The War of Restoration of the Dominican Republic – another example of a war won by the least likely contender – provides an example. War against the Spanish attempt to recolonize the country ensued in 1863, with an army of Dominican liberals amounting to some 15,000 troops against a Spanish army of some 51,000 plus 12,000 Dominican auxiliaries (Clodfelter, 2017, 306). "Spanish might indicated the occupation would succeed" (Eller, 2015, 118) had it not been for an unexpected yellow fever epidemic killing thousands of Spanish troops – casualties were up to 10,000 at the end of the war – which seems to be the main explanation for the outcome (Cruz, 2018, 251).

Another completely exogenous event that could have caused the withdrawal of Spain in both the Chincha Island and Restoration wars was the end of the American Civil War. The Franco-Mexican War provides yet another case where the side that seemed clearly bound to lose – the liberal army of Benito Juárez – experienced a turn of fate, thanks to this unexpected shock. Had the surrender of the Confederacy taken place one year later, it is possible that the liberals would have been completely crushed (Shawcross, 2018, 225).[6]

To summarize, we can be quite certain that in all of the wars we are analyzing, fortuitous events played a notable role in defining the outcome. This is easy to identify, because these events were followed by changes in the course of the war – in the cases of decisive battles, they ended the war – and almost invariably favored the party that would have been bound to lose if we were to consider the size of the armies involved in the fight and the previous course of the war.

For the most consequential wars in Table 5.1, the War of the Pacific and the Paraguayan War, conventional wisdom has it that the Peruvian and Paraguayan defeats were evident from the outset. Yet the element of chance is to be found everywhere in the voluminous historiography of these wars.

5 The events leading to the Chincha Islands War – also known as the Spanish–South American War – are covered in more detail in Chapter 8.

6 The events relating to the Second French Intervention in Mexico are covered in more detail in Chapter 9.

The most serious historiography on the Paraguayan War unanimously points to several accidents that determined the outcome. The first set of contingent developments has to do with the Argentine reaction. The Paraguayan president, Francisco Solano López, had reason to believe that the government in Buenos Aires would allow him passage to support his allies in Uruguay and war would be limited to that front. He counted on his Uruguayan allies to resist the opposition leader, General Venancio Flores, and was certain that Argentine provincial *caudillos* would rebel if authorities in Buenos Aires dared to declare war. In particular, he thought General Justo José de Urquiza, leader of the province of Entre Ríos, would rebel against Buenos Aires. Historians agree he might have been correct in this assessment, but he was unlucky to declare war right after Urquiza had achieved an agreement with Argentine president Bartolomé Mitre (see Mazzuca, 2021). López delayed the invasion for slightly too long due to weather conditions (Whigham, 2002, 418) and thus "opened the Uruguayan version of Pandora's box" (Williams, 1979, 199). Argentina declared war on Paraguay and sped up the signing of the Treaty of the Triple Alliance on May 1, 1865 – a secret treaty that committed Argentina, Brazil, and Uruguay to fighting together until López was finally defeated. Argentina became the main theater of operations for the Paraguayan invasion. Counterfactually, Argentine neutrality could have secured a Paraguayan victory, for the Paraguayan army of some 60,000 men was vastly superior and three times larger than the Brazilian army at the outset of hostilities.

Yet the die would be thrown once again during the Battle of Riachuelo on June 11, 1865 – the first Paraguayan defeat. George Thompson (1869) reports the confession of a Brazilian naval officer stating that the battle could have easily ended in a Paraguayan victory had they tried to board the Brazilian navy. Apparently Paraguayan commodore Ignacio Meza's original plan to do this was frustrated by a change in river currents that delayed the operation until after daybreak, allowing the Brazilians to spot the Paraguayan offensive and counterattack. A contemporary said, "If those nine vessels had been captured *I am certain* Lopez would have been victorious for he would have instantly appeared before Buenos Aires or Montevideo and, by threatening a bombardment, compelled them to make terms with him" (Masterman, 1870). Professional historians agree that Meza's bad luck might have cost Paraguay the war (Doratioto, 2002, 151).

Finally, historians also agree on a similar depiction of the Battle of Yatay, on August 17, 1865, which decided the retreat of Paraguayan land forces. Paraguayan colonel Antonio de la Cruz Estigarribia had divided his forces between the margins of the Uruguay River when the weaker of his two detachments was encountered by chance by the advanced guard of the allied army. Estigarribia decided to abandon his column on the other side of the river, expecting an attack on his side that never took place. Had he not made this unfortunate decision, Paraguay could have won the battle (Doratioto, 2002, 180; Whigham, 2002, 365).

The aforementioned narratives do not exhaust the many instances in which chance played a role during this war, many of which are explored in Chapter 7.[7] Yet they should be enough to illustrate the many ways in which the whims of weather, river currents, and fortuitous decisions might have changed the course of the hostilities leading to the final Paraguayan defeat.

Let us turn finally to the War of the Pacific. In the initial phases of the war, Chile – the eventual winner – was outnumbered two to one by the combined land forces of Bolivia and Peru, and the Peruvian navy was at least as strong as the Chilean, if not superior. Much unlike conventional wisdom would suggest, "the immediate outlook did not look promising" for Chile (Collier and Sater, 2004, 130–131). According to Bruce Farcau (2000, 47), "It is a natural tendency, when looking at a war in retrospect, to see the outcome as inevitable ... [but] a closer look will demonstrate that the two sides were much more evenly matched than the results might indicate and, at a number of junctures during the conflict, the issue was much more of a 'near run thing' than has generally been recognized."

The first, clearly fortuitous, event that might have decided the War of the Pacific was the Battle of Iquique on May 21, 1879. At the time, the Peruvian fleet counted four ironclads against two ironclads of the Chilean navy, which had been sent north. The situation in Iquique clearly favored Peru, with two ironclads confronting two small wooden vessels. One of these vessels was the schooner *Covadonga*, which the Chileans had taken from Spain at Papudo. Adding to its myth, the crew of the Chilean schooner tried to board the Peruvian ironclad *Independencia*, which repeatedly tried to ram it to no effect. In the end, "the Peruvian ship turned to starboard, in direction to the reef, right after one of the helmsman had fallen, wounded by a shot from the *Covadonga*. The only ruddler of the *Independencia* was on deck" (Manson, 1971, 87). The *Independencia* hit the reef and had to be scuttled. The set of events leading to the sinking of the *Independencia* is an example of contingency, or at least a "combination of Chilean cunning and Peruvian ill-fortune" (Sater, 2007, 177). The *Covadonga* had attacked, disobeying orders, survived cannon fire, somehow managed to drag the *Independencia* with it, and finally sunk it by a lucky shot, hitting a helmsman while the ironclad ran across a rock no one knew was there. Had any of these elements not been present in this chain of events, the *Covadonga* was more likely to have been defeated, yet the Chileans scored a decisive victory by eliminating a key Peruvian ship.

[7] For example, by mid-1866 the allied forces were very close to abandoning every hope of invading the well-defended Paraguay border. Mitre, commander of the allied forces, sat with López at Yataití-Corá on September 11, 1866, and both convened on the terms of a possible peace treaty that would have ended hostilities. With time, this would certainly have been seen as a Paraguayan victory or at least a draw. The possibility of peace was frustrated after the stupendous Paraguayan victory in the Battle of Curupaití on September 22, 1866, which led the Paraguayans to believe they could negotiate better terms – which, of course, they did not.

Despite having lost the *Independencia*, the Peruvians continued the fight. The *Huascar* – their remaining ironclad – had the advantage of being faster than any other ship and, commanded by the skillful Admiral Miguel Grau, invariably escaped its pursuers and continued to harass the Chilean coast. It would take another stroke of luck for the Chileans to stop the continued Peruvian offensive. On October 8, 1879, two Chilean ironclads – the *Cochrane* and the *Blanco Encalada* – spotted the *Huascar* and started to chase it. As usual, Grau fled until the point where he had only one contender in firing range, then turned to face the enemy. The first shot of the *Huascar* pierced the bow of the *Cochrane* and the projectile landed on its deck. The Battle of Angamos would have been over if this charge had exploded, but it did not. Instead a subsequent shot from the *Cochrane* killed Grau on the spot and the *Huascar* was boarded within the following hour (Manson, 1971, 115).

After Iquique and Angamos, the Chilean victory at sea was decided, but still many reasons prevented the small Chilean fleet from effectively blockading the powerful port of Callao. Other events of the land campaign were also decided by chance. The mysterious retreat of a Bolivian army that never arrived at the battlefield and a very close battle in Tarapacá are only two examples of how a small turn of fortune could have led to a different outcome. These and other events are covered in Chapter 8, which is devoted in large part to this war.

The short historical narratives in this section support the assumption that defeat and victory depended on contingent events and were determined largely by chance. In the case of short wars, this becomes evident when the descriptions of one or a few decisive battles are reviewed. In the case of longer wars, the contingency of their outcome is also evident by the fact that combat was protracted for years, with defensive and offensive campaigns on both sides. Finally, although victors developed relatively larger armies in the years following the war, there is no evidence that victors had larger armies at the outset of hostilities. Quite on the contrary, a case-by-case evaluation seems to show that those states with smaller armies tended to win.[8]

Importantly, the random selection of the treatment – that is, defeat – is not an assumption in DID models, as it would be in randomized controlled trials and other methodologies. It is not necessary that we believe this for the models in the next section to produce reliable estimates. These models rely on the much narrower assumption that confounders varying across countries are time invariant and time-varying confounders are country invariant – two twin claims researchers usually refer to as a parallel trend assumption. Yet having at least unveiled the important element of chance will give us more reason to trust the results that follow.

[8] Systematic evidence for this was already presented in Table 5.6.

5.2 TREATMENT (DEFEAT), OUTCOMES, AND COVARIATES

Because classical bellicist theory predicts that losing states will change trajectories after the outcomes of war are revealed while winners will continue on the same trajectory, my main treatment variable in all models is the defeat in the wars listed in Table 5.1.

There are two aspects of these wars that should be taken into account. First, not all of them were equally intense or affected contenders in the same manner. Even within each of these wars, some countries mobilized more than others and did so for longer periods. This should raise concerns about heterogeneous treatment effects, which are not an issue in the context of some estimators like the SCM but need to be considered in the context of a DID estimation.

Second, the precise ends of these wars can be a subject of debate. One might consider that the Paraguayan War, for instance, was decided after the siege of Humaitá in 1868, which led to the fall of Asunción in less than a year. Most scholars consider the end of military operations in 1870 as the moment when the war ended. Yet the withdrawal of the occupying forces in 1876 might still be proposed as an alternative end date. All this is to illustrate that in some of these wars, the treatment might be located some years before or some years after the end dates in Table 5.1, a point that I consider in my robustness checks.

In order to identify the effects of war outcomes on the infrastructural power of the state (Mann, 1988), I focus on state spatial and social control (Soifer and Vom Hau, 2008). The dimension of spatial control, reach (Soifer and Vom Hau, 2008), or range (Kurtz and Schrank, 2012) refers to the state's capability to effectively connect its territory and population (O'Donnell, 1993; Herbst, 2014). I use railroad mileage as an indicator of such capacity (Banks and Wilson, 2015), although railroads proxy state capacity in myriad different ways. As Marcus Kurtz (2013, 14–15) eloquently puts it:

> At the dawn of the twentieth century in South America, no public good was more important from the perspective of state building (and economic development) than the construction of a national rail network, for rails at this point in time were the only efficient way to transport people and goods over substantial distances where riverine transport was not available and they were effectively the arteries that cemented territorial unity and the formation of a single national market. Indeed, because railways permitted the central state to effectively project force throughout the national territory – which in the past was exceedingly difficult because the movement of troops over large distances was very costly and slow – the endemic regional rebellions on the continent began to come to an end. (Kurtz, 2013, 14–15)

Railroads provide an approximation like no other for the territorial reach of the state (Herbst, 2014), but they also serve as a proxy for state infrastructural and despotic powers more broadly (Mann, 1988). To grant a concession to railway companies, states needed first to exercise control over those territories.

If the state was to build the railroad, as it often did,[9] the enterprise required important mobilization of resources, a corps of engineers, and an unfathomable number of public employees. But even if a concession to a foreign company was granted, large bureaucracies were required to tax and regulate the sector.

Already in the construction phase, as railway companies extended their reach, telegraph lines, post offices, police stations, and many other manifestations of state presence were deployed along the way. The train made it profitable to exploit lands previously inaccessible, so the state had to register those lands. The usual foundation of new towns along the railroads required the presence of state agents, from school teachers to tax collectors and judges. This whole dimension of state expansion was less important in Europe, where existing townships were connected by the train, than it was in the Americas, where the train arrived first, making an immensity of land available to the local population and newly arrived immigrants (Callen, 2016).

Finally the train also facilitated the movement of people on an everyday basis, which also enhanced the capacity of the state. Central authorities were now able to deploy bureaucrats and troops to the peripheries by the thousands and cover immeasurable distances in a matter of hours. Trains expanded the reach of the press, allowing people to stay connected with news and developments in the capitals and allowing central authorities to effectively communicate the law and keep a fluid contact with their officials. Because of all these properties, railroads are widely attributed a central role in expanding the national state in the late nineteenth century (Paredes, 2013; Soifer, 2015).

To assess social control I focus on the extractive element of state capacity, using a measure of national government revenue per capita (Banks and Wilson, 2015). The detailed discussion provided in Section 3.4 already explains why this should be considered a good measure of state capacity in the context of nineteenth-century Latin America.

9 Many studies have demonstrated the central role played by the state in this regard. Railway historians now clearly associate the uneven spread of railroads throughout Latin America with factors akin to state capacity, such as institutional stability and the provision of government subsidies, which attracted foreign investment that would otherwise never have arrived (Sanz Fernández, 1998). In the context of the state formation literature, Ryan Saylor (2014, 66–71, 96–99) has provided a detailed discussion of how railroads in Argentina and Chile should be seen as a public good provided by the state. The state played a central role in the planning, financing, and regulation of this means of transport in many other cases as well, with Brazil, Mexico, and Uruguay standing out (Herranz-Loncán, 2014). In most of these cases, foreign capital provided little more than locomotives. The design, engineering, and labor that went into the construction and running of the network relied on state-owned companies. Although the specific role played by the state varied from country to country, "the build-up of state capacity was a necessary condition for railway expansion and also, to a large extent, for export expansion in Latin America during the first globalization" (Bignon et al., 2015, 1277). In other words, railroads, already an indicator of state infrastructural power – in the form of territorial reach and control – also required other dimensions of state capacity – such as extractive capacity – to precede them and were themselves a cause of economic growth, not the other way around.

TABLE 5.2 *Outcomes: General descriptive statistics*

Variable	Mean	Std. dev.	Min.	Max.
Railroads	1,294 miles	3,071 miles	0 miles	19,240 miles
Revenue	6.36 USD p/c	5.89 USD p/c	0.59 USD p/c	33.35 USD p/c

Source: Banks and Wilson, 2015.

TABLE 5.3 *Outcomes: Descriptive statistics by country*

		Railway miles			Revenue p/c (USD)	
Country	Min.	Mean	Max.	Min.	Mean	Max.
Argentina	329	6,578	19,240	4.41	11.84	24.42
Bolivia	0	229	798	1.08	1.97	3.98
Brazil	272	5,779	15,445	2.88	5.18	8.69
Chile	211	1,866	5,008	4.50	16.53	23.40
Colombia	66	265	708	0.76	1.96	3.17
Costa Rica	0	169	486	7.21	11.50	17.22
Dominican Rep.	0	64	150	1.47	3.89	8.03
Ecuador	49	136	380	1.51	2.87	6.31
El Salvador	0	57	191	2.55	4.66	8.42
Guatemala	0	190	502	1.00	4.70	10.45
Haiti	0	18	64	1.60	4.34	6.98
Honduras	0	46	150	2.17	3.37	5.45
Mexico	150	6,004	15,804	1.86	2.52	4.06
Nicaragua	0	80	191	1.92	3.77	7.23
Paraguay	45	97	232	0.59	2.30	6.55
Peru	150	798	1,656	1.68	9.98	24.37
Uruguay	0	656	1,575	9.70	18.57	33.35
Venezuela	0	260	533	2.07	3.60	6.45
All	0	1,294	19,240	0.59	6.31	33.35

Source: Banks and Wilson, 2015.

Some descriptive statistics of these outcomes are included in Table 5.2. A look at standard deviations in particular will help interpret the substantive result of the DID models and the synthetic control models provided later. In Table 5.3 I provide more detailed descriptive information about these two outcomes of state capacity by looking into each country in the sample. Although the variable for railroad mileage is not always monotonic, maximum railroad extension corresponds in all cases to the extension of the railway network in 1913, while the minimum corresponds to the extension in 1865. Countries that developed the most extensive railway networks are also the largest countries in the region, suggesting we should control for territorial size in our analyses. However, the table also shows that the extension of the railway network was not only a function of territorial size. Chile, for example, laid nine times more track than Venezuela, seven times more than Colombia, and six times more than Peru, all larger countries.

The evolution of revenue, calculated in current US dollars, is clearly not monotonic in all cases. Revenue also peaks at different moments in time depending on the country we look at, and while the overall trend is declining for some countries, it is positive for others. The revenue of the national government is already in per capita figures, which helps control for the size of population. A quick look at the data reveals that population is far from the only factor driving variation in revenue extraction. While Uruguay, a country with a small population, has the highest value (33.35 USD), Paraguay, a country with a similarly small population, presents the lowest value (0.59 USD).

Figure 5.1 provides a look at the evolution of railroad mileage and per capita national revenue. The subfigures for railroads clearly exemplify the increasing trends in railroad construction during that era. The first inauguration of railway lines in Latin America took place in Mexico in 1850 for a track connecting the port of Veracruz with El Molino and in Peru in 1851 for a train linking the port of El Callao with Lima. By the start of the series in 1865, Mexico and Peru had laid 150 miles of track and most countries in the region were building their first lines. Therefore the progression starts at a level very close to zero. The rate of growth thereafter suggests that these developments were steady and resilient to shocks that affected the region as a whole.

The figures to the right distinguish between the group of countries that will be defeated throughout the period and the trend for winners. They plot the means for each group with a confidence interval of 90 percent, confirming that losers developed less state capacity on average. In the case of railroads, the gap increases with time, producing a statistically significant difference in means by the year 1895. At the end of the series, winners had on average laid some 5,000 more miles of railway than losers.

Figure 5.1 also shows how the average per capita revenue in Latin America suffered considerable variation, and it suggests the importance of the international context. Fluctuations in foreign trade might be at the core of this phenomenon, and that is a factor to be taken into consideration. However, winners and losers also tend to diverge in revenue extraction. Note that during the decade from 1870 to 1880, both groups are virtually matched at some 5 USD per capita of revenue, and the difference only starts to grow after this violent decade. By the end of the series, winners extract on average 11 USD per capita, while losers extract some 4 USD per capita. As with railroads, the difference between the means of the two groups becomes significant with time. This also provides evidence of parallel trends in the prewar period, an assumption that will be key to my DID models.

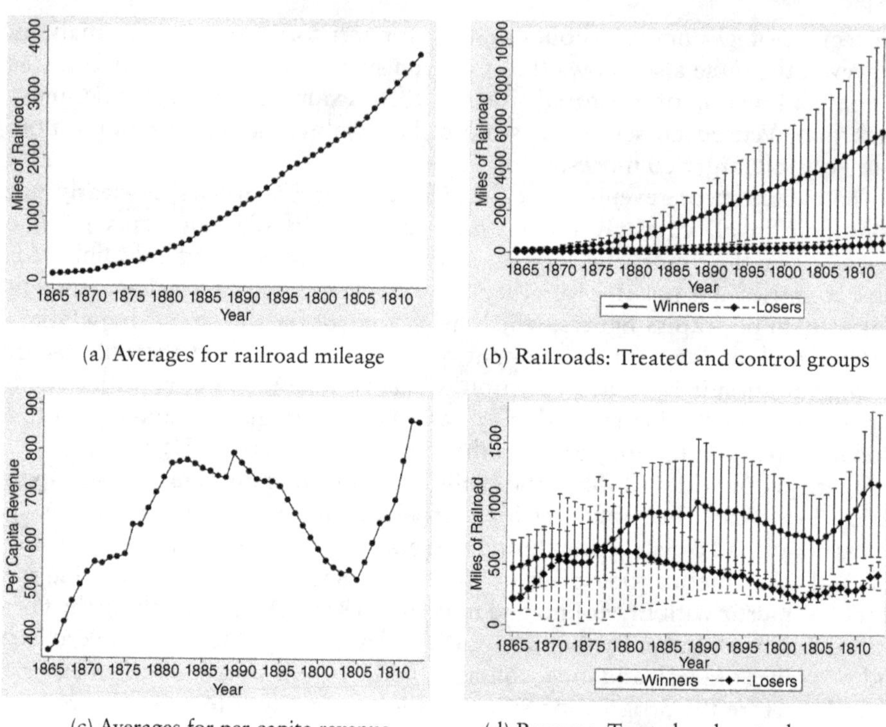

(a) Averages for railroad mileage

(b) Railroads: Treated and control groups

(c) Averages for per capita revenue

(d) Revenue: Treated and control groups

FIGURE 5.1 Descriptive statistics on revenue and railroad mileage

The gap between winners and losers is suggestive but still far from conclusive. One important step before we turn to estimating the effects of defeat is to consider which factors we are omitting that might have affected war outcomes and levels of state capacity, therefore confounding our results.

On the one hand, there are factors that might explain war outcomes. Military superiority is perhaps the most intuitive (Desch, 2002). Although weaker countries very often win wars (Arreguin-Toft, 2005, 1–18), it is commonly believed that having a stronger army should be a good predictor of war outcomes. The size of the military is the best available proxy for military superiority at the time (Singer, 1988), given the lack of systematic data about military equipment and training (Madrid and Schenoni, 2024).

Relatedly, Tilly himself suggested that there could be a relationship between territorial size and victory in a coercion-intensive path to state formation – a relationship explored in recent literature (Abramson, 2017; Cederman et al., 2023) – and highlighted the importance of state finances, which underlie military power and provide the thrust to sustain war efforts in the long term (Wayman et al., 1983). I therefore include measures of territorial size and per capita expenditure to control for these factors (Banks and Wilson, 2015).

Another popular argument suggests that democracies tend to win wars (Reiter and Stam, 2002). Due to the extended use of electoral fraud and the limited rights of large parts of the population, it is unclear whether one could consider any Latin American state to have been democratic at that time, yet it is still true that some had functioning legislatures. This indicator provides at least a proxy for the types of mechanisms – for example, public debate about the war, accountability of the leader – highlighted by this literature.

Finally, besides bullets, wallets, and ballots (Henderson and Bayer, 2013, 310), there is a fourth argument in the war outcomes literature suggesting that education creates an advantage on the battlefield by increasing levels of nationalism (Posen, 1993) and also by providing better-trained and more capable soldiers. The number of students enrolled in primary school for every 100,000 inhabitants (Banks and Wilson, 2015) provides a good proxy for this.

These factors do not provide an exhaustive summary of the literature on the determinants of war outcomes, but they do include the main possible confounders that vary across countries and times.[10]

On the other hand, there are factors that can be associated with higher revenue or larger railway networks. Foreign trade, for example, can be a very important factor affecting revenue – via customs duties – and providing a key incentive for investment in railroads connecting productive areas and ports (Bignon et al., 2015). Since Latin American economies were largely export oriented at the time, I will use exports per capita as a proxy for this factor.

Territory and population are also important confounders in this regard. The sheer size of the territory might have justified long extensions of track connecting different areas of the country. The concentration of the population in large urban areas can also facilitate taxation (Andersson, 2018) and provide incentives for the construction of railroads connecting large cities. This is yet another reason to consider territorial extension and add urban population to our list of relevant controls.

Table 5.4 provides a complete list of the variables I will use in my models, including those that will be used as controls. The list includes characteristics

[10] Part of this literature points to alliances (Henderson and Bayer, 2013) and cultural or idiosyncratic factors such as military doctrine (Biddle and Long, 2004), but since factors like alliances and doctrines do not vary during the wars under consideration, these invariant factors will be controlled for by the two-way fixed effects in my generalized DID models. The same is true for factors that the state-building literature might deem important in determining the results of warfare, such as the presence of servile labor (Kurtz, 2013), the centrality of a main urban hub (Soifer, 2015), and the type of colonial institutions (Mahoney, 2010), all taken care of by country-fixed effects. Year-fixed effects also take care of possible country-invariant characteristics like commodity booms (Saylor, 2014).

TABLE 5.4 *Variables and sources*

Variable	Function	Indicator	Source
War outcome	Treatment	1 after defeat	S&W
Railroad mileage	Outcome	Miles of line	B&W
P/c revenue	Outcome	In current USD (0.01)	B&W
P/c expenditure	Control	In current USD (0.01)	B&W
P/c exports	Control	In current USD (0.01)	B&W
Size of the military	Control	Military personnel (1,000)	B&W
Effective legislature	Control	Four-point scale	B&W
School enrollment	Control	Per capita students (0.0001)	B&W
Urban population	Control	In cities over 100,000 (1,000)	B&W
Size of territory	Control	Area in square miles	B&W

Note: B&W = Banks and Wilson, 2015; S&W = Sarkees and Wayman, 2010.

TABLE 5.5 *Confounders: Descriptive statistics*

Variable	Mean	Std. dev.	Min.	Max.
P/c expenditure	664	599	52	3,318
P/c exports	1,142	1,040	190	6,146
Size of the military	11.946	22.752	0.001	354
Effective legislature	1.55	0.72	0	3
School enrollment	8	59	0	150
Urban population	157,332	349,572	0	2,381,000
Size of territory	1,106,463	1,920,959	21,393	8,500,000

that vary both in time and across countries, since the two-way fixed effects in the DID models take care of country-invariant factors – for example, financial shocks – and time-invariant factors – for example, cultural or idiosyncratic characteristics. Table 5.5 provides some descriptive statistics of these covariates. Information about them will help interpret their coefficients in the models and is also illustrative of their variance.

Finally, Table 5.6 shows that winners and losers did not differ notably in any potential covariates of victory and defeat before wars took place – a balance test that further backs the parallel trends assumption in my DID models. By the year 1865, none of the differences in means between the two groups had reached a *t*-value of 1.96. The results for the size of the military, the most theoretically important confounder in my list, are particularly interesting. It would seem that losers had larger armies on average than winners before wars started to take place.

TABLE 5.6 *Pretreatment balance in covariates*

Covariate	μ Winners	μ Losers	*t*-value
P/c expenditure	483.45	288.71	1.09
P/c exports	960.54	578.14	1.00
Size of the military	10,000	14,428	−0.58
Effective legislature	1.36	0.71	1.90
School enrollment	0	0	–
Urban population	90	0	1.57
Size of territory	1,425,308	571,571	0.92
Observations	11	7	–

5.3 DIFFERENCE-IN-DIFFERENCES

To estimate the effects of war outcomes on these two dimensions of state capacity, I use a generalized DID model (Gelman and Hill, 2006, 228).

$$Y_{ct} = \lambda_0 + \lambda_D D_{ct} + \lambda_\alpha \alpha_c + \lambda_\delta \delta_t + \varepsilon. \tag{5.1}$$

The units of analysis in the model are country-years. The key treatment variable is coded one for every year after a defeat (D_{ct}), and the outcome is an indicator of state capacity (Y_{ct}). Other model parameters for Equation (5.1) include α_c for country-fixed effects and δ_t for year-fixed effects.

If, once triggered, wars are like a coin toss or the roll of a die, like our empirical and theoretical discussion suggests, then model (5.1) would correctly identify the causal effect of defeat on state capacity levels.

The model offers a good approximation of the effect of exposure on defeat even if the time-invariant characteristics of countries were theoretically relevant, for these are controlled for by the fixed effects.[11] In other words, the more specific assumption underlying the model is that no time-varying confounders affect the probability of winning a war.

Despite all the theoretical and historical reasons previously presented, some might still contest this assumption, arguing that there are relevant confounders varying across countries and time that are not being captured by the two-way fixed effects in the model. In my previous discussion of factors that might make countries more likely to win a war, I identified military superiority, wealth, regime type, and level of education as factors possibly related to war. I also discussed how factors like territorial size and volume of export could affect not only the outcomes of war but also the state capacity outcomes of interest.

11 In these models, country-fixed effects account for permanent characteristics of countries – for example, geography and stable cultural factors – while year-fixed effects help control for time trends that are shared by all countries in the sample – for example, commodity shocks, and financial crises.

All these possible factors in selecting countries for treatment are represented by the term X_{ct} in Equation (5.2).

$$Y_{ct} = \lambda_0 + \lambda_D D_{ct} + \lambda_\alpha \alpha_c + \lambda_\delta \delta_t + \lambda_X X_{ct} + \varepsilon. \tag{5.2}$$

This new model still assumes that the ignorability condition is met once we control for the observable covariates listed in Table 5.4.

A key identifying assumption in DID models is that state capacity trends would be the same in the absence of treatment. One common way to test for this is to look at the effects before, during, and after defeat in what some refer to as a modified Granger causality test (Angrist and Pischke, 2008, 171–179). This model (5.2) includes, therefore, an exploration of three leads of the treatment that test for these parallel trends. Three lags of the treatment are also included to test for time-varying treatment effects.

Other specifications of model (5.2) include slight changes in coding as a robustness check, one of them changing the end dates of the war from the end of hostilities to the end of occupations and the other capturing variation in the severity of the war outcome.[12]

To further address endogeneity concerns associated with the existence of time-varying unobservables, I use a lagged dependent variable model in Equation (5.3), which might help complement the fixed effects model detailed earlier by producing a lower bound estimate of our parameter of interest (see as an example Holbein and Hillygus, 2016, 365). We can be highly confident that our "true" parameter resides between these brackets even in the presence of unobservable confounders (Angrist and Pischke, 2008, 246).

$$Y_{ct} = \lambda_0 + \lambda_D D_{ct} + \lambda_Y Y_{c,\,t-1} + \lambda_X X_{ct} + \varepsilon. \tag{5.3}$$

Equation (5.3) is similar to Equation (5.2), except that it takes out the two-way fixed effects and includes a one-year lag of our indicator of state capacity.

Results for all three models when applied to railroad mileage as a first-state capacity indicator of interest are summarized in Table 5.7. In all models, results are negative and statistically significant as expected. If we believe war outcomes were effectively assigned as-if randomly, loser states are expected to lay 935 fewer miles of track than their counterparts, a result that is significant at a $p < 0.005$ level. The effect is reduced to 214 miles in the model with confounders, but this result is still substantive if we consider the descriptive statistics in Table 5.3 and remains significant at a $p < 0.05$ level. Importantly, the results of the difference-in-differences model with confounders (5.2) do not change substantively if we change the date on which the war ends – from the end of hostilities to the end of occupation – nor does it change when we

[12] Model $(5.2)_{\text{host.}}$ is my baseline coding, with losers acquiring a value of 1 when the hostilities end. Model $(5.2)_{\text{occup.}}$ introduces a slight change by introducing the treatment after the end of military occupation. Finally, model $(5.2)_{\text{sev.}}$ codes the treatment for more severe wars with a value of 2 in order to capture possible differences between more and less severe defeats.

TABLE 5.7 *Difference-in-differences and lagged models for railroads*

	(5.1)	$(5.2)_{host.}$	$(5.2)_{occup.}$	$(5.2)_{sev.}$	(5.3)
Treatment/ defeat	**−935***** **(163)**	**−214*** **(93.7)**	**−224*** **(88.7)**	**−165*** **(82.5)**	**−11.3**** **(4.23)**
Expenses p/c	–	−0.223* (0.107)	−0.226* (0.105)	−0.243* (0.116)	−0.001 (0.012)
Exports p/c	–	0.471*** (0.102)	0.468*** (0.103)	0.470*** (0.102)	0.009 (0.007)
Military size	–	4.44 (2.47)	4.47 (2.48)	4.42 (2.46)	−0.199 (0.149)
Legislature	–	−372*** (122)	−372*** (121)	−365*** (124)	8.11 (6.69)
Schooling	–	−4.61 (2.72)	−4.65 (2.69)	−4.54 (2.72)	0.356 (0.304)
Urbanization	–	8.63*** (0.349)	8.62*** (0.349)	8.61*** (0.349)	−0.030 (0.053)
Territory	–	−0.001*** (0.000)	−0.001*** (0.000)	−0.001*** (0.000)	0.000** (0.000)
Outcome $_{t-1}$	–	–	–	–	1.04*** (0.006)
Observations	882	882	882	882	864
Two-way FE	YES	YES	YES	YES	NO
Clustered SE	YES	YES	YES	YES	YES
Treatment $_{t-1}$	–	−9.57 (191)	−8.86 (212)	−16.9 (181)	–
Treatment $_{t-2}$	–	32.0 (190)	33.8 (195)	54.9 (157)	–
Treatment $_{t-3}$	–	−154 (140)	−230 (132)	−172 (101)	–
Treatment $_{t+1}$	–	61.0 (172)	78.0 (188)	53.7 (156)	–
Treatment $_{t+2}$	–	33.1 (166)	8.02 (173)	24.0 (161)	–
Treatment $_{t+3}$	–	−222 (139)	−185 (137)	−155 (136)	–

Note: Standard errors in parentheses ($p < 0.05^{*}$, $p < 0.01^{**}$, and $p < 0.005^{***}$).

consider the difference between more and less severe wars. The last model (5.3) should be interpreted otherwise, as a lower bound for a possible substantive effect. This lagged model suggests that the effect of losing a war on railroad mileage is robust, and defeated states comparatively lose at least eleven miles of track.

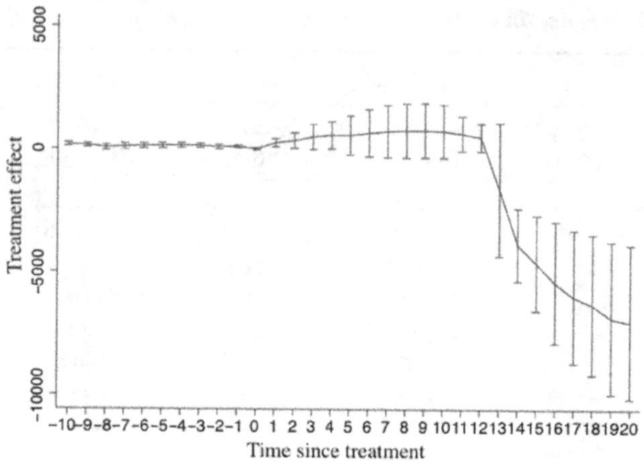

FIGURE 5.2 Plot of lags and leads for DID on railroad mileage

Three leads at the bottom of Table 5.7 (5.2) test for secular trends – that is, the possibility that losers were already on a downward trajectory with regard to railway construction. The insignificant results on the leads of the treatment in the second, third, and fourth columns should provide sufficient evidence that a common trend assumption is met. Interestingly, when time trends are included, the first three lags are not significant either, suggesting that the effect picked up by the models does not take place immediately after the defeat. This is also in line with the theory. The negative effect does not result from the kinetic or destructive effect of the war itself – for example, the destruction of existing rails – but is rather due to some divergence that takes place long after warfare has ended.

This last finding is particularly relevant and merits the question of how long it takes for the effect to take place. To answer this question I plot a longer series of lags (10) and leads (20) in Figure 5.2. Note that these are actual lags and leads of the estimated effect, not the treatment (Autor, 2003).

To calculate these I use a procedure recommended by de Chaisemartin and D'Haultfoeuille (2018), which provides additional advantages. First, it allows for the possibility of heterogeneous treatment effects. Because we know each of these wars had a different intensity, we can deduce that the average treatment effect calculated in our previous models might be obscuring important variation in the average treatment on the treated. Second, this fuzzy approach to DID (de Chaisemartin and D'Haultfoeuille, 2019) relaxes the assumption that the treatment rate does not vary over time. This is more in line with our theoretical prediction that the dynamics taking place after war are self-reinforcing.

The model I use is akin to model (5.2) in Table 5.7, including the same set of covariates. It produces the plot of lags and leads in Figure 5.2, which demonstrates a great fit with our theoretical predictions in two important ways. First, the trend of both winners and losers does not differ from zero in the pre-treatment period, neither substantively nor statistically. Second, the difference between treatment and control groups increases with time, becoming statistically significant thirteen years after the defeat, as shown by the 95 percent confidence intervals.

Figure 5.2 reassures us that our models are not picking up the destructive consequences of defeat in the short term but rather longer-term effects mediated by institutional dynamics, which set countries onto different trajectories for decades. Note that the size of the effect continues to grow twenty years after the defeat, when these countries had had enough time to overcome the immediate effects of warfare. This is indicative that the negative dynamics triggered by the defeat have been internalized and are reproducing in a self-reinforcing or path-dependent manner.

Let us turn now to our second outcome of interest: per capita revenue as an indicator of the extractive capacity of Latin American states. Almost the exact same models are applied to test the effects of this outcome. The only minor change is that I have removed territorial size from the list of control variables, given there is no theoretical reason to believe this would be correlated with revenue – as it was with railroad extension – and the territorial factor is probably already controlled for by the country-fixed effects.

The results of the models for revenue are in Table 5.8 – figures are in cents of current USD – and are also clearly aligned with our expectations. Under the assumption of randomized treatment assignment, losers collect 4.62 USD less than winners do. A quick look back at the descriptive statistics in Table 5.2 reveals that the negative impact is huge considering the regional average is 6.36 USD with a standard deviation of 5.89 USD. According to the summary statistics in Table 5.3, more than half of the countries in our sample collected, on average, less than that amount.

In the model (5.2) with confounders, the effect is reduced to 0.83 USD, a much more reasonable yet still substantive amount, and remains significant at a $p < 0.005$ level. This figure remains relatively robust despite variations in end dates and the severity of wars. Insignificant leads and lags in model (5.2) also show support for the parallel trends assumption and the possibility that effects might take place beyond three years after the end of the war.

Finally, the lagged model (5.3) shows that the effect of losing a war on revenue extraction is robust under a more stringent specification and suggests defeated states collect at least 0.19 USD less than their counterparts.

In Figure 5.3 I once again calculate pre- and post-treatment effects for my model (5.2) with confounders. The results are once again in line with my expectations. In only three out of ten lags is the difference between treatment and control significantly different from zero, and the divergence is still very small and broadly in line with a parallel trends assumption. After the military defeat, the difference grows steadily with time – not immediately afterward – and becomes statistically significant six years after it. Although the effect seems to stabilize some thirteen years after the treatment, it remains negative at statistically significant levels until the twenty-year lag.

TABLE 5.8 *Difference-in-differences and lagged models for revenue*

	(5.1)	(5.2)host.	(5.2)occup.	(5.2)sev.	(5.3)
Treatment/ defeat	**−462***** **(56.9)**	**−83.0***** **(12.9)**	**−74.2***** **(12.8)**	**−69.7***** **(13.2)**	**−19.4*** **(7.64)**
Expenses p/c	–	−0.853*** (0.020)	−0.855*** (0.020)	−0.843*** (0.021)	0.779*** (0.024)
Exports p/c	–	0.051*** (0.012)	0.050*** (0.012)	0.049*** (0.011)	0.039*** (0.008)
Military size	–	0.605*** (0.149)	0.615*** (0.153)	0.601*** (0.148)	0.069 (0.089)
Legislature	–	31.2*** (7.79)	29.9*** (7.80)	34.8*** (7.89)	4.32 (7.55)
Schooling	–	−0.518 (0.374)	−0.562 (0.372)	−0.427 (0.383)	0.219 (0.267)
Urbanization	–	−0.027 (0.030)	−0.027 (0.030)	−0.028 (0.029)	−0.026 (0.016)
Outcome $_{t-1}$	–	–	–	–	103*** (12.5)
Observations	882	882	882	882	864
Two-way FE	YES	YES	YES	YES	NO
Clustered SE	YES	YES	YES	YES	YES
Treatment $_{t-1}$	–	−0.456 (34.2)	−0.239 (26.5)	−03.36 (37.3)	–
Treatment $_{t-2}$	–	−16.9 (30.7)	−24.9 (25.9)	−14.1 (29.1)	–
Treatment $_{t-3}$	–	−14.4 (21.2)	−13.2 (18.6)	−19.8 (18.1)	–
Treatment $_{t+1}$	–	−12.7 (34.9)	−6.65 (32.9)	−6.28 (37.5)	–
Treatment $_{t+2}$	–	−24.3 (166)	−3.51 (30.0)	−37.4 (30.0)	–
Treatment $_{t+3}$	–	−17.4 (26.4)	−21.9 (23.4)	−6.35 (17.9)	–

Note: Standard errors in parentheses ($p < 0.05^{*}, p < 0.01^{**}$, and $p < 0.005^{***}$).

Overall, the DID analyses presented in this section provide strong support for the hypothesis that defeat in war had enduring negative effects on indicators of state capacity. These effects remain significant when controlling for confounders and a one-year lag of the dependent variable. The effects also did not take place during or immediately after the war – for example,

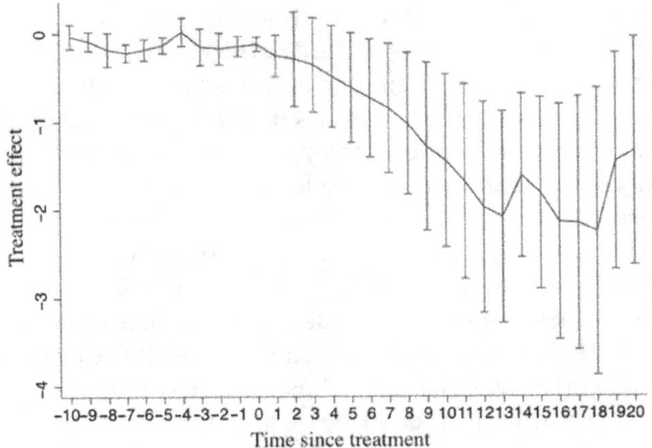

FIGURE 5.3 Plot of lags and leads for DID on revenue

during occupation – but rather over the long term and by some mechanism that permitted their reproduction and accumulation.[13]

5.4 SYNTHETIC CONTROL METHOD

In this section I start to narrow down the focus of my analysis to address the Paraguayan War and the War of the Pacific, which will be the subject of Chapter 7 and Chapter 8, respectively. These are the two major Latin American wars of the late nineteenth century and those where the effect I am tracing should most clearly take place. The Paraguayan War (1864–1870) was the greatest war in Latin American history.[14] It confronted Paraguay with Argentina, Brazil, and Uruguay, resulting in an estimated 250,000 to 400,000 battle deaths. The War of the Pacific (1879–1883) pitched Chile against Bolivia and Peru, but this time it was the alliance that was defeated. With some 16,000 battle-related deaths, this is clearly the second-bloodiest conflict between two Latin American countries in this period.

In the following analysis I will focus on the effects these events had on Paraguay and Peru, the two main losers of those wars.[15] I once again focus on

13 This is the first work to pick up these effects, although the results are in line with a sparse literature that predicts an effect of defeat on regime instability (de Mesquita et al., 1992, 643) and decreasing international reputation (Clare and Danilovic, 2010, 873) within a ten-year window after the conflict (Barnhart, 2021, 206).

14 It is actually the bloodiest interstate war in the history of the Americas, standing second only to the American Civil War if we consider all episodes of organized political violence. The anarchy that followed the Mexican Revolution might be the only historical process that led to more violent deaths, but it would be incorrect to portray it as a war.

15 Bolivia is not included in the analysis because Bolivian forces fought only at the beginning of the war and the fight resulted in relatively few (920) battle deaths. This means the War of the Pacific was not particularly severe for Bolivia. According to the parameters explained in

losers and not winners, for the change in trajectory that classical bellicist theory predicts takes place only on the losing side after the war outcome is revealed.

Looking at individual cases can help address some of the limitations of the regression techniques I use in Section 5.3. Qualitative researchers are aware that Paraguay and Peru are very different from each other and thus might require a different set of comparison cases from which to draw inferences. Yet regression extrapolates from all cases in the sample without careful consideration of these counterfactuals (Kennedy, 2014, 280). To address these problems I use the synthetic control method. This method uses information from a donor pool to construct a synthetic or counterfactual case that best resembles the treated case – for example, Paraguay or Peru – in theoretically relevant pretreatment characteristics. In other words, the SCM uses a panel of other countries – in this case, all other Latin American countries – and applies weights to extrapolate counterfactual values that we can then compare to those of the actual case (Abadie et al., 2015, 501). The cross-validation technique used to choose these weights is the following:

$$\sum_{m=1}^{k} v_m (X_{1m} - X_{0m} W)^2, \qquad (5.4)$$

where $X_1 - X_0 W$ measures the difference between the pre-intervention characteristics of the treated unit and a synthetic control, and v_m is a weight that reflects the relative importance assigned to the m-th variable when we measure the discrepancy between $X_1 - X_0 W$ (Abadie et al., 2015, 497). The variables I utilize for X_1 and X_0 are those labeled as controls in Table 5.4.

I start by looking at railroad mileage. The aforementioned statistical procedure selects the countries at the bottom of Table 5.9 and assigns them the weights described there to produce our comparison. In the case of Paraguay, for example, the donors that produce the best match for railroad mileage in the pretreatment period are Colombia (0.682), El Salvador (0.221), and Haiti (0.088). These cases and weights also produce the balance of covariates between the synthetic and the real case that is also summarized in the table. With the exception of territorial size and the presence of an effective legislature, the counterfactual proves to be a perfect match in almost every characteristic.[16] Colombia also plays an important role as a donor for the Peruvian counterfactual (0.625) but is complemented by Argentina (0.191) and Chile (0.184) in order to generate a similar best match for the covariates and the treatment in the pretreatment period. The match in covariates is less impressive in this case, at the expense of a more impressive match of the

Table 3.4, this was not a case of mobilization. The same applies to Uruguay during the War of the Triple Alliance.

[16] Note that we are working with a limited donor pool composed of Latin American countries alone. Because the composition of the synthetic control might be sensitive to the inclusion of specific countries in the sample, I explored several robustness checks in which I eliminate the main donor and rerun the analyses.

TABLE 5.9 *Paraguay and Peru railroad SCMs: Balance and weights*

Paraguay railroad SCM

Predictor	Treated	Synthetic
Expenditure p/c	167.2	166.9
Military size	56	4.4
Exports p/c	443.4	444.1
Legislature	0	1
Schooling	0	0
Urbanization	0	0
Territory	268,000	757,832
Railroads in 1865	45	45
Railroads in 1869	45	45
Colombia	v_m =	0.682
El Salvador	v_m =	0.221
Haiti	v_m =	0.088

Peru railroad SCM

Predictor	Treated	Synthetic
Expenditure p/c	1,765	421.7
Military size	14.7	6.2
Exports p/c	1,123	852.9
Legislature	1	1.6
Schooling	0	0.16
Urbanization	46.1	79.3
Territory	1,300,000	1,294,673
Railroads in 1865	594	612
Railroads in 1882	150	142
Argentina	v_m =	0.191
Chile	v_m =	0.184
Colombia	v_m =	0.625

pretreatment trends in railroad mileage, which can be seen in Figure 5.4. Importantly, the general trends in the figure and the results that I report are robust with the exclusion of Colombia from the donor pool.

After considering the counterfactual or synthetic cases in Table 5.9, we can look at Figure 5.4, which plots the effect of defeat on railway mileage in Paraguay and Peru compared to that on their counterfactual. In the figures on the left-hand side, the real cases are represented by a bold line, while the synthetic cases – or the extension they would have achieved had they avoided defeat – are represented by the dashed line.

In the case of Paraguay, the progression seems very similar to that of our DID models, with the gap between the real and the synthetic Paraguay being initially small and increasing with time until it reaches some 150 miles by the year 1900 – that is, thirty years after the treatment.

The placebo tests on the right-hand side show that the substantive results are statistically significant. In this chart the zero on the Y-axis indicates that there is no difference between the synthetic control and the actual case. The lines represent seventeen replications of the same model that replace Paraguay and Peru with other countries, represented by gray lines. The effect on the treated cases is represented by the bold line.

Figure 5.4(b), for example, shows that Paraguay was virtually the only country to be negatively affected and set on a downward trajectory in c. 1870. These placebos provide strong support for my hypothesis. The divergence of the real Paraguay from the synthetic case is clearly not due to random chance or secular trends affecting many cases ($p < 0.1$).

The Peruvian counterfactual in Figure 5.4(c) also matches the real case very closely during a prewar period that is relatively longer in this case, convincingly showing that when Peru lost the war, the progress of railway construction

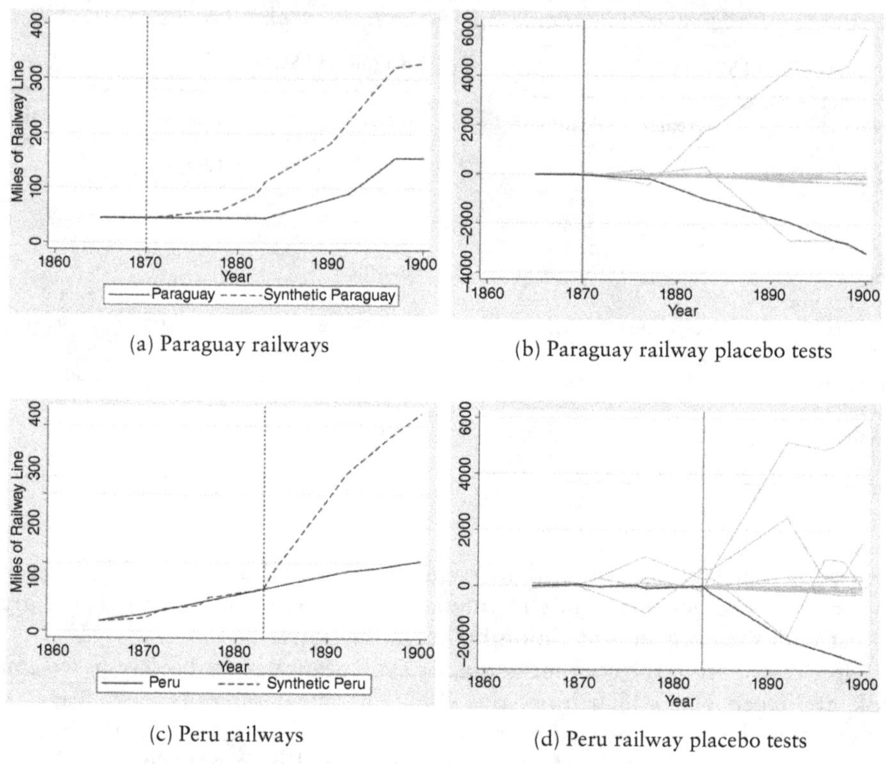

(a) Paraguay railways

(b) Paraguay railway placebo tests

(c) Peru railways

(d) Peru railway placebo tests

FIGURE 5.4 Effects of defeat on railroad mileage in Paraguay and Peru

slowed down. Home to the first railways in South America as early as 1851, Peru was set onto a clear negative trend when compared to others.

The placebo tests for Peru are also very reassuring. These tests show that no country was affected like Peru by a shock in that particular year and that the effect is unlikely to be due to random chance ($p < 0.05$).

My final analyses turn to revenue. Table 5.10 shows the counterfactual cases selected by the SCM and how they match our cases of interest in pretreatment trends and covariate characteristics.

The results are plotted in Figure 5.5. Here too, in the case of Paraguay, the negative effect of the defeat is clear. This is evident in the decline suffered by the real Paraguay – the bold line. In the placebos, we can corroborate the fact that almost no other country suffered a similar decline in revenue collection until 1890, and the results are again significant for both Paraguay ($p < 0.1$) and Peru ($p < 0.05$).

In the case of Peru, we should consider the extraordinarily high value of revenue in the pretreatment period, which seems to be the main reason why the best-matching counterfactual at hand is still far from reaching Peruvian

TABLE 5.10 *Paraguay and Peru revenue SCMs: Balance and weights*

Paraguay revenue SCM

Predictor	Treated	Synthetic
Expenditure p/c	167.2	114.2
Military size	56	2.2
Exports p/c	443.4	274.0
Effective legislature	0	1.3
School enrollment	0	0
Urban population	0	0
Territorial size	268,000	1,045,328
Revenue in 1865	121	88.8
Revenue in 1869	59	82.4
Colombia	v_m =	0.949
Haiti	v_m =	0.051

Peru revenue SCM

Predictor	Treated	Synthetic
Expenditure p/c	1,765	1,316
Military size	14.7	2.6
Exports p/c	1,123	1,525
Effective legislature	1	1.3
School enrollment	0	0
Urban population	46.1	0
Territorial size	1,300,000	51,000
Revenue in 1865	576	925
Revenue in 1882	1,741	1,698
Costa Rica	v_m =	1
Others	v_m =	0

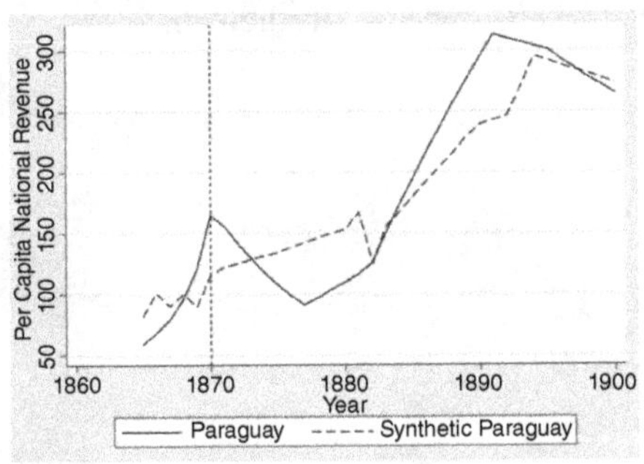

(a) Paraguay revenue

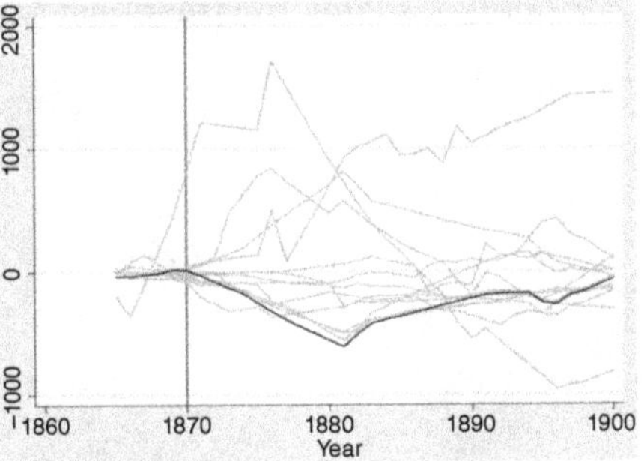

(b) Paraguay revenue placebo tests

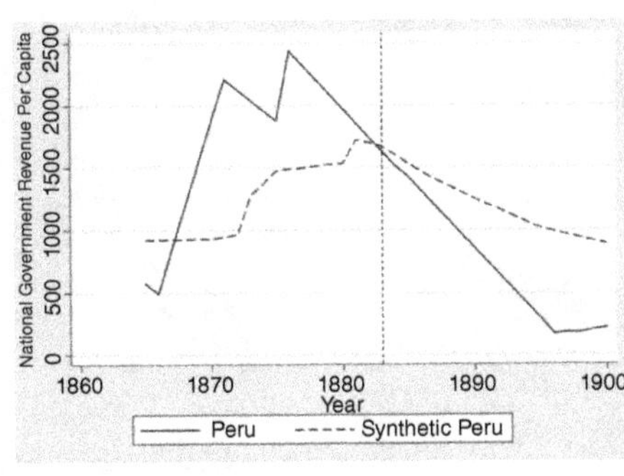

(c) Peru revenue

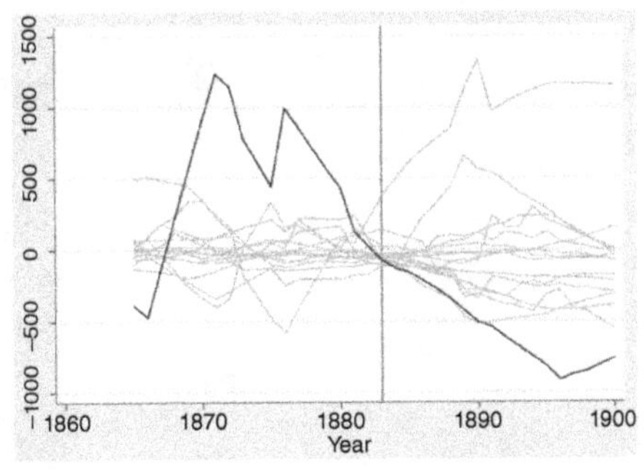

(d) Peru revenue placebo tests

FIGURE 5.5 Effect of defeat on revenue in Paraguay and Peru

extraction levels. Even if we eliminate Costa Rica from the sample – the case that singlehandedly produces the synthetic case in this particular model – the second-best match continues to lack a good pretreatment fit, although the posttreatment gap grows bigger. This is in line with my case narrative in Chapter 8, where I argue that Peru was undergoing a process of state formation immediately before the war.

The timing of the treatment is yet another factor to consider in the Peruvian case. It is clear that the decline in revenue starts before the end of the war – probably in its first stages. This issue will also be discussed in the case study. Here it is worth mentioning that this is in line with our intuition that key battles – which in the case of this war took place at the very first stages – might be more relevant as a critical juncture than the year of a peace treaty, which in the case of the War of the Pacific only took place after the Chilean army had been occupying Lima for years.

Importantly, both analyses show that the impact of losing a war was negative and statistically significant and withstand several checks like changing the donor pool, changing the treatment year, and eliminating predictors.

6

The State Capacity Ranking c. 1900

Were nineteenth-century war outcomes a main cause of state formation in Latin America? Previous statistical analyses looking at the effects of militarized interstate disputes (MIDs) and war outcomes on indicators of state building offer some support for this hypothesis. Yet critics could still argue that, although statistically significant, the effects of warfare might have been substantively irrelevant and even marginal compared to other factors. This potential criticism is difficult to address with a regression-type approach. Did nineteenth-century wars truly define the fate of Latin American states in the long term?

To address this question, this chapter explores the possible determinants of the rank ordering of Latin American state capacity c. 1900. This has become a somewhat standard plausibility test in the literature (Mahoney, 2010, 5; Kurtz, 2013, 11–16; Soifer, 2015, 13), which also allows me to compare the merits of my classical bellicist explanation with those of other explanations in the literature and replicate those analyses. By pursuing this "causes of effects" (Goertz and Mahoney, 2012) approach to my research question, I demonstrate that war outcomes not only have a significant effect on state formation but are also a very important cause. Since the ranking of state capacity in 1900 has hardly changed, this chapter demonstrates that the outcomes of wars in the nineteenth century could explain intraregional variation in state capacity in the present day.

This chapter is divided into three sections. In Section 6.1 I use fuzzy-set Qualitative Comparative Analysis (fsQCA), a technique that produces a unique type of inference in terms of the necessity and sufficiency of certain conditions for an outcome, replicating a similar analysis by Mahoney (2003). In Section 6.2 I use correlations to evaluate how war outcomes were associated with a broad set of state capacity indicators at the turn of the century, replicating an analysis by Soifer (2015). Finally, in Section 6.3 I consider the timing of the formation of the hierarchy c. 1900, deriving a set of hypotheses to be tested via a case-by-case analysis of longitudinal data in Part III.

6.1 QUALITATIVE COMPARATIVE ANALYSES

James Mahoney (2003) unveiled the interesting feature of Latin American development that motivates this chapter. He noted that the levels of development of Latin American states relative to one another have remained almost the same during the twentieth century, pointing to a path-dependent effect of some processes that took place before that. He also identified a novel way of analyzing this phenomenon, using fsQCA to look for conditions that might have been necessary and/or sufficient for some countries to be relatively at the top or bottom of this ranking.

One key feature of fsQCA is that it requires thinking of indicators – for example, revenue per capita – in terms of conditions that are either present or not. Therefore it is the *level* of these indicators that has to be evaluated in relation to the different countries in a (usually small) sample and then coded on a fuzzy scale from 0 to 1, which determines the extent to which a condition is present. Consider revenue per capita in the year 1900 as an example. Chile would be a full member (membership = 1) of the set of countries with high revenue, featuring the highest value (22.03 USD) in the region. The country with the lowest revenue per capita at the time, Peru (2.18 USD), would receive the lowest value for membership (0), while other countries like Argentina (10.69 USD or 0.83 membership) or Venezuela (3.83 USD or 0.33 membership) would fall somewhere in the middle of the scale.

Table 6.1 shows the resulting coding. The values for economic and social development are from Mahoney (2003, 77). Following his standard, I will also code all my conditions and outcomes of interest using a seven-point scale. In this particular table I include two alternative outcomes of interest: per capita measures of GDP and primary school attendance by the year 1900.

As expected, the Maddison data for GDP per capita in the year 1900 (Bolt et al., 2018) correlates highly with the measure of economic development provided by Mahoney (2003, 76), which is also based on GDP per capita and a few other indicators, such as telephones and automobiles per capita. Yet Mahoney's conditions are measured as an average for the 1900–1990 period, which introduces some extemporaneous factors we might not want in our analyses. As Mahoney (2003, 55) notes, Venezuelan GDP per capita skyrocketed after the oil industry consolidated in the 1920s. Oil-rich countries in general receive a boost in this dimension, and still other twentieth-century developments might affect the ranking c. 1900 at its margins. Therefore a strict focus on the values at the turn of the century is better suited as an outcome measure.

Notice that the work of Mahoney (2003) is concerned with socio-economic development rather than state capacity. Of course these two phenomena are

TABLE 6.1 *Ranking of development in Latin America c. 1900*

Country	Economic dev.	Social dev.	GDP p/c	Schooling p/c
Chile	0.83	0.83	0.83	0.67
Uruguay	1	1	1	1
Costa Rica	0.67	1	0.67	0.83
Brazil	–	–	0.33	0.33
Argentina	1	1	1	1
El Salvador	0.17	0.17	0.17	0.33
Ecuador	0.17	0.33	0.33	0.5
Guatemala	0.17	0	0.5	0.5
Mexico	0.83	0.33	0.67	0.67
Colombia	0.5	0.5	0.33	0.33
Venezuela	1	0.5	0.33	0.17
Honduras	0	0.17	0.5	0.83
Nicaragua	0	0.17	0.5	0.33
Bolivia	0	0	0.17	0.17
Paraguay	0.17	0.5	0.17	0.5
Peru	0.33	0.17	0.17	0.33

Notes: The coding for economic and social development is taken from Mahoney. For GDP, per capita thresholds (in USD) are 3,000, 2,000, 1,400, 1,000, 800, and 600. For primary school attendance per 100,000 inhabitants, thresholds are 800, 600, 500, 400, 300, and 200.
Sources: Mahoney, 2003; Banks and Wilson, 2015; Bolt et al., 2018.

highly correlated and even confounded in the literature. Yet it will serve our analysis better to focus more narrowly on indicators of the latter. For reasons that were already discussed, revenue extraction and government expenditure on a per capita basis, as well as railroad mileage and the volume of post mail, should be considered indicators of state capacity with high internal and external validity for the nineteenth century.[1] I summarize the fuzzy scale they produce in Table 6.2.

Overall, highly populated countries might be slightly penalized by our use of per capita figures. Something similar might happen with countries of great territorial extension when we consider railroad density. Brazil might be the clearest example of both. Yet the fact that the indicators in Table 6.2 tap into the same underlying concept of state capacity is relatively clear by the comparable rankings that they produce.

1 The post office was a quintessential expression of state capacity in the nineteenth century. In some countries postal and telegraph services were the single most important public employer and the biggest and most complex civilian bureaucracy (Acemoglu et al., 2016, 63). These were the most important means by which the acts of the state were transmitted, from the passing of legislation to everyday administrative decisions. In conjunction with the train, the post mail and the telegraph allowed states to integrate their agents across vast territories, keeping officials in the capital connected with bureaucrats and military in every corner of the country.

TABLE 6.2 *Ranking of state capacity in Latin America c. 1900*

Country	Revenue p/c	Expenditure p/c	Railroads	Post mail p/c
Chile	1	1	0.67	0.83
Uruguay	1	1	1	0.83
Costa Rica	0.67	0.67	1	0.67
Brazil	0.33	0.5	0.17	0.33
Argentina	0.83	0.67	0.67	1
El Salvador	0.33	0.5	0.83	0.33
Ecuador	0.5	0.5	0	0.33
Guatemala	0.33	0.5	0.5	0.5
Mexico	0.17	0.17	0.83	0.67
Colombia	0.17	0.17	0	0
Venezuela	0.33	0.67	0	0.5
Honduras	0.33	0.33	0	0
Nicaragua	0.17	0	0.17	0.67
Bolivia	0	0	0	0.17
Paraguay	0.17	0.5	0.17	0.33
Peru	0.33	0.17	0	0.5

Notes: The thresholds for my seven-point scales are determined so that an equal number of states fall into each category. For revenue and expenditure per capita, thresholds (in USD) are 15, 10, 5, 4, 3, and 2. For railroad mileage over square miles, the thresholds are 0.12, 0.1, 0.08, 0.06, 0.04, and 0.02. Finally, for letters received by postal mail per capita, thresholds are 50, 15, 10, 4, 2, and 1.
Sources: Banks and Wilson, 2015; Bolt et al., 2018.

So far I have focused on several indicators of development and state capacity – that is, definitions of my outcome of interest. Now fsQCA analysis requires that I similarly code potential causal conditions that might explain these outcomes. In his analysis, Mahoney (2003, 78) does this for a set of explanatory variables, such as the density of indigenous populations, the prominence of labor-intensive estates, the relevance of mineral and tropical exports, and the relative strength of liberal and conservative parties. After performing a series of analyses, his findings pointed to the density of indigenous populations and the strength of liberal elites from 1700 to 1850 as key explanatory conditions.

My main conditions of interest are war outcomes, which I also code along a seven-point scale following two steps. First, I distinguish consequential defeats and victories from minor events. If a country ended up victorious (Great V) or defeated (Great D) after a large mobilization – defined as losing half its army during a war that results in more than 5,000 casualties and lasts two years: see the procedure in Table 3.4 – that country acquires the highest value (1) for Victory (fuzzy V) or Defeat (fuzzy D), respectively.[2] Second, I code all remaining cases as departing from the center (0.5) of the scale and moving one step up per

[2] Mexico is the only country that went through both a severe victory and a severe defeat. I thus give Mexico a value of 0.5 on this scale.

TABLE 6.3 *Ranking of military success in Latin America c. 1900*

Country	minor d	minor v	v–d	Great V	Great D	fuzzy V	fuzzy D
Chile	0	2	+2	1	0	1	0
Uruguay	0	1	+1	1	0	1	0.17
Costa Rica	0	1	+1	1	0	1	0.17
Brazil	1	1	0	1	0	1	0.33
Argentina	2	1	−1	1	0	1	0.33
El Salvador	1	2	+1	0	0	0.67	0.33
Honduras	1	2	0	0	0	0.67	0.33
Colombia	0	1	+1	0	0	0.67	0.33
Mexico	0	0	0	1	1	0.5	0.5
Guatemala	2	2	0	0	0	0.5	0.5
Venezuela	0	0	0	0	0	0.5	0.5
Ecuador	1	0	−1	0	0	0.33	0.67
Nicaragua	2	1	−1	0	0	0.33	0.67
Bolivia	2	1	−1	0	0	0.33	0.67
Paraguay	1	0	−1	0	1	0.33	1
Peru	4	1	−3	0	1	0	1

Sources: Sarkees and Wayman, 2010, and own coding from Tables 3.2 and 3.4.

minor victory (minor v) and one down per minor defeat (minor d), as listed in Table 3.2. The resulting scale is in Table 6.3.[3]

The key statistic in fsQCA tests for necessary conditions is "consistency," and this refers to the degree to which the causal condition is a superset of the outcome. The higher the consistency of a condition, the more likely it is to be necessary for the outcome. Consistency scores are usually considered to be high above a 0.8 threshold.[4] When I replicate the analyses done by Mahoney (2003, 83) for the determinants of economic development, victory shows a significant necessary condition (consistency = 0.90), although strong liberal elites are still more relevant (consistency = 1). Things change slightly when I include GDP per capita in 1900 – ostensibly a more reliable and valid measure for the reasons discussed earlier. Victory (consistency = 0.95) and strong liberal elites (consistency = 0.97) are now virtually tied.

Victory performs even better (consistency = 0.94) when we look at social development, relegating liberal parties to the second-best explanation

3 One interesting algebraic feature of Qualitative Comparative Analysis (QCA) is that it allows for causal asymmetry – that is, the conditions that lead to victory, not necessarily defeat, and vice versa (Schneider and Wagemann, 2012, 81). This asymmetry is incorporated into my concept (Goertz, 2020). It can be readily seen in Table 6.3 that the fuzzy score for defeat is not the negation of victory (¬ victory) but rather a different indicator that specifically captures the experience of defeat.

4 I conduct these analyses using the software fsQCA (Ragin and Davey, 2016) and check the results using the Duşa (2018) QCA package for R, since the way in which these statistics are calculated varies slightly.

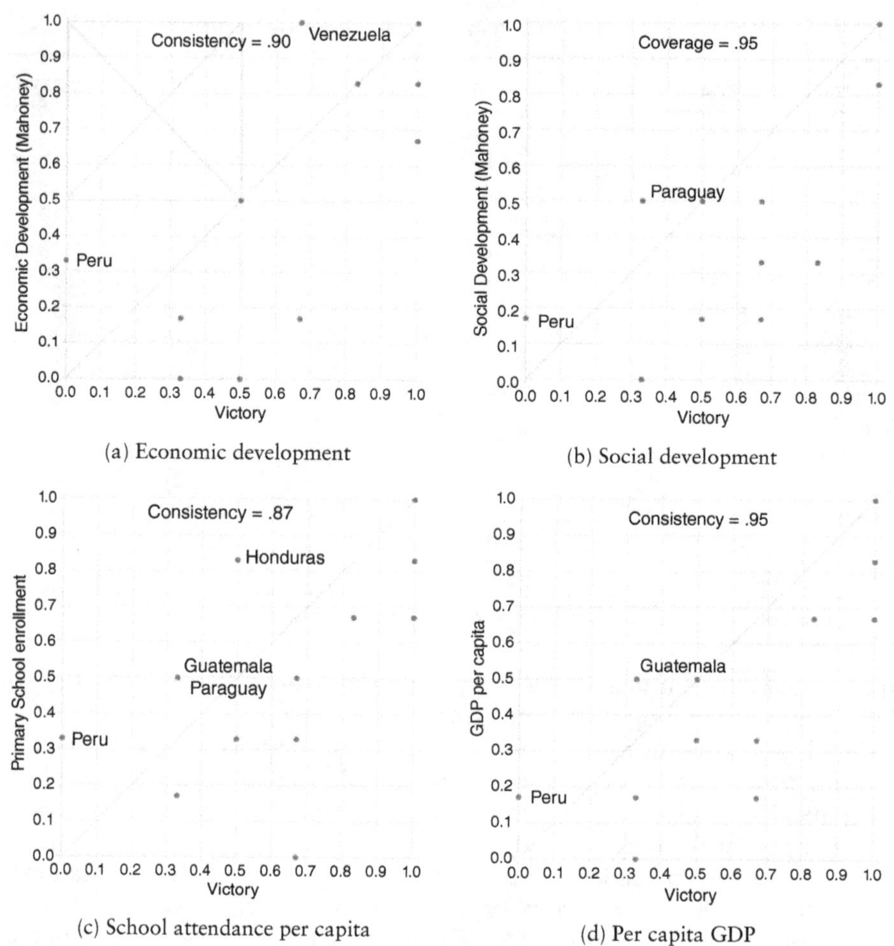

(a) Economic development

(b) Social development

(c) School attendance per capita

(d) Per capita GDP

FIGURE 6.1 Necessity of victory for high development at 1900

(consistency = 0.92). Both conditions appear to be equally necessary (consistency = 0.87) for schooling rates c. 1900.

The results for my fsV (victory) condition can be seen in Figure 6.1. The cases that fall below the diagonal line support the hypothesis that victory is necessary to achieve high development, while the cases above that line – in the figures I provide their names – contradict this hypothesis. It is clear that only a few cases – out of a total of fifteen – are located above the line.

It is important to note the distance between the above-the-line cases in Figure 6.1 and the diagonal line itself. This distance also affects the consistency scores. The fact that all the off cases are still close to the diagonal means none of them fundamentally challenges our conclusions.

Finally, it is also important to look at the distance between the below-the-line cases and the diagonal. This can indicate whether the necessity is trivial or

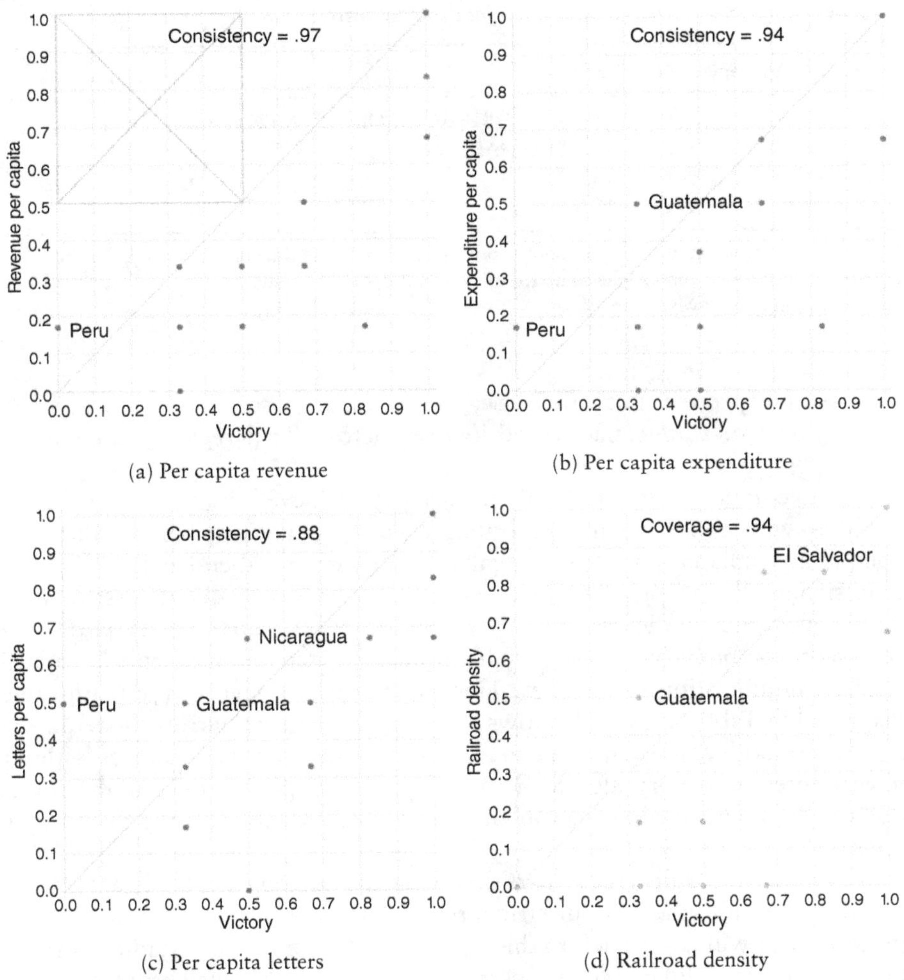

(a) Per capita revenue

(b) Per capita expenditure

(c) Per capita letters

(d) Railroad density

FIGURE 6.2 Necessity of victory for high state capacity at 1900

not. In this case we can see that besides being highly consistent, the necessary condition is not trivial, for several cases cluster close to the diagonal and many cases tend to accumulate in the upper-right quadrant. These analyses show that positive war outcomes are more of a necessary condition for high development, both social and economic, than any conditions considered in previous analyses with the exception of one: having a strong liberal elite.

Turning our attention toward state capacity in Figure 6.2, victory continues to show high consistency. The upper-left quadrant marked with a cross in Figure 6.2(a) – like that in Figure 6.1(a) – is always free of cases, which means that victory is a consistently necessary condition for state capacity from a

TABLE 6.4 *Truth table: Conditions leading to state capacity*

Liberals	Victory	N	Cases	High revenue (%)
1	1	7	ARG; CHI; URU; SAL; COL; CR; MEX	57
0	0	4	BOL; ECU; PAR; PER	0
1	0	1	NIC	0
0	1	1	HON	0

Note: This example features the results for revenue per capita as the main outcome, but the countries in each row remain the same for all four indicators discussed.
Source: Ragin and Davey, 2016.

crisp-set perspective. Put otherwise, there are no cases that score high on development or state capacity and low on victory. That region is completely empty.

If we compare the levels of consistency achieved by victory in these analyses with those of the conditions used by Mahoney (2003), the only competing explanation is, once again, having strong liberal elites. The fact that strong liberal elites and victory are both individually necessary with high consistency indicates that they will probably show up as part of a sufficient combination leading to high state capacity if we apply standard csQCA minimization procedures. This can be readily seen in the truth table displayed in Table 6.4, which shows how high-revenue countries cluster in the row where both conditions are true. It is also telling that the countries without liberal elites or victory also tend to cluster. Although not exactly the same, this can be interpreted as a problem akin to collinearity in a regression-type approach.

It remains to be discussed how these two factors relate. This is a question about sequence for which our strict cross-sectional focus on the year 1900 is of little use. I will come back to this issue, however, in my case studies to show how victory consolidated liberal parties and not the other way around.

6.2 CORRELATIONAL ANALYSES

The fsQCA analyses above are the most suitable to answer the question about the necessity and/or sufficiency of war outcomes to generate state capacity or development, but they are not the only way in which scholars have analyzed cross-sectional data c. 1900. One common alternative has been to look for simple correlations. Hillel Soifer (2015, 34) follows this intuition when he evaluates a key variable in his argument: the primacy of a single urban hub.

Soifer argues that in countries where a single city predominated and elites saw state building as a center–periphery dynamic, the deployment of central bureaucrats toward the peripheries led to a more capable state

TABLE 6.5 *State capacity c. 1900: Correlations in the literature*

	Railroad density	Census	Literacy	Military exp.
Victory	0.7*	0.54	0.62*	0.84*
Urban primacy	0.53	0.25	0.45	0.46
Intensive labor	−0.39	−0.24	−0.45	−0.2
Liberal elite	0.65*	0.32	0.47	0.44

$p < 0.05$*.

(Soifer, 2015, 20). He thus explores a correlation between the primacy of the largest city and four indicators of state capacity c. 1900: the total number of censuses conducted so far, military expenditure, levels of schooling, and railroad density. To do so, he provides his own measure of urban primacy – which I take as a given in my replications. Then he shows positive Pearson correlation coefficients ranging from 0.3 to 0.65 (Soifer, 2015, 34–38).

In this section I set out to replicate this analysis with some minor enhancements. Because Soifer loses important information by transforming all his continuous indicators into an ordinal scale, I use the original continuous data when possible. I also use Spearman's coefficients instead of Pearson's, since the former are better suited for correlations that include at least one ordinal variable – such as his measure of urban primacy or my previously described measure of victory. Since Soifer codes urban primacy for eleven Latin American countries – he essentially excludes Central America – I replicate the analysis on those same cases. Finally, I also include data on liberal elites (Mahoney, 2003, 83) and how labor intensive an economy was (Kurtz, 2013, 35).

Table 6.5 shows that urban primacy, liberal elites, and victory correlate positively with Soifer's indicators of state capacity, while labor intensity correlates negatively – all in line with extant theories. Yet victory fares much better than the alternatives, and it is the only variable that significantly correlates ($p < 0.05$) with railroad density, literacy, and military expenditure. Only Mahoney's liberal elites correlate significantly with railroad density, but even then victory outperforms it substantively.

This evidence is not enough to discard Soifer's argument, which posits urban primacy as a necessary – but not sufficient – condition, which has to be accompanied by the deployment of central bureaucrats to have an effect. There might be other ways to better test that hypothesis.[5] Similarly, this simple correlation analysis should not be taken as definitive proof against the other hypotheses. These analyses show, simply, that when basic techniques previously applied in the literature are replicated including the outcomes of wars as an alternative explanation, this new variable outperforms others.

5 QCA analyses would do a better job of testing his specific hypothesis than correlations do.

TABLE 6.6 *State capacity c. 1900: Other correlations*

	Mail p/c	Cables p/c	Revenue p/c	Railway miles
Victory	0.56	0.27	0.63*	0.61*
Urban primacy	0.47	−0.17	0.52	0.37
Intensive labor	−0.54	0.30	−0.42	0.09
Liberal elite	0.54	0.41	0.49	0.22

$p < 0.05$*.

This type of analysis could easily be replicated using other available indicators of state capacity, many of which we have discussed already. Table 6.6 shows another set of correlations using variables previously discussed. It is possible that these indicators provide a better grasp on state capacity than those used before. Railroad density measures tend to underestimate the size of large countries, while military expenditure could be high due to the corporative influence of the armed forces, not necessarily entailing a stronger state vis-à-vis society. Measures of taxation – like revenue – tap more clearly into our concept of interest, as does the provision of public goods like the railroad, postal services, and the telegraph.

The results of these simple correlations show that victory continues to outperform its alternatives. Again, it is the only variable to achieve statistical significance in its relation to per capita revenue and railroad mileage – the two indicators we are most interested in, given their internal and external validity – and it predicts the per capita volume of post mail better than others. The only exception seems to be the number of telegrams per capita, which is better predicted by liberal elites. In both tables the presence of liberal elites continues to perform as the second-best explanation. The other alternative explanations do not pass this simple test.

Another way to look at the tightness of these correlations is to eyeball a series of corresponding scatterplots with a regression line through them. The correlations in Tables 6.5 and 6.6 are represented in this way in Figure 6.3. In the case of military expenditure, railroad density, per capita revenue, per capita mail, and per capita telegrams, I use a logarithm of base 10 to illustrate the better fit of an exponential function. The figures should leave no doubt about a correlation between nineteenth-century war outcomes and all these indicators of state capacity measured c. 1900.

Although they do not perform well in these analyses, the primacy of a single urban hub and the importance of labor-intensive economies are variables that, just like liberal elites, could be endogenized in our account of how war outcomes affected state capacity. It is clear in the history of Costa Rica and Colombia, for example, that war was an important factor in breaking the deadlock between San José, Alajuela, and Heredia in the former and Bogotá and Cali in the latter. Similarly, Brazilian history illustrates well how defeat

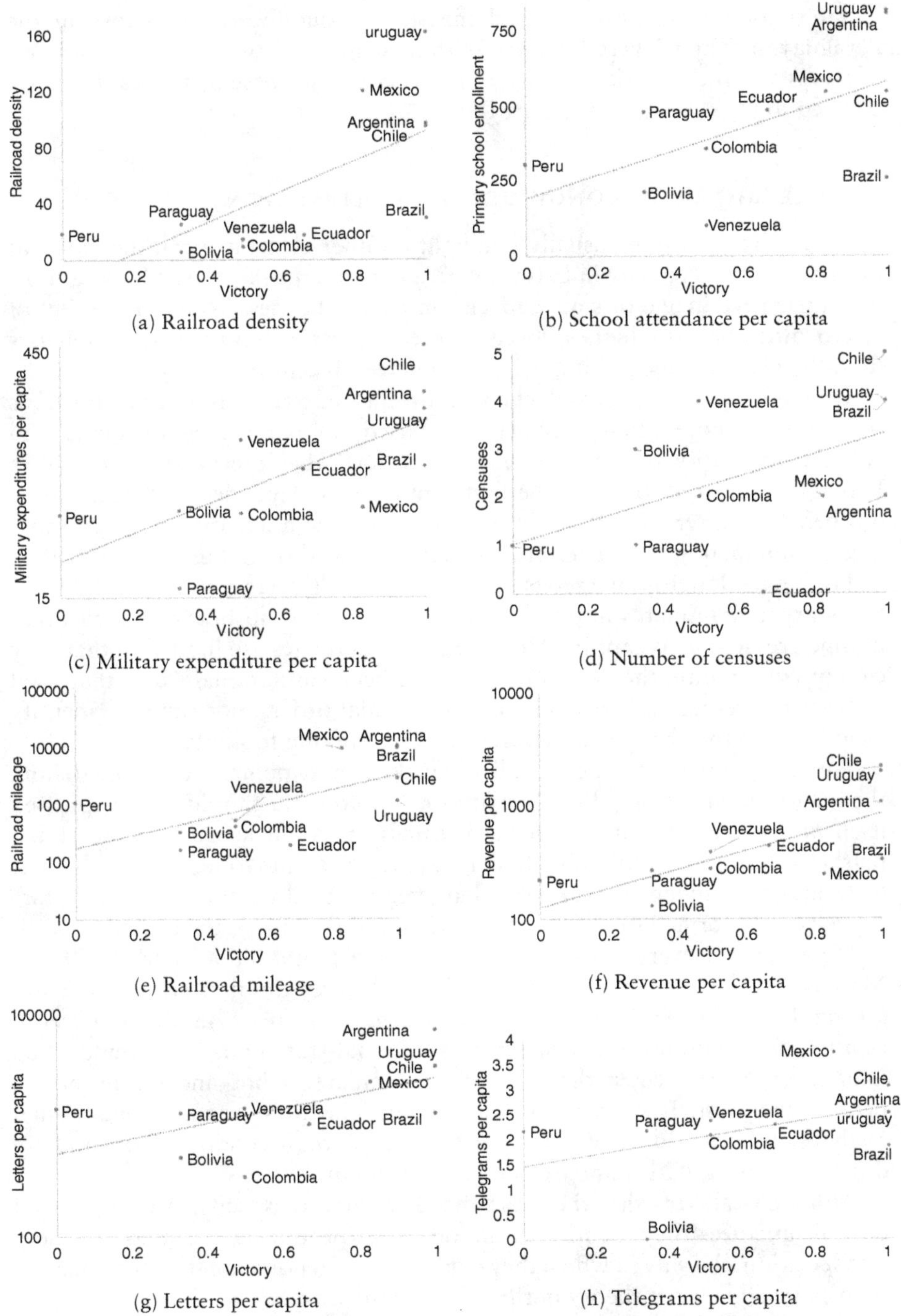

FIGURE 6.3 Correlates of victory c. 1900

in international war strengthened the slave economy, while victory in the Paraguayan War triggered a process that would end with the emancipation of slaves and the abolition of slavery in the country. These dynamics are better covered in my case studies in Part III.

6.3 THE BIG FLIP: LONGITUDINAL COMPARISONS

Comparative historians usually highlight another element when they look at the map of state capacity in Latin America c. 1900: the fact that it looks almost like a negative image of state capacity in colonial times. While the capital of viceroyalties had the highest levels in the eighteenth century, the peripheries took the lead at some point during the nineteenth century.

One relatively overlooked element of this narrative is *timing*. Previous studies have noted that explanations based on natural endowments and colonial institutions often overlook a key fact: that the greatest change in Latin America took place in the first century of independence (Abad, 2013), not before or after. Therefore there must have been a juncture at which those factors, interacting with a certain context, produced the center–periphery flip.

Looking at longitudinal series – like we did in Chapters 4 and 5 – is therefore necessary to illuminate our puzzle from an angle that snapshots at a single point in time are unable to capture. However, those statistics are limited in that they cannot corroborate the switch of positions between national states that used to be at the center and periphery of the colonial orders, nor can they identify exactly when the change in the state capacity ranking took place.

James Mahoney (2003, 54) explicitly tackles these points. According to him, the long-term effect of colonial institutions *in potentia* should have expressed itself *in actu* at the point when Latin American countries entered the global market in around 1870. Hillel Soifer (2015, 97) seems to agree that the first fifty years after independence were characterized by domestic unrest, and state capacity only formed in a "liberal era" closer to the end of the century.

However, not every author agrees with expecting a flip around the 1870s. Marcus Kurtz (2013, 38) also quite clearly locates the first critical juncture setting Latin American state-building trajectories apart in the nineteenth century, but he points "at their birth as national-state units" in around 1820 (Kurtz, 2013, 36), when the division between free labor and servile orders became manifest. It is clear that statements like these require longitudinal analyses, are not addressed when one looks at a cross-section c. 1900, and are difficult to check with standard statistical techniques.

Although all of the theories above point to specific variables and critical junctures they identify as important in producing a center–periphery transposition, the way in which they explain this phenomenon is less persuasive than classical bellicist theory in three important ways.

First, none of them explain why this ranking solidified in the twentieth century and changed during the late nineteenth century alone. Previous authors will argue that a window of opportunity opened during that critical juncture that remained closed forever before and after, an argument that is broadly in line with the comparative historical approach to temporal location of causes (Mahoney and Thelen, 2015, 20–24). Yet there is another, simpler way to answer the same question: by asking which factor was present in the late nineteenth century – thus producing mobility – and absent in the twentieth century – resulting in stiffness. To my knowledge, no scholar has so far pursued this non-barking-dog line of explanation for this particular puzzle, which leads directly to war. Because arguments about critical junctures need two propositions to produce observational expectations about timing – what Soifer (2012) called permissive and productive conditions; for example, incorporation into the global economy *and* colonial institutions (Mahoney, 2010) – an argument that works solely with one proposition – war – should be considered superior by the law of parsimony.

Second, while Mahoney's theory explains the center–periphery flip by reference to colonial institutions, my classical bellicist hypothesis can also explain the center–periphery inversion by reference to the Independence Wars – which severely hurt the defeated colonial centers and bolstered victorious peripheries. The campaigns of Bolívar and San Martín involved extraction and mobilization efforts that remain unmatched in Latin American history. As measured by battle deaths, duration, and the size of the contenders, the Wars of Independence were the Latin American equivalent of the Napoleonic Wars. It is therefore fair to assume they had a long-lasting impact.[6]

Third, while previous scholars highlight a single point in time as a region-wide critical juncture – for example, c. 1870 – my theory has time-varying dyad-specific junctures that more precisely adjust to changes in trajectories. In other words, classical bellicist theory produces more specific predictions and measures itself against a higher bar when put to the test against alternative hypotheses. Much like Mahoney (2003) and Soifer (2015), my hypothesis points to the late nineteenth century as a period of heightened state building. Warfare became more frequent and intense in this period as well. Yet I would also expect wars that happened during the first half of the short nineteenth century to affect the trajectory of Latin American states as well.[7]

6 Unfortunately Latin American countries did not really exist as sovereign entities by then, which means these cannot be really defined as interstate wars and makes interstate comparisons impossible. Since the *cabildos* acted as a clear locus of power in that era, future research could take a look at how patriotic and royalist cities were affected by those wars. What we know about that seems to suggest that the latter were severely affected, while revolutionary cities were boosted, although in cases like Mexico, where the royalists won the war, the relationship was inverted (Arias and de la Calle, 2021).

7 The aforementioned Argentina–Brazil War (1825–1828), in which these countries ended up losing their claims to Uruguay, was seen as a serious defeat by domestic audiences on both sides and devastated their early state-building efforts. Similarly, the War of the Peru–Bolivia Confederation (1836–1839) shattered the prospects of this rising power and consolidated the Chilean state-building project early on. Three prominent cases of these eras make it onto our

Early nineteenth-century wars are key to understanding changes in individual trajectories, even if these events happened in an era before incorporation into the global economy, trains, telegraphs, and public schooling.

Thus the different observational implications between these theories and mine are clear. They have to do mostly with the timing of change (Mahoney, 2003, 54). While Kurtz locates his critical juncture c. 1820 and Mahoney and Soifer do so c. 1870, my prediction is that states will be affected at different moments depending on when they fight a war. One feature of wars as critical junctures is that they do not happen only once, nor do they affect the whole universe of cases simultaneously – with the exception of independence wars. Of course, war outcomes are not case specific either. They affect all countries involved in a conflict – a dyad at the very least – at the same time. Yet this feature allows subsets of states to be affected differently and thus captures variance that has previously been unexplained.[8]

In Figure 6.4 I provide a simplified depiction of the long-term observational expectations of classical bellicist theory at the macro level. Due to the case-specific expectations that the theory produces, the accuracy of this figure can only be corroborated by the case studies in Part III. While Chapter 5 already demonstrated that the timing of changes in state capacity trajectories corresponded to the end of wars in a full panel of Latin America between 1865 and 1913, my case studies will show that these statistical summaries are corroborated on a case-by-case basis, and I will illustrate the effects of pre-1865 wars on the trajectories of Latin American states by looking at available proxies of state capacity and qualitative historical sources.[9]

In this illustrative example I attribute an arbitrary average effect to the occurrence of victory or defeat, respectively, in some severe nineteenth-century wars that occurred in South America and Mexico (Sarkees and Wayman, 2010). The existence of this effect we can infer from our findings in Chapter 5.

short list of high mobilization in Table 3.4: the defeat of Mexico by the United States (1846–1848), the successful Uruguayan defense of Montevideo (1843–1851), and the victory of Costa Rica against the American filibuster William Walker (1856–1857).

8 Soifer (2015, 88) has noted that the argument about a center–periphery inversion struggles to explain the divergence in state capacity between colonial centers like Mexico vis-à-vis Peru, as well as peripheries like Chile vis-à-vis Colombia. Mahoney (2010, 190) identified this as well and suggested that in order to capture the unexplained variance, "attention in the search for causes must gravitate toward interstate warfare. For what really gave Chile and Costa Rica an advantage over the other four nations was their ability to elude the adverse consequences of international war – consequences that fell upon Paraguay, Honduras, Nicaragua, and El Salvador quite tragically." Overall, an argument that focuses on war outcomes ends up being more parsimonious, for the initial inversion could be attributed to the independence wars and adjustments to subsequent wars.

9 Many of the indicators used in previous sections were unavailable for the period before 1865. This is the case for railroad mileage, mailing, schooling, revenue, and expenditure (Banks and Wilson, 2015).

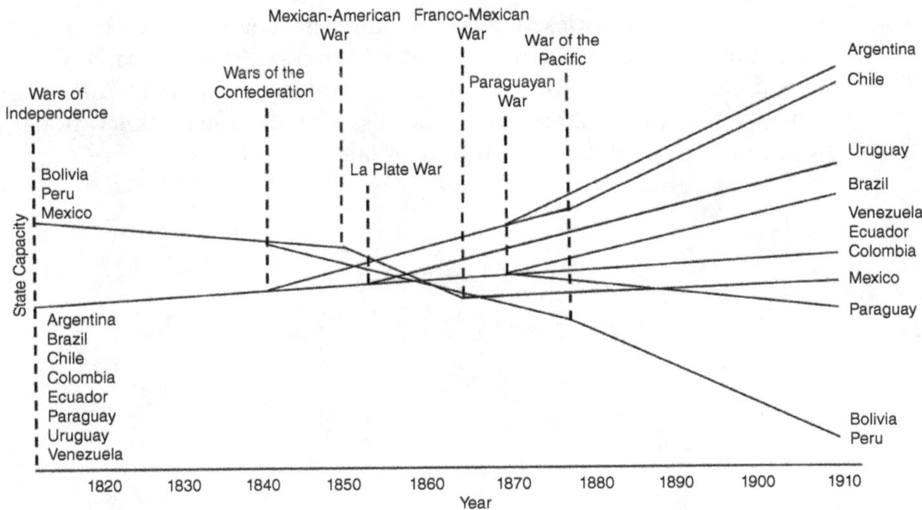

FIGURE 6.4 Outcomes, paths, and the hierarchy of state capacity

On the left-hand side, I show colonial centers – Bolivia, Mexico, and Peru – as departing from a baseline of higher state capacity (Mahoney, 2010, 51) and being negatively affected by the independence wars. Conversely, I locate colonial peripheries, winners of the independence wars, in an ascending trajectory that departs from a lower baseline.

Throughout the twentieth century, countries are affected individually by victory and defeat after these wars, which can consolidate or reverse – as in the case of Mexico – their ascending or declining trajectories.

The hierarchy c. 1900 on the right-hand side of the graph, as well as the trajectories leading to it, matches the interpretation of previous scholars with striking precision.[10]

Figure 6.4 sets the roadmap for what is left of this book. The case studies that follow in Part III trace the kinds of forking paths represented in the figure by looking at how wars led to mobilization in all cases before they set winners and

10 For Mahoney (2010, 5), for instance, the ordering of these countries regarding economic development features Argentina, Uruguay, Chile, Venezuela, Mexico, Colombia, Peru, Paraguay, Ecuador, and Bolivia. For Soifer (2015, 13), a ranking of average state capacity c. 1900 features Uruguay, Chile, Argentina, Brazil, Venezuela, Mexico, Paraguay, Colombia, Bolivia, Ecuador, and Peru. Marcus Kurtz (2013, 11–16) displays a very similar ordering. Note that this illustration excludes Central American and Caribbean states. In order to facilitate interpretation, I only included wars that were particularly severe. To more easily read this figure, pick a country of your choice on the right-hand side and follow its trajectory backward. This will show whether and when they are expected to be affected by war outcomes.

losers onto divergent trajectories. In this sense, there is a comparative case study element to them: We can always look at least at two states at the same time. The analytical narratives provided should show evidence from many different angles that systematically matches these and the many other observational implications of the classical bellicist argument laid out so far.

PART III

CASE STUDIES

7

War and the State in the River Plate

If one is looking for how war made the state in Latin America, the obvious place to start is the Paraguayan War (1864–1870). Called the War of the Triple Alliance by the victorious allies – Argentina, Brazil, and Uruguay – and known in the defeated Paraguay as the *Guerra Guasú* – the Guarani for Great War – this is "the one dog of war that definitely did bark" (Centeno, 2002, 56). It was the deadliest international war between 1815 and 1914, head to head with the Crimean War (Bethell, 1996, 20), and only second to the American and Chinese civil wars if we include all forms of violent conflict.

Recent studies, however, tend to circumvent "Latin America's Total War" (Wilson, 2004) and question its effects on state capacity (Kurtz, 2013, 104; Saylor, 2014, 92; Saylor and Wheeler, 2017). This chapter provides the most detailed discussion of this case in the literature and provides an overarching account of international conflict in the River Plate basin, showing how state capacity moved with the ebbs and flows of military success in this subregion.

The narrative is organized to match the four stages of my theory. In Section 7.1 I depict the evolution of the balance between central and peripheral elites in Argentina and Brazil from independence to the rise of the tensions leading to the Paraguayan War. This first section also shows how the Great Siege of Montevideo (1843–1851) might have been a key historical juncture helping to explain Uruguayan exceptionalism. Then Section 7.2 illustrates how preparation for war led to incipient state formation amid polarization in all major contenders in the Paraguayan War.[1] Next Section 7.3 looks closely at contingent developments on the battlefield and the consequential impact they had on the domestic front. Finally, Section 7.4 discusses the institutions left by the war and their long-term effects on state capacity.

[1] Uruguay mobilized below our requirements for stringent warfare and is therefore not considered in detail, although similar dynamics might have taken place.

7.1 EARLY WARS AND THE URUGUAYAN MIRACLE

One of the geographical areas with the highest state capacity in Latin America today, the basin of the *Rio de la Plata*, was once a poor, unpopulated periphery of the Spanish Empire. The region was considered of little worth until the Portuguese started to expand southward in the eighteenth century, threatening Spain's strategic control of its rivers. This prompted Spain to create the *Virreynato del Rio de la Plata* in 1776, with its capital in Buenos Aires. The city has gained prominence since then, but in comparison to other colonial capitals, it was still a minor commercial and military outpost at the time of independence.

The Wars of Independence prompted a central elite of *unitarios* in Buenos Aires to form and build the state we now know as Argentina. Yet the Constitution of 1819, a centralist charter responding to the necessity of fighting Spain, was harshly contested by a peripheral elite of *federales* who took advantage of the absence of the Buenos Aires army – having defeated Spain in Chile, the army under San Martín had decided to sail to Peru in a risky and uncertain campaign – and defeated the *unitarios* in the Battle of Cepeda on February 1, 1820, devolving power to provincial *caudillos* and their local militias. Only after the final victory against Spain was achieved in the Battle of Ayacucho of December 9, 1824, were central elites in Buenos Aires empowered to attempt a new constitution for the *Provincias Unidas del Rio de la Plata* and recentralize power.

The case for a strong central state was facilitated by an impending external threat. The Brazilian Empire claimed one of the River Plate provinces, the *Banda Oriental*, as their own *Provincia Cisplatina*. Under the pressing need to organize against the aggressor, a constitution was swiftly passed, and Bernardino Rivadavia, a liberal and prominent *unitario*, became the first Argentine president on February 8, 1826, only days before actual warfare began.

Tulio Halperín Donghi (1982, 12) estimates that during the first year of the Argentina–Brazil War, the Argentine state spent 3.17 GBP per capita, some three times the governmental expenditure of Great Britain. To sustain this enormous fiscal burden, the government resorted to the usual suspects: tariffs, inflation, and loans. To secure customs revenue, Rivadavia sanctioned the *Ley de Capitalización*, which federalized the city of Buenos Aires and its customs, source of 75 percent of the province's revenue (Lynch, 1985, 633). Yet, due to the blockade of the Buenos Aires port, tariffs alone provided only meager revenue, so he established the *curso forzoso* in April 1826 – the compulsory use of the national currency for all transactions, which would allow the state to impose an inflation tax (Halperín Donghi, 1982, 162). The remaining deficit had to be financed through debt – which in 1825 accounted for at least 53.74 percent of all revenue (Halperín Donghi, 1982, 156), most of which was covered by a Baring Brothers loan that required collateral in the form of a mortgage on lands that had to remain in public hands. Rivadavia formalized this in May 1826 through the *Ley de Enfiteusis*, a law appropriating all land not formally acquired by ranchers or *estancieros*, who now had to rent it from the Argentine state.

Although "the policy of Rivadavia struck at too many interest groups to succeed" (Lynch, 1993, 19), mounted on a series of initial victories, Rivadavia made substantial progress toward the formation of a strong Argentine state. The landed elites of the Buenos Aires province who had lost their precious customs, monetary freedom, and lands waited in silence, hoping for an opportunity to rebel.

The Brazilian independence process was rather peaceful in comparison to that of its Hispanic neighbors. Unlike Spain, Portugal could do little to project power across the Atlantic, although the young Brazilian Empire had to confront a Portuguese army of 5,000 men and 13 warships in 1822, which offered a tenacious resistance in the city of Salvador (Bethell, 1989, 35). These initial victories against Portugal and increasing tension with the *Provincias Unidas* paved the way for a centralist Brazilian constitution as well, sworn on March 25, 1824. Centralization in Rio de Janeiro also generated harsh reactions in the peripheries. On July 2, 1824, three provinces of northeastern Brazil – Pernambuco, Ceará, and Paraíba – declared the secession of the *Confederação do Equador*. Yet the situation of impending war in the River Plate helped reinforce centralist tendencies and a 10,000-strong army was deployed, which crushed the rebellion in two months. The constitution was upheld and conscription implemented for the first time to fight the *Guerra da Cisplatina*, although these measures continued to be unpopular and resented by a peripheral elite of *liberais*, particularly in Rio Grande, the most affected province.

After three years of fighting between Argentina and Brazil, the war ended in a stalemate. The Treaty of Montevideo of August 27, 1828, established the independence of Uruguay, a significant territorial loss for both contenders. The outcome favored the British and the newly independent *orientales* but was portrayed as a defeat by peripheral elites in Argentina and Brazil waiting to overthrow the project of the central elites.

In Brazil the liberals became stronger in parliament and managed to downsize a seditious army and strengthen their local militias (Werneck Sodre, 1979, 105). On March 13, 1831, a rebellion took place in Rio de Janeiro, which epitomized state weakness. During the so-called *Noite das Garrafadas*, discontented Brazilian liberals attacked the central elite monarchists in an episode that forecast civil war. These tensions eventually led to the abdication of the emperor in favor of his son, Dom Pedro II, on April 7, 1831.

This decision was seen as a concession to peripheral elites and led to the collapse of the incipient Brazilian Empire (Buarque de Holanda, 1972, 27). "If before 1831 the instruments of law and order were in the oppressive hands of the central government, now they fell into the oppressive hands of the locally powerful" (Bethell, 1989, 66). A series of reforms in 1831 and 1832 decentralized criminal justice and the security forces. The army was further downsized from 30,000 to 14,342 men in two years, and the number went down to merely 6,000 by the end of the decade (Werneck Sodre, 1979, 130). Now the militias of the National Guard, commanded by locally elected officials, were largely in control of organized violence. The reforms would severely undermine the authorities of Rio de Janeiro and ultimately the territorial integrity of the national state. During the following decade Brazil faced the bloodiest rebellions in its history. The most important of these rebellions, the *Revolução Farroupilha* – Ragamuffin War – caused the de facto secession of Rio Grande, the state that had more seriously mobilized for the war against the United Provinces (Buarque de Holanda, 1972, 25).[2]

In Argentina the situation was similar. When news spread of the infamous peace terms, Rivadavia had to resign. The national authorities were dissolved and Argentina de facto defaulted on its debt to Baring Brothers. The province of Buenos Aires recovered all its territory and its sovereignty and did away with the complex tax reforms of Rivadavia, which had reduced the proportion of tariffs to 83 percent of national revenue (Garavaglia, 2014, 35). The army tried a last attempt at rescuing the state-building project. General Juan Lavalle, a military man returning from Brazil and very much invested in the process of state formation, deposed Manuel Dorrego, the leader of the peripheral elite of *estancieros*, on December 1, 1828, and subsequently ordered his execution. Lavalle's revolution was done "against rural conservatism, caudillism, and provincialism, and in an attempt to restore the system of Rivadavia" (Lynch, 1985, 634). Yet after the loss of the *Banda Oriental*, peripheral elites had the momentum, and Juan Manuel de Rosas, the new leader of the *federales*, soon retook the governorship of Buenos Aires, starting a three-decades-long intermittent civil war between *unitarios* and *federales*. The country was reorganized in the form of a very loose confederation with no unified monetary or tax system and virtually no access to foreign credit, putting the prospect of a centralized Argentine state to rest for decades.

The balance between peripheral and central elites remained largely unchanged until a war against the Peru–Bolivian Confederation (1837–1839) followed by a French blockade of the port of Buenos Aires (1838–1840) that

[2] When the *gaúchos* started their rebellion in Rio Grande do Sul, the northern state of Para was also experiencing the *Cabanagem*, a protracted conflict that spread throughout neighboring states and ended with the death of 30,000 men – 20 percent of Para's population. In Bahia 1,800 were killed during a five-month siege of Salvador that brought the *Sabinada* rebellion to its knees. Finally the *Balaiada* rebels in the state of Maranhão – near Para – managed to put up a force of 11,000 men – equivalent to the entire Brazilian army at the beginning of the war with Argentina (Bethell, 1989, 68–75). The anarchy also reached the states of Mato Grosso, Goiás, Pernambuco, and Minas Gerais (Buarque de Holanda, 1972, 180–189, 198–204, 401–402). Forecasting rebellion in other parts of the country too, in his 1836 *Fala do Trono* regent Feijó also "referred to the widespread and growing disregard for the authorities and warned that the country's basic institutions were threatened" (Bethell, 1989, 76).

forced the provinces to recentralize some authority in the hands of Rosas, then president of the Argentine Confederation. War prompted a veiled return of state building under a federal system. While the province of Buenos Aires spent 27 percent of its total budget on the military by 1836, the proportion increased to 49 percent in 1840 and 71 percent in 1841 (Lynch, 1985, 642). When this drain of resources created resentment among the peripheral elite of *federales*, Rosas's military subdued them.[3]

With all provinces aligned behind him, Rosas also put up an eight-year siege of Montevideo (1843–1851). This episode has gone relatively unnoticed in the local historiography, which tends to focus on the feats of José Gervasio Artigas in the previous decades, but it could explain Uruguayan exceptionalism in terms of state capacity until the present day.

In February 1839, Fructuoso Rivera – leader of the *colorado* party in Uruguay and ally of the Argentine *unitarios* – declared war on the Argentine Confederation, initiating what Uruguayans call the *Guerra Grande* (1839–1851). Argentina had been supporting opposition leader Manuel Oribe – leader of the *blancos* and ally of the Argentine *federales* – and responded to the declaration by sending a large contingent of soldiers to besiege Montevideo. Although it is sometimes depicted as an Uruguayan civil war, Argentina contributed for almost eight years with half the 12,000 men that surrounded Montevideo (Schurmann and Coolighan, 1956, 332; Méndez Vives, 2014, 54), which makes this effectively an international war. Soon a *Gobierno de la Defensa* formed in Montevideo and gathered support from a large liberal coalition including Argentine *unitarios* in exile, Brazilian *liberais*, and even European volunteers, including an Italian legion under the command of Giuseppe Garibaldi. This international coalition lobbied for support in European capitals, which led to a long French–British blockade of the port of Buenos Aires (1845–1850), another important militarized interstate dispute.

Importantly for our argument, the *Guerra Grande* was truly big for a tiny country like Uruguay. With a total population of some 100,000 at the time (Schurmann and Coolighan, 1956, 343),[4] the population of Montevideo during the siege (1843–1851) is calculated at around 31,000 inhabitants, out of which 5,000 were part of the national army (Méndez Vives, 2014, 57). Put otherwise,

3 "First, the governor of Entre Rios, Pascual de Echague, moved away from the influence of the powerful Estanislao López and submitted himself unconditionally to Rosas. Then Corrientes, resentful of its economic subordination, declared war on the new metropolis; but the defeat and death of Governor Berón de Astrada at Pago Largo on March 31, 1839, brought Corrientes too under the aegis of Buenos Aires. Now there was only Santa Fe. Its governor, Estanislao Lopez, was the most powerful of the provincial caudillos, experienced in the politics of the confederation and possessing a reputation equal to that of Rosas. But Rosas waited and in 1838 Lopez died.... In each of the eastern provinces, therefore, Rosas succeeded gradually in imposing allied, dependent, or weak governors" (Lynch, 1985, 645).

4 The first national census was conducted in 1852 and counted 132,000 inhabitants in all the territory, of which 34,000 were in Montevideo. It is not clear, though, how much the population diminished during the siege (Nahum, 1999, 38).

one out of every six individuals within the city walls – virtually all the male population between fourteen and thirty years of age – was conscripted into the army. Naturally, everyone else in the city lived in a wartime economy for a decade. Montevideo was constantly mobilized, virtually all resources were devoted to the cause, and volunteers supported the efforts on the front by providing clothing and provisions for the soldiers and healthcare for the wounded. In the Battle of India Muerta (1845) alone, the armies of Rivera lost somewhere between 600 and 1,700 men – an equivalent of 2 to 5 percent of the population of Montevideo or the population loss of France during the Napoleonic Wars. The epic proportions of the *Guerra Grande* are properly represented in *Montevideo, or The New Troy*, a novel by Alexandre Dumas that compares the episode to the ancient epitome of warfare.

Dumas was not the only observer. At the time, the war in the River Plate was seen by liberals around the world as a major battle between civilization and the barbarism of a despotic Argentine regime. Argentine exiles were themselves an important minority of 4,000 in Montevideo and were joined in 1842 alone by some 5,000 French and 2,000 Italians (Zum Felde, 1967, 160). The degree of mobilization of Montevidean society and these foreign brigades helped fuel the myth. At the beginning of the siege, two fortresses were restored, trenches were dug, and a wall was built all around Montevideo, which would hold for eight years. Slaves inside those walls were freed and conscripted into the army. Liberals from Europe and the Americas contributed to the formation and training of an incipient bureaucracy and military and developed a system of public education. Garibaldi himself became a math teacher. The University of the Republic and the Institute for Public Instruction, the institution in charge of primary education, were founded during the siege. Government offices like the customs also grew impressively, partly because of the French and British blockade of Buenos Aires, which diverted much of the trade in the River Plate toward the port of Montevideo (Schurmann and Coolighan, 1956, 333, 344).

Under such circumstances, it was logical that the greatest cleavage in Uruguayan politics became that "between *doctors* and *caudillos*, that is, between the city and the countryside" (Zum Felde, 1967, 159). Four years into the siege, General Venancio Flores, leader of the defending forces and a *caudillo* himself, had lost his political leverage. After India Muerta and the initiation of the French–British blockade of Buenos Aires, it was clear that it was not his *gauchos* anymore but Europeans who were fighting the war. Thus he was forced into exile in Brazil by the *doctores* or urban elements of his party. The central elites thereafter started to converge on a broader state-building coalition aimed at confronting the peripheral elites of the countryside across party lines.

Finally, in 1851 Brazil intervened in the war and freed Montevideo in a campaign that, as we will see, affected the destiny of Argentina as well. The victory of Montevideo was experienced as a Uruguayan national victory by the masses, the partisan cleavage failed to trickle down, and families separated by the walls of the city were reunited (Somma, 2015, 416). The victory also restructured Uruguayan politics, consolidating a coalition of the urban segments of the *blanco* and *colorado* elites that coincided on the necessity for modernization and state building to fence off future invasions from Argentina and even from Brazil – since the latter neighbor had now taken advantage of the situation to settle a long-standing territorial dispute, chipping away at Uruguayan territory.

As classical bellicists would expect, the split in the peripheral elite of *colorados* broadened the state-building coalition, and Juan Francisco Giró, a *blanco*, became president. Taking advantage of Uruguayan bureaucratic capacity immediately after the war, Giró was able to conduct the first national census in 1852 – that is, a decade or two before countries like Argentina, Brazil, or Peru could conduct their first census (Nahum, 1999, 38). This "pink" coalition, also known as *fusionismo*, was, importantly, reliant on the bureaucracies and military elements developed in Montevideo after eight years of siege (Reyes Abadie and Vázquez Romero, 1998) and became dominant for at least a decade.

Overwhelmed by the hegemony of the central elite of *doctores*, Oribe and Flores, the two dominant *caudillos* of yore, formed a coalition against them in 1853, which was opposed by a Liberal Union now formed by the urban elements of both traditional parties. Many measures taken by *colorado* president Gabriel Antonio Pereira (1856–1860) and his *blanco* successor Bernardo Prudencio Berro (1860–1864) exemplify this fusion of the elites against *caudillismo* and the traditional parties. For example, they banished warlords from their own parties and penalized the use of partisan insignia in public. The fight between *blancos* and *colorados* – admittedly still bitter and violent – now centered mostly on access to a centralized Uruguayan state that both parties agreed upon. Peripheral elites – of the type we find in other countries, asking for a small state and decentralization – were notably marginal in the Uruguay that came out of victory in this Great War.

Historians of Uruguay have long been amazed at "how great an abyss existed between the Uruguay we find toward the end of the Guerra Grande … and that which was born in 1900" (Barran and Nahum, 1978, 18, in López-Alves, 2000, 54). Sebastián Mazzuca (2021) properly traces back the formation of the Uruguayan state to this consensus of liberal elites, noting that in Uruguay, both *blancos* and *colorados* were liberal, and that the agreement between the *doctores* – that is, the heads of the parties in Montevideo – was the foundational and defining moment setting Uruguay apart from its neighbors. This raises the question of how Uruguay was able to accomplish such a feat. The answer lies in how the war effort created these cross-partisan bonds and how victory strengthened central elites in Montevideo and the military. Uruguay, just like Chile on the other side of the Southern Cone, was becoming a serial winner; it was the only winner of the Argentina–Brazil War (1825–1828) and had now succeeded once again. Although playing a secondary role, it would soon score

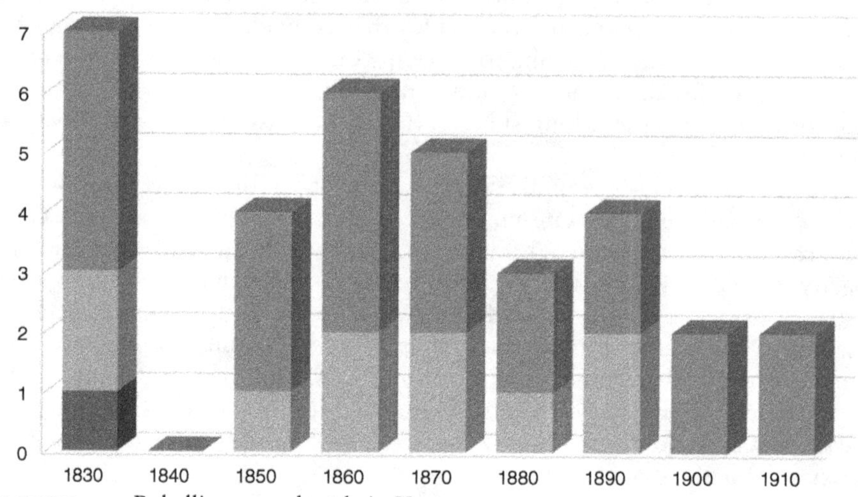

FIGURE 7.1 Rebellions per decade in Uruguay

a third consequential victory during the Paraguayan War, which would lead to further consolidation of its national parties and military.

Figure 7.1 shows the evolution of rebellions in Uruguay. Rebellions are defined as any open defiance of the state monopoly on violence by a political group with more than 500 members (Madrid and Schenoni, 2024). The lack of rebellion onsets in the 1840s already shows the degree of cohesiveness that was produced by the rebellion of Oribe – which started in 1839 – and the eight-year siege. The declining trend in revolts that follows these events is clearly in line with our expectations. Uruguay, however, is a case of a high rebellion rate compared with Chile and Costa Rica, the other outliers in state capacity in Latin America, which has puzzled other scholars. This could be explained by the lack of profound social cleavages and the bipartisan competition (Somma, 2016). However, after the Revolution of the Spears (1870–1872), where the *blancos* fought the *colorados* to reach a power-sharing agreement, the coup attempts and factional revolts in Uruguay are usually short-lived. The Revolution of the Spears is known in Uruguayan history as the first time when a regular army with modern weaponry effectively repressed a traditional *caudillo* militia. The use of lances and *boleadoras* disappeared due to the consolidation of modern armed forces (Madrid and Schenoni, 2024). From then on, the fate of political factions was fundamentally decided by the resort to factions within the armed forces, which became a decisive actor in politics (Acevedo, 1934).

The turbulence in the River Plate did not only affect Uruguay. As we have seen, Argentina underwent a process of centralization during the siege, which also prompted recentralization in Brazil. As the siege went on, liberals were forced to accept the *maioridade* – coming of age – of Emperor Pedro II and empower Rio de Janeiro to counterbalance Rosas. The size of the Brazilian army grew once again and rebellions against this *regresso* – for example, in São Paulo and Minas Gerais in 1842 – were suffocated. This relative return of order is impressive when compared to the previous decade. The only relevant example of a local rebellion seems to be that of the *Revolução Praieira* – Beach Revolution – in Pernambuco (1848–1850), a relatively minor episode leading to some 815 deaths over two years (Buarque de Holanda, 1972, 236–241, 406–412). A series of centralist reforms were enacted, starting with the 1842 criminal justice reform – giving back the authority to designate judges and police chiefs to the minister of justice (Bethell, 1989, 80) – and ending with the 1850 reform of the National Guard, which also eliminated the elective principle for designating officers, now appointed from Rio de Janeiro or the provincial capital. "The reforms of 1842, 1845, 1847, 1850, all partial, resulted from the River Plate threats that started to grow, once again" (Werneck Sodre, 1968, 1979, 135).

Finally, in 1851, Pedro II intervened in the war on the side of Montevideo and, in alliance with the governor of Entre Ríos, Justo José de Urquiza, defeated the armies of Buenos Aires and deposed Rosas (Lynch, 1985, 648). The defeat of the Argentine Confederation in the Battle of Caseros on February 3, 1852, is often depicted in Argentine history as the end of a civil war between Rosas and Urquiza, but Brazilian and Uruguayan historiography more accurately represents the episode as a severe international defeat that left the state formation process in Argentina shattered once more. One year after the war, the capital was moved to the city of Paraná to reflect the new leadership of Entre Ríos. In turn, Buenos Aires effectively seceded from the Argentine Confederation from 1853 to 1859. The equilibrium between central and peripheral elites was very fragile, and although negotiations had started to reunify Argentina in 1859, Buenos Aires fought the Confederation again in 1861. The negotiations that took place thereafter allowed Argentina to come together again as a single political unit (Mazzuca, 2021), but by the time the Paraguayan War started in 1864, Argentine unity arguably remained a fragile political equilibrium between central and peripheral elites, subjected to the pendular shifts in power between Buenos Aires and the provinces.

Conversely, the strengthening of the central elites characterized Brazil in the years following victory in the La Plata War. After decades of secessionism and civil war, "a search for accommodation, fear of party strife and effort to head off extreme reformist demands characterized national politics from 1853 to 1868" (Bethell, 1989, 145). The army was now composed of 16,000 men and 1,400 officers – still a small number but much larger and more professional than a decade before – and would remain roughly at that level until the Paraguayan War (Werneck Sodre, 1979, 92, 135). An increasingly cohesive cadre of bureaucrats also began to form, and Brazil achieved complete currency autonomy – that is, monopoly rights to issue *milréis*, the national currency (Levy and Andrade, 1985, 35).

7.2 STATE BUILDUP AMID POLARIZATION

While in Argentina, Brazil, and Uruguay, state building danced to the rhythm of international victory and defeat, the state of Paraguay developed modestly but steadily in between them.[5]

In colonial times Paraguay was already characterized as a "paranoid's paradise," threatened constantly by the native tribes of the Chaco forest and Portuguese incursions, which had already forced settlers to organize themselves in a rather martial and authoritarian fashion (Williams, 1979, 5). With independence, the threats surrounding Paraguay did not diminish. Paraguay declared its own separate independence in 1813, opposing not only the crowns of Spain and Portugal but also the elites in Buenos Aires who claimed it as an Argentine province. Surrounded by enemies, local elites declared José Gaspar Rodríguez de Francia *Supremo Dictador*, triggering a process of power centralization that was famous at the time for what we would now call totalitarian undertones. Francia not only repressed royalists and partisans of the *porteño* cause but, for example, prohibited marriage between *peninsulares* – born in Spain – and *criollos* – white people born in the Americas – and banned the former from even commenting on politics. Aware that the peripheral elite of *estancieros* was a threat to his state-building efforts, Francia sought strong popular support,[6] imprisoned schemers, confiscated their property, and built a considerable army. It is estimated that some 500 members of the local elites were in prison by 1840 (White, 1989, 107) and around 3,000 men served in the military by 1830 (Chaves, 1985, 227), a huge

[5] The historiography of Paraguay during those years, like that of the Paraguayan War, is complex and controversial. In a nutshell, one could talk of four historiographical waves. The first one, during the late nineteenth century, represents the view of a contemporary (Thompson, 1869; Rengger, 1987), a British engineer who witnessed many major events. The second wave during the first half of the twentieth century is heavily ideological, portraying Paraguayan leaders as tyrants and upholding the virtues of the victorious nations. A third, revisionist, wave is also very ideological in its critique of the role of Great Britain and victimizes Paraguay (Chiavenatto, 1979; Pomer, 1981). My conclusions rely more heavily on the fourth wave, which situates the war in the broader context of Latin American state formation and is far more rigorous and sophisticated in methodological terms (Doratioto, 2002; Whigham, 2002; Capdevila, 2012). I do my best here to rely on statements that are not contested by any particular side of the debate, and my own archival research in American and British archives.

[6] He formed a battalion of grenadiers made up exclusively of commoners and promoted lower classes to the higher ranks in the army (Maestri, 2016, 114). Returning the favor, "the people preferred to back the dictatorship, which provided support and protection vis-à-vis the declining oligarchy of landowners, now under the power of the state" (Andrada e Silva, 1978, 165). This strategy proved very effective in detecting and dismantling conspiracies.

number considering population size and the fact that the Spanish bureaucracy and military in colonial times were "minimal" (Williams, 1979, 11).

Francia was also able to implement the system of taxation Rivadavia had tried with no success in Argentina: the lease of public land in return for an annual rent. Collecting these taxes required an army of bureaucrats, the *alcabaleros*, to be present throughout the territory (Rengger, 1987, 113), often accompanied by officials running the state-owned *tiendas del estado* – shops that rented tools for rural labor. As early as 1840, Paraguay seemed to be considerably ahead of its neighbors in the provision of a wide range of public services.[7] Overall, Francia's measures "strengthened the state, repressed banditry, organized the army and reinforced the borders by building diverse forts" (Maestri, 2016, 109), while a system of passport control and border patrols shielded the country from foreign influence.

After the death of Francia in 1840, the Paraguayan elite aligned around Carlos Antonio López, a more outward-thinking leader who quickly and successfully sought international recognition of Paraguayan independence. The Argentine Confederation under Rosas vociferously condemned this recognition and war was declared on two occasions – in 1845 and 1850 – but neither came to an actual confrontation. Yet a War Ministry was created in Paraguay, military expenditure skyrocketed, and a foundry was established in the township of Ybycuí. A state monopoly over the production and trade of yerba mate and timber helped fuel militarization and the expansion of industries related to war.

Argentina finally recognized Paraguayan independence after Rosas was defeated in 1852, but neighboring countries continued to resent the Paraguayan control of the waterways,[8] and the growing threat posed by the Brazilian navy – whose access to rivers increased after victory in the La Plata War – pushed Asunción to enhance its river defenses and open its own shipyard.[9] Still,

7 The degree of development of Paraguayan public education has been particularly controversial due to a revisionist literature insisting that "in 1840 Paraguay was a country without illiteracy" (Chiavenatto, 1979, 27) and that there was "not a single illiterate" until the Paraguayan War (Maestri, 2016, 168). This has been rightly dismissed as a purely ideological statement, but there is probably some truth to the myth, given that Paraguay did instate mandatory schooling early on and provided buildings, educational materials, and teachers (Peters, 1996, 347).

8 Brazil had a vested interest in keeping the navigation of all rivers in the River Plate wide open, as they constituted the only route via which Brazil could access the inner province of Mato Grosso. Part of this province – beyond the Apa river – was claimed by Paraguay as its own. The Brazilians therefore resented the attempts by Asunción to exert sovereignty over the Paraguay and Paraná rivers and the relentless building of river fortresses that could eventually block their passage.

9 The British investments of Blyth & Co. helped build the *Tacuarí* – the flagship of the Paraguayan fleet – and provided the services of William Whytehead, a world-renowned civil engineer who became Chief Engineer of the State upon his arrival in Asunción in 1855. His colleague Thomas Smith was named Ship Constructor of the State; he built two steamers in 1856 and one per year during the next three years (Williams, 1979, 181–182). British engineers and machinists like these were paid an extravagant salary to work on the foundry of Ybycuí, set up a modern weapons factory in Asunción, build a train connecting the foundry and the factory, channel a river to provide power for these incipient industries, and begin the mining of iron ore.

with new commercial ships and the River Plate navigation routes wide open, Paraguayan foreign trade doubled in a decade (Tate, 1979, 47–50), and due to the American Civil War, cotton became a sizable taxable export after 1861 (Abente, 1987, 58). This boom gave Paraguay access to financial markets with a first credit of 5,000 GBP in 1855 and a new credit of 52,000 GBP in 1862. These credits facilitated the construction of a train connecting Asunción with the township of Paraguarí, some forty miles of track that put Paraguay neck and neck with its neighbors in the development of this transport technology. In 1865, López would ask for a third credit of 5 million GBP, offering a concession for a railway to Bolivia in return. This would have been one of the most impressive railway projects and engineering feats in South America, but the war frustrated the project (Pastore, 1993, 10).

In 1862 mandatory military service was instituted for all males between seventeen and forty years of age – this would be extended to sixty during the war. The training of some 50,000 soldiers began almost immediately, and the military started to draft war plans.[10] The death of the Paraguayan leader on September 10, 1862, was followed by a meeting of the Paraguayan Congress in which the increasing cohesion of the central elites became evident, as did the polarization with the peripheral elites. The motion that the leader's son, Francisco Solano López, become the new president was contested by peripheral elites soon accused of conspiracy and sentenced to five years in jail (Doratioto, 2002, 42).

According to the estimates provided by Leslie Bethell (1996, 6), Paraguay already counted an army of between 28,000 and 57,000 men, plus 28,000 reservists, at the outset of hostilities. In the course of the war, Paraguay would lose at least 80,000 men on the battlefield – that is, virtually all its adult male population or some 25 percent of the total population. In relation to a population of 300,000 to 400,000, the Paraguayan mobilization effort simply knows no parallel in Latin American history.

Such a military effort was made possible by a strong state. Thanks to years of pro-state policies fostered by fear of external invasion, on the eve of the war, the Paraguayan state owned 90 percent of the national territory and 80 percent of domestic and foreign trade (Doratioto, 2002, 44). It had become "a dynamic, dictator-directed, semi-industrialized, semi-militarized, financially sound nation" (Williams, 1979, 1). The "extraordinary cohesiveness of Paraguay" was indeed very promising even in the event of a war on several fronts against the "badly divided nations" of Argentina and Brazil (Schweller, 2008, 85–89). On the battlefield, "the Paraguayans counted with an outstanding discipline, and impressive logistical cohesion that the allies could

10 Historians do not always agree on the preparedness of this army, and some insist that the fifty battalions that were formed were undermanned, with only the Asunción battalion approaching 1,000 men. But by any estimate the Paraguayan army was at least double that of Argentina or Brazil at the time (Williams, 1979, 204).

never achieve," says Whigham (2016, 12), "and a nationalism that could feed the popular sentiment when the stomachs have known no food for considerable time."

By 1864 the foundry of Ybycuí, "an industrial complex with no parallel in Argentina, Brazil, or any other place in Hispanic America" (Pomer, 1981), was producing swords, cannons, rocket launchers, industrial machinery, and even steam locomotives. The Paraguayan navy of steamers was heavily armed, and the line of fortresses over the Paraguay river was also enhanced by chains, mines, and torpedos. The most important of these forts was Humaitá, an impregnable complex with the largest concentration of artillery pieces in all of Latin America. "Built on high ground twenty or thirty feet above the river, bounded on either side by swamps, armed with an estimated two hundred guns or more, Humaitá was famed in Europe as the Gibraltar or Sebastopol of South America" (Warren, 1949, 237). Finally, the telegraph arrived in Paraguay in 1864, and lines were extended that connected all their line of fortresses with Asunción in a period of months.

Brazil had become much more stable since liberals previously in favor of extreme decentralization had agreed to a *política de consiliação* – a policy of increasing centralization respecting some provincial autonomy, which had been stable since 1852. Yet the renewed tensions in the River Plate led to increasing polarization in the cabinet, provoking the rise of Zacarias de Góis e Vasconcelos, a moderate liberal, to the position of prime minister in 1864 (Carvalho, 2009, 21).

Of immediate concern was the situation in Uruguay, once again the epicenter of political tension. On April 19, 1863, Flores, the leader of the Uruguayan *colorados*, returned to his country with the intention of overthrowing President Atanasio Aguirre, leader of the *blancos* in government. The cabinet in Rio de Janeiro, concerned that radical liberals in the southern provinces of Brazil would offer military support to the Uruguayan rebels, sent Counsellor José Antonio Saraiva to facilitate a compromise between *blancos* and *colorados*. As negotiations failed and the cabinet fell, the new Zacarias cabinet was compelled to take additional steps and presented an ultimatum to Aguirre.[11] The Brazilian ultimatum of August 4, 1864, played into the hands of the Uruguayan president, who used it to entice the Paraguayans into the war.

[11] As a moderate liberal, Zacarias tried to avoid this confrontation, but the domestic situation called for it. João Batista Calógeras, a liberal officer in the Ministry of Foreign Affairs, put it this way: "All our policy in this issue was misguided from the beginning. We started by sending a special mission, carried by a threat of revolution of the rio-grandenses siding with Flores, who try to extend their influence in the eastern state … we sought satisfaction for claims forfeited twelve years ago, while the eastern state had many other claims against us. This was a true provocation, moreover, for when we presented those claims the government of the Uruguayan Republic was, and continues to be, dealing with a revolt that it cannot tame, and that is sustained, overall, by the Brazilians siding with Flores" (Doratioto, 2002, 65).

Aguirre knew these developments would be perceived by a paranoid López as a threat to Paraguayan sovereignty.

In effect, López sent a note to the Brazilian government on August 30, 1864,[12] explaining that the stability of the *blancos* was a guarantee of Paraguayan security, peace, and prosperity, and Asunción would intervene with its own forces should any military action take place against the government in Montevideo (Doratioto, 2002, 51). On August 31, 1864, the day after receiving the Paraguayan promise to retaliate, Zacarias stepped down. The prospect of mobilization was debilitating the peripheral elite of liberals. His successor, Francisco José Furtado, had to fulfill his promise, and on October 12 he effectively sent Brazilian troops across the Uruguayan border, prompting Paraguay to react. On November 11 the Paraguayans captured the Brazilian ship *Marquês de Olinda* as it sailed up to Mato Grosso. On December 13 they formally declared war on Brazil and launched an offensive to take the province.

Brazil's 18,000-man army was initially far from ready for a war with an army like Paraguay's, which had been drilling for years and was three times larger. True, Brazil had a large National Guard of 200,000 men scattered across the country, but it was unclear whether these local militias were prepared for the task or could even be mobilized. By the end of the war, 25,000 to 50,000 Brazilians – some say 100,000 – had died on the battlefield, which illustrates the extent of mobilization thereafter (Bethell, 1996, 9), but "the lack of military preparedness of the Empire at the outset of the Paraguayan War is agreed among historians" (Peres Costa, 1990, 257). To enlarge the army the *Voluntários da Pátria* was created on January 7, 1865, a corps of volunteers between eighteen and fifty years old. These volunteers and the officers of the National Guard who participated in combat were offered an extra salary, a pension, and rapid promotion if they demonstrated valor (Doratioto, 2002, 114). The war plans presented by the Marquess of Caxias[13] on January 20, 1865, anticipated that a 45,000-strong army would be needed to take the fortress of Humaitá, allowing the Brazilian fleet to supply a siege of Asunción. In this way "the Paraguayan War, due to its magnitude and the need to build up the national state instead of regional forces, put an erstwhile secondary military apparatus of the Empire at the forefront: the regular army" (Salles, 1990, 59).

Recruitment, however, was extremely difficult and generated great tensions, primarily at a local level:

> The situation evidenced in the sources is dramatic: runaways, fights, aggressions, attacks to the escorts, mutilations, hurried marriages, clashes between local groups, and tensions due to the assignment of labor to the war, among other elements, expose the difficulties

[12] Information about this document and the reasoning behind it is in a letter to Earl Russell of October 24, 1864. British National Archives FO/420/18, p. 24.

[13] Caxias was a central character during the war. He had fought in every war since independence and acquired the title of General at the age of thirty. After the War of Independence, he became the only duke in the Brazilian Empire. Caxias is now considered the Protector of the Brazilian Army.

of mobilization and the fear of the authorities that it would result in the imperial government's expansion over the businesses of the localities. (Izecksohn, 2009, 403)

To finance this effort, the expenditure of the central government tripled during the initial years of the war (Villela, 1999, 41; Carvalho, 2007, 264). The main source of revenue for the state consisted of an increase in taxes on foreign trade and debt but above all inflation (Izecksohn, 2009, 405). Three foreign loans were issued between 1860 and 1865, totaling 11 million GBP, but credit was scarce thereafter, and on September 12, 1866, a law conceding a monopoly of the Treasury on the issuing of notes made it possible to finance the deficit via seigniorage (Villela, 1999, 19). Convertibility to gold had been virtually suspended since the 1864 financial crisis known as the *Quebra de Souto*, allowing the expansive monetary policies to stimulate the growth of war-related industries like steel and textiles. The economy of Brazil grew 9 percent per year during the war, faster than ever before during the nineteenth century (Goldsmith, 1986, 25). Of course, "the war also modernized Brazil's infrastructure and rudimentary state organization, which suddenly and unexpectedly became responsible for the recruitment, training, clothing, arming, and transportation of a large standing army engaged in a war beyond Brazil's borders" (Bethell, 1996, 110).

One aspect of this had to do with the construction of railways. Railroad construction had started in Brazil back in 1852 with the concession of specific profitable lines to European companies, but developments were slow and only sixty miles had been built before the war. During the war, the Pedro II railway line gained great impulse. Unlike others connecting populated suburbs, this particular line was intended to connect the states of Minas Gerais and São Paulo with Rio de Janeiro, the capital city and main hub of the recruitment effort. The construction of the line progressed very slowly until 1864 due to lack of capital, its economic unattractiveness, and the orography of the territory. Yet the Brazilian state saw its strategic purpose, took over, and finished the line during the war years.[14] The Paraguayan interventions in Mato Grosso and Rio Grande do Sul provided an important incentive for the government to expand the railroad to those provinces as well. In particular, "a line of penetration in Paraná, leaving the coast in direction to Mato Grosso, was one alternative foresaw at the time to enhance communications by land with that

[14] Construction involved a set of tunnels and bridges, protection against landslides, and locomotive power to climb steep hills, making it a veritable marvel at the time but also a very costly endeavor. As one author puts it: "In 1865 the company was without resources to continue the construction works and the state extinguished the contract and took over the project. This decision provoked a heated discussion involving politicians and engineers, over the question – still relevant – of the role of the state in the matter. The second section of the Pedro II Railway Line, besides being an important engineering work for the time, was, importantly, a practical school for engineers. There was formed the first nucleus of Brazilian train engineers, many of whom would become known by building their own railways or in other activities" (Telles, 2011, 46).

province, which became imperative due to the Paraguayan War" (Telles, 2011, 86). The line connecting Sao Paulo with the port of Santos was also sped up and inaugurated in 1867.

In Argentina, as well as in Brazil, the campaign effort was to be initially financed by debt and by increasing the money supply, which required a notable effort on the part of the state to control currency and financial markets. Until 1862 two currencies circulated in Argentina: the *peso plata* – silver peso – in the Confederation and the *peso papel* – paper peso – in Buenos Aires, increasingly in disuse after decades of inflation. Thus one of President Bartolomé Mitre's first measures after Argentine reunification was to establish the *peso fuerte* as the only official means of payment for state wages and purchases, somewhat restoring the capacity of seigniorage to the national state (Cortes Conde, 1989, 22). Yet, knowing that financing deficits by printing money had caused monetary strain in the past, the Argentine government initially kept a low monetary base (Chiaramonte, 1971, 58) and issued new debt with Baring Brothers for some 2 million GBP or 20 percent of the cost of the war, something Argentina had not done since the time of Rivadavia and the war against Brazil back in 1824 (Platt, 1983). To secure further credit, the national government passed a Law of Free Banking, which broke the virtual monopoly of the Bank of the Province of Buenos Aires over domestic credit, allowing banks in Córdoba, Santa Fe, and Entre Ríos to issue debt. Overall, public debt tripled during the war from 6.2 percent of GDP to some 20 percent (Ferreres, 2005, 526).

These debts were accompanied by an impressive increase in revenue due both to foreign tariffs and domestic taxation. "From 1864 to 1868 fiscal revenues increased 57 per cent and revenue from import rights even more, some 126 per cent" (Cortes Conde, 1989, 40). The total revenue of the national government jumped from 2 percent of the GDP to 5.5 percent during the war (Ferreres, 2005, 483). In his case study of Argentina, Marcus Kurtz (2013, 104) shows this large relative increase in revenue extraction during the war (see Oszlak, 1982, 27), but this fact usually goes unexplored in the literature. Ryan Saylor (2014, 92) also dismisses this clear increase in extraction due to the absence of a fiscal reform aimed at taxing landed elites directly (see also Saylor and Wheeler, 2017). Yet these interpretations put the bar too high, resulting in an underestimation of the real impact of the aforementioned policies. The creation of the *Oficina de Cambios* in 1867 and the Law of Free Banking were key steps toward a truly national financial system, and the war was financed, importantly, through increasing pressure on the domestic consumer, both via seigniorage and inflationary taxation, as well as increases in the value of imports. This inflationary policy triggered the coercion–extraction cycle, leading in late 1866 to important rebellions or *montoneras* – rural guerrillas – in the Argentine inlands, led by the *caudillo* Felipe Varela – which were explicitly against inflation and conscription.

The effort to increase governmental revenue was directly associated with the expansion of the armed forces. The Argentine national army had only 6,000 troops at the moment the war broke out, so Congress hastily legislated on recruitment in order to secure support from all provinces for an army of 10,000 plus 15,000 national guards. The former peripheral elite of *autonomistas* – that is, *federales* from Buenos Aires – were the first to align with Mitre. Eventually the province provided almost half of the recruits, although it represented only 30 percent of the national population (Garavaglia, 2016). The support of the province of Entre Ríos was key, and Urquiza – the local warlord – agreed to contribute with 8,000 troops of his own. But some 3,000 men deserted from his camp on July 3, 1865, and when he tried again to put together an army of 6,000, his troops deserted once more. In the end 1,000 troops from Entre Ríos arrived at the battlefield (Baratta, 2019, 67).

The rebellions in Entre Ríos illustrate the situation of those peripheral elites for whom loyalty was too costly and who chose to exit.[15] These rebellions were initially few, but they grew in intensity and frequency after partial defeats on the battlefield. Moreover, recruitment was very difficult in virtually all provinces. Córdoba, San Juan, and Tucumán sent fewer troops than expected and excused themselves on financial grounds and because of practical difficulties. Troops from Salta arrived tardily, and battalions coming from Catamarca, San Luis, La Rioja, and Santiago del Estero deserted on their way to the battlefield.[16] Desertion continued once the conscripts arrived at main national hubs, like the port of Rosario, from where troops were shipped up north (Garavaglia, 2016, 118). So-called *enganchados* – foreigners who volunteered for the pay – were the most likely deserters (De Marco, 2003).

Despite all these problems, the Argentine army was eventually able to harness some 31,843 men from all provinces, amounting to some 1.7 percent of the population (Garavaglia, 2016, 109). Leslie Bethell (1996, 9) estimates the army on the frontlines amounted to 15,000, but the total increase in the ranks must have been greater, since battle deaths amounted to somewhere between 10,000 and 18,000. Since Argentina barely had arms for a third of that force, Brazil issued a short-term loan of 200,000 GBP, which was entirely used to purchase rifles.[17] No other Argentine war, civil or international, produced

15 Lopez Jordán, an officer of Urquiza, wrote just before rebelling: "You call to fight Paraguay. Never, my general, those people are our friends. Call us to fight porteños and Brazilians. We are ready. Those are our enemies." And the leader of the rebellion continued to argue: "I will stay in Entre Ríos, where I will be of more use as a counterweight to the march intended by Justo [José de Urquiza], which is not favorable to us. If I cannot resist persecution, then I will seek refuge in the Paraguayan army with a group of men of importance, carrying with me forces from Santa Fe, Córdoba, and other provinces. It is not possible to live with the porteños anymore. I prefer Calfucurá [a native Mapuche chief widely regarded as an enemy of the nation] to them" (Carcano, 1941, 219).

16 According to María Victoria Baratta (2019, 60), one of the factors affecting conscription was partisan struggles. Because officials in charge were probably seen as *unitarios* supporting Buenos Aires, provincialism undermined the legitimacy of the enterprise.

17 Letter of Mr. Edward Thornton to Earl Russell. June 8, 1865. British National Archives FO/420/300, p. 8.

such a level of mobilization. For Buenos Aires elites the battlefront had not been so far away since the Wars of Independence. All of it contributed to a general feeling that the war with Paraguay was a national endeavor of historical proportions. Moreover, unlike in previous campaigns where men were separated into provincial units, Argentine soldiers from different origins were mixed into the same battalions, all of which helped build a sentiment of brotherhood.

The war also favored the advancement of the railroad network. Before the war, the only two working railway lines in Argentina were the *Ferrocarril Oeste* and the *Ferrocarril del Norte*. The former covered forty miles by 1864 and the latter only fifteen (López, 1994, 370–386). Projects to connect large cities by train had been discussed since 1853, but no real progress had been made since then (Rebuelto, 1994, 69). The war prompted the first big concession to a railroad company in Argentine history: that of the *Ferrocarril Central Argentino*, which would cover the 246 miles between Cordoba and Rosario. This was the main route used for the transportation of recruits during the war and the main route the army had to use to quell rebellions in the inner provinces. Negotiations moved swiftly just before the outbreak of the war (López, 1994, 49). By 1866 the railroad covered 121 miles – tripling the extension of the national railway network in a matter of two years – and the whole extension of 250 miles was finalized on April 13, 1870, with the state fully supporting the project as a strategic priority.[18]

7.3 THE PARAGUAYAN WAR (1864–1870)

At the moment the Paraguayan War effectively broke out, two distinctive camps were clearly identifiable in all three main contenders, one in favor of the war and state building, the other against them. This equilibrium between *conservadores* and *liberais* in Brazil, *unitarios* and *federales* in Argentina, and *lopistas* and *liberales* – mostly in silence, jail, or exile – in Paraguay was very fragile and fundamentally depended on what happened on the battlefield.

18 The strategic rationale for connecting the main city of inland Argentina with the port of Rosario was clear, but the economic rationale was clearly unfavorable: "This was not, like the Ferrocarril Oeste, a matter of building 10 kilometers of railroad, departing from a populous city. The Central Argentino united two populations, both smaller than Buenos Aires, and separated by 400 kilometers of desert, still reachable by the attacks of indigenous tribes; in all the possible trajectory of the train there were no populated places of importance, nor cultivated land, no nothing, in sum, anything that could contribute to the traffic of the line" (Rebuelto, 1994, 82). In 1865 the company also built the Boca–Barracas line and a railroad connecting Buenos Aires and the port of Ensenada. The *Ferrocarril Oeste* and the *Ferrocarril del Norte* also expanded notably during the war, and the plan for a *Ferrocarril Primer Entrerriano*, connecting the key province of Entre Ríos, was also devised during the war.

By late 1864 many observers believed that, Paraguay having conquered Mato Grosso, López would be willing to sign for peace.[19] Yet López decided to send his army to Montevideo, marching through Corrientes in Argentina and Rio Grande in Brazil. The plan depended on two key premises: that Aguirre would hold on and that Mitre would allow safe passage and stay neutral. López had an ace up his sleeve. He was certain that if Buenos Aires decided to intervene on the Brazilian side, the provinces of the littoral led by Urquiza would side with him. In fact, rumors had been recently circulating in Asunción that "Urquiza is organizing his troops for the conquest of Buenos Aires."[20]

According to one authority:

> The marshal's [Solano López's] plan was ambitious but not insane. Its slender logic rested for the most part in the resilience of the Blanco Party in Uruguay and on the putative support of Argentine "allies" in the intervening territories. Yet, to paraphrase Proudhon, the fecundity of the unexpected far exceeds the stateman's prudence; when Solano López did eventually drive south, he missed his opportunity by three months. Paysandú had fallen. Flores had assumed the presidency at Montevideo. And, for better or for worse, Urquiza had cast his lot with the national government. (Whigham, 2002, 418)

Facing the Argentine denial of free passage, López took the port of Corrientes on April 13, 1865, generating the rallying around the flag one would expect after a foreign attack on national soil. *La Nación*, the newspaper of president Bartolomé Mitre, published the following, much in line with classical bellicist theory: "All parties have disappeared.... We have long maintained this: the only possible and popular war among us would have been an Argentine war, done to reject a foreign attack or to avenge the injuries inflicted to the nation. An Argentine war done by our own causes, in name of the honor and rights of the Argentine people and which will have all Argentines under its flag" (Baratta, 2019, 56).

This reflex of public opinion made it politically impossible for many peripheral elites to oppose Mitre when he declared war on Paraguay. A series of letters written by the prominent intellectual Juan Bautista Alberdi denouncing the war as benefiting Buenos Aires and Brazil more than the Argentine provinces were immediately shunned, Alberdi was portrayed as a traitor, and his image was forever stained by them. Although some, like Alberdi, suggested that Mitre harbored intentions of entering the war (Rosa, 1964), the perception of foreign diplomats from the United States and the United Kingdom at the time was that Argentina intended to "observe the strictest neutrality"[21]

[19] Letter of Mr. Edward Thornton to Earl Russell. January 20, 1865. British National Archives FO/420/300, p. 19.

[20] Dispatch from Ambassador Charles Washburn to Secretary of State William H. Seward. November 21, 1863. US National Archives RG/128/1, p. 3.

[21] Letter of Mr. Edward Thornton to Earl Russell. November 22, 1864. British National Archives FO/420/300, p. 14.

unless attacked and was expected to "use every possible exertion compatible with its honor to stay neutral."[22] Yet the invasion of the national territory left few options available, and on May 1, 1865, Argentina, Brazil, and Uruguay – now governed by the *colorado* Flores – signed the Treaty of the Triple Alliance, a secret pact that ensured coordination of the three powers during the campaign until López was deposed from power in Asunción.

The Paraguayans continued their march undismayed, and a column reached Rio Grande a few days after the treaty was signed. The liberal government of Furtado, which was taken by surprise by the Paraguayan invasion of Mato Grosso in December 1864 and failed to react in a timely manner for a second time, was harshly criticized. Only a few days after the event, the conservative Marquess of Olinda became the new president of the Council of Ministers.[23] Public opinion now sided with conservative figures like the Admiral of the Navy, the Marquess of Tamandaré, and war brought the liberal interregnum to a sudden end. A rallying around the flag similar to Argentina's strengthened the central elites, and the emperor himself decided to journey to the province to provide some symbolic leadership and reunify the forces.

The first battle of the war took place on a little river south of Corrientes, where the Brazilian fleet was anchored. The Battle of Riachuelo on June 11, 1865, was decisive, for it determined which navy would be in control of the rivers for the rest of the war (Crespo et al., 2012, 14). In the first chronicle of the Paraguayan War, written by the contemporary George Thompson (1869), the event is depicted as one of high contingency: "Thompson reports a Brazilian confession assuring that the battle was a touch and go, and might have been a Paraguayan victory had Meza immediately gone alongside instead of running down past the enemy," says historian Harris Warren (1949, 226), who also remembers the persuasive words of yet another contemporary, George Frederick Masterman (1870):

> This battle of four hours and a half really decided the war, for it gave the allies the command of the river. If those nine vessels had been captured *I am certain* Lopez would have been victorious for he would have instantly appeared before Buenos Aires or Montevideo and, by threatening a bombardment, compelled them to make terms with him. (Masterman, 1870, cited in Warren, 1949, 226)

The result of the battle, however hazardous, was a victory for the Brazilian navy, denying the waterways to the Paraguayans, who started to use mines, chains, and fortresses – mostly around Humaitá – to defend themselves against river-based incursions. All the pressure was now on Colonel Antonio de la Cruz Estigarribia, in Rio Grande. The land forces of the alliance were slowly deployed, and López exploited the element of surprise to score a big win in

22 Dispatch from the Buenos Aires Consulate to Secretary of State William H. Seward. December 15, 1864. US National Archives RG/59/M70/11, p. 2.

23 "The lack of preparation of the *gaúchos* is related to the change of the Rio de Janeiro cabinet in May 1865" (Doratioto, 2002, 178).

the southernmost Brazilian province. William G. Lettsom, British consul in Montevideo, evaluated the situation this way:

The movements of the Uruguayans, Argentines, and Brazilians are so slow in the war they are carrying against Paraguay, that I cannot report to your Lordship that any decided steps have been taken by the allies this month. There has neither been a victory to encourage, nor a defeat to exasperate any of them. I may say without fear of contradiction that in this Republic [Uruguay], at least, the war against Paraguay is decidedly unpopular ... from what I learn, it seems that the Brazilian government is alarmed at the probability of a general rising of the slave population ... Should this reported state of affairs in Brazil prove to be true, that country may probably be induced to settle its quarrel with Paraguay as speedily as possible.[24]

On August 17, 1865, the first land battle of the war took place. Estigarribia had divided his forces between the margins of the Uruguay River, and the weaker of his two forces was encountered by chance by the advanced guard of the allied army. In the Battle of Yataí, 10,800 allied forces were confronted with 2,900 Paraguayans and killed half of the latter. Just before the battle started, Estigarribia decided to abandon his column on the other side of the river, expecting a parallel attack on Uruguaiana that never arrived. Had he not made this unfortunate decision, historians agree that the result of the battle could have been different (Doratioto, 2002, 180; Whigham, 2002, 365). In any case, the outstanding victory of the *Fuerzas de Vanguardia* led by Flores discouraged the leaders of some incipient rebellions from conscription in the Argentine provinces. Mitre himself proclaimed, "This triumph is going to heal everything" (Carcano, 1941, 224).

In Brazil as well, the cabinet of the Marquess of Olinda consolidated as a product of the victories in Riachuelo and Yataí. The enthusiasm and support for the campaign was such that the emperor and his noblemen wanted to be present to collect the triumph after the siege of Uruguaiana. The Brazilian military had to argue heatedly with the Argentine and Uruguayan allies to delay the final blow against Estigarribia's forces (Doratioto, 2002, 185).[25]

After the defeat in Uruguaiana, López ordered his last column to retreat across the Paraná River. He had lost some 18,000 of his best troops in the first act of the war. These initial defeats had the immediate effect of generating division within the Paraguayan ranks and bolstering opposition and the conspiracies of peripheral elites in exile. The most telling episode was the defection of General Wenceslao Robles, who remained in charge of half of the

24 Letter of Mr. William G. Lettsom to Earl Russell. July 30, 1865. British National Archives FO/420/300, p. 45.

25 The victory in Uruguaiana also had a transformative impact on the way Pedro II saw the future of nation building, making him realize slaves could contribute to Brazil as soldiers and freemen, and emancipation would allow him to claim a higher moral ground (Peres Costa, 1990, 313). In this way, the victory weakened the peripheral elites' opposition to abolition.

army by the Paraná River.[26] Like many other officers, Robles was arrested, charged with treason, and executed.

The members of the alliance declared that the end of the war was near, but the line of Paraguayan fortresses, marshes, and woods along the border would lead to a protracted second phase of the war.

As the offensive phase of the war dragged on – now the goal of the allies was the invasion of Paraguay – the Uruguaiana honeymoon was diluted and the Marquess of Olinda started to face opposition in the cabinet. The war of positions wore out the central elites bit by bit. Tensions were due, first and foremost, to the difficulty of conjuring up all necessary means to continue the fighting. Olinda had to issue a decree by which the *Voluntários da Patria* were not voluntary anymore and ultimately suspended the system, initiating mass recruitment into the army, a policy that severely hurt landed elites all over the country.

Almost a year after Yataí, the tide favoring the peripheral elites had become unstoppable. Foreign diplomats with high stakes in deciphering the outcome of the war saw little hope for the allied cause:

> In my judgment I may be in error, yet the more calmly I review the whole course of the war, judging of the future by the past, the less I think it probable that the allies, by force of arms at least, will be likely to effect what at the outset they looked upon as a mere child's play.[27]

Olinda resigned on August 3, 1866, two weeks after the Brazilian defeat in the Battle of Boquerón on July 16. The liberal Zacarias returned to power as leader of the *progressistas* – now a mix of conservatives and moderate liberals still in favor of the war. Contributing to tensions on the Brazilian home front was a meeting between López and Mitre in Yataití-Corá, which raised suspicion that the Argentine government – also worn out by the stalemate and facing increasing domestic opposition – might unilaterally agree to end hostilities. These prospects put pressure on the Brazilian war cabinet to hurry an offensive over the main defense line in Curupaití, leading to a political crisis of great dimensions between army officials who pressed for an immediate offensive and the liberal Minister of War, Ângelo Moniz da Silva Ferraz, who had hopes for a negotiated peace.[28]

26 "He does not follow the Marshall's military commands. Murmurs to him in front of his officers. Receives correspondence from Paraguayans in the exile inciting a rebellion. It is said in San José [the residence of Urquiza] that Urquiza favors him as a possible replacement for López.... On the morning of July 23, Minister of War, General Barrios, presents himself in the headquarters at Empedrado and arrests Robles by order of the Marshall [López], receives his sword, and with a sentinel carries him as a prisoner to Humaitá" (Carcano, 1941, 225).

27 Letter of Mr. William G. Lettsom to the Earl of Clarendon. June 20, 1866. British National Archives FO/420/300, p. 13.

28 "What seems fundamental to understand the political crisis is the inevitable interaction between the dynamics of the war and that of the political struggle. The hardening of the latter coincides with the transition from a strategic defense to a strategic offense and, therefore, the new

In the end the allies convened on an offensive, but the Battle of Curupaití of September 22, 1866, ended in a major blowback for them. Losses in their ranks amounted to 4,043 men against a mere ninety-two Paraguayan battle deaths. Some 40 percent of Argentine troops and 20 percent of Brazilian soldiers were disabled in that battle (Carcano, 1941, 264). The effect was absolutely demoralizing and led many to forecast a Paraguayan victory in the war:

> The military expertise of López and the Paraguayans was thought brilliant and capable of frustrating any new attempts. In Buenos Aires, Montevideo, and Rio de Janeiro, the event was scowled at and all the South American press considered it to be fatal for the allied operations. At the same time, divisions among the generals and commanders were made public, and every news and rumor, more or less credible, foresaw the breakup of the alliance. (Schneider, 1902, 133)

When news of the defeat arrived in Rio de Janeiro, the opposition of the peripheral elites became emboldened. Zacarias was forced by the emperor to name Caxias – a known conservative – as commander in chief of the Brazilian forces, provoking the resignation of Silva Ferraz and the defection of many other liberals. The situation put the coalition in parliament on the brink of collapse (Carvalho, 2009, 25). Measures had to be taken to placate the liberals and avoid civil war. The Marquess of Tamandaré – a prominent conservative and Admiral of the Navy – was called to the court to explain the inaction of the Brazilian fleet in Curupaití, which the Argentines saw as the major cause of the defeat. General Manuel Luís Osório – a well-known liberal – was named commander of the third corps of the army by Caxias and given a prominent place in the campaign. Still, liberals in Rio de Janeiro continued to oppose Zacarias, and hostilities continued with increasing resolve.

In Argentina the effect of the Curupaití catastrophe was even worse. News of the defeat was followed by scattered mutinies until *federal* leader Felipe Varela returned from his exile in Chile and unified the rebellions under an antiwar banner (Bragoni, 2010). His influence soon extended throughout the country and plunged Argentina into civil war (Baratta, 2019, 88). In November, Mitre dispatched the fifth column of the army, 1,000 men under the command of General Wenceslao Paunero, to fight the *montoneras* in the provinces. In December he sent 4,000 additional men. Half the Argentine army was now fighting a civil war. The rebellion of Varela is a clear example of the extraction–coercion cycle, or how the resistance to mobilization for war can lead to the development of the domestic security forces. The main motive for the popularity of this anti-war movement seemed to be resistance to the recruitment effort. In a letter to Mitre, Paunero describes the war as "a phantom that

challenges that the war presented, generating pressures over the politics of the Empire. The crisis would reach its paroxysm with the cabinet of Zacarias, but is already visible in the difficulties experienced by Olinda to conciliate politics and war. The difficulties of the strategic offense would become patent after the Curupaity setback, but their seed is in the preceding months" (Peres Costa, 1990, 338).

has these people terrified" (Baratta, 2019, 49). Conscription was therefore suspended to avoid provoking more insurrections (Garavaglia, 2016, 125), and forces on the Paraguayan front would not rise beyond 10,000 for the rest of the conflict.

In the capital city of Buenos Aires the political situation was no better, forcing Mitre – until then commander in chief of the allied forces – to leave the battlefield on February 9, 1867. Having promised that Argentine troops would be in Asunción in just three months, two years later Mitre was being mocked in the press and insulted on the streets. Intellectuals wrote widely condemning the war and calling Mitre a *porteño* despot and a slave of the Brazilian Empire for having signed the Treaty of the Triple Alliance, which had by then become public. Finally, the *autonomistas* left Mitre's coalition.[29] Baring Brothers suspended the issue of the second part of a 2.5 million GBP loan, putting the government under serious financial strain (Vedoveli, 2019, 56), and foreign diplomats analyzing the situation evaluated that the defeat would "lead to the breakup of the alliance."[30] The US consul in Buenos Aires said:

> Any impartial observer of the affairs here is forced to the conclusion that the Paraguayan War is ruinous in its effects, morally as well as materially, causing mourning in thousands of families; no wonder then that there is a growing impatience for its speedy termination all over the Argentine Republic.[31]

In Paraguay, Curupaití had the opposite effect: It became a symbol of national unity (Capdevila, 2012, 32). The Paraguayan press, formerly harshly repressed, now reflected the enthusiasm of the central elites. A new publication titled *El Centinela* read "Long live democracy! Long live Paraguay! Long Live the Champion of the Century, the hard-working Marshall López! Liberty or Death! Down with Slavery!" (Williams, 1979, 220). Many other newspapers and theater plays glorifying the war effort started to circulate. In this climate of overwhelming support, López pardoned political leaders who had been imprisoned. One such case was that of Fidel Maíz, a former classmate of López who had opposed his candidacy for president and purportedly cried "Curupaití! Place of my second birth!" (Williams, 1979, 196) upon his release.

Endowed with this overwhelming popularity, López saw that it was possible to extract the unimaginable from the population. If it was not for the victory of

29 "The fervor of the liberal elites at the beginning of the war dissipated with the publication of the treaty of the triple alliance and the defeat in Curupaití. Since the end of 1866 the *autonomismo* started to criticize the alliance with Brazil and the protraction of the conflict. The federal uprisings and the inaction in the front provoked increasing criticism during 1867" (Baratta, 2019, 91).

30 Letter of Mr. William G. Lettsom to Lord Stanley. November 4, 1866. British National Archives FO/420/20, p. 20.

31 Dispatch from Amb. Alexander Asboth to Secretary of State William H. Seward. December 15, 1866. US National Archives RG/69/17, p. 12.

Curupaití, "it is hard to reconcile the ghastly tool of the war and the growing sacrifices of the Paraguayan people with a decision to collect money for an equestrian statue of the Mariscal, or with the massive collections in all parts of the republic of thousands of pesos to prepare a golden sword for presentation to López on his 1867 birthday" (Williams, 1979, 221). Convinced that the war was over, mothers allowed their children from twelve to fifteen years old to be conscripted, while the Paraguayan state took advantage of the patriotic fervor to arm households and hospitals.

By 1867, rebellions and a cholera outbreak were taking a heavy toll on Argentine and Brazilian troops, and López felt so emboldened, he attacked the enemy lines in Tuyutí, killing 6,000 of his own men. The strategy was to show resolve and let diplomatic pressure bring the allies to the table. The United States in particular was showing great animosity toward the purpose of the Triple Alliance of imposing a government on Paraguay and, together with the United Kingdom, Chile, Bolivia, Peru, and Ecuador, started to exert pressure to achieve a peaceful settlement (Sanchez Quell, 1935, 155; see also Peterson, 1932). Time worked now in Paraguay's favor.

After Curupaití the stalemate dragged on for more than a year, corroding the project of central elites in both Argentina and Brazil. In the latter case, the pressing opposition of the liberals led Caxias to present his resignation. The emperor rejected it, but he knew that the decision between Caxias and the liberals – that is, between continuing the war or surrendering – could not be postponed for much longer.

The only hope for the allies was now to break through the river defenses at Curupaití and Humaitá and transport their forces upstream. For this impossible mission the allies needed to use Brazilian warships, which made it easy for the peripheral elite of liberals in Rio de Janeiro to denounce the plan as an Argentine conspiracy to sink the entire Brazilian fleet. Although the Passage of Curupaití on August 15, 1867, successfully avoided the 22 cannons in that fortress, some 505 were waiting upstream in Humaitá. The emperor seemed unwilling to take the risk, and Mitre, the main promoter of the offensive strategy, had to return to Buenos Aires and leave the war theater after the sudden death of his vice-president led to renewed opposition to the war effort.

Just when the situation in Buenos Aires and Rio de Janeiro was reaching a head and peace negotiations seemed inevitable, the emperor surprisingly approved the plans. It was a very risky bet, but on February 19, 1868, the Brazilian fleet managed to break the chains blocking the Paraguay River and sail toward Asunción and shell the city. The Passage of Humaitá meant that Paraguayan forces in the Humaitá fortress had to be diverted upstream.

News that López was abandoning Humaitá tilted the balance toward the war coalition in Brazil. Now it was the central elite of conservatives that had the upper hand against the peripheral elite of liberals, and Zacarias was hanging by a thread. The fortress of Humaitá stood now as the only thing preventing the fall of both Paraguay and the Brazilian liberal cabinet.[32]

The concurrency between the conservative takeover in Rio de Janeiro and the events on the Paraguayan front suggests a clear connection between these events. Zacarias left the São Cristóvão Palace on July 14, 1868, refusing to offer his consent to form a conservative government and opposing the plans to attack the fortress, which had been recently approved. Pedro II used his *poder moderador*[33] to name a conservative, the Viscount of Itaboraí, to preside over the Council of Ministers. On July 16, Caxias commanded Osório to lead a fearless offensive against Humaitá, which was defended by only 3,000 Paraguayans – a quarter of the usual garrison. Osório lost more than 1,000 of his men, but the attack demonstrated the determination of the allies to take the fortress, and the Paraguayans abandoned the position on July 28. The campaign against Humaitá had lasted two long years, but now the fortress had fallen, progress proved easy. Allied forces entered a deserted Asunción only a few months later, on January 1, 1869.

Humaitá marked the end of a political era in Brazil known as the *conciliação*. The rapid succession of four ministers in four years – the most rapid in the fifty-eight-year reign of Pedro II – gave way to a new era of conservative hegemony and stability governed by these central elites. The events surrounding the fall of Humaitá are widely seen as a main hinge in Brazilian history. "All historians are unanimous in considering this crisis of July 1868 to be the seed of the fall of the Empire," says Manuel Torres (1968, 95), "even if it also gave birth to one of the most splendorous times in Brazilian history: the conservative decade of 1868–1878, ten years of great progress." Those in the peripheral elite of liberals that did not adapt to the new order of things abstained from participating in the elections of January 1869, but being too weak to rebel, their defection only accentuated the central elite's hold on the state.[34] On the other hand, a

32 "By mid 1868, however, the forward movement slowed. Stalemate in the front worsened the conflict in Rio, where the Legislature had reconvened, for it suggested that Caxias was unwilling to risk a defeat because of continued concerns about cabinet support.... The conservatives, if they had been willing to topple the cabinet in February, they since decided not to do so. They were apparently persuaded by the Council discussion or their perception of the emperor's wishes or, most probably, both. Both had made it clear that a change in the cabinet to suit the soldier was unacceptable politically and reconciliation, at least initially, was the best face to put on matters. They were also persuaded, though, that Zacarias's fall was simply a matter of time and opportunity; the emperor's support for Zacarias had been fatally undermined by his obsession with victory" (Needell, 2006, 243).

33 The "moderating power" was the capacity of the monarch to dissolve the chamber, change judicial sentences, and name ministers. This moderating power played a key role "in the consolidation of national unity and the stability of the political system of the Empire" (?, 233) but could only be used without generating a political crisis when international victories or similar events gave the emperor sufficient political clout.

34 Among them, a radical group that still envisioned the demise of the central state founded the *Clube Radical*. These radicals quickly developed a national structure and adopted a program that promoted decentralization, freedom of education, and even a locally elected police force

majoritarian faction of the liberals – those we have referred to as *progressistas* – were forming a new grouping more in line with the pro-state consensus forming around the conservatives.

> And so, in 1869, the best and largest partisan program of the Empire enters the scene, the Liberal Party, traumatized by the veiled yet efficient coup by the Marquess of Caxias against the cabinet of Zacarias de Góis e Vasconcelos, under the excuse of reanimating the efforts in the Paraguayan War … the program, properly understood, presents much more sobriety than any previous [liberal] one. (Chacon, 1981, 37)

The 1868 crisis also illustrates the role played by the armed forces in this reconfiguration of the domestic balance of power between central and peripheral elites. For some authors, the outcome was not really a win for the conservatives, nor a defeat of the liberals, but a victory of the state altogether, represented by its strongest – and now glorious – corporation: the military.[35]

After Humaitá there was a great deal of certainty that the allies would sooner or later win the war. Since political stakes in the battlefield were now low, after taking Asunción, Caxias left the command of the army in the hands of the Count of Eu, a member of the royal family who was much less involved in politics.

A coalition of central elites including the *autonomistas* was also reestablished in Argentina, where developments on the front might have been of great consequence in fostering the candidacy of Domingo Faustino Sarmiento for the presidency. Sarmiento was the ambassador of Argentina in the United States, and, having no political affiliation, "his name had been proposed by members of the officer corps that had participated in the war" (Sabato, 2001, 26). He was seen as a promoter of the fight against the rebellious *caudillos* and a supporter of the war effort and therefore a strong army and national state. Sarmiento had fought the last rebellion of the *federales* and had lost his foster son in Curupaití. Yet he was far from popular at the time. According to his best biographer, "To explain how Sarmiento became presidential candidate – a man not considered a normal politician and detested for attacking everyone in the press – one should look at the political situation" (Galvez, 1950, 275),

and judiciary. Rescuing the liberal *Ato Adicional* of 1834, the radicals asked for the end of the moderating power of the emperor and the constitution of municipal militias led by officials named locally by the municipal chambers. But the radicals were stuck in the regency period, the order of things had changed dramatically, and they stood no chance against the overwhelming majority supporting the central state (Carvalho, 2009, 40).

35 "Because the crisis had at its epicenter the confrontation between the General [Caxias] and the President of the Council [Zacarias], it was also seen as the beginning of military interference in political life and even a pre-announcement of the *questão militar* which precedes the proclamation of the Republic.… It was not that the commander was being chosen for being member of a party in the cabinet, it was the cabinet that was being chosen because of the General, the *raison d'etat* imposing itself to the logic of partisan life" (Peres Costa, 1990, 421, 450).

meaning the need for a figure that could represent the army and the nation as values above and beyond partisan strife.

Initially, Sarmiento did not harbor much hope for his candidacy. Most observers expected that the dispute would be resolved between Urquiza and Rufino de Elizalde – Mitre's minister of foreign affairs – with the former representing the peripheral elites' clamor for peace.[36] Until October 9 the very results of the election would be contested, given that revolts in Corrientes and Tucumán had prevented peaceful elections. Sarmiento stayed in the United States, where he was awarded an honorary doctorate by the University of Michigan on June 28, 1868. Yet as the siege of Humaitá came close to an end, his candidacy consolidated. Urquiza's candidacy was not feasible anymore in the context of a victorious national army, and Mitre's and Elizalde's reputations were badly damaged after years of antiwar propaganda.

As classical bellicist theory would expect, the winning coalition expanded to incorporate pro-state elites beyond Buenos Aires and the military. Sarmiento, a provincial candidate and an independent – therefore palatable for the now-realigned peripheral elites – became the personification of a renewed alliance between *autonomistas* and *liberales* – that is, central elites – now determined to see the war to its end. In the words of Argentine intellectual Leopoldo Lugones (1988, 239), "Sarmiento was to take the difficult middle path between the extremes. Neither the provinces over Buenos Aires, not Buenos Aires over the provinces. The Nation above all." But above all, as Hilda Sabato (2001, 26) put it, "Although he was not a military man, his victory reflects the growing influence of the army after the campaigns against the federalist caudillos and the war."

Under the new circumstances, Sarmiento decided to travel back. He was informed of his victory aboard his ship and arrived only five weeks before his inauguration. The US ambassador, Henry Worthington, described his arrival in Buenos Aires as follows:

> Neither Mr. Sarmiento's election nor his arrival here were accompanied by demonstrations of feeling as to furnish any assurance for a quiet and satisfactory beginning of his executive duties, for besides the natural insubordinate element among the people, and the disappointment of his unsuccessful rivals, the continued war with Paraguay exercises a remarkable influence over the minds of the people. It is undoubtedly true that Mr. Sarmiento was nominated for the presidency through the influence of those who opposed the war and the alliance. Mr. Elizalde, Minister of Foreign Affairs was his most formidable opponent, and the entire influence of the war party as well as the present administration was exerted on his behalf. Yet when Mr. Sarmiento arrived here it was ascertained from him, that he was in favor of the war until the terms of the triple alliance were carried out.[37]

[36] Dispatch from the Buenos Aires Consulate to Secretary of State William H. Seward. May 13, 1868. US National Archives RG/59/M70/11, p. 34.

[37] Dispatch from Amb. Henry Worthington to Secretary of State William H. Seward. September 11, 1868. US National Archives RG/69/17, p. 25.

After taking office on October 12, 1868, Sarmiento continued to use the army to quell the rebellions. The victory in Humaitá changed the domestic balance in favor of the national army. Varela and his allies were consistently defeated by the *Ejército del Interior* in all battles from then on. By November 7, 1868, Varela was already in Bolivia asking the local authorities for asylum, and his last forces were defeated on the battlefield on January 12, 1869. After the fall of Asunción, even more forces from the Paraguayan front were diverted to fight the few remaining rebels. The pacification of Argentina was such that the first national census could be conducted in 1869 without major disruption.

Paraguayan politics were also radically changed by the defeat of López in Humaitá. Asunción was impossible to defend with only a few thousand troops, and it was abandoned. At this point, the demographic catastrophe was clear. López recruited the few able men left and encouraged the enlisting of slaves and *libertos* across the country, yet the home front had collapsed completely. With the Brazilian army determined to hunt him down, the last year of the war until the Battle of Cerro Corá, on March 1, 1870, must have been extremely difficult for those in the entourage of López.[38]

Figure 7.2 shows a timeline highlighting the main events described in this section. Of particular interest to us is the concurrency of events on the battlefield and political consequences in the domestic realm in all three contenders. The narrative and figure clearly show that defeats on the battlefield strengthened the position of peripheral elites, and partial victories strengthened central elites, all in a matter of days, providing smoking-gun evidence in favor of classical bellicist theory. At least three critical events – distinguished by horizontal lines on the figure – are important: the initial allied victories in Riachuelo and Yataí, the allied defeat in Curupaití, and the final allied victory of Humaitá. The fact that these three events produced the expected reaction in all three countries results in nine crucial tests all aligned with our expectations.

7.4 FORKING PATHS AFTER THE WAR

Historians have long agreed that "there was a fairly widespread belief in Paraguay's long term potential" (Tate, 1979, 65) at the time the Paraguayan War broke out. But if the Paraguayan state was ever on a course of consolidation, this Great War would change that forever. Of course, the demographic consequences of the war were evident immediately. The most conservative estimates situate battle deaths at 25 percent of the population

[38] "In 1868, El Mariscal, beset with defeat, perhaps hearing rumors of dissatisfaction, and himself in poor health, gave in to a carnival of paranoia, envisioning a vast, silent plot to depose and kill him ... arrested a thousand or so unfortunates, he turned them over to drumhead military tribunals, and, after brutal tortures, overworked firing squads did away with many hundreds, including Francisco's two brothers, his two brothers-in-law, dozens of ranking government and military personnel, the bishop, and the last five hundred foreigners, including many a diplomat" (Williams, 1979, 223).

Paraguay	Brazil	Argentina	Year	Battlefield
			1864	
Outstanding popular support for López and mobilization of 60,000				Paraguayan intervention in Mato Grosso
	Fall of Furtado's Cabinet (Liberal) and progressive strengthening of the central elite of conservatives	War coalition forms including Urquiza	1865	Paraguayan intervention in Corrientes
	Mobilization of 30,000	Mobilization of some 25,000		Battle of Riachuelo Battle of Yataí (Paraguayan defeats)
Widespread desertions and execution of officers	Olinda Cabinet (Conservative) consolidates	Mitre's coalition expands including autonomistas and last rebellions are quelled	1866	
	Conservative cabinet falls			Battle of Boquerón Battle of Curupaití (Paraguayan victories)
Presidential pardons and surge in support for López	Silva Ferraz and radicals leave a consolidating Zacarias Cabinet (Liberal)	Caudillo Felipe Varela starts a civil war in the wast	1867	
Mass mobilization to go on the offensive	Conservatives are severely weakened	4,000 troops diverted to quell the rebellion		Battle of Tuyutí Passage of Curupaití
Diplomatic overtures	Zacarias Cabinet (Liberal) Weakens and falls	Autonomistas abandon Mitre's coalition Mitre leaves the front	1868	Fall of Humaitá (Paraguayan defeat)
Anarchy in Asunción	Itaboraí Cabinet (Conservative) consolidates	Sarmiento is elected president and the war coalition is restored		
López leaves Asunción but distrusts and executes most of him entourage			1869	
		Varela uprising is defeated		
Death of López			1870	Cerro Corá (Paraguayan defeat)

FIGURE 7.2 Paraguayan War timeline

(Bethell, 1996, 9), and some 60 to 69 percent of the total population of Paraguay was lost – either killed or displaced – during the war (Whigham and Potthast, 1999). The war also cost Paraguay almost all the territory it disputed to Argentina and Brazil – some 30 percent of the territory over which it claimed to be sovereign before the war (Crespo et al., 2012, 11) – and since the occupation forces had no interest in conquering or reconstructing the country, Paraguay suffered the destruction of defenses like Humaitá and industries like the Ybycuí foundry.

The great economic, military, and demographic blow suffered by Paraguay has led observers to naturalize the chronic underdevelopment of the country as the inevitable consequence of this destruction. However, John Stevens, US ambassador to Paraguay, who arrived in 1870, did not feel like that:

> It is safe to say that the newspapers and other accounts of the numerical loss of life and existing hopelessness of the country are an exaggeration. There is left alive of the original population a larger proportion that had been represented. The financial status is far from hopeless. As the Lopez government paid his soldiers comparatively nothing, the loss of the war left a small debt to be provided for by the new government. Calculable real state of Asunción belongs to the government. How successful the people of Paraguay will be in maintaining a future government and in recovering from the material consequence of the war depends largely on the answer to the following questions: What will be the future policy of Brazil towards Paraguay. And what will be the conduct of the men introduced into the country by the war, especially into its commercial and political capital.[39]

The fate of Paraguay, in other words, was not sealed by the sheer destruction but was cemented afterward by the institutions that consolidated after the defeat. Right after the fall of Asunción, the central elite of *lopistas* who helped build an impressive Paraguayan state were completely replaced by their opponents returning from exile. "The Paraguayan state was organized right after the conflict with elites proceeding from the two camps controlled by the winners," says Luc Capdevila (2012, 35): "The opposition to Francisco Solano López that fought him under the Argentine flag, and partisans of marshal López that, captured by the Brazilians, were then reestablished to balance the relation with the Argentine ally." In fact, throughout the occupation years, "Everyone sought the backing of the occupation armies to further his ambitions" (Lewis, 1986, 478), which worked against any attempt to restore Paraguayan state capacity. The heroes of the war, who were martyred and enshrined during the war, were erased from the official history (Caballero Campos, 2013), together with their ideas of strengthening the army and the state.

In this context a triumvirate followed by some provisional governments supervised the return of exiled families and the formation of several political *clubes* – the seeds of a new political system. The first constitutional president, Cirilo Rivarola (1870–1871), was a known deserter who became a Brazilian

39 Dispatch from Amb. John Stevens to Secretary of State Hamilton Fish. September 8, 1870. US National Archives RG/128/3, p. 19.

spy. He massively privatized fiscal lands and the Asuncion–Villarrica railway and eliminated the tariffs on the exports of yerba mate and timber, benefiting a few families of *estancieros* who soon became the most powerful political actors.

Rivarola was succeeded by Salvador Jovellanos (1871–1874), who drastically reduced the army. These reforms led some remaining officers to leave Asunción and join the revolt of a war hero, Major José Dolores Molas. After the revolt was crushed by the occupying forces, Jovellanos signed the peace treaties that lost Paraguay most of its territorial claims and also asked Baring Brothers for a 403,000 GBP loan that famously ended up in the pockets of his cabinet. He was succeeded by Juan Basutista Gill, who, unable to pay public employees and creditors, privatized most remaining public buildings and lands. In 1876 the army was reduced to a mere 400 men (Kallsen, 1983, 33), a size hardly sufficient to maintain internal order (Warren, 1985, 31).

When the occupation forces left the country, Paraguay, once thought to be one of the most cohesive nations in the Americas, was left with a broken identity and a severely damaged state (Capdevila, 2014). Political instability was rife. One president, one ex-president, and a main candidate for president had been murdered in the span of two years. The most notable of these events was the rebellion of October 29, 1877, in which a handful of patriots – a few veterans who had the support of the police and their bodyguards – orchestrated a failed coup. Together with Molas, four prominent politicians died during the revolt. The country was subsequently plunged into anarchy.

General Bernardino Caballero was elected president after a coup on September 4, 1880. Caballero was a patriot who had fought to the end with López and thus could bring some representation to former *lopistas* trying to find a space in politics, reinstating order. Yet his presidency was severely constrained by his debt holders, and "the land sale laws of 1883 and 1885 led to a wholesale alienation of [what was left of] the public domain" (Lewis, 1986, 480). A two-party system started to consolidate around the *colorados* and the *azules*, both of which supported a minimal state policy. As one author notes: "Battles between the two parties were often bitter and bloody, for personal and family loyalties were involved in choosing sides" (Lewis, 1986, 482).

These centrifugal dynamics and outbursts of violent, almost feudal, rebellion were facilitated by the virtual absence of a proper army, justice, and police. Having been reduced to a few hundred men, the army was still very small by 1890 – 2,500 soldiers – yet the bureaucracy in general had been so radically reduced that these few soldiers alone consumed one-fifth of the state's resources. The postwar partisan and military institutions, all imbued by an anti-state bias, consolidated minimal levels of state capacity in the long term.

Although the effect of the war on railroads and revenue in Paraguay has been thoroughly documented in Chapter 5, a look at the trends in Figure 7.3 illustrates some of the effects of the war by comparing all three contenders along additional indicators of interest for which we have reliable data covering the entire nineteenth century. One of these is the number of permanent diplomatic

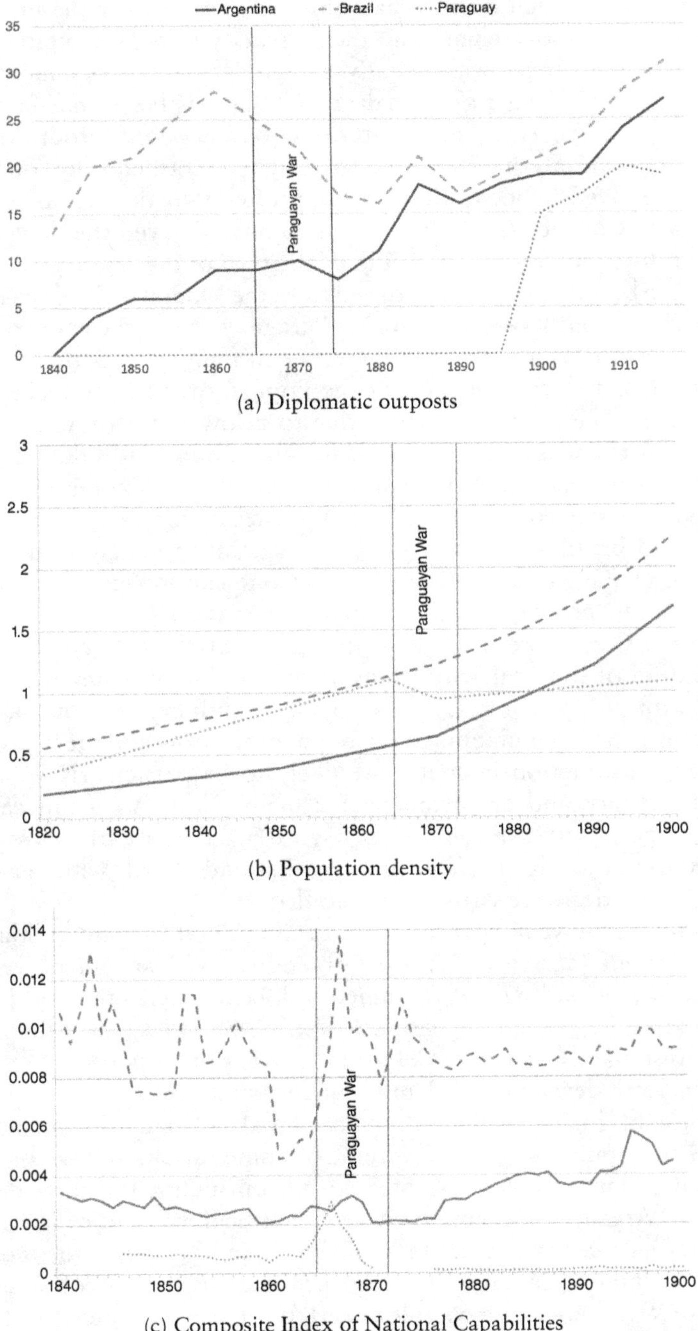

(a) Diplomatic outposts

(b) Population density

(c) Composite Index of National Capabilities

FIGURE 7.3 Postwar trajectories in Argentina, Brazil, and Paraguay

representatives that each country had abroad – a proxy for the international recognition of their sovereignty and their capacity to deploy diplomats. Data on diplomatic exchanges was initially gathered by scholars concerned with international status (Singer and Small, 1966) and has been since updated and expanded by the Correlates of War project (Bayer, 2006). From the figure it seems clear that the international legal sovereignty (Krasner, 1999) of Argentina and Brazil received a boost after the war, after two decades of stagnation in this regard. Conversely, the war seems to have delayed the deployment of Paraguayan foreign missions almost until the turn of the century.

Population density measures retrieved from the Maddison Project (Bolt et al., 2018) show a similarly bleak picture for Paraguay. While the country seems to have been growing at a higher rate by virtue of immigration, the war had the double effect of reducing the size of the population and producing a flatter postwar trend. The latter was partly due to a lower birth rate – due to the decimation of the male population – but most importantly due to a change in migration patterns – now Paraguayans started to emigrate and European immigration to the country plummeted. In clear contrast, immigration to Argentina and Brazil accelerated after the war. Unfortunately GDP per capita measures for Paraguay are unavailable, but one can imagine the impact this had on economic productivity and global output as well.

Finally, the Composite Index of National Capabilities (CINC) provides an approximation of state capacity from the perspective of material capabilities. The indicators that comprise this index – military personnel, military expenditure, urban population, total population, iron and steel production, and energy consumption in coal – are likely to be particularly valid for the nineteenth century and are available for many Latin American cases back to 1840 (Singer, 1988). In the case of Figure 7.3 they clearly show wartime mobilization and a ratchet effect in Argentina and Brazil, while Paraguayan material capabilities were virtually dismantled.

In Argentina, the year 1870 marks a turning point in state building. Tulio Halperín Donghi (2005, 31) notes: "Argentina lived an era of very quick progress in the second half of the nineteenth century ... [although] the pace of progress of independent Argentina is, until 1870, slower than that of Cuba, still in Spanish hands." Charles C. Griffin (1962, 519) concurs: "This country, one of the least developed and most underpopulated parts of the Spanish empire at the beginning of the century, outdid all other Latin American states in rapidity of population growth, volume of immigration, mileage of railroads constructed and in expansion of foreign trade during the last three decades of the century." Argentina, "facing the war at a critical moment of its formation, consolidates its recently acquired national unity, and contains the *montoneras* and local rebellions" (Carcano, 1941, 236). Historians also agree that before the Paraguayan War there was a complex overlap between provincial and national identities affecting all institutions of the state (Rabonivich, 2015), including the organization of the armed forces (Di Meglio, 2018). Yet "a Herculean effort was made in all the country to confront the conflict and after five years, over the ashes of common sacrifice, a more vivid idea of the Argentine community had arisen" (Romero, 1956). One authority summarizes the institutional impact of the war as follows:

> In spite of provincial traditions and caudillo resistance, central power and national organization survived and took root. They were assisted by the growth of institutions with an Argentine dimension, the press, the postal service, the National Bank, the railway system. But two particular agencies promoted national identity and unity: federal justice and the national army. By law of 1862 a national judiciary was established, and in 1865–68 the Argentine Civil Code was drawn up. The supreme court and the various lower courts completed the structure of the modern state.... The executive had the right of intervention in the provinces, a right which became more effective once it was backed by a national army. By decree of 26 January 1864 the government created an army of 6,000 men distributed between artillery, infantry and cavalry. A Military Academy was established in 1869 and the formation of a professional officer corps was begun. The law recruitment of 21 September 1872 anticipated national conscription ... the army gave the president real power and enabled him to extend the executive's reach into the furthest corners of Argentina. (Lynch, 1985, 656)

This quotation does not do proper justice to the impressive change in the Argentine public education system that was initiated by Sarmiento. During his tenure, national investment in education quadrupled and some 800 new schools were created (Rock, 1985, 130), earning him the nickname of *padre del aula* – father of the classroom – immortalized in an anthem to Sarmiento that students in Argentina sing to the present day.

Another impressive institutional change that goes unnoticed in the quote is that of Argentine parties. Unlike most politicians of his time, when Sarmiento was elected he had no party of his own, nor was he clearly aligned with any of the contenders (Campobassi, 1962, 231), yet the experiment took hold thanks to the incredible partisan convergence between *autonomistas* and *nacionalistas* – or *liberales* – right after victory. Sarmiento's inauguration was the first peaceful presidential transition in Argentine history, and his administration witnessed the birth of the *Partido Autonomista Nacional*, a structure that consolidated the state-building coalition in the long term. The new party would govern uninterruptedly until 1916, presiding over the period of most rapid growth in Argentine history (Rock, 2002).

The triumphant army was also one of the main factors sustaining Sarmiento and bonding the alliance of central elites. After the Paraguayan War, every rebellion was rapidly quelled. In 1870, Sarmiento intervened in the province of Entre Ríos after the *caudillo* Ricardo López Jordán – the leader of many wartime rebellions – rebelled once again, this time assassinating Urquiza. Before the war, Mitre thought it was impossible to intervene in a province like Entre Ríos that could marshal a force of 12,000 men on its own. Now Sarmiento put up a force of 8,000 well-equipped, seasoned military in a matter of weeks and defeated the rebels in months.

As the main tool for securing internal peace, the national army never left the political scene. Army officers started to define key strategic objectives. In 1872 the military defeated Calfucurá, the leader of the main Mapuche threat on the southern border. Only four years later, the army marched under the command of Julio Argentino Roca – a veteran who had lost his father, two brothers, and two cousins in Paraguay – to effectively incorporate all the territories of Patagonia into the national realm. Coming back from the campaign, the army defeated the militias of Buenos Aires, who had rebelled against the president, Nicolás Avellaneda, and a law was passed prohibiting provincial authorities from forming military forces by law – this was the end of militias in Argentina. Furthermore, the National Guard was integrated into the army as a reserve force of 65,000 men (Nunn, 1983). The armed forces never quite left the political scene thereafter. Because Chile and Argentina were engaged in a formidable arms race, with both countries importing increasingly sophisticated weaponry and nearly going to war on several occasions between 1898 and 1902, when Chile instituted universal obligatory military service in 1900, Argentina followed in 1901. In 1899, Argentina also received a German military mission to reform its army, something Chile had done immediately after victory in the War of the Pacific.

This momentous victory against the militias of Buenos Aires in 1880 also allowed for the federalization of the city and port of Buenos Aires, a project thought impossible since the time of Rivadavia. "The victory of Roca was that of the central State" (Halperín Donghi, 2005, 143). Roca would eventually become the leader of the *Partido Autonomista Nacional* and remain the central figure in Argentine politics until his death in 1914.

The stability of the coalition of central elites was accompanied by the transformation of the opposition. The provincialist *federales* had no real place in a new situation where threats of secession and opposition to centralist policies were no longer credible. The new situation gave rise to the Unión Civica – latter called *radicales* – a segment of the Argentine elite that had no quarrel with state formation but asked for free and fair elections, rightly accusing the *Partido Autonomista Nacional* of fraud. The *radicales* put up several rebellions against the state – all of them repressed – but although their opposition was strong and sometimes violent, the new division meant no relevant Argentine party really questioned state formation anymore.

Shortly after the war, debt services amounting to some 60 percent of the total revenue started to cause financial strain, and Argentine elites had to face the same dilemma they had faced four decades before: pay or default on the debt with Baring Brothers. This time Argentina decided to honor its debt by increasing import duties and taxing consumer goods, which in turn consolidated state revenues in the long term (Chiaramonte, 1971, 181; Cortes Conde, 1989, 117, cited in Saylor and Wheeler, 2017, 401). A convertibility with gold in place since 1867 provided a strong base for the expansion of the domestic financial market, which continued to develop via the creation of the Banco Hipotecario in 1872 and many other smaller financial institutions. The state continued to resort to credit through a set of new instruments such as the swap of bonds for land recently occupied by the army. Even though this reckless expansion of the domestic financial market might have led to the Baring crisis in 1890, the result of it was its stricter regulation by an ever-growing bureaucracy (della Paolera and Taylor, 2001, 49).

Finally the war had also set Argentina on a self-reinforcing trajectory regarding the expansion of the railroads. Sarmiento gave his first speech as elected president in Argentina in the town of Chivilcoy on October 3, 1868, arriving on a train built only two years before and promising to continue its development (Di Privitellio, 2016, 21). On April 18, 1870, Sarmiento inaugurated the line connecting Córdoba and Rosario, which had been initiated at the beginning of the conflict. In less than a decade, the Buenos Aires to Rosario line – some 180 miles – and many other lines interconnecting small townships across the province of Buenos Aires were also open. Immigrants settled in colonies along the railway lines, expanding the agrarian frontier and generating more revenue for the state in a positive feedback that led to more investment in trains (Rebuelto, 1994, 148).

The extension of the *Ferrocarril Central Argentino* some 348 miles to the north, connecting Córdoba to Tucumán, exemplifies the key role played by the state in the design of the railway network. The decision was driven by the need to reach that outermost part of the country where low state presence usually encouraged rebellions and neighboring threats. Construction began when populations in the region were still small and there was no clear economic gain to pursue, yet state infrastructure fueled a lucrative sugar industry in Tucumán after the line was finished.

One prominent alternative hypothesis for the Argentine case is that export-led economic growth starting in the 1870s led to state formation (Saylor, 2014), but this inverts the causal order unveiled by generations of historians. In one of the most sophisticated analyses of the process to date, Samuel Amaral (2002, 1) recognizes the decisive importance of institutional stability and the rule of law – beyond other factors like the incorporation of new land, which were also made possible, thanks to the strength of the military after the war.

In Brazil it is also the consensus that the Paraguayan War gave birth to a new military that would play a central role in domestic politics (Bethell, 1996, 112; see also Izecksohn, 2002). "Until the Paraguayan War the army continued to play a virtually negligible goal in the affairs of the nation," says June E. Hahner (1969, 3), yet "the war with Paraguay greatly increased the political strength of the Brazilian army. Not only did the army grow in size, but its officers acquired a new sense of military spirit and pride."[40]

40 Underpinning the consolidation of the military corporation was the professionalization of the military corps, which before the war resembled an improvised militia. Now the military academies were full of students and reproduced the memoirs and feats of war heroes, creating a cohesive corporation (Castro et al., 2004, 14). Modern warfare had also trained a corps of

First and foremost, "the politicization of the war brought as a corollary the militarization of politics" (Peres Costa, 1990, 414). The heroes of the war, like General Osório – he who led the charge against Humaitá – were granted titles and exalted by the emperor. As parties competed for the support of officers, the military started to take seats in the cabinet more than ever before in the reign of Pedro II (Carvalho, 2007, 55, 103). Quickly the army took over the National Guard and by 1873 wielded a monopoly on violence throughout Brazil.[41]

The Paraguayan War also led to politicization within the armed forces. The navy, for example, benefited after the war when Brazil bought two ironclads, two corvettes, two monitors, and two transport ships. By 1872, Brazil's was considered the sixth most powerful fleet in the world, and this "golden age" of the Brazilian navy (Soares Alsina, 2015, 61) ensured officers in this force were supportive of the monarchy. Yet the same could not be said of the army, where overall troop reduction and a slowdown in the rate of promotions (Schulz, 1994, 294) led dissatisfied soldiers to openly oppose the monarchy in a process known in Brazilian historiography as *questão militar* – the military question.[42] As Nelson Werneck Sodre (1979, 138) notes, the army started to identify with the middle class in their claims for open political participation, which bolstered the demands for a republican regime.

Partisan life after the war is often characterized as a *retrocesso conservador* – a conservative setback (Carvalho, 2009, 21; see also Lynch, 2014) – given the overall convergence toward the position of those central elites. The Republican

military engineers and helped establish the image of a professional military man, a full-time technician distinct from the mere man of bravery (Peres Costa, 1990, 501).

41 Immediately after the Paraguayan War, the National Guard counted more than 600,000 members, seven times the size of the state bureaucracy (Carvalho, 2007, 158), and although the dominance of landed elites over the national guards was severely undercut, these were still subnational militias. To weaken the National Guard and local interest, its participation in the front was diminished from 74 percent in 1866 to 44 percent three years later, a change to which landowners gladly acquiesced but which ultimately favored the army (Bethell, 1989, 155). The National Guard reform of 1873 finally transferred most of its duties to the army and left local militias virtually powerless.

42 Imbued with the intellectual spirit of positivism, young cadres began to question the rigid social structures of the empire, corruption, and clientelism and placed meritocracy at the core of their values and political demands (Peres Costa, 1990, 525). Already in 1871 a military faction planned a coup d'état against the royal family, taking advantage of the departure of Pedro II for Europe (Oliveira Lima, 1989, 109). The most important of these coup attempts was probably that of 1879, when the war and navy commissions in parliament proposed a reduction in the number of officer positions across the armed forces. The bill met fierce resistance from the military, who brought the issue to the press. A group of officers in Rio Grande threatened a rebellion, and the pressure successfully prevented the bill from passing, setting an important precedent for civil–military relations (Hahner, 1969, 13). This trend continued until the proclamation of the Republicvia a military coup: "The relation between the war of the Triple Alliance and the Military Question is without any doubt deep and even explicit in the dialogue of 15 November 1889, between Marshall Deodoro da Fonseca, chief of the military uprising and the Viscount of Ouro Preto, president of the last Council of Ministers" (Peres Costa, 1990, 16).

Party, founded in December 1870 – a few months after the end of the war – institutionalized this for decades. In its program former liberals came to emphasize the republican aspect of their project while abandoning their former quest for decentralization. Their motto, *centralização-desmembramento, descentralização-unidade*, conveyed a renewed view of federalism as a way to consolidate national unity and strengthen the state instead of contesting it. "The long list of reforms to the electoral system, the police, the judiciary, the National Guard, disappeared from the Republican agenda, gobbled by the change in the system," says José Murilo de Carvalho (2009, 41). "Presenting itself as politically radical for denying the system as a whole, the new party cooled the political debate and drained the reform agenda, reducing it to the system of government alone."

This swift movement to the center that liberals took after the war was concomitant with a similar change – perhaps even more impressive – in the conservative camp. The Viscount of Rio Branco, a conservative elected prime minister in 1871, gathered support for a swift application of all liberal reforms in ways that enhanced the state-building process. For example, the reforms effectively separated the functions of the police and the judiciary – a liberal demand – but did not allow for their local appointment. Rio Branco also enacted the Law of Free Birth by which children of slaves would be granted freedom, and he even set up a state fund for the emancipation of adults (Bethell, 1989, 158). This produced a division between traditionalists, or *saquaremas*, and modernizers – moderates within the conservative party – on the issue of abolition and might have marked the end of the Conservative Party itself: "In 1871 the state divided the party and alienated its key constituencies; it had effectively broken with the party ... 1871 was the party's most significant defeat" (Needell, 2006, 314).

These partisan transformations had a correlate in big changes that took place during the war, such as the emancipation of slave combatants and the rise of a manufacturing and coffee industry in São Paulo, which promoted free labor (Salles, 1990). With the old elites and plantation economy gone, the cleavage between republicans and modernizers, both of which supported further expansion of the state, took center stage in Brazilian politics. These parties differed mostly on how the state was organized and who should have the right to access government – that is, the regime. "The great social and political debate [about the state] almost disappeared ... it was as if all other options were closed and the only alternative was between republic and empire" (Carvalho, 2009, 42). The war thus acted as a veritable critical juncture in the history of Brazilian party politics. As liberal Joaquim Nabuco put it, "The Paraguayan War had such a decisive influence on our national destiny that it is possible to see it as a turning point in contemporary history" (cited in Peres Costa, 1990, 464).

Of course the military and political parties were far from the only institutions changed by the Paraguayan War. Several bureaucracies of the state were fundamentally restructured due to the war, which played a key role, for example, in the development of the foreign service (Cervo and Bueno, 2011, 142; Almeida, 2017, 211). But the role state institutions played in the expansion of the railroad system is perhaps the most illustrative.

Brazilian railroad construction was changed incredibly after an 1869 law introducing a uniform gauge for the whole country. "From this moment on the Brazilian [state] participation in studies, projects, and construction increased, and the system became, in a few years, almost completely national" (Telles, 2011, 60). By 1870 the state-owned *Estrada de Ferro Dom Pedro II* alone was employing 7,000 men, more than half the size of the Brazilian army at the beginning of the war and half of the railroad workers in the country. Capable of financing most projects, the Brazilian state felt more and more comfortable regulating the sector, offering more limited concessions, and deciding the projects of strategic interest that would be open for public bidding.[43] The war experience and involvement of the military were also behind a great effort to extend the railroads to the south:

> The Paraguayan War showed the precariousness of transport in the south of Brazil and the pressing need to rectify this. Engineers were assembled to solve two problems: the so-called Strategic Network of Rio Grande do Sul, and communications with Mato Grosso. For Rio Grande do Sul there was a special law (Law 2.397 of 1873) that authorized the construction, backed by the government, of a railroad linking the coast and the provincial capital to attend strategic interests. A diagonal line linking Porto Alegre [the capital of Rio Grande do Sul] to Uruguaiana [the largest Brazilian city invaded by Paraguayan troops] was built, together with radial lines linking different points in the border to the port of Rio Grande. Engineers and military officers had a long discussion over which would be the best hub for the lines connecting the border. (Telles, 2011, 83)

The strategic line connecting Paraná with Mato Grosso took more than a decade but eventually became a reality thanks to a powerful military lobby including the support of General Osório himself (Osório, 1915, 745; Peres Costa, 1990, 505).[44]

[43] The new narrow-gauge system was favored due to strategic concerns – it was different from the gauge used by neighbors – even if European investors preferred the previous system. In 1871 the concessions to foreign investors were reduced from ninety to fifty years. In 1872 the gauges were regulated by the state by law – until then each company could choose its own. To incentivize the declining foreign investment, the Imperial Government promulgated a new law in 1873, paying each company a fixed amount of 30 contos for each kilometer of railroad built while also reducing the concession of the lines for thirty years. Even though the terms were strict, "the new legislation permitted the rapid development of railroad construction in Brazil. Some 90 per cent of all railroads built during the empire [until 1889] has to be credited to this law" (Lima Neto, 2001, 126–132).

[44] The plans designed by Antonio Rebouças back in 1868 had to be subsequently abandoned due to lack of state resources, but General Osório, now Marquess of Herval and later war minister, never stopped lobbying for the line based on its purely strategic necessity. The project finally became possible when the French *Cie. Générale des Chemins de Fer Brésiliens* invested in it by 1879. Construction of this railroad – with no clear economic purpose – became a veritable

In sum, as Ricardo Salles (1990) succinctly puts it:

> As a total war affecting in different ways all of society and requiring the resources and centralized action of the government, the Paraguayan War was one of the defining moments in our history ... the country lived in that period the most profound transformation of its social structure: the decadence of the slave economy and the expansion of free-labor coffee production in the west of Sao Paulo, the expansion of service infrastructure, the rise of manufacture, shipyards, and small factories, urbanization, European immigration, and the growth of the urban middle class. From a political perspective, this was accompanied by the strengthening of a new sector – the great landowners of the west of Sao Paulo – in the dominant class, the foundation of the Republican Party, the emergence of the abolitionist movement, and the increasing opposition of slaves to captivity. That process would lead to two other defining events: the abolition of slavery in 1888 and the proclamation of the republic in 1889. (Salles, 1990, 55)

Figure 7.4 shows the evolution of rebellion in our three main cases of interest. Paraguay sees, as expected, an increase in rebellions after the war. It is in fact one of the few states in Latin America to experience such an increase in a general context in which national armies are strengthening and therefore either repressing or deterring rebellions of political groups outside the state more or less consistently (Madrid and Schenoni, 2024). Although the decrease in different categories of revolt is evident in Argentina and Brazil, some characteristics of the remaining revolts that favor the classical bellicist argument even remain unseen – for example, the fact that "all revolutionary attempts launched after 1862, including those originating in 1874 and 1880, were defeated" (Sabato, 2001, 9).

Finally, victory in the Paraguayan War was also followed by a further modernization of the state in Uruguay, even if its consolidation – meaning the effective monopoly of violence – would take longer to be established due to its peripheral participation in the war (Panizza, 1997). After his initial and decisive feat against the Paraguayans in the Battle of Tayaí, Venancio Flores soon managed to align the Uruguayan elites behind him and achieve a series of remarkable accomplishments, like the civil code (1865), the first telegraphic service (1866), and the commercial code (1868). His successors inaugurated the first railway line (1869) and introduced cable cars and running water to Montevideo (Nahum, 1999, 47).

The rebellions against the *colorado* hegemony – like the one of Timoteo Aparicio (1870–1872) – were not so much against the state as intended to allow rural sectors to participate in the expansion of the Uruguayan state. The

odyssey due to the roughness of the terrain and thickness of the forests. Some 12,000 men worked on the project and thousands died from malaria. The railroad not only allowed for the transportation of bureaucrats, military, and police, it also changed the landscape of the backward societies of inland Brazil. Because British and local companies insisted that no slave labor should be employed in the construction works, the railroad was also disruptive of local orders by promoting the use of free labor (Telles, 2011, 56).

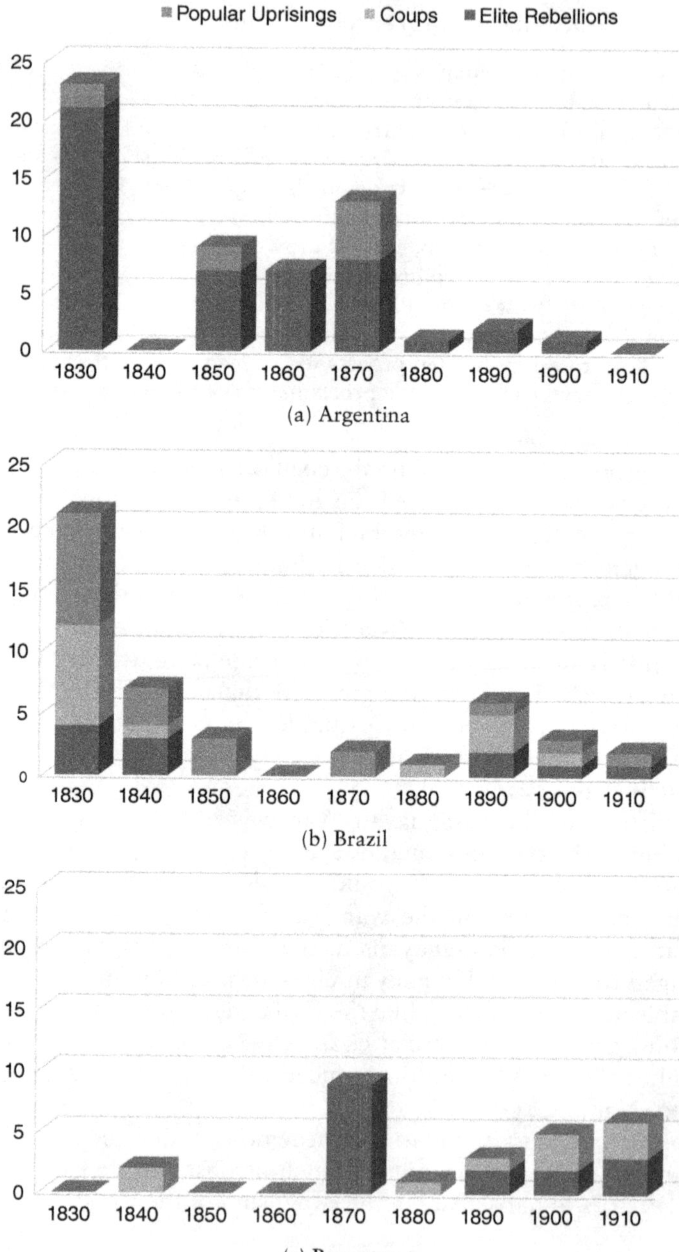

(a) Argentina

(b) Brazil

(c) Paraguay

FIGURE 7.4 Rebellions per decade in Argentina, Brazil, and Paraguay

manifesto of the rebellion shows that early on, struggle in Uruguay was driven by concerns regarding regime type – that is, access to the state – rather than local or parochial demands:

> We must again make our voice heard to satisfy the votes of our fellow citizens who have spontaneously pronounced in favor of the restitution of constitutional order. The flag we raise is that of the Nation, not that of any particular party with exclusivist aspirations which, even if reasonable, should not be imposed upon future generations. (Arozteguy, 1889, 13)

The so-called militarist period was followed by the government of the *doctores* – the wise men within both parties – who wanted to supersede previous differences and build an interpartisan consensus around a strong bureaucratic state. They decided the destiny of the country during the presidencies of Lorenzo Batlle (1868–1872) and José Ellauri (1873–1875). In 1871 the *Asociación Rural* was founded, which already showed a radical change in the strategy of the peripheral elite of *estancieros* now aligned behind the state formation process, promoting the fencing, registration, and taxation of cattle in exchange for infrastructural expansion from Montevideo. The role of landowner was clearly differentiated from that of the *caudillo* (Finch, 1981, 5).

Then the military took on a prominent role in fostering state expansion during the administrations of Lorenzo Latorre (1876–1880) – a hero of the Battle of Estero Bellaco in the Paraguayan War – and Máximo Santos (1882–1886). "This date [1876] marked the start of a long-term process of strengthening the state's authority over the whole national territory" (Panizza, 1997, 677). Schooling in particular spiked after Latorre passed a new law of public education in 1877. As Fernando López-Alves (2001) has noted, the Uruguayan military were not as almighty as their peers in Argentina, where all rebel armies had been virtually eliminated by 1880. Probably if Uruguay had participated with more soldiers in the Paraguayan War, it would have amassed a similarly powerful force, yet parallel forces continued to exist in Uruguay. It must be emphasized, however, that those armies fought not against the state but for partisan participation in the state, much in the way of the Argentine *radicales*. "By 1904, Aparicio Saravia was still challenging the central power in Montevideo with a force that also called itself the national army" (López-Alves, 2001, 165), because his main goal was not to dismantle the state but for the *blancos* to become part of the project.

The state-building consensus was fundamentally evident in a consistent policy of taxation during the last four decades of the century. Duties were always above 20 percent, "rather surprisingly for a small, export dependent country in the heyday of the gold standard" (Kurtz, 2013, 203). During these years Uruguay continued to be very violent. The assassination of political leaders and coups were unnervingly usual, and civil wars continued to shatter the country as late as 1897 and 1904, but the motives of these rebellions were fundamentally about participation, and state capacity grew progressively.

"By the last quarter of the nineteenth century there was a progressive consolidation of state power" (Panizza, 1997, 671).

It is remarkable that the three countries that won the Paraguayan War escalated the hierarchy of state capacity to the very top by the year 1900, starting from very humble origins. In the eloquent words of Mazzuca, "an imaginary South American country combining the Argentine *Pampa Húmeda*, the entire territory of Uruguay and the state of Rio Grande do Sul in Brazil ... would have been an economic powerhouse similar to Australia, and perhaps even stronger" (Mazzuca, 2017, 29).

8

War and the State in the Pacific

The War of the Pacific is the war between Latin American states with the second-highest casualty rate in the nineteenth century. Although it has been considered a case where bellicist mechanisms should show up (Centeno, 2002; Mahoney, 2010), recent studies have dismissed its state-forming impact (Kurtz, 2013, 89–94; Saylor, 2014, 64–65; Soifer, 2015, 208).

This chapter provides the most detailed discussion of this case in the state formation literature by focusing on the winner, Chile, and the main loser, Peru.[1] The comparison should be illuminating, since both countries were comparable across important characteristics of their states – for example, the size of armies, navies, bureaucracies, and budgets – and were impacted similarly by important economic confounders such as commodity booms and the 1873 crisis (Cavieres and Aljivín de Lozada, 2005; Paredes, 2013, 17).[2]

My narrative is organized into four sections. In Section 8.1 I depict the evolution of the balance between central and peripheral elites in Chile and Peru from independence to the middle of the century. Then Section 8.2 illustrates how preparation for war led to state formation amid polarization, and Section 8.3 looks at the effective evolution of the campaign with one eye on domestic politics. Finally, Section 8.4 discusses the institutions left by the war and their long-term effects.

1 Bolivia mobilized below my requirements for stringent warfare and is therefore not considered in detail, although similar dynamics might have taken place and are summarily highlighted.

2 Chile was as mineral dependent as Peru in the nineteenth century and thus was subject to similar fluctuations in these prices. Chile and Peru profited from a boom in copper and silver, followed by booms in guano and nitrates, most of which were exploited by entrepreneurs from both countries.

8.1 EARLY CONFLICTS AND STATES IN THE PACIFIC

As the capital of the Viceroyalty of Peru, Lima sat atop the South American hierarchy of state capacity in colonial times. Spain "inflicted upon Peru the largest, most powerful, prestigious, and best-paid bureaucracy to be found in all of South America" (Pike, 1967, 25). Offices of the Spanish Crown and the Catholic Church covered the city. The University of San Marcos in Lima educated *criollo* elites from all over South America, and until the late eighteenth century, the accountants of the merchant guild of Lima supervised a strict monopoly over all imports and exports in the subcontinent. No other city had more tax collectors or military.

The contrast with Chile could not be starker. It would have seemed impossible at the time for this minor silver-mining *Capitanía* in the extremity of the empire – a land of no economic, cultural, or strategic importance – to steadily rise to the highest ranks of state capacity, much less displace the mighty Peru. In this section I briefly consider how defeat and victory in war early after independence leveled the playing field between the two, so that Chile and Peru were not so different in terms of state capacity when they clashed yet again in 1879.

The long story of Peruvian defeats begins with the Wars of Independence. In 1820 the *Libertador* José de San Martín organized a naval expedition from the Chilean port of Valparaiso to take Lima from Spain. Having achieved this goal, he declared the independence of Peru on July 28, 1821, and oversaw the establishment of its first flag, national anthem, currency, public schools, and national library. Yet his *Ejército de los Andes* counted only 4,000 men against a 23,000-strong Spanish army still concentrated in the highlands. After meeting with Simón Bolívar in Guayaquil, he decided to make room for the stronger of the two (Roel Pineda, 1982, 284) and left the country with the prophetic words: "Peruvians, I leave you having established national representation; if you trust it unwavering, hail victory, if not anarchy will devour you" (Basadre, 2005, 42).

The *realistas* in Lima were profoundly uncomfortable with the new order. Accepting the new state of affairs meant subservience to former subordinate elites from peripheral regions of the empire (Pike, 1967, 43). Soon after San Martín left, asking Limanians to "unite as is necessary!" the elites divided. Liberals supported an invasion by Bolívar, who disembarked in the port of Callao on September 1, 1823. However, Peruvian sentiments were in general opposed to the Great Colombian intervention, and many conservatives still hoped the Spanish troops would retake the city.

The Constitution of 1823 limited the executive powers of Limanian authorities and strengthened Congress by making it unicameral. The president was to be elected by the legislators, and ministers could veto presidential decrees (Basadre, 2005, 85).[3] After Bolívar's landing, conservative forces in

[3] Bolívar said of the Limanians, "[They have] one hand to act, and twenty heads to deliberate; I already foresee the fatal consequences of such vicious principle," and Marshall Sucre opined, "The army has no leaders, the country is as divided in factions as are the troops."

the city rebelled against this state of affairs (Basadre, 2005, 45, 64, 74). A royalist force took the Callao despite the bravery of the *Ejército de los Andes* – epitomized by the heroic defense of the Real Felipe fortress by the legendary black soldier Falucho – which eventually disbanded, leaving the country in the hands of the Great Colombian army. In two years of resistance the pro-Spanish forces were reduced from 6,000 to 376. However vain, the rebellion stood as a testament to Limanian conservatism (Pike, 1967, 60).

The death sentence of the Callao rebellion and Limanian conservative elites, however, was decided in other latitudes. Bolívar's victory in the Battle of Junín, on August 6, 1824, and Marshall Antonio José de Sucre's victory in Ayacucho on December 9 of the same year put an end to the military campaigns of the Wars of Independence once and for all. Paradoxically, the defeat of Spain also weakened Bolívar, whose legitimacy as Liberator depended on the continuity of the Spanish threat.

When Bolívar finally returned to Bogotá, the Peruvian elites could successfully oppose his unification projects and dismantle his dictatorship. Nonetheless, Limanian conservatives were utterly weakened, struggled to rebuild an army, and could not project power to the viceroyalty over which they formerly presided. The absolute hegemony of Bolívar's army in the region encouraged peripheral elites in Upper Peru to form a new country, independent from Lima. In 1825 they declared, "If from Romulus, Rome; from Bolívar, it is Bolivia" and offered the presidency to the Liberator. A flattered Bolívar supported the secession but gave the presidency to Sucre.

Despite its destruction and mutilation, "Peru emerged from the wars of independence as potentially the most powerful nation in the Pacific coast of South America" (Farcau, 2000, 13), maintaining a relatively highly trained bureaucracy and military and a sophisticated tax structure (McEvoy and Rabinovich, 2018, 20). Yet intraelite conflict continued to be rife during an "age of caudillismo" extending from 1823 to 1845 (Pike, 1967, 56), which impeded Peruvians from making use of all their inherited wealth and power.

As one would expect, after Bolivian independence, friction between Great Colombia and Peru was all too frequent and quickly resurfaced when the absence of the Spanish threat led to an abrupt reduction of Bolívar's army and domestic conflict in Colombia as well. The president of Peru, José de La Mar (1827–1829), took advantage of this to launch an intervention in Bolivia and Ecuador in 1828, leading to a war with Great Colombia. The war ended in a stalemate – similarly to the Argentina–Brazil War, it was eventually interpreted as a defeat on both sides – and plunged Peru into a civil war and the weak government of Agustín Gamarra (Pike, 1967, 63).[4]

4 General Gamarra would have a difficult time consolidating his power. He had to confront several rebellions all over the country, a plot led by Vice-President La Fuente, and continuous opposition from Congress, leading him to close the legislature in 1832 (Basadre, 2005, 252). When the National Convention chose Luis José de Orbegoso (1833–1836) as his successor, civil war ensued, with *gamarristas* resisting for four months in the highlands. Further rebellions continued to

The Peru–Great Colombia War also led to the breakup of Great Colombia. In Ecuador, peripheral elites who used to favor Ecuadoran annexation to Peru turned their backs on their southern neighbor after a long occupation and unsuccessful defense of the city by La Mar. Elites in Quito who were historically closer to Colombia also became wary of Bolívar's and Sucre's influence and demanded more autonomy. The result was the formation of an incipient Ecuadoran nationalism that congregated around the figure of independence hero Juan José Flores.

Similarly, conservative elites in Venezuela rallied around another hero of the Independence Wars, José Antonio Páez, in the hopes of gaining sufficient autonomy to avoid the grandiloquence and follies of Bolívar. These two charismatic military leaders became the first presidents of these two independent countries after Bolívar announced his resignation from the Colombian presidency and died soon thereafter (Davis, 1983).

With Colombia in civil war and no other external threat looming on the horizon, central elites in Caracas and Quito had no reason or excuse to build a strong state in subsequent decades, a context that favored peripheral elites in both countries and prevented the formation of strong central armies and bureaucracies, leading to a situation of intermittent civil war. Venezuela's army, for example, was reduced to a mere 1,000 men by 1830 (Centeno, 1997, 1571) – probably the smallest in Latin America as a proportion of total population. The central government therefore remained tiny, and the country faced 166 revolts between 1830 and 1903 as a result (Arraíz, 1991, 32).

After the breakup of Great Colombia, some sectors of the Peruvian elite sought the reintegration of Upper Peru one more time. Andrés de Santa Cruz, president of Bolivia since 1829, was now being courted by factions in the Peruvian civil war who, unlike him, were unable to consolidate power. In 1836 the two countries formed the Peru–Bolivia Confederation, and Santa Cruz was declared its *Supremo Protector* for a ten-year period. Santa Cruz moved the capital to Tacna and started to build a centralized army and bureaucracy there, a move that was immediately opposed by peripheral elites in Bolivia and Peru, many of them having fled into exile in Ecuador and Chile. It soon became clear that the infrastructure, population, and wealth of the Peru–Bolivia Confederation made it the greatest South American military power of its day, and this was soon perceived as a threat by its neighbors, leading to a new war.

The War of the Confederation (1836–1839) provides a brief, elegant example of the mechanisms at work in the bellicist approach. Bolivian victory legitimized Santa Cruz, whose position was further strengthened when Argentina and Chile declared war against the Confederation. In the following

characterize the Orbegoso era. In 1835, during one of his many absences a mutiny took place in the Real Felipe fortress. The rebels were quelled, but General Salaverry, seeing that the president would not return, proclaimed himself *Jefe Supremo del Perú*.

years Santa Cruz expanded the army and bureaucracy and issued a civil code, a penal code, and a commerce code and reorganized tax collection before defeat in the Battle of Yungay on January 20, 1839 effectively destroyed his project and both Bolivia and Peru collapsed into anarchy once more.

After the secession from Bolivia, Gamarra retook the Peruvian presidency and was ratified as *Restaurador del Perú* in Lima. But soon a new rebellion broke out. Gamarra declared war on Bolivia for harboring a rebellious leader and died fighting the Bolivian army in the Battle of Ingavi of November 18, 1841. The Peru–Bolivia War was yet another international defeat for Peru – the third since independence. In the words of two celebrated historians:

> The defeat of Peru in Yungay (1839) followed by the humiliation of its army at Ingavi (1841), started to show the consequences of what could be understood as the "ten-year-war": the constant fight between rival factions not only was subsuming the country in economic crisis and political chaos, but also started to seriously affect its capacity to seriously defend itself from neighbors and regional rivals; in particular Chile, where the port of Valaparaiso had started to replace the Callao as the first port in the South Pacific. On the other hand, the country emerged from the war more divided than ever. (McEvoy and Rabinovich, 2018, 28)

Watching the travails of its neighbor from close by, Chile slowly started to climb the ladder of state capacity in the Pacific. When the Wars of Independence started, Santiago was a poor, isolated colony at the edge of the empire. Chilean revolutionaries had to instate a mining tax and an average 30 percent customs tariff to finance their nascent independent army and bureaucracy,[5] but they soon had their independence taken away by Spain in 1814. A proverbial crossing of the highest mountain range in the continent by the *Ejército de los Andes* provided the much-needed foreign support for a decisive victory in the Battle of Chacabuco on February 12, 1817. After it, Bernardo O'Higgins, leader of the Chilean forces, was declared *Director Supremo*, and a swift consolidation of the state took place: "Within nine days of Chacabuco, O'Higgins decreed the formation of a military academy and by the end of the year the new Army of Chile of nearly 4,800 men was larger than the Army of the Andes" (Collier and Sater, 2004, 37).

In the following years, Chile's trade doubled, along with its mining output, state revenue, and the size of the port of Valparaiso. "Between 1818 and 1823 Chile showed considerable promise ... had assembled a formidable navy, had secured a large British loan, and gained the recognition of the United States" (Burr, 1974, 12). Yet with the withdrawal of the *Ejército de los Andes* from Peru and the subsequent fall of O'Higgins, divisions ensued between conservatives and liberals – called *pelucones* and *pipiolos* – and a series of constitutions were drafted, all of them of short duration. None of these attempts managed to consolidate one party, and they ended in a brief civil war won by the

5 Unlike in the territories of Bolivia and Peru, other revenue sources like the Indian tax did not exist in those latitudes (Sanchez-Albornoz, 1978).

conservatives at the Battle of Lircay on April 17, 1830. General Joaquín Prieto, the leader of the conservative forces, was elected president, but Diego Portales soon emerged as the strongman behind the new regime, and a new centralist constitution was passed in 1833.

The first years of the conservative government were relatively calm in the international realm, allowing Portales to restructure the armed forces. The *Escuela Militar* was reopened, offering a conservative curriculum, and liberal soldiers were discharged to ensure cohesion. While the military were offered pay rises (Arancibia Clavel, 2007, 130) and paid on time (Nunn, 1976, 41), a law fixing the size of the army at 3,000 men was passed in 1834, which reduced the weight of military expenditure in the total budget to just 37.5 percent (Somma, 2011, 397).

However, the professionalization of the army hid broader dynamics. One of the smallest and least populated countries in South America, Chile tried its best to avoid international friction, but provocations from its neighbors put constant pressure on Santiago. Lima, for example, defaulted on its post-independence debt to Chile and began to raise tariffs on the imports from this southern neighbor – at a time when Peru was the destination of 50 percent of all Chilean exports. The prospect of conflict with Peru led to the institution of the *catastro* in 1834, a real estate tax used mostly with the end of preparing for war (Edwards, 1932, 146). Although there was a limit to the size of the army, the Civic Guard was enlarged considerably. By 1835 this militia corps already consisted of 30,000 men, which allowed the professional armed forces to be fully focused on equipping and training exclusively for international warfare (Wood, 2011, 86).

Tensions reached boiling point when Santa Cruz formed the Peru–Bolivia Confederation. "With relations with Peru strained to the utmost, the Chilean government asked a number of wealthy citizens for a secret loan for the purchase and equipment of warships" (Burr, 1974, 36). Unlike Portales, who thought Chile should claim a more prominent role in the Pacific,[6] many thought it bold to oppose the mighty Confederation and were unwilling to pay the price, but soon enough the Santa Cruz government became involved in a plot to unseat the conservatives, which ended in the seizure of the Peruvian sloops *Obregoso* and *Monteagudo* and with Chile declaring war on the Confederation.

[6] "The Confederation must disappear forever. We must dominate forever in the Pacific" (Cruz and Feliú Cruz, 1936, 453, cited in Collier and Sater, 2004, 65), he declared. Portales's reasoning was clear: "Chile's position in relation to the Peru–Bolivian Confederation is untenable. It can be tolerated neither by the people nor by the government, for it would be equivalent to suicide ... the confederation must forever disappear from the American scene. By its geographical extent; by its larger white population; by the combined wealth of Peru and Bolivia, until now scarcely touched; by the rule that the new organization, taking it away from us would exercise in the Pacific; by Lima's larger number of cultured white people closely connected with influential Spanish families; by the greater intelligence, if indeed inferior character, of its public men, the Confederation would soon smother Chile" (cited in Burr, 1974, 38).

When the War of the Confederation (1836–1839) started, Chileans were shocked by the suspension of guarantees and the court-martial of members of the elite. Discontent fueled a conspiracy against the tyrannical Portales, who was kidnapped by military officials and assassinated on June 6, 1837. The revolt was subdued, however, and instead of stopping the war, the assassination of Portales galvanized the war effort. After Portales's pompous funeral, the war was taken as a holy enterprise and the initial army of 3,000 tripled in size, leading to a concurrent expansion of taxes and the central bureaucracy (Cid, 2011, 2013; Serrano, 2017).[7]

After victory in the Battle of Yungay on January 20, 1839, troops paraded through Santiago in the most important celebration since independence. According to Collier and Sater (2004, 68), "Victory in this war undoubtedly enhanced the international prestige of Chile. It reinforced the commercial hegemony of Valparaiso. The country's finances bore the strain with remarkable ease. It seems likely, also, that the war helped consolidate the grown sense of Chilean nationality." It is unlikely that the *República Conservadora*, a Latin American exception in terms of political stability, would have consolidated as it did had Chile lost the war. Between 1830 and 1837 there were at least twenty attempts to overthrow the government (Heise, 1978, 207), yet when President Prieto finished his second five-year term on September 18, 1841, power transitioned peacefully to General Manuel Bulnes, the victor of Yungay, who governed uncontested for two terms. His successor, Manuel Montt, would also be able to govern under the constitution for another ten years.[8]

The conservative regime also doubled the size of the security forces – mostly the Civic Guard – and state bureaucracy and transformed them qualitatively. According to Samuel Valenzuela (1985), the Civic Guard in Chile had played a prominent role in enacting fraud during elections in the 1830s. Yet the war diminished the factionalism within this force early on in Chile and increased their professionalism and status. Hilda Sabato (2018, 107) notes that "government officials and military commanders did not spare words of honor to the guards as bulwarks of liberty and order." Figure 8.1 shows the evolution of revolts in the cluster of countries covered in this chapter, showing the absence

7 Unfortunately, scholars who have studied Chile in the state formation literature have overlooked the effects of this war (López Taverne, 2014; López Taverne and Fernández Abara, 2018). Saylor (2014, 64) skips the War of the Confederation and claims, "Chile's only international war between 1848 and 1879 was a brief naval war with Spain," but this time span excludes the possibility that progress in that era was due to the long-term effects of the victory against the Confederation.

8 Chile had to face two insurrections in 1851 and 1859 that pitched local elites against central ones at the beginning and end of the Montt administration, but these were mild disagreements when compared to the situation of South American countries in general and were rapidly repressed (Collier and Sater, 2004, 113). In the decades after the revolts, "Chile made more progress than any country in Latin America in consolidating a party system, institutionalizing these differences" (Paredes, 2013, 134; see Scully, 1992).

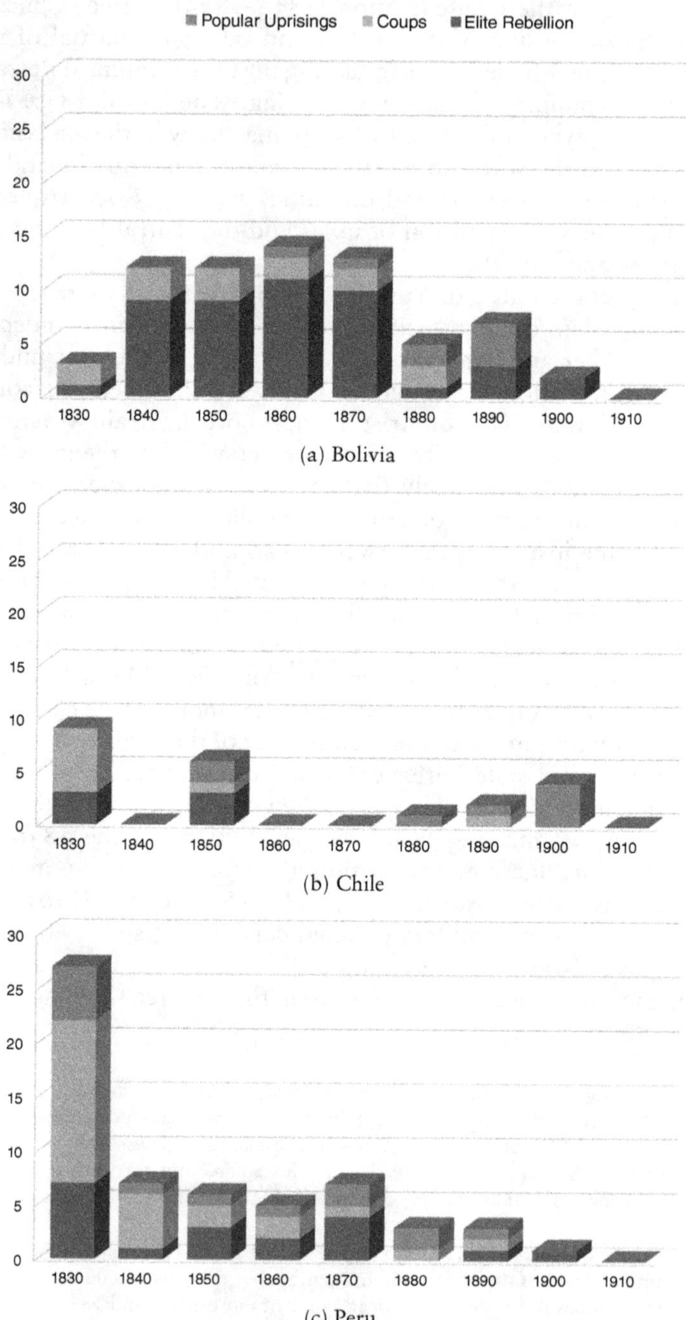

(a) Bolivia

(b) Chile

(c) Peru

FIGURE 8.1 Rebellions per decade in Bolivia, Chile, and Peru

of rebellion onsets in Chile during three of the four decades after the conflict, an impressive feat in Latin America at that time (Madrid and Schenoni, 2024).

Beyond the security forces, the Chilean Normal School was founded in 1842 and directed by future Argentine president Domingo Faustino Sarmiento, who is likely to have formed his ideas about state building during his exile in Chile (Blumenthal, 2019). The *Oficina Central de Estadística* was also founded in 1843, and Chile instated the first Civil Code of Latin America in 1850. Conservatives also implemented new internal taxes, and collection of domestic duties increased by about 50 percent after the war (Paredes, 2013, 136).

8.2 RESOURCE BOOMS, CRISES, AND MOBILIZATION

Tensions between Chile and Peru entered a second phase by the middle of the century as a result of the discovery of rich resources on the Pacific coast – guano first and then nitrates – which once again fueled international competition.

In Peru a guano boom helped fertilize Ramón Castilla's presidency, bringing some much-needed political stability. Early on, the discovery of guano aligned pugnacious sectors of the Peruvian elite behind the project of a stronger state that could help administer and protect these resources. International tensions helped Castilla foster domestic reforms. He created the accounting office that would draw up the first official budget of Peru in 1847, and he reopened the Bellavista academy to professionalize the military. Having successfully repressed rebellions in 1848 and 1849, Castilla started building South America's first working railway line in 1851, connecting the Callao port with Lima. During his second term, he reorganized the territorial administration through the *Juntas Departamentales* and the *Ley de Caminos*, which effectively allowed Lima to be connected to the rest of Peru. Slaves were freed, and Indian tribute and the tithe were abolished in 1854. This was a big blow to elites engaged in quasi-slave labor in the highlands, both in the agricultural and the mining sector.[9] Castilla's state-building project was eventually consolidated by his centralist constitutions of 1856 and 1860.

This process of reform and modernization was justified mainly by the need to defend guano from the United States,[10] European powers, and regional competitors like Bolivia and Chile, all of which had set their eyes on the white

9 Freeing the indigenous populations from the burden of the tribute, the law substantially increased their freedom of movement, affecting plantation economies, which started to rely on cheaper Chinese labor.

10 Castilla exploited the colonial prestige of Peru to put forward the idea of a South American collective security regime and organized a conference in 1847, after the Mexican–American War. The United States had become a threat to Peru as well. In 1850, US president Millard Fillmore expressed that given how valuable Peruvian guano had become, Washington should employ "all the means properly in its power" to secure its import at convenient prices. In 1852 the United States instituted a formal claim over the Lobos Islands.

gold of the seabirds. Castilla's maxim "If Chile buys one warship, Peru must buy two" (López, 1980, 46) exemplifies the preoccupation with this southern neighbor, which, although relatively weak, had been able to inflict important military blows on Lima in the near past. Paradoxically, however, Chile would become the most indispensable Peruvian ally against an unexpected Spanish invasion.

Using citizen protection as a pretext, the Spanish navy occupied the guano-rich Chincha Islands – source of roughly 70 percent of Peru's revenue – on April 14, 1864, and asked authorities in Lima for compensation reaching back to the Wars of Independence. Overwhelmed by the Spanish fleet, the Peruvian government signed the terms of the Vivanco–Pareja Treaty on January 27, 1865 (Saint John, 1992, 70), but this sudden capitulation caused outrage and civil war. General Mariano Ignacio Prado took the presidency on November 28, 1865, and decided to continue the fight, joined by Bolivia, Ecuador, and Chile. During the war Chile withstood a long shelling of Valparaiso and inflicted an important defeat on the Spanish navy by capturing the corvette *Virgen de Covadonga* during the Battle of Papudo on November 26, 1865 (Farcau, 2000, 54). Yet Chile mobilized little for the war – buying only two British wooden corvettes for its navy and maintaining its army and tax structures untouched – when compared to Peru, where Prado took the opportunity to implement new taxes and invest heavily in the armed forces.

The Chincha Islands War, which was portrayed as a victory by Prado, brought Peruvian state building to new levels. Noting that the Spanish squadron largely outgunned all South American fleets combined (Farcau, 2000, 16), Prado ordered the purchase of the first two armored ships in Latin American naval history – the ironclads *Independencia* and *Huascar*. The purchase required a great fiscal effort, and when the ships finally arrived after the war, they significantly altered the balance of sea power between Peru and Chile.

In Santiago, concern about the geopolitical environment mounted in the following years. While the Peruvian navy coming out of the Chincha Islands War largely outsized and outclassed that of Chile, Bolivia was more forcefully claiming its territorial rights on the Pacific coast, and by the end of the decade, Argentina had built a powerful military on the other side of the Andes with which to render effective its claims to Patagonia. The responsibility to mobilize in order to catch up with its neighbors fell into the hands of President Federico Errázuriz Zañartu (1871–1876), former secretary of war during the Chincha Islands War. After a long period of conservative hegemony, now a conservative–liberal alliance – including the so-called *nacionalistas* and *radicales* – embodied the project of the central elites. The liberal attempts to laicize and further centralize the Chilean state aligned Church and landlords in an opposing coalition of peripheral elites (Eyzaguirre, 1977, 127). In 1873, however, the "fusion" government collapsed after a conservative minister issued a decree allowing Catholic schools to conduct their own exams and grant degrees.

The liberals around Errázuriz aimed to increase the power of the state vis-à-vis the Church, expand the army and navy, and build railways to the north and south of Chile. After the line connecting Santiago to Valparaiso was finished in 1863 – some 110 miles – only 25 miles had been built in a decade. Realizing that progress was much slower than in Peru – where some 850 miles had been built already – the Chilean state bought the entire railway network in 1873 (Alliende, 1993, 55). By the end of his mandate, Errázuriz had nationalized much of the fragmented railway network, doubled the size of the army, bettered its equipment, and partly restored the naval balance in the South Pacific through the purchase of two ironclads, the *Cochrane* and the *Blanco Encalada*, launched in 1874 and 1875, respectively.

Yet all this progress came at great expense. Soldiers, bureaucrats, and state purchases had to be paid for by export duties, affecting mostly agriculture and metal mining precisely when the world economic crisis was starting. In 1873 a sharp decline in the prices of copper, silver, and wheat was already evident. Wheat producers were particularly affected due to the rise of multiple competitors (Collier, 1993, 27). The situation caused considerable strain on landlords, who organized to roll back the liberal reforms. A state-owned foundry set up in 1865 – which produced a large variety of items from industrial machinery to arms – had to be closed in 1874 due to the pressure of these peripheral elites. A Code of Commerce was instituted in 1874 and a Code of Mining in 1875, trying to unify the regulation of export markets and make taxation more efficient. The reforms were much needed to continue building up state capacity and military might, for the value of Chilean foreign trade, which had increased fivefold in the last thirty years, providing abundant revenue for the state, was now plummeting (Collier and Sater, 2004, 75). Facing much domestic opposition, the liberals had to concede on the diplomatic front as well. In 1874 Chile agreed on a territorial settlement that granted Bolivia sovereignty over Antofagasta in return for a twenty-five-year moratorium on export taxes. The treaty seemed to secure a *modus vivendi* for both parties at the expense of important Chilean concessions in the long term.[11]

When liberal leader Aníbal Pinto became president on September 18, 1876, everything indicated the conservative opposition would continue getting stronger. During his first year in office, peripheral elites were successful in passing a cut of state expenditure and blocking several attempts at new taxation. But the domestic equilibrium of forces changed drastically when Bolivia imposed a new ten-cent tax on the *Compañía de Salitres y Ferrocarriles de Antofagasta* on February 14, 1878, in clear violation of the 1874 treaty and triggering the chain of events leading to the War of the Pacific.

[11] Tensions with Buenos Aires, which had also mounted due to overlapping territorial claims in the Andes and the Magellan Strait and the incorporation of the two ironclads into the Chilean navy, were eventually resolved as well.

Following some initial attempts to see if Bolivia would back down, and amid the relentless lobbying of the saltpeter industry, Pinto formed a new cabinet and decreed the inconvertibility of banknotes, which became legal tender, allowing the state to increase the money supply via credits to commercial banks. In the subsequent months tariffs were increased and taxes on inheritance and property were imposed on the wealthy (Collier, 1993, 28). The increase in taxation very rapidly faced the resistance of peripheral elites not directly affected by the Bolivian tax (Ortega, 1984), including vociferous opposition from the landed elites and the Church.[12]

The military situation of Chile at the time was indeed critical. Its army had some 2,841 men divided into four battalions, which outnumbered the 1,675-strong standing army of Bolivia, but rumors of a secret defensive treaty between Bolivia and Peru also suggested the army of the latter – amounting to some 5,557 men – could be brought into the conflict (Sater, 2007, 46, 51, 59). If the armed militias of such an alliance were considered as a reserve army of sorts, it would amount to 120,000 men against a Chilean national guard of 7,000 (Sater, 2007, 44). The Chilean navy would also be under serious pressure. Although Chile had its two new armored frigates, the *Cochrane* and the *Blanco Encalada*, the Peruvian navy had two new ironclads, the *Manco Capac* and the *Atahualpa* – formerly the USS *Oneota* and the USS *Catawaba* – alongside the *Huascar* and the *Independencia*.[13] Other reasons for concern were the smaller Chilean economy and population, the fiscal constraints that the state was facing, and a long tradition of fighting alongside foreign allies, which this time did not exist.

During a period of escalation between Bolivia and Chile, elites in Santiago were unsure about the role of Peru. Siding with President Pinto were many in the Chilean elite who did not believe in the existence of the defensive alliance. Yet the signals sent by Lima were confusing and concerning. While the Peruvian diplomacy had offered its good offices to help reach an amicable solution, the Peruvian navy had decommissioned all Chilean sailors in its ships, and the army began to drill. Such was the situation when the Pinto government started to consider a landing in the port of Antofagasta to defend Chilean investments from the threat posed by Bolivian authorities there.

[12] Discord with the Catholic Church arose during 1878 due to the attempt by the liberal government to appoint a moderate to the archdiocese of Santiago after the death of an *ultramontane* cherished by the conservatives. Pinto's candidate was rejected by the Pope, who claimed *patronato* – the right to name his bishops – leaving the Chilean state and the Holy See in a situation of open confrontation during the entire war.

[13] Five smaller wooden ships completed each fleet. Part of the Chilean historiography claims that the "pacific attitude of Chile, maintaining a much inferior army to those of either Peru or Bolivia, and a much inferior navy to that of Peru, showed the sole preoccupation of the Chileans to work in and outside their territory, contrasting with the Bolivian and Peruvian post-independence history of permanent revolutions and large standing armies" (Benavides Santos, 1972, 8).

The situation in early February 1879 is properly represented by the British ambassador to Chile, who wrote to the Foreign Office in the following way:

> I regret to say that the chances of a peaceful settlement between Bolivia and this country appear to have much diminished.... But the very uncertain attitude of Peru causes at present great uneasiness here, as it is generally believed that she is secretly in league with Bolivia and that she may at any moment throw off the mask and interfere with effect by means of her powerful ironclads. The landing of a force in Antofagasta is always a matter of danger on account of the surf, and if to this be added the presence of possible hostile ironclads, the difficulties of Chile would indeed be great. The government meanwhile is in the greatest straits for money, and though a public spirited banker is said to have come forward and guaranteed to the government large sums for the thorough prosecution of the war, I fear that even his resources, large as they are, may be unequal to the strain.[14]

Chilean troops disembarked in Antofagasta on February 14, 1879 – exactly one year after the tax had been passed. When Bolivia declared war on March 1, 1879, the Chilean ambassador in Lima met with President Prado and asked for his reassurance that Peru would remain neutral. Prado confessed the existence of the defensive alliance with Bolivia on the spot. Soon afterward, on April 5, 1879, Chile formally declared war on both Bolivia and Peru.

From 1879 to 1880 the revenue of the Chilean state doubled from 124,406 to 242,126 pesos. Almost all of it came from tax revenue, which rose from 110,124 to 227,716 pesos. Of this increase, internal taxes covered the largest share. Income from foreign duties only increased marginally from 63,540 to 87,010 pesos, since global trade was still stagnant. Indirect taxes rose from 91,452 to 151,032 pesos, but this was only halfway from covering the war expenditure. The rest was covered by specific taxes – which rose from 25,247 to 60,402 pesos – and taxes to the mining industry, which doubled, all in the same year (Díaz et al., 2016). "In May 1879, in desperation, Congress passed the *mobiliaria*, a property tax it had rejected the previous year. But the new tax on its own could not defray the cost of the war." According to Collier and Sater (2004, 143), "Still urgently in need of cash, the government appealed to the banks ... with the government's supply of specie almost exhausted, Pinto authorized the printing of paper notes, which the banks had no choice but to accept." By mid-1879 a British diplomat evaluated: "The property and income taxes are being rigorously enforced, and several millions of paper dollars have been issued, thus, for the moment, the country is enabled to pay her way and carry on the war."[15]

14 Letter of British Ambassador to Chile Mr. Francis Pakenham to the Secretary of State for Foreign Affairs Robert Gascoyne-Cecil, Marquess of Salisbury. February 10, 1879. British National Archives FO/16/202, p. 35.

15 Letter from the head of the British Legation in Santiago to Ambassador Mr. Francis Pakenham. July 15, 1879. British National Archives FO/16/202, p. 217. By the end of the war in 1884, revenue was at 323,015 pesos and taxation at 300,349, tripling prewar levels (Díaz et al., 2016). The increase corresponded mostly to domestic taxes, although inflation should be considered when interpreting these figures.

Virtually all governmental expenditure in 1879 was devoted to building up the army and constituting four civic battalions in Antofagasta, organized with local militias. The extent of the mobilization undertaken by Chile during the first year of the war was truly impressive:

> The 2,000 men the army had in February increased to 10,000, without counting the civic militias. The soldier that now had the pride of his uniform and victories was a few months before a peaceful worker. Now he has all he needs to defend the honor of his flag, the arsenals are full of weapons and projectiles, and all was done with few resources, imposing the most severe and rigorous administration. All the military organization and the administrative service was financed with national revenues, and emission of currency worth 12 million pesos. (Bulnes, 1976, 116)

The character of Chilean mobilization for the War of the Pacific is somehow misconstrued in the state-building literature. Ryan Saylor (2014, 65), for example, states that the war was funded through paper emission – implying it was not funded through taxation – when tax collection more than doubled, and domestic taxes imposed upon the rich were of particular importance. Importantly, Saylor does not discuss the fact that state building during the War of the Pacific took place amid a global financial crisis that temporarily removed the key permissive condition in his theory – the commodity boom – as well as access to foreign credit (Queralt, 2019, 723; see also Sater, 1985).

Also Marcus Kurtz (2013, 89–94), who does show an uptick in the evolution of Chilean tax revenue during the war,[16] chooses to represent this as a case where state building preceded war and elites consensually chose to go to war to further build up the state.[17] Yet this interpretation of the war as purposively sought after by the Chilean elites runs counter to serious

[16] In a figure showing the evolution of Chilean tax revenue (Kurtz, 2013, 69), the largest relative increase in the series takes place during the War of the Pacific (1879–1883). The figure also shows that every large increase before and after that is concurrent with war or military standoffs. It is clear that Chile increased taxation notably during the War of the Confederation (1836–1839) and the Chincha Islands War (1864–1866). Increases in taxation after the War of the Pacific peak and decline concurrently with de-escalation after the 1891 Matta-Reyes Protocol with Bolivia, Argentina's acceptance of a 1902 arbitration award settling a contentious border, and after a dtente with Argentina and Brazil was reached in 1912, stopping the so-called "dreadnought race" and setting the basis for the ABC Pact of 1915. Another figure (Kurtz, 2013, 155) shows a clear correlation between the Beagle Crisis – which in late 1979 almost ended in war between Chile and Argentina – and a new peak in tax collection (see also Thies, 2005).

[17] In his words: "It was the construction of an elite consensus in Chile around the desirability of *initiating wars of conquest* – from which the dominant classes expected to benefit – that turned military conflict into a component of the process by which an effective administration was constructed. Successive conflicts – with the Araucanian Indians to the south, with Spain, and repeatedly with Peru and Bolivia – were both initiated by the Chilean state and used to justify the expansion of the public powers, the creation of an effective standing army, the imposition of substantial new tax burdens, and the creation of major public infrastructure" (Kurtz, 2013, 90). Although most readers would take this as a concession to bellicist theory (Sambanis et al., 2015), Kurtz proceeds to argue that the Chilean case is not amenable to the conflict-centric approach because it is a case of deliberate expansionism.

historiographical debates highlighting division in the upper echelons of Chilean society, important opposition to the war, and the breakup of hostilities as an outcome that Pinto himself tried to prevent. According to one of the most respected historians of the war, "The need for recruits caught Pinto by surprise" (Sater, 2007, 60). Landowners saw their activities largely affected by conscription, and lower classes felt the weight of war terribly, having their young conscripted and either losing them or getting them back maimed by the effects of modern warfare. The war also forced the Chilean state to radically change its fiscal system, introducing new taxes the rich would have probably resisted in the absence of *force majeure*.

The issue of Peruvian mobilization before the War of the Pacific is no less controversial and requires a close look. As discussed earlier in this section, Peru had gone through a process of considerable state formation and military buildup during its guano boom. Emboldened by his victory against the Spanish fleet, Prado clung to power until 1868, fostering further reforms to strengthen and modernize Peru. Facing declining guano exports, his minister of finance, Manuel Pardo, sought an important tax reform as a way of balancing the state accounts, creating an income tax – called "personal tax" – equivalent to twelve days of payment per year (Hunefeldt, 2004, 129). Pardo also instituted stamp duties, increased the *contribución predial* – a property tax directly affecting the landed elites – and created professional offices in charge of tax collection, until then in the hands of local government (Planas, 1998, 194). The project was resented by peripheral elites, eventually causing the fall of both President Prado and Minister Pardo.

Despite this temporary setback, the Peruvian state had grown impressively by the year 1870, particularly with regard to its bureaucracy – which doubled in a decade, reaching some 10,000 men – and public infrastructure (Hunt, 1984). "The guano money spent in this way by the state implied a true diffusion throughout the territory of a new figure: the public official." As Contreras and Cavieres (2005, 182) put it, "Be it in the form of a judge, policeman, a customs officer, army captain, teacher, or civil engineer ... these men represented at the local level something like a missionary."

The process of Peruvian state making thus showed some continuity after the Chincha Islands War. Prado's successor, José Balta (1868–1872), renegotiated the rights to exploit the islands and granted them to Dreyfus & Co., a French company, and was granted two important loans in London in 1870 and 1872, the first for 11 million GBP and the second for 22 million GBP, which included a mortgage on guano exports and the railroads to be constructed with that money. This ensured the continuity of railroad construction – at a pace of some forty miles per year – but in the context of declining guano revenues, state expansion had now become much more burdensome, soaking up virtually all public investment (Farcau, 2000, 18).

Pardo ran for president in 1872 under the banner of the Civil Party and with the slogan "Turn guano into railroads." Since his time as minister, Pardo and his *civilistas* had come to represent an increasing urban middle class and sought to compensate for the declining guano boom by increasing public participation in the affairs of the republic (McEvoy, 1999, 229). His ticket was resented by peripheral elites, and a coup was even attempted by the defense minister, Tomás Gutiérrez, to prevent him from taking office after winning the election by a landslide. The preoccupation of the peripheral elites was justified. In his inauguration as the first civilian president of Peru, Pardo announced an ambitious fiscal and administrative reform of Congress. The main project was the decentralization of both revenue collection and governmental expenditure in the *Concejos Departamentales*, a reform that strengthened the central state by decentralizing the fiscal burden and contesting the power of local *caudillos* and landlords via more powerful bureaucracies and political parties at the subnational level (McEvoy, 1997, 140).[18] Pardo also expanded public education, created a college for the bureaucracy, and established a school of naval officers. To keep rebellious militias in check, he created a centralized National Guard and enforced meritocratic rules of promotion (McEvoy, 1994, 112). As everywhere else in Latin America, these state-building attempts met with fierce resistance. The most prominent opposition leader was Nicolás de Piérola, who, having taken part in Gutiérrez's rebellion, rose in arms again in 1874 with the support of landed elites affected by taxes and local elections (McEvoy, 1997, 146).

When Peru was hit by the 1873 crisis, Pardo, very much aware that passing a personal tax could result in his destitution, turned to saltpeter in the Tarapacá region. In 1873 he decreed the *estanco*, by which the Peruvian Congress limited the production of saltpeter to a maximum tonnage and established a fixed price at which the state could buy the resource (Bulnes, 1976, 24), but, facing several problems with companies trying to evade the law, the Peruvian government authorized expropriation in 1875, a policy that severely affected Chilean interests (Pereyra Plasencia, 2010, 86). During his last year in government, Pardo coordinated some of these policies with Bolivia, a country with which he had signed a defensive alliance on February 6, 1873. Making use of these fiscal reforms, schooling extended throughout the territory, and some ports were modernized while others were built from scratch and connected to the expanding railway network.[19]

The *civilistas* conducted the first-ever Peruvian census in 1876, which counted 2,661,997 inhabitants. The census crowned a decade of great progress for Peru, but one that had also taken place in the midst of a grave debt crisis.

[18] Peruvian intellectual José Carlos Mariátegui (1959, 183) evaluated that the *Concejos Departamentales* were a smart way of undermining local orders, for they were too complex for the *caciques* and feudal lords to participate in yet contained important functions of the modern state. In other words, the project decentralized "without limiting the power of the central government" (Mucke, 1998, 77) and enhanced the state overall.

[19] Railroad construction was continued even in the absence of foreign credit after 1872. Overall, "between 1868 and 1876 ten railway lines were initiated in Peru, all of them connecting ports in the coast with productive centers in the inlands" (Contreras and Cavieres, 2005, 184).

Unable to make ends meet, Lima defaulted on its debt with bond holders and renegotiated the exploitation of its guano reserves with yet another French company, the Société Générale de Paris.[20] The economic crisis put the Civil Party in a weak position for the 1876 elections. Pardo did not harbor much hope and worried that the opposition would roll back his reforms, but his concerns were quelled when the opposition chose Prado – whom he had served as minister a decade before – as their candidate. As a celebrated Peruvian historian puts it:

> The candidate proclaimed by the opposition was the man under whom he started his career as Minister of Finance, an ally back in 1872 for whom a ship was waiting to bring him back from Chile in case the rebellion of Gutiérrez had continued; he was not, therefore, an enemy, and would not take decisive measures against him. Pardo opted, therefore, for what some have called a "waiting period." He would give the *civilismo* time to change leaderships, calm its passions and heal the wounds that the exercise of power opens. He would wait until the next parliamentarian elections and the 1880 presidential elections to return to power. (Basadre, 2005, 132)

With Prado as president again, the real opposition to state building continued to come from Piérola, who led yet another two military rebellions against Prado in 1876 and 1877,[21] but the 1878 parliamentarian elections resulted in an overwhelming victory for the Civil Party, and Pardo returned to the country to take up position as senator. The momentum was clearly with the *civilistas* when Pardo was assassinated on November 16, 1878. Instead of weakening the central elites, the event led to an immediate alignment of Prado and the *civilistas* controlling Congress under a "national fusion" (Basadre, 2005, 133–141). The alliance would only become stronger as a result of the impending war with Chile. Army enlargement and fiscal reform had become a priority, and the affected peripheral elite of *pierolistas*, invariably against these projects, was forced out of the governing coalition.

When Chilean forces occupied the city of Antofagasta, war drums sounded in Lima and all across Peru, and "heading the movement was the *civilista* party of Pardo" (Bulnes, 1976, 36). In April the *civilista* caucus passed a 3 percent tax on the utilities made by industries and registered workers. This law was soon followed by another reinstating a personal tax – akin to Pardo's during the Chincha Islands War – that obliged "every Peruvian able man between 21 and 60 years old to contribute with four *soles* per semester to the Department of the Interior" (Rosario Pacahuala, 2011, 196). These two bills were followed by three other taxes: on movable capital, on property, and on the export of sugar,

20 A number of holdouts remained, who were finally satisfied by a new renegotiation in 1878, but debt with Dreyfus & Co. remained a great burden and the situation of Peru was clearly one of financial strain (Miller, 2011, 170).

21 Piérola rebelled against the new Prado administration twice – in La Cotera on October 19, 1876, and following a mutiny on the *Huascar* on May 6, 1877, which proclaimed him the Supreme Chief of Peru. Fearing that the Prado government would respond to the continuous pressure of peripheral elites, the *civilistas* also rebelled soon after the *Huascar* incident.

which directly affected the elites (Basadre, 2005, 192). Congress also debated a law to increase all customs duties by 25 percent and authorized the emission of 70 million *soles*, which forced individuals to bear a notable inflation tax in the absence of convertibility.

The numerous taxes sanctioned by the Peruvian state in this short period seem to contradict the claim that "the Peruvian elite in fact continued its refusal to approve tax levies to defend itself, even as the Chileans actually invaded" (Kurtz, 2013, 76).[22] As Soifer (2015, 19) has noted, such a narrative "struggles to explain the case of prewar Peru" and "mischaracterizes it as one in which state building never emerged rather than its correct classification as a case in which a concerted state-building effort failed." This is particularly true under the *civilista* government of Pardo and as Peru prepared for war under Prado during 1878 and 1879. Although conscription was limited in the initial stages of the war – which made sense, since the Peruvian army was already double the Chilean forces at the outset of hostilities – virtually all males were leveraged in late 1880 to defend Lima, also contradicting the claim that "elites were reluctant to resist the Chilean invaders, as doing so would require joining with and arming the (long-restive) local peasantry" (Kurtz, 2013, 76).

One reason why previous authors missed the extent of mobilization in the prewar period might be that Peruvian decisive defeats in the War of the Pacific took place early on, by the end of 1879, which hindered mobilization during the next three years of conflict. As I show in the following sections, the subsequent demobilization and abrogation of tax reforms was a consequence of military defeat, just as classical bellicist theory would expect. I therefore agree with Soifer that in the "immediate postwar" Peru "the weakness of the state ... undermined state development efforts during the prewar period" (Soifer, 2015, 119–120).

8.3 THE WAR OF THE PACIFIC (1879–1883)

At the outset of hostilities, the situation was such that Chile was clearly outnumbered by the allied armies on land and closely matched, if not superseded, by Peru on the sea. Although it could be argued that Chilean troops were better trained and the two Chilean ironclads were of a slightly superior class, the reality was that numbers favored Peru, with two times the ironclads and soldiers of its opponent – and this without considering Bolivia.[23]

[22] The source supporting this claim is an obscure short history of Peru (Werlich, 1978). The conclusions drawn here rest on a much more comprehensive review of the historiography about the war in both English and Spanish.

[23] This statement requires some context, for it has been the subject of notable historiographical debate. The mischaracterization of the balance of forces at the outset of the War of the Pacific has a clear origin in the radically distorted versions of the war that appeared in Chile and Peru after it, usually understating their own forces at the outset of hostilities to highlight the valor of their men. This has apparently confused the assessment of foreign historians as well. For

If the Peruvian army was not better trained or equipped, it had to do with rather exogenous and fortuitous factors. Some arms purchases were unduly delayed, and troops had to be decommissioned due to the fiscal crisis – this was also true in Chile, where some 700 men were dismissed in 1878 alone, but both arms procurement and conscription would swiftly change this balance (Sater, 2007, 46, 61).

The first stage of the war would concentrate on the maritime front. Chile began a blockade of the port of Iquique on April 5, 1879, the very same day it declared war on the allies. Knowing it was outnumbered and the mighty Callao fortresses had been able to repel a much more powerful Spanish fleet, the Chileans hoped the blockade would force a fight near Iquique. Yet the chances that the Chileans could hold in Iquique were dim. The British ambassador, Francis Pakenham, recommended actions were taken in case the Peruvian fleet broke the blockade and proceeded to bombard Valparaiso:

> The Chilean ironclads are, commander Boys [captain of the HMS *Pelican*] says, handy and efficient vessels, but owing to want of practice, some doubt may be felt as to their power of maneuvering with rapidity and skill sufficient to enable them to avoid or parry the attack of the Huascar ram. If the Peruvian force should prove victorious, there is nothing to hinder them from appearing off this place [i.e., Valparaiso] and commencing a bombardment.... In view of this possible contingency I have silently commenced preparations for receiving temporarily at my cottage 3 miles off about 100 of the wives and children of the British citizens of this place.[24]

Surprisingly, the Peruvian response took a long time, and after a month the impatient commander of the Chilean navy, Juan Williams Rebolledo, devised a reckless plan to dynamite the Callao. Persuaded that the Peruvians would continue to adopt a defensive position, the bulk of the Chilean fleet sailed north, failing to notice that, at the very same time, Peru had sent the best of its

example, Bruce Farcau (2000, 20) writes: "On the eve of the War of the Pacific, Peru found herself in a state of virtual bankruptcy with a political landscape littered with real corpses. Her army of twenty-five hundred men was inadequate even for simple police duties in a huge nation of nearly three million people. Even her formerly dominant navy had already been qualitatively outclassed by the Chileans. Her president, while experienced in both military and political affairs, had no identifiable power base of his own, and the nation had been in a state of virtually constant civil war for years with the corresponding disruption in economic life." This reading of the prewar situation justifies the outcome but fails to properly represent the situation. I take the evaluation of William Sater (2007, 42, 97) – who provides more documentation – when I conclude that the Peruvian army was double the Chilean with 5,557 men. I also concur with Sater when I refer to the navies of the two countries being virtually matched and the Peruvian fleet being quantitatively superior. My conclusions also rely on primary sources – British and American diplomatic sources – that should be neutral in this regard. The US ambassador, for example, evaluated that "The navies of Peru and Chile are equal in point of strength." Letter of US Ambassador to Chile Thomas A. Osborn to Secretary of State William M. Evarts. April 3, 1879. US National Archives M10/30RG/57, p. 2.

24 Letter of British Ambassador to Chile Mr. Francis Pakenham to Secretary of State for Foreign Affairs Robert Gascoyne-Cecil, Marquess of Salisbury. April 7, 1879. British National Archives FO/16/202, p. 48.

navy – the ironclads *Huascar* and *Independencia* – to break the Iquique blockade. The domestic pressure to engage in battle had been as fierce in Lima as it was in Santiago:

> The government will be compelled soon to make a forward movement of some kind or lose the confidence of its people; the great masses of whom are ignorant and impulsive and easily led by demagogues or ambitious aspirants to revolutionary movements. Piérola, the champion and favorite of the Church party, is probably ready to avail himself at the first favorable occasion.[25]

Thus when the Peruvian ironclads arrived at Iquique, they were surprised that the Chileans had left only the corvette *Esmeralda* and the sloop *Covadonga*, two wooden ships largely outgunned and outclassed by the forces that were coming for them.

The Battle of Iquique took place on May 21, 1879, and provides a neat example of the fortuitous events that usually decide key battles. When the nineteen cannons of the *Independencia* confronted the two cannons of the *Covadonga*, the situation must have looked like a sure victory for the Peruvians. Yet, disobeying the orders of Arturo Prat, captain of the *Esmeralda*, the Chilean sloop closed up as the snipers kept firing on deck to prevent the Peruvian gunners from reaching the cannons. When both ships were side by side, the captain of the *Independencia* threw all the weight of his heavy ironclad against the sloop, trying to ram it. After the maneuver both ships drifted toward the shore and the *Independencia* unexpectedly hit a reef.[26]

Virtually at the same time, a combat between the *Esmeralda* and the *Huascar* was taking place. This was supposed to be an easy win for the Peruvians as well, since the cannons of the old Chilean corvette were unlikely to harm their mighty ironclad, and land forces in Iquique were helping by opening fire from the coast. Yet when Admiral Miguel Grau tried to ram the *Esmeralda*, Prat and his crew showed impressive valor and tried to board the enemy, sacrificing their lives. The *Huascar* tried ramming the corvette for a second and third time until it was sunk with its colors still up high. When the combat ended, the Peruvian fleet was in awe. Their plans to blockade and shell Iquique and Antofagasta were suspended. Rebolledo wrote:

> Huascar and Independencia should have concluded in one hour with the Esmeralda and Covadonga. Subsequently, they would have followed until Antofagasta, taking all of our transport ships. Afterwards they could have set Antofagasta on fire and all of our coast would have followed. The heroism of our sailors has saved us and through it, an event that should have brought us death, brought us glory and material advantages,

[25] Letter of US Ambassador to Peru Isaac P. Christiancy to Secretary of State William M. Evarts. May 12, 1879. US National Archives T-52/32.

[26] Lieutenant Theodorus Manson says of these last moments: "According to the logbooks of both Captain Moore and Condell [the Peruvian and Chilean captains, respectively], the tiller of the Peruvian ship turned to starboard, in direction to the reef, right after one of the helmsmen had fallen, wounded by a shot from the Covadonga. The only rudder of the Independencia was on deck" (Manson, 1971, 87).

for the exchange of the Esmeralda for the Independencia is very advantageous. Yet here, between us, God may grow tired of protecting us if we continue to be so clumsy. (Bulnes, 1976, 57)

Historians across the board highlight the element of chance in the Battle of Iquique. "This utterly unexpected encounter had far-reaching implications," as Sater (2007, 177) puts it, for "thanks to a combination of Chilean cunning and Peruvian ill-fortune, Pinto's fleet accidentally won a significant strategic victory." The *Independencia* was finally scuttled, resulting in a considerable advantage for the Chilean navy, and Prat became something of a "secular saint" (Collier, 1993, 30), his death giving impulse to the war much like in the case of Portales back in 1837.

Still, the opposition to the war in Santiago, headed by the conservatives, turned all of its attention toward the *Huascar*. The Peruvian flagship continued to harass the Chilean shores. Until Grau and his powerful ironclad were brought to their knees, it was impossible to ensure the safety of the coastal cities, much less think of safely transporting troops to the north. Rebolledo acted as an agent of these peripheral elites, insisting on keeping the strategic defense and thus allowing Grau to harass Chilean ports and vessels. But Rebolledo had been responsible for sending the fleet to the Callao and leaving the *Covadonga* and the *Esmeralda* unprotected in Iquique, and his days as commander were numbered.

The situation after the battle of Iquique remained a draw in the view of a British diplomat:

Since the naval engagement of Iquique … no fight of any consequence has occurred between the belligerents. The Chilean government, even if it desires mediation, dares not mention such a measure at the present moment. The population of this Republic is in a fever of impatient excitement for the war. The intention that Peru shall be made to pay dearly for the costs of the war as well as the innate hopes that this country will be enriched by the result of the war is so formidably rooted in the Chilean mind that, without Peru be utterly crushed, she could not accept the terms to which Chile would at present subject her. As Peru has as yet suffered little loss, I do not doubt her pretensions will be also exaggerated. Thus, until a decisive blow is given and received, it is to be feared that the war must be prolonged.[27]

By August the situation had worn out the conservative cabinet of Antonio Varas, who had been entertaining a peaceful resolution. "Pinto organized the new ministry with a new program: exclude the Conservative Party and support [Colonel Emilio] Sotomayor in the north with all vigor" (Bulnes, 1976, 67). Rebolledo was dismissed, and Chile finally adopted an offensive strategy in the sea (Sater, 2007, 150–152). Pinto was very wary of making this move, but popular sentiment had started to strengthen radicals in the war party. The US ambassador reported the situation in the following manner:

27 Letter from the head of the British Legation in Santiago to Ambassador Mr. Francis Pakenham. July 15, 1879. British National Archives FO/16/202, p. 217.

President Pinto is exceedingly conservative and disposed to "make haste slowly" but public sentiment is pressing him forward and has just made it necessary for him to change the Commander in Chief of the navy. There is a very general demand for an aggressive campaign.[28]

Even then, more than three months passed before the two Chilean ironclads – the *Cochrane* and the *Blanco Encalada* – spotted the *Huascar* in the distance and started to pursue it. Grau initially fled, but noting the *Cochrane* was in firing range and the *Blanco* was far behind, he turned to his pursuers, starting the Battle of Angamos of October 8, 1879. The *Huascar* shot first, a cannonball piercing the bow of the *Cochrane* and landing on its deck. By a miracle the projectile never exploded (Manson, 1971, 115). A few minutes later, a lucky shot by the *Cochrane* destroyed the turret of the *Huascar*, killing Grau. Lacking their leader, the Peruvian sailors were forced to surrender their ship before they could scuttle it. "The loss of the Huascar produced a profound impression in Peru … Grau was its pride, and the Huascar its glory" (Bulnes, 1976, 77).

With central elites in Santiago strengthened by the Angamos victory, a military offensive on land became feasible. In particular, the conscription of the largest national army Chile had ever seen had become a politically tenable objective. Now every young Chilean man wanted to share the glory of Prat and take part in a victory that seemed entirely plausible now that a fleet of Chilean transport ships could carry the army of Sotomayor to the north to take the port of Iquique. But even if Chilean primacy on the sea was incontestable now, things on land appeared much more evenly matched according to foreign observers:

Chile, thus far has, by her own mode of carrying on the war, conferred a great favor upon Peru and Bolivia, by transferring the field of operations to the very locality which they would naturally have chosen: the point where their forces can readily form a junction and operate in concert. And they seem to be now acting in entire harmony, having an efficient combined land force in that region of between 28,000 to 32,000 men, which can be readily concentrated. And the Chilean fleet is too small compared with the size of the Pacific Ocean to seriously to endanger the free water communication between field operations and the Peruvian base at Callao. Such is substantially the condition of military affairs today. It is liable to be changed at any time, but no one can foresee just what that change is likely to be.[29]

The campaign developed swiftly during the month of November. The port of Pisagua was captured on November 2, 1879, cutting transport lines connecting Iquique with Tacna and blocking reinforcements that the Bolivian president Hilarión Daza and Prado could send from their headquarters there and in Arica. On November 19, a detachment of the Chilean army under the command of

[28] Letter of US Ambassador Thomas A. Osborn to Secretary of State William M. Evarts. July 24, 1879. US National Archives M10/30/RG/57, p. 18.

[29] Letter of US Ambassador to Peru Isaac P. Christiancy to Secretary of State William M. Evarts. July 20, 1879. US National Archives T-52/32.

Sotomayor and his 6,500 men confronted an allied army of some 9,000 men for the control of a well. The Battle of Dolores was a close call, decided by a timely charge of the Chilean forces against the flank of the allies when they were climbing a hill to take the artillery. Under siege, Iquique was surrendered on November 22.

Grasping the momentum, Sotomayor took notice that the Peruvian general Juan Buendía had retreated there with his 4,500 troops and sent a detachment of 2,300 in pursuit under the command of Colonel Luis Arteaga. The Battle of Tarapacá on November 27 lasted the whole day, with the Chileans and the Peruvians attacking five different times each. At many moments the Chileans thought they were defeated and were close to withdrawing (Benavides Santos, 1972, 55) but persisted and in the end took Tarapacá, with Arteaga losing almost a quarter of his soldiers, either killed or severely wounded, and losing a chance to finish the Peruvian army (Bulnes, 1976, 108).

The takeover of Tarapacá had contradictory effects in Santiago. On the one hand, the last battle of the campaign had ended in the unnecessary loss of some 800 men, either killed, captured, or severely wounded, which represented roughly a third of the army at the outset of the war.[30] On the other hand, Chile had now conquered the Tarapacá province, which worked in favor of the war party. In this situation, it would be the domestic victory of the peripheral elites in Bolivia and Peru that would, more than anything else, boost the position of Chilean central elites.

Bolivian president Daza was stationed with his troops in the northern town of Arica when the attack on the port of Pisagua took place, and he left in the direction of Iquique to offer support, but his troops were unable to cross the Atacama Desert and he turned back in an episode that was and still is depicted by Peruvians as a desertion and a betrayal. After the infamous retreat, he stayed stationed with his troops in Arica, where he was notified of the sequence of battles that followed and remained ready to fight a Chilean advance to the north. Yet his image had suffered greatly, both in Lima and La Paz. He was pictured as a coward, and this "arrived to the ears of Daza in Tacna, who spoke of massacring and avenging his enemies." Although "all he wanted was to return to the highlands" (Bulnes, 1976, 112), he received notice of his destitution by a coup led by General Eleodoro Camacho while he was still in Peru, on December 28, 1879.

The situation was no less critical in Peru. After Tarapacá, Prado decided to leave his headquarters in Arica and march back to the capital. The masses had filled the streets of Lima during the nights preceding his arrival and had to be violently repressed. The city was boiling when the president arrived; the

30 This cost Lieutenant Colonel Francisco José Vergara – a key partisan of the strategic offensive – his position. Immediately after the battle Vergara was recalled to Santiago to explain what had happened, and he gave a bleak description of the situation on the front and prospects of a Chilean victory.

cabinet and all the *civilista* legislators who had pushed for war were targeted by the angry mob.

Facing a situation of virtual anarchy, Prado dismissed his cabinet and called Piérola to the House of Pizzarro. "Piérola was, without a doubt, the most prestigious man in the country at the time, a prestige acquired by his continued fight against those who governed" (Bulnes, 1976, 111). Prado asked him to join his government as a minister and organize a new cabinet, but the *caudillo* refused.

The Peruvian president probably foresaw that the situation was headed for civil war, and "rather than thrust the country into a political maelstrom, Prado boarded a ship sailing to Panama" (Sater, 2007, 209).[31] Upon his departure, a coup took place on December 23, 1879. Piérola had taken the city without firing a single shot, thanks to the support of the archbishop and two bishops, who helped ensure the peaceful surrender of the *civilistas* and their supporters in the armed forces (Barros Arana, 1979, 165).

Piérola had been a vociferous antiwar public figure. On May 24, 1879, he had written from Valparaiso denouncing the Limanian elites, who in his view had stirred up the crisis (Basadre, 2005, 195). After a year of war, and with national sentiments boiling, he could not openly oppose the war effort anymore, but Peruvian peripheral elites hoped he would soon surrender to acceptable terms. Immediately after taking office, Piérola surrounded himself with these peripheral elites, announcing a new constitution that eliminated the legislature and created a council of state, including notables from the main families and the archbishop of Lima (Farcau, 2000, 106). To further weaken the *civilistas*, he divided the army in Tacna into two, so that Admiral Lizardo Montero – its commander and a member of the Civil Party – could not challenge him politically (Sater, 2007, 209). It was clear from the beginning that most of these reforms would hurt state capacity and thus the war effort, but Piérola seemed persuaded that a Chilean invasion of Lima by land was impossible and he would be able to find a political solution.

Several other measures taken by Piérola illustrate the collapse of the efforts made by central elites in the previous decade. After his coup the national railways were sold to British companies and Peru reassumed the 4 million GBP debt to Dreyfus & Co. that was defaulted on in 1876, giving the company broad rights over guano exports in exchange for a short-term loan that never arrived. Short of foreign support and that of the Limanian middle class, Piérola sought support "in the clergy and the indians" (Bulnes, 1976, 121). Knowing Santiago was at odds with the Vatican, he wrote to Pope Leon XIII asking for his blessing and gave numerous concessions to the Church. He also sought the support

[31] Some historians state that upon leaving the country, he sincerely hoped he could return with more foreign support (Saint John, 1992, 114; Farcau, 2000, 101). He asked for the authorization of Congress to make trips to the United States and France in search of the arms and warships needed to continue the war effort.

of powerful *caciques* by investing himself as *Protector de la Raza Indígena*, a colonial title by which he could directly attend to any judicial case involving these local leaders. All the reforms were at the same time directed to weaken the *civilistas*, who allegedly preferred "the Chileans rather than Piérola" (Basadre, 1931, 139, cited in Bonilla, 1980, 191).

Although a result favorable to Chile was virtually decided after the Piérola coup, the war dragged on for another three years as the Peruvian leader realized signing the Chilean terms would be signing his own political death certificate. Thus the war entered a new phase: the Chilean invasion of Peru.

Elites in Santiago were divided on whether it was the right time to attack Lima. While Pinto and Domingo Santa María, then minister of war, advocated a more conservative move against Tacna as the next step, Sotomayor insisted that Chile should take Lima and assemble for this purpose an expeditionary force of 12,000 men.[32] It was clear that the effort would require doubling the size of the army – now 10,000 strong – since at least 6,000 men had to stay in Tarapacá to defend the province. The position of Sotomayor was echoed in Congress, in particular within a faction of *liberales* led by Domingo Arteaga Alemparte, who presented a motion to annex the regions conquered by the army. Although a majority of the lower chamber opposed the motion, the episode illustrates how emboldened the war party was at the time (Bulnes, 1976, 115).

In this context preparations started for the 1881 presidential elections. For the first time in Chilean history the liberals were completely hegemonic. It soon became evident that the only two possible candidates with serious chances were Sotomayor and Santa María. After Sotomayor's unexpected death on May 20, 1880, all ministers resigned, leaving Pinto with full capacity to form a new cabinet of his liking (Barros Arana, 1979, 264, 275). It was clear that the support for Pinto and his favorite for succession, Santa María, was overwhelming. General Manuel Baquedano became the commander of the army and scored two new victories in the Battle of Tacna on May 26 and the Battle of Arica on July 7, which consolidated this situation.

The loss of Tacna and Arica led to renewed hysteria in Lima, where the *civilistas* publicly criticized the dictatorship after months of silence. Divisions ensued within the army as well when Montero accused Piérola of having no military training and failing to understand the necessity of strengthening the state by collecting taxes and conscripting more soldiers, even if this meant hurting his initial coalition. Facing the real possibility of an invasion, these

[32] Sotomayor was by far the most salient figure of the war party in favor of an offensive. One faction of the Liberal Party wanted him back in Santiago to run for president, but Pinto refused his requests to return and Sotomayor continued with the troops. Santa María wrote to Sotomayor explaining that a continuation to Lima – which would no doubt be necessary if the goal was territorial annexation of the entire Atacama Desert – would meet opposition worldwide and probably hurt the prospects of an enduring peace. The debate soon transcended to the public sphere and led to important controversies in the press, dividing Chileans once again between those in favor of a defensive posture and those for an offensive strategy.

critiques prompted Piérola to hurry a shipment of weapons from Europe and institute conscription of all able men between eighteen and fifty years old. He also reinstated the personal tax in yet another form (Contreras, 2005, 94), severely sanctioned the ranchers that collaborated with Chile, confiscated ecclesiastical goods, and punished as traitors those landlords who refused to contribute to the cause with men or coin (Basadre, 2005, 215). Yet Piérola's belated transformation to the cause of the central elites could do little to sway other peripheral elites, who were very much discouraged by the developments on the battlefield.

Right after the triumph in Arica, a debate was held in the Chilean Congress regarding the need to take Lima. Negotiations were unpopular, but the military goal seemed out of reach. The Chilean navy had bombarded the Callao on April 22 and again on May 10, 1880, and the best-fortified port in all of Latin America proved impregnable. Furthermore, the new technology of the torpedo was proving very effective at keeping the fleet offshore, virtually leveling the field in the sea (Sater, 2007, 161). All three Chilean ironclads – the *Blanco*, the *Cochrane*, and the *Huascar* – were almost blown up by torpedos on different occasions. Fire from a fortress in the Callao sank the *Covadonga* and displaced a turret of the *Huascar*. Wary of the Callao defenses, Chilean troops had disembarked far from the port and encircled and besieged the city of Lima on land.

During the year between the fall of Arica and the final assault on Lima, several negotiations took place. As a result of these efforts, a conference took place on board the USS *Lackawanna*, where plenipotentiaries from Bolivia, Chile, and Peru and the US ministers in those nations convened for peace talks from October 22 to 27, 1880. Peru took this opportunity to request the devolution of all lands and battleships taken by force, a condition that was rejected by Chile. Still, knowing the costs of the campaign, Pinto would have gladly signed the terms if it was not for the pressure of an emboldened radical wing of the war party. According to the US ambassador in Chile:

> So strong was the opposition to the movement immediately preceding the conference that I am confident the government would have gladly retraced its steps in that matter if it could have honorably done so. The country was exceedingly sensitive upon the subject, and there was very great danger that the government would fall.[33]

Back in Santiago, Deputy José Manuel Balmaceda vociferously defended a final offensive, saying that "peace was to be found in Lima or nowhere," for Chile "cannot stay with the weapon on its shoulder and suffer the cost of war without keeping the spoils of victory" (cited in Bulnes, 1976, 170). After the failure of the peace negotiations, the Santiago government decided to take Lima and force a surrender, but this would require an incredible effort. According to

33 Letter of US Ambassador Thomas A. Osborn to Secretary of State William M. Evarts. February 24, 1881. US National Archives M10/30/RG/57, p. 38.

one account, the army plus all reservists in the country barely reached 25,000 by 1880. These numbers were doubled in a matter of months to 27,000 on the front and some 42,000 total – an army larger than Argentina's at the height of the Paraguayan War. A single detachment in Araucania – now facing revolts due to the power vacuum in the region – was 4,500 (Benavides Santos, 1972, 117).

The Peruvian army also mobilized greatly for the defense of its capital. The army of Lima was comprised of the armies of the center and the north plus all able men from eighteen to fifty years old living in the city or the vicinity, virtually "the entire male population of the capital" drilling every day and making a force of 25,000 to 32,000 men (Sater, 2007, 259, 274).[34] The armies of both countries at this point had acquired dimensions that would have been impossible to conceive of just one year before. Lima was in a state of full mobilization, with yet another battery of taxes being levied from the elites.[35]

After its defeat in the Battle of Chorrillos on January 13, 1881, the Peruvian army retreated to a second line of defense, heavily armed with trenches and machine guns. Yet General Baquedano charged again, and after the Battle of Miraflores on January 15, 1881, Lima was finally abandoned. Piérola left the city to mount a resistance in the highlands, the six fortresses surrounding the Callao were destroyed, and the seven remaining ships of the Peruvian fleet were sunk. The Peruvian economy completely collapsed. The *billetes fiscales* issued by the government became worthless, and due to the lack of trust in the government-issued currency, silver coin became the de facto means of payment thereafter.

Defeat produced the divisive effects classical bellicist theory would expect. Peruvian peripheral elites in occupied Lima named Francisco García Calderón provisional president on February 22, 1881, who reinstated the previous constitution and started peace talks. A former minister of Prado and close to the *civilistas*, García Calderón named Montero his vice-president, gaining the support of the Army of the North.[36] Since Piérola still claimed to be president, he declared all participants in the new cabinet in Lima to be traitors under the penalty of death and called for a Congress to be held in Ayacuacho on June 6, 1881. Yet the American diplomatic intervention on the side of García Calderón

34 According to another estimate, the *ejército de línea* amounted to some 20,000 men and the militias to another 25,000, totaling 45,000 men (Benavides Santos, 1972, 127).

35 "To finance this new citizen reserve army, the Peruvian government imposed a special tax upon the propertied classes whose rights and interests the army was called upon to defend and protect. It is interesting to note that the government did not collect this tax: instead, the authorities hired a tax farmer, who, in return for a 5 per cent commission, contracted to amass the funds, which the government promised to use solely to provide equipment to the military" (Sater, 2007, 272).

36 The Peruvian army was divided into three forces: the armies of the south, the center, and the north. While these had so far acted under the command of Lima, in the new situation each army became almost completely independent and often confronted the others.

increased hopes that a face-saving peace could be achieved, weakening Piérola's position before his men (Burr, 1974, 156). Eventually Andrés Avelino Cáceres – Piérola's commander of the Army of the Center – took charge of the resistance in the sierra.

On the Chilean side, both the consolidation of the party in power and constitutional continuity seemed secured by victory. Confident that surrender would soon follow, Pinto ordered his battalions' most important military commanders back to Chile. Many of these men would vote in the June elections, which featured only one ticket with the name of Santa María. The central elites formed a highly cohesive bloc, and no opposition party dared present an alternative to the state-building wartime coalition. Baquedano, the only figure that could match Santa María in popularity, stepped down from the contest (Sater, 2007, 299).[37] On September 18, 1881, Santa María succeeded Pinto as the new president of Chile in the most ordered of contexts. Unlike Pinto, the incoming president did not have to seek congressional alliances in order to govern. Now the *liberales* were running the state alone and virtually unchallenged.

The fall of Lima opened the last long act of the war, characterized by two years of Peruvian resistance in the inlands. While the Chileans were hopeful that García Calderón would accept a peace treaty conceding Tarapacá and selling Tacna and Arica, they soon realized the terms would be unacceptable as long as the *montoneras* continued to shine a light of hope. In this situation Chile would have to defeat the *caudillos* Cáceres and Piérola and occupy the departments of Junín and Arequipa with some 5,000 men each. The 12,000 Chilean troops stationed in Lima – some 1,000 out of service due to endemic diseases – would not be fit for the task.

The peace terms proposed during this period could have been accepted if it were not for the deep divisions that persisted among Peruvian elites. As long as "*civilistas* and *pierolistas* combatted each other with the same hatred they felt for the invader – or perhaps more – all efforts to conciliate were rejected, for the offenses against each other were too grave and the submission of one faction to the other was impossible." As Bulnes (1976, 226) notes, "The only thing they agreed upon was in rejecting the Chilean claims."

Finally, General Miguel Iglesias – who succeeded Montero as chief of the Army of the North – formed a new government in Cajamarca and issued the *Manifiesto de Montán*, calling for a peace treaty. At this point Peru was so worn out and badly divided that it could not drive out the Chileans even if, as a US diplomat noted, this was not an impossible task:

> The situation of Peru itself is that of a state without credit, without arms, and without resources, as it is without spirit to defend itself. The entire force of the enemy in the

[37] Baquedano then left the party, leading to a fracture of the state-building camp. The exclusion from the coalition of the charismatic wartime leader who had conquered Lima explains in part why Chile would experience a civil war between two statist factions soon afterward.

country does not exceed 18,000 men of all arms, a force so small that the weight of numbers, armed only with machetes, would overcome it were the Peruvians united and determined. But they are badly divided while anarchy and lawlessness has possession over large areas of the country ... it is apparent to me that the Peruvians, if left free to elect, could not organize a government. Their party antagonisms and personal feuds are too bitter, while personal interests govern all alike.[38]

Finally, the Chilean government would organize a final campaign to subdue the rebels. In the Battle of Huamachuco on July 10, 1883, 1,300 Chilean soldiers defeated the 4,000-strong army of Cáceres. Grasping the momentum, Iglesias and the Chilean occupying forces in Lima signed the Treaty of Ancón on October 20, 1883. The treaty stipulated the permanent secession of Tarapacá to Chile and a ten-year concession of Arica and Tacna, after which local referendums would decide which country had the right to buy each territory. A few days after the signatures, an expedition was organized to take Ayacucho, which departed on October 24, 1883, and was victorious every step of the way. Having secured this victory and the election of Iglesias as Peruvian president, the Chilean forces left Lima in August 1884.

Figure 8.2 provides a synthesis of this section, showing the concurrence of events on the battlefield and changes in the domestic balance between central and peripheral elites. At least three events clearly produced the expected domestic reaction: the late 1879 Chilean victories on land and sea, the early 1880 Peruvian defeats in Tacna and Arica, and the 1881 occupation of Lima all strengthened the coalition of central elites in Chile and weakened it in Peru.

8.4 THE AFTERMATH: DIVERGING INSTITUTIONS AND CAPACITY

In his national message of 1883, Chilean president Santa María threatened to use all the power of the state to attack the peripheral elite of conservatives, in particular its clerical wing. Tension with the Pope had remained high despite all attempts by Santiago to conciliate the election of a moderate archbishop. During the war, the Catholic Church clearly favored Peru, in particular after Piérola made the Archbishop of Lima a member of his council of state. Resenting the intransigency of the Pope, Santa María announced a program to remove all births and deaths registers from the hands of the Church and transfer them to the state. Moreover, he instituted civil marriage, ensured freedom of religion, and allowed the burial of people of any faith in cemeteries hitherto Catholic (Blakemore, 1993, 37). Balmaceda, then minister of the interior, was charged with implementing the new policies, winning him the utmost hatred of the conservatives.

[38] Letter of US Ambassador to Peru Seth L. Phelps to Secretary of State Frederick T. Frelinghuysen. October 3, 1883. US National Archives T-52/38.

Peru	Chile	Year	Battlefield
Prado aligns with the civilistas broadening the war coalition and mobilizes	Pinto conforms an all-liberal cabinet excluding the peripheral elite of conservatives	1879	Occupation of Antofagasta Battle of Iquique (Chilean victory) Battle of Angamos Battle of Tarapacá (Chilean victories)
Piérola performs a coup backed by peripheral elites against the war	Strengthened, the war coalition now draws plans for the annexation of Southern Peru	1880	Battle of Tacna Battle of Arica (Chilean victories)
Piérola's coalition weakens and civilistas have the political upper hand	Emboldened, Chilean central elites support plans to invade and occupy Lima General Baquedano received as a war hero	1881	Fall of Lima (Chilean victory)
Piérola leaves for Arequipa and eventually joins Cáceres in civil war against Lima, producing the de facto secession of the southern departments Rebellion of Iglesias produces the de facto secession of the northern departments	Minister of War Domingo Santa María wins the election unopposed Chile sends a new expeditionary force	1882 1883	Battle of Huamachuco (Chilean victory)
Weak Iglesias government reliant on Chilean troops	Liberal hegemony		Treaty of Ancón

FIGURE 8.2 War of the Pacific timeline

The presidency of Santa María, which looked undoubtedly authoritarian from the perspective of a conservative minority, was vastly legitimated by the military victory. With broad popular support and the backing of the returning Chilean forces, the ruling party won the 1885 parliamentary elections by a landslide. Although fraudulent and violent, the elections showed the extent to which *liberales* were now hegemonic, for only one conservative deputy was elected. In the 1886 presidential elections, Balmaceda became the liberal candidate and won with 98 percent of the vote.[39] The war arguably helped consolidate the liberal party, which was comparatively weak before the war, into a strong organization with wide nationalistic appeal to the masses (Remmer, 1984, 18).

The consolidation of the central elites was also favored by economic developments. As we have seen, Chile entered the war in a context of international recession and lack of international credit. The resort to debt monetization could have proven catastrophic, but after the war a virtual monopoly over the nitrate trade provided Chile with substantial assets and revenue to build the necessary confidence in the currency. "As the nitrate took over from copper and silver, the material progress undergone in the half-century or so before the war soon begun to look modest in comparison with the boom of the 1880s" (Collier, 1993, 31). As territorial expansion consolidated, "from a contribution of 5.52 per cent of national revenue in 1880, export taxes on nitrate and iodine (a by-product) rose to 33.77 per cent in 1885, and to 52.06 per cent in 1890" (Blakemore, 1993, 41). In this way Chile could have become a victim of a Dutch disease, but it managed to avoid it through investment and taxation (Palma, 2000).

Much of this surplus was destined to fuel public investment in one particular infrastructural project above all: railroads. The War of the Pacific had highlighted the inefficiencies of operating multiple lines under different administrations, so Santa María called Congress to an extraordinary session and by law of January 4, 1884, all lines were put under the control of a single director general. The *Empresa de Ferrocarriles del Estado de Chile* was born, which in 1884 administered some 500 miles of rail (Alliende, 1993, 56). Once president, Balmaceda designed a plan to expand the railroads 2,000 miles in six years (Sagredo, 2001, 45). "The main component of Chilean spending was railways ... around 30 per cent of the public budget in this period was used in constructing railways" (Paredes, 2013, 140, in Humud, 1969, 58). The expansion of the state during the Balmaceda administration is difficult to exaggerate:

39 Again, the liberals ran virtually alone. The Partido Nacional and Partido Radical proposed José Francisco Vergara – yet another state builder and key figure who favored offensive campaigns during the war. The conservatives did not participate. The *nacionales* and *radicales* would thereafter become the opposition, joining the so-called freelance liberals or *liberales sueltos*, for whom "the practice of electoral intervention had become odious" (Blakemore, 1993, 42).

There was to be heavy public spending on major construction projects such as railways and docks, and in social investment, particularly education, colonization, and municipal buildings. Additional expenditure was also allocated to the strengthening of Chile's military capabilities, including new ships off the line, and adequate barracks and military schools.... A new ministry of industry and public works was created in 1887, and within a year it was assigned more than one-fifth of the national budget, while the ministry of education took one-seventh.... Government intentions were translated into action: from a school enrollment of some 79,000 in 1886, the number rose to 150,000 in 1890; railway construction was pushed ahead, assisted in the south by the bridging of the Bío-Bío, Chile's wildest river; the great dry dock at Talcahuano was completed and a canal was built along Santiago's own river, the Mapocho. (Blakemore, 1993, 47)

The creation of the Ministry of Public Works – whose corps of engineers was in charge of supervising all private infrastructural projects in the country and expanding public ones – was a powerful development. It created a new bureaucracy with a powerful capacity for lobbying and consuming a large extent of the public revenue (Guajardo, 2007). Yet the state institution that most clearly consolidated after the war was the military.

The state-building literature has paid limited attention to how the War of the Pacific transformed the Chilean military and its relation to politics. Authors like Hillel Soifer (2015, 208), who note how the size of the Chilean military spikes during the war, point to the demobilization of most of the army after the war as a reason to dismiss the topic. Similarly Ryan Saylor (2014, 65) argues that this war did not lead to state formation because most of the army demobilized once the war was over. Yet both authors report that after the war, the army remained at least 60 percent larger than it was before the war.[40]

Far more important than this permanent increase in the size of the armed forces is how the war "forced the army into the lives of civilians to an extent not seen before" (Collier and Sater, 2004, 137), the role that the military would come to play in politics, and the level of professionalization that the armed forces would acquire after the war. Chile became known as "the Prussia of Latin America" and developed one of the most influential and strongest militaries in the region.

The new political role of the Chilean army is hard to overstate. Sotomayor had become the most popular political figure in the country after the Tarapacá campaign, and his successor in the command of the army, Baquedano, became equally popular after him. The charismatic leadership and prestige acquired by these military men made them central political figures.

As a corporation, the armed forces were strengthened by victory as well, and they used this political influence to push for the expansion of the southern frontier, fighting the Mapuche tribes, who had risen in Araucania in 1880–1882. "Victory achieved, seasoned troops were sent south where they inflicted a

40 No matter the sources we use and the time periods we compare, the relative increase in the size of the military between the pre- and postwar periods in Chile is very clear. That the size of the army would shrink comparatively after the war is only natural, for after the occupation of Lima was over, there was little reason for such a force.

final and irrevocable defeat upon the rebels" (Blakemore, 1993, 43; Jones, 2013, 124). New forts were built in Temuco and Villarrica, and the military oversaw the colonization of the south, opening agencies in Europe that recruited more than 10,000 settlers in a decade.

In the following years a process of institutional reform began that would make the Chilean military the most modern of Latin America by the end of the century. "The push for thorough reform was irresistible. Modernization was backed by a powerful coalition of civil-military leaders" (Resende-Santos, 2007, 131). In 1885 a German delegation arrived in Chile with the mission of reorganizing the military. After reforming the Military School, the delegation founded Chile's Military Academy in 1886 and subsequently established specialized schools for the infantry, cavalry, and engineers (Arancibia Clavel, 2007). Officers started to be regularly sent to Europe for training. In 1889 and 1890 two German loans were extended to finance the acquisition of Mauser rifles, beginning a broad modernization of equipment that would last at least a decade.

In the elections of 1888, the peripheral elite of conservatives would be utterly defeated once more, and they could only return to being a relevant force as part of a coalition, moderating their program in a way that approximated the *nacionales* and others mostly concerned with free and fair elections. Besides the moderating influence of the pretorian army, the War of the Pacific consolidated a new class of politicians, different from the conservative *estancieros* of yore. Most of the Chilean elite now engaged in the type of commercial and financial activities that depended very much on the state protection of their property and orderly administration of national resources. As an authority puts it:

> When Chile was winning the War of the Pacific, during the presidency of Santa María and then with Balmaceda, we find that the social strata from which state leaders used to come since colonial times – i.e., the *haciendas* – had suffered a great transformation. To the landowners now followed rich copper and silver miners, pioneers of the saltpeter industry, and bankers. (Góngora, 1994, 48)

The transformative effect that the war had had on Chilean politics became clear in 1891. As often happens with leaders that preside over a swift concentration of power immediately after victory, Balmaceda soon entered into a bitter confrontation with the legislature, which by 1889 had started to veto his ministers and in late 1890 decided it would not approve the budget for the following year. On January 1, 1891, after Balmaceda tried to pass the budget by presidential decree, Congress voted to depose him, triggering a constitutional crisis. Admiral Jorge Montt offered his support to the legislators, who sailed north on the *Blanco Encalada* and the *Esmeralda* to organize the rebellion. Thereafter, a confrontation between the army and the navy defined the partisan struggle. At the end of the day, the military had taken hold of the state. Baquedano became president for a brief period, and Montt himself oversaw the reforms in favor of a more parliamentarian system as the new president. The process of state modernization and military mobilization accelerated.

Chile became the first Latin American state to introduce mandatory military service in 1901 (Resende-Santos, 2007, 136). While the military expanded its influence, state bureaucrats ran a quiet revolution in accounting, transport, and construction (Crowther, 1973), as "the political deadlock may have made it easier for engineers and bureaucrats in these sectors to gain autonomy by presenting themselves as a non-political force" (Paredes, 2013, 164). Maritza Paredes (2013, 166) shows that from 1900 to 1918, the number of employees in the Ministry of the Interior increased sixfold – from 1,935 to 13,828 – while the state bureaucracy tripled in size overall.

The civil war of 1891 brought about a new period in Chilean political history known as the Parliamentary Era (1891–1925), characterized by clearer limits to the power of the president and the organization of the party system around two coalitions: the *Coalición Conservadora* and the *Alianza Liberal*. During this new era the friction between the two coalitions revolved not around state building but mostly around the democratic nature of the political regime – that is, the rules to access the state. Most of these conflicts, however, were resolved institutionally. Only one radical revolt took place in 1905, which was quickly quashed. The new role of the military as overseer of politics and protector of the state led to a consensus over the fact that education, justice, policing, and statistics could not be fully delegated to local leaders and the Church, as in the times of the conservative republic.

In the following years Chile and Argentina engaged in a formidable arms race, with both countries importing increasingly sophisticated weaponry and nearly going to war on several occasions between 1898 and 1902. The victories of Argentina and Chile in the largest wars of nineteenth-century South America certainly contributed to strengthening their militaries, energizing nationalist sentiments, and stiffening their position with regard to their territorial disputes. This rivalry continued to fuel state building on both sides of the border.

While the negative effects of the War of the Pacific on revenue collection and railway construction in Peru over the long term has been clearly documented in Chapter 5, Figure 8.3 looks at some proxies of state strength that are available for Bolivia, Chile, and Peru throughout the nineteenth century to illustrate how the pattern generalizes to them. A look at permanent diplomatic representation abroad (Singer and Small, 1966; Bayer, 2006), for example, shows how, despite a larger Peruvian diplomatic network, Chile takes over in the following decade.

Similarly, GDP per capita measures from the Maddison Project (Bolt et al., 2018) show Chile on a clear upward trajectory since the beginning of the series – which matches our knowledge about victory in the War of the Confederation (1837–1839) – and receiving a clear boost after the War of the Pacific. Conversely, Peru enters the series on a relatively flat or downward

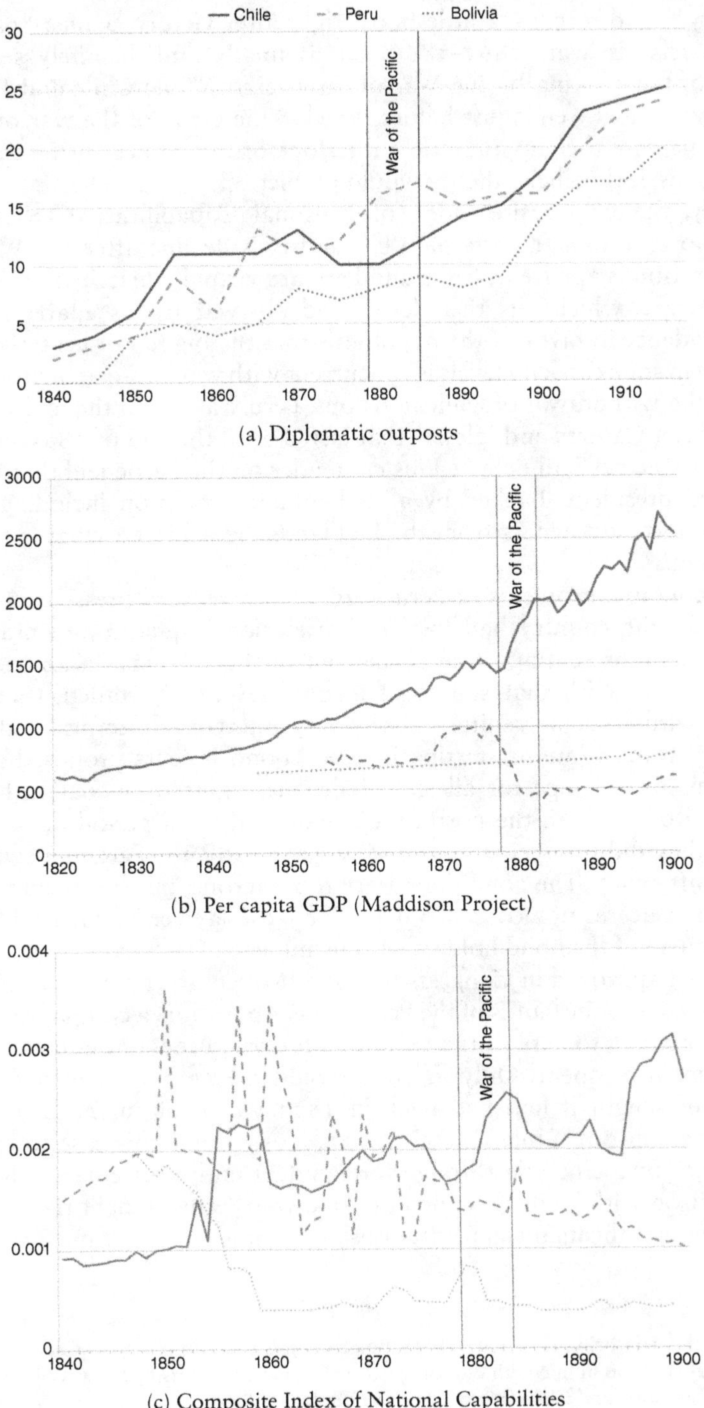

(a) Diplomatic outposts

(b) Per capita GDP (Maddison Project)

(c) Composite Index of National Capabilities

FIGURE 8.3 Postwar trajectories in Bolivia, Chile, and Peru

trajectory[41] and receives a little boost right after victory against Spain in the Chincha Islands War (1865–1866) but is finally and definitely sent to the bottom of the ranking by the War of the Pacific. While Chile and Peru seem to follow parallel trends just before the war, the effect of the war outcome is to both increase the gap and affect the slope of the two countries in the long term, as classical bellicist theory would predict.

Finally, the Composite Index of National Capabilities (CINC) (Singer, 1988) shows a similar pattern. While Bolivia's decline after the War of the Confederation is apparent, Chile and Peru are virtually matched until the War of the Pacific, which sets their levels and postwar trends apart. The figure shows evidence in favor of the hypothesis that the big flip or center–periphery inversion in state capacity levels is concurrent with wars instead of other shocks.

With the withdrawal of Chilean troops, Peru was left in the midst of a civil war between Cáceres and Iglesias that lasted until the end of 1885. It was not until after Cáceres had defeated his contender on the battlefield that he would be elected president. Backed by a civil–military coalition including military *caudillos* and landowners from the highlands, he achieved what is known as a *pax cacerista*.

The economic problems of Peru were, of course, very pressing. As a result of the war, the country had lost territories rich in guano and nitrates, the two exports representing some 70 percent of the customs duties collected in pre-war years. With that source of income severely curtailed, Cáceres had to settle with foreign creditors in the very unfavorable terms of the Grace Contract. In negotiations starting in 1886, bond holders proposed a general settlement in exchange for all state railroads, rights over coal and mercury mines and oil fields in the north, plus guano, all for a period of seventy-five years. If they did not secure a rent of 700,000 GBP, the Peruvian state would pay the difference. The conditions were too onerous, but under dire financial conditions Cáceres named Pedro del Solar – the lawyer of Michael P. Grace, representative of the bond holders – prime minister. Del Solar managed to have the contract approved in Congress by 1889 (Miller, 2011, 173–194). Peruvian trains passed into the hands of the Peruvian Corporation, a company created by the bond holders to exploit the existing infrastructure without compromising any further investment. Only in 1910 would the Peruvian railroad network recover the length it had had back in 1875 when the financial crisis froze railroad expansion. While Queralt (2022, 43–45) uses this case to exemplify the perils of financing war through foreign debt under extreme conditionality, a comparison with Chile demonstrates that this Peruvian debt trap was not a consequence of the financial institutions of the time but of the impact of defeat.

[41] Despite the data being censored, other estimates suggest the trajectory was negative until the 1860s. This is also in line with our knowledge of Peruvian defeats by Great Colombia (1828–1829), Argentina and Chile (1837–1839), and Bolivia (1841).

To ensure governability, Cáceres also struck a fiscal decentralization deal with the eighteen departments that comprised Peru. His law of fiscal decentralization, passed in 1886, could not have been more different from that of the *civilistas*. As his own proponents recognized, this new law did not entail administrative decentralization – and therefore bureaucratization at the local level – but decentralization of revenue alone, strengthening the traditional orders led by peripheral elites (Manrique, 1988). Deputy Eleuterio Macedo – a vociferous opponent of the Grace Contract and the Peruvian Corporation – said of the law, "This will lead to disorder, and the most absolute lack of a system of government" (cited in Planas, 1998, 245). Under the new law, the departments were responsible for collecting most of the taxes (Contreras and Cueto, 2004, 176), including the old Indian tribute – abolished three decades before – which was reinstated in 1885 (McEvoy, 1997, 260). In the absence of administrative decentralization or a strong revenue source for the national state, this tilted the balance of power in favor of the *breñeros* – the soldiers of Cáceres, who became powerful strongmen at the level of the departments and municipalities (McEvoy, 1997, 289). All in all: "The Cáceres government of the immediate postwar period had sought political stability and fiscal recovery via radical decentralization that empowered local elites." As Soifer (2015, 119) notes, "The consequences both in fiscal terms and in terms of stability were strikingly negative, as highlighted by the weakness of the state during this period."

The clearest casualty of the war was the *civilista* project of state formation. "The war with Chile in 1879 ended up exterminating the social, political, ideological, and even geographical bases of the project" (Nieto and Vito, 2005, 150). One problem of Peruvian politics after the war seems to be a virtual deadlock between the coastal and urban elites – those who used to back the Partido Civil on the one hand and the traditional rural and highland elites on the other (Cotler, 1978). Also a new dynamic of fragmentation ensued, which cut across many strata of society, not just the central and peripheral elites. The political stage could be more properly pictured as a continuous fight between peripheral elites. "The destruction of the oligarchical state, as a product of the Chilean invasion and occupation, provoked the direct confrontation between the leaders and subordinates, as well as between the different political factions, *caciques* and *caudillos*" (Bonilla, 1980, 203). Regionalism would be accentuated by the rise of briefly successful local clans (Gilbert, 1977). Traditional elites from the highlands would secure patronage and local autonomy in exchange for electoral support for the executive (Miller, 1976). Instead of state officials, now *gamonales* would be in control of politics at the local level. Maritza Paredes notes how this contrasted starkly with Chile:

In Chile, competing sectors and interests, which coexisted with interlocking, elitist networks, led to the creation of institutional forms of negotiation, the building of strong political organizations and a greater institutional involvement of elites in policy making. This resulted in the development of state capacity. Such a thing did not occur in Peru. Instead, in the case of Peru, the most significant aspect of elites at the time was that they continued to be fragmented along regional lines. (Paredes, 2013, 212)

Although the former central elite of *civilistas* had initially seen Cáceres as the only possible solution to the postwar chaos, soon the situation became critical, as the *caudillo* began to institute an authoritarian and militaristic regime with no place for the central elites of yore. In 1890 he personally selected his vice-president and right hand, Remigio Morales Bermúdez, as his successor. Bermúdez "represented the military sectors, specially the *breñeros* now deeply embedded in the Peruvian state apparatus" (McEvoy, 1997, 290), and thus was harshly resented by both civilians and factious military from different corners of Peru, who would not accept a Cáceres dictatorship for long. This opposition would eventually be spearheaded by the surreptitious Piérola, who escaped jail once again in 1890 and started planning a coup from abroad.

Several rebellions took place in the army and navy during the Cáceres and Bermúdez administrations, particularly due to the huge reduction in army size that took place after the war. While Chile had an army that had quadrupled in size a decade after the war, the Peruvian military was at roughly prewar levels and with much lower salary and education. The last cohort graduated from the Military College in 1877 and the officers running the armed forces were largely unprofessional. Equipment was a cause for great concern as well. The case of the navy was particularly critical. Having scuttled all its fleet, Peru was only able to acquire one cruise ship after the war and at great effort. Once the greatest navy in Latin America, the Peruvian fleet was comparable to that of Ecuador – its smaller neighbor to the north – at the same time as Chile was entering a dreadnought race against Argentina and Brazil.

After the death of Bermúdez, Piérola supported the candidacy of del Solar from his new exile in Valparaiso, but Cáceres was quick to retake power. Foreseeing the continuation of the Cáceres dictatorship, a great coalition formed around Píerola to support a coup. Even the *civilistas* participated in the general rebellion that led Piérola to government in 1895, now considered by them the lesser evil. Economic growth provided some stability from then on, but the Civil Party had drastically reduced its aspirations. No relevant reforms took place that could return Peru to its previous glory in the Pacific.

9

War and the State in Mexico and Central America

Despite being the largest country in Hispanic America, Mexico has been conspicuously absent as a case study in the recent state formation literature (Kurtz, 2013; Saylor, 2014; Soifer, 2015). Only Mazzuca (2021, 270) covers the case in some detail, pointing out that although Mexico has been always considered a case of state failure due to its chronic fiscal problems, weak armies, and territorial losses, the "hidden success" of Mexico – in particular its capacity to monopolize violence since the 1870s – has remained unaddressed and deserves more attention.

In this chapter I show that war is a key missing piece of this Mexican puzzle. The threat of European and American invasion fueled early state-building attempts. After the war against the United States (1846–1848), which resulted in the loss of half its territory, Mexico collapsed into an era of anarchy. While local threats to peripheral elites – for example, the Caste Wars in Yucatán – and Washington's concern with the stability of its southern border prevented further territorial disintegration, only victory against France can explain Mexico's increases in state capacity since the 1870s.

This case is unique in that it combines a great defeat in the Mexican–American War (1846–1848) and a great victory in the Franco-Mexican War (1861–1867), both producing the long-term effects on the military and political parties that are to be expected according to classical bellicist theory. This chapter will look at how these and other conflicts relate to constitutional changes, the charismatic legitimacy of figures such as Santa Anna, Benito Juárez, and Porfirio Díaz, and the balance between central and peripheral elites.

My narrative is organized into four sections. In Section 9.1 I follow the evolution of the Mexican constitution from that of an empire (1822–1823) to that of a federal republic (1824–1835) and a unitarian republic (1836–1846) as it responds to external pressures. Then Section 9.2 illustrates the bellicist dynamics that took place during the Mexican–American War and its aftermath.

Leaving Mexico in a state of post-defeat collapse, I propose a brief detour to focus on Costa Rica in Section 9.3 – which, like Uruguay, is a curious outlier in state capacity levels until the present day. In this section I show how Costa Rican exceptionalism could be explained by its victory in the National Campaign (1856–1857) against American filibuster William Walker. Finally, Section 9.4 goes back to Mexico, testing bellicist predictions during the Second French Intervention and discussing the state institutions left by victory.

9.1 FROM INDEPENDENCE TO THE TEXAN REVOLUTION

As with Peru, the other colonial center in Spanish America, the independence of Mexico is better understood as a defeat of creole elites and the colonial state. Unlike on the peripheries of the Spanish Empire, the revolution was not led by prominent urban aristocrats but by priests representing disenfranchised elements of society. Very much like Lima at the time, Mexico City – capital of the Viceroyalty of New Spain – remained loyal, and conspiracies by members of the elite were "uncovered and crushed without difficulty" (Alba, 1982, 9). After the popular revolts led by Miguel Hidalgo and José María Morelos (1810–1815) were quelled, the independence movement became a rural guerrilla scattered across the country, with Vicente Guerrero as the most prominent of these outcasts. Since peripheral *caudillos* opposed the central state, in the Mexican case mobilization of royalist militias generated state capacity, while insurgents undermined it (Arias and de la Calle, 2021). Independence, overall, was a state-weakening event (Fowler, 1998).

Only when independence became inevitable did elites rally around Agustín de Iturbide, a royalist general who repressed the early independence movement. Iturbide drafted the Plan de Iguala of February 21, 1821, which offered the crown of Mexico to the Bourbons. Spanish general Juan O'Donojú had to accept the terms of this plan at Veracruz for *realistas* in Mexico City to be comfortable with it, and it was only after four members of the Spanish dynasty rejected the offer that Iturbide was crowned Emperor of Mexico himself. As novelist Octavio Paz (1982, 51) put it, "These differences influenced the later history of our countries. The Independence movement in South America began with a continent-wide victory: San Martín liberated half of the continent, Bolívar the other half. They created great states and confederations." Mexico lacked this initial impulse.

Mexican independence thus did not see the formation of regular republican armies that characterized the South American experiences. Instead the richest kingdom of the Spanish Empire imploded both politically and economically. The minting of coins declined from 222 million pesos per year before the Wars of Independence to 10 million thereafter (Bazant, 1991, 3). The Catholic Church, a pillar of the colonial political order, was decimated in its ranks and lost almost two-thirds of its economic power due to the decline of the tithe

(Bazant, 1985, 425). The royal bureaucracy virtually lost all power, which was transferred to a factional army.

Factionalism among conservatives was rife. Bourbonists requesting the coronation of a European monarch continued to be a powerful political club in Mexico City. Meanwhile, liberals impugned Iturbide and saw him as the leader of a counterrevolution (Brading, 1985, 56; Mallon, 2010, 285). The alliance between Church, state, and landed elites, which was necessary to centralize power (Brading, 1991, 642), forced the conservative government to pursue a revolutionary rhetoric, leading conservatives like Lucas Alaman (1985, 582) (cited in Shawcross, 2018, 83), to express that "the generation that witnessed [Mexican independence] was fooled in such a way that it came to believe the opposite of what it saw."

Although Iturbide succeeded in forming a coalition of conservatives and liberals and was crowned emperor on July 21, 1822, only weeks after his coronation he had imprisoned nineteen members of Congress and several army officers (Bazant, 1985, 428). The hostility of his adversaries led him to close Congress on October 31 of that same year, and, facing a republican rebellion of the armed forces commanded by General Antonio López de Santa Anna, he was forced to abdicate on March 19, 1823. In the process, Mexico lost Central America and power shifted to a peripheral elite of local *caudillos* – the heroes of the early independence movement – and liberals.

During the first quarter century after independence, the main cleavage in Mexican politics was that between conservatives and liberals. Conservatives, which in this first stage tended to be centralists and monarchists, were predominant in Mexico City. As Victor Alba (1982, 12) puts it, "The capital and the wealthy cities formed a world apart, they were the state, their leading figures were men who fought against independence for eleven years and accepted it only to appropriate it." Yet after the failure of those elites to keep the country together, the pendulum of power swung to the side of the liberals, who were mostly of federalist persuasion and concentrated in more peripheral regions.

The federalist Constitution of 1824 reflected the centrifugal tendencies we would expect to prevail after the defeat of Mexico City by the peripheries. During the tenure of Guadalupe Victoria (1824–1828), attempts at centralization were prevented. Alamán, who had been named Minister of State in 1825 and succeeded in attracting an important influx of British investment (Bazant, 1985, 430), was ousted from government in less than a year, and with that, the last attempts at centralization were virtually suspended. "Alamán's defeat was a triumph for the centrifugal forces in Mexico" (Byrd Simpson, 1982, 65).

When a conspiracy to restore Spanish rule was discovered in January 1827, Guadalupe Victoria was forced to expel the Spanish middle class of *gachupines*, key to the administration and the army. Centralist conservatives were widely accused of treason, and peripheral *caudillos* like Guerrero, who wanted nothing less than the preservation of the autonomy of their feuds, gained more influence

(Bazant, 1991, 10). Finally, despite losing the elections, Guerrero took power after the Parián Riot of 1828 and allied with Santa Anna (Arrom, 1988, 12). In the next six years, Mexico would be governed by twelve heads of state, three of whom rose to power through rebellion (Anna, 1998).

During this period the figure of Santa Anna began to gain prominence. Initially at the service of peripheral elites like the liberal Guerrero, Santa Anna built a reputation on the battlefield (Byrd Simpson, 1982, 62) and quickly became a central figure around whom other warlords would converge when facing an external threat. On July 26, 1829, when a small Spanish contingent attempted to reconquer Mexico, the invasion "served to cause a temporary lull in the factional political conflict as the nation rallied to the call for unity" (Bazant, 1991, 11). In the Battle of Tampico, 8,000 Mexicans easily defeated a detachment of 3,500 royalists, boosting the legitimacy of Santa Anna, who leveraged the strategic location of his feud, Veracruz, to become the main military leader. Veracruz was the main port on the Gulf of Mexico and would be attacked systematically by foreign powers throughout the nineteenth century, providing Santa Anna with numerous opportunities to promote himself as a national hero. After Tampico, for example, Santa Anna was named Benemérito de la Patria, the highest honor bestowed by the Mexican government.

The war with Spain also prompted Guerrero to expel *peninsulares* residing in the country and reform the tax system, "shifting the burden onto medium and large businesses, foreigners, and the rich" (Henderson, 2007, 63) and raising tariffs. The abolition of slavery on September 15, 1829, only four days after victory in Tampico, also shows how the national state momentarily strengthened vis-à-vis *hacendados* and local elites. However, the impact of this militarized dispute – total battle deaths were around 350, short of a war as conventionally defined (Clodfelter, 2017, 301) – was limited and "the patriotic fervor did not last long" (Henderson, 2007, 64). Although the conservatives did win the elections in 1830 and Alamán was given a central role in the cabinet, only limited state-strengthening reforms could be implemented. In the new climate of international peace, centrifugal tendencies resumed.

In a way, the meagre size of the royalist detachment demonstrated that Spain could not retake Mexico anytime soon and strengthened Guerrero as a *caudillo*. Now outside the government, he initiated a new revolt against Mexico City. When he was captured and executed, the death of this national independence hero of indigenous background led to widespread rebellion against the national government. In 1832 Santa Anna rebelled too and took control of the Veracruz customs, forcing the resignation of the sitting president. He thereafter won the 1833 elections and retired to his feud, leaving his vice-president, Valentín Gómez Farías – a radical liberal – in charge of limiting special jurisdictions, reducing the size of the army, and decentralizing power to subnational states.

Yet in the following year or so, the political mood in Mexico City started to change. In the state of Texas, the power shift from central to peripheral elites was coupled with an influx of foreign settlers. These Texians (English-speaking settlers) had refused to accept the abolition of slavery, leading the Mexican government to ban new settlers in 1830. Yet, taking advantage of Santa Anna's revolt in 1832, Texians expelled Mexican troops from the state and threatened secession if their demands were not met (Vazquez, 1997). Indirectly, this meant the possibility of a war with the United States and thus triggered a new process of centralization. According to Justo Sierra (1982, 106), "a war with Texas did not preoccupy the Mexicans; what did overcast the entire period of centralism was the fear of a war with the United States."

Santa Anna, who had initially supported Gómez Farías's decentralization, noted that public support was swinging back to the conservatives and switched allegiances in 1834. After quelling a rebellion in the state of Zacatecas, he returned to Mexico City, dissolved Congress, and governed as a dictator for eight months. Then he hand picked a conservative Congress and suspended the constitution. The conservatives were back in power, and with them the project of centralization gained new impulse.[1]

The suspension of the federalist constitution under Santa Anna sent shivers down the spines of local elites, who feared the end of their autonomy. Some historians adduce that "when centralization triumphed during 1834 in the person of Santa Anna, the Texans refused to accept his new constitution" (Bauer, 1974, 5). Other historians assert that "the fear of losing Texas was used by a small group of centralists to strengthen their position that federalism favored secessionism" (Vázquez and Meyer, 1985, 50). That the two processes were intertwined is clear by Sam Houston's call for volunteers of December 12, 1835, being closely followed by Santa Anna's proclamation of the new constitution, usually referred to as the Seven Laws, on December 15. The Seven Laws curtailed the autonomy of states, turning them into mere departments with governors appointed by the president. Spain recognized the independence of Mexico in that same year, further reinforcing the conservative constitution and the coalition behind it.

1 As in the case of Brazil, the clear identification of liberals and conservatives with the state formation process – that is, as central or peripheral elites – is rather difficult, at least until the *liberales puros* take the center of the liberal stage in the 1850s. Conservatives, for example, tended to favor a centralized government while liberals favored federalism, which in general reinforces local elites and weakens the national state. Liberals in the opposition, on the other hand, were courted as local allies by external actors like the Americans – who would quietly support the Texan Revolution in 1836 – and the French – who would blockade Veracruz during the so-called Pastry War of 1838 – since they focused mostly on preserving the autonomy of Mexican states and reducing the influence of the army (Shawcross, 2018, 58). Yet despite their centralist inclinations – related to their monarchical, traditionalist views – conservatives also backed the interests of parochial and peripheral elites, such as the Church and landowners. Therefore, later in the century, when liberals promoted the centralization of state functions like education and civil registry, they were better represented as peripheral elites. Here I use the term "conservative" to refer to "a group of politicians who were more inclined to preserve colonial institutions in post-independent Mexico" (Shawcross, 2018, 9).

The rebellion in Texas thus provided new fuel for the centralist project. "New taxes were levied, one on top of another" (Sierra, 1982, 108), although low productivity made it difficult to collect enough to maintain a large standing army. After a costly victory at the Alamo on March 6, 1836, which emboldened Santa Anna to continue the campaign, he was defeated in the Battle of San Jacinto on April 21 and taken prisoner. Less than a month after the defeat, revolts against the central government ensued throughout Mexico. In Yucatán, angry local elites, who had seen prices and taxes increase due to the war with Texas, rose up in arms on May 2, 1836, and declared a return to a federalist constitution. A federalist *pronunciamiento* followed in Oaxaca on June 5, 1836. A few months later a revolt ensued in Veracruz, the very state of Santa Anna, which would last two years. Due to the decimation of the army, military presence in the north of the country was also reduced, leading to what historian Brian Delay (2008) called the War of the Thousand Deserts (1831–1846), referring to the intermittent violence against the Comanches, Apaches, Kiowas, and other tribes in northern Mexico, where the reach of the central authorities was timid at best.

As a prisoner, Santa Anna signed a document recognizing Texan independence and was freed in the spring of 1837, but he soon questioned the legitimacy of this declaration and was able to retire again to Manga de Clavo, where he concentrated on restoring his public image by dictating a version of the war in Texas "in which he won all the victories and his subordinates suffered all defeats" (Byrd Simpson, 1982, 72). Meanwhile, "the specter of war with Texas, which seemed certain, and with the United States, which seemed probable, served Santa Anna's purposes" (Sierra, 1982, 111). In fact, as the policy of the United States turned from neutrality to one of "graduated pressure" (Bauer, 1974, 13), the centralist republic founded in 1836 proved more resilient than one would have predicted after the defeat in San Jacinto (Costeloe, 1993).

In the end, Santa Anna's opportunity to return to the national scene came in the form of a French blockade and occupation of the port of Veracruz on November 27, 1838. Santa Anna commanded the Mexican offensive and lost a limb fighting the invaders. His left leg was amputated and buried with all military honors, contributing to his legend of sacrifice for Mexico. When the French finally left Veracruz on March 9, 1839, ending the so-called Pastry War of 1838–1839, Santa Anna resumed his centralization project by increasing the size of the Mexican army and repressing revolts in Coahuila, Nuevo León, and Tamaulipas – which tried to form the Republic of the Rio Grande – as well as secessionist attempts in Tabasco and Yucatán. Santa Anna entered his second presidency amid many troubles but on a trajectory of state consolidation (Henderson, 2007).

Mobilization and new taxes in the context of these interstate militarized disputes triggered a coercion–extraction cycle. One prominent example is the *derecho de consumo*, a 15 percent increase in import taxes sanctioned in 1839, which provoked much discontent in ports like Veracruz. This led to a series of disturbances "known as the *plan mercantil*, on the basis of its origin being the call by both overseas and Mexican merchants and traders for the repeal on the taxation on foreign goods" (Boyd, 2010, 164). Interestingly, some revolts, like that of Mariano Otero in Jalisco, did not request a return to a federalist constitution but just lower taxes. The legitimacy of the centralist constitution was still high due to the situation in Texas and the threat from the United States. In 1842 the Mexican army managed to take back San Antonio from Texas on two occasions but was later forced to withdraw. In 1843 the states of Sonora, Puebla, and Oaxaca faced federalist revolts, while the Yucatán government de facto reattained autonomy with the withdrawal of the national army. A truce between Texas and Mexico was mediated by France and Great Britain, although Mexico continued to reject its independence and Santa Anna declared that annexation to the United States would be seen as a declaration of war (Bazant, 1991, 19).

In May 1844 a draft of a treaty annexing Texas was submitted to the United States Congress, forcing Santa Anna to reiterate his ultimatum. He then "coerced loans from the *hombres de bien*, seizing and auctioning off the goods of those who resisted ... preyed on the church's wealth through forced loans and confiscations [and] raised taxes nearly across the board" (Henderson, 2007, 128) and asked the Mexican Congress for a 4-million-peso appropriation, but "politicians had been milking the cow of a chimerical Texas campaign for years" (Henderson, 2007, 130), and passing the bill proved impossible. Aware that he could not win a war without this support, Santa Anna agreed to recognize Texas's autonomy in November 1844 in exchange for an indemnity from the United States and guarantees offered by Britain and France. The proposal was deemed unacceptable by the conservative General Mariano Paredes, who revolted against his government. When Santa Anna left the capital to quell the rebellion, his replacement was overthrown by General José Joaquín Herrera. Santa Anna was defeated in Puebla soon afterward and fled into exile.

Herrera, a liberal close to exiles in Louisiana and Texas, was inclined to strike a deal with the United States as well. In May 1845 he agreed to recognize the independence of Texas if its government would reject unification with the United States. Yet Texas accepted annexation with the United States on July 4, 1845, forcing Herrera to become a partisan for centralization or resign. His government started conscripting for the army and levied a 15-million-peso contribution from elites and the Church (Henderson, 2007, 150), leading to a notable transformation of the liberal party, with the peripheral elites of the *liberales puros* withdrawing their support for the *liberales moderados* that sided with Herrera (Santoni, 1996, 44). The crisis needed a strong, committed centralist leader, so Paredes, leader of the conservative opposition, marched into Mexico City on January 2, 1846, determined to uphold Mexican territorial integrity at all costs.

9.2 THE MEXICAN–AMERICAN WAR (1846–1848)

Unlike Santa Anna, Paredes was a consistent conservative who envisioned that the war effort would have to be accompanied by the consolidation of a strong legal authority of the state, in opposition to the charismatic authority that the *caudillos* had been wielding. As he put it in his first public address, "We seek a strong, stable power which can protect society; but to govern that society, we do not want either the despotic dictatorship of a soldier or the degrading yoke of the orator" (Bazant, 1991, 20). Thus the conservative central elites embarked on a whole-hearted state-building effort, while the peripheral elites did what they could to limit the process.[2]

At the outset of hostilities, it was difficult to determine whether Paredes would lose or win this war. While the Americans sent a detachment of some 2,000 men led by General Zachary Taylor, the Mexican army on the Rio Grande was almost three times as large and was supported by another 12,000 soldiers waiting relatively nearby in Monterrey (Guardino, 2016, 50). The most recent historiography on the war concludes that the armies were not so dissimilar in motivation and experience.[3] If anything, the United States had the significant advantage of a larger economy and a fitter navy, while Mexico's finances before the war were in bad shape, leaving the economy more vulnerable to blockades (Guardino, 2016, 6). These factors, however, were far from relevant in the short term and were completely irrelevant on the war front. Therefore "many Mexican politicians and generals believed they could defeat the United States … Mexicans also did not see the effervescent religious pluralism of the United States as a positive and were acutely aware of both nativist and racial tensions." They even saw these things as "evidence that the United States was a country about to fall apart." Of course, "in 1861 the United States did explode, even if this explosion came fifteen years too late for Mexico" (Guardino, 2016, 76).

To further substantiate the view that the final result of this war was essentially unforeseeable – after all, this is a war where the superiority of the United States is widely assumed – I pay particular attention to reports of diplomats trying to assess the situation. As with all other wars in my case

[2] For example, when Alamán suggested the possibility of crowning a monarch to further centralize, legitimize, and strengthen the state, General Juan Álvarez rebelled with 3,000 troops, asking for the replacement of Paredes and the return of Santa Anna – now exiled in Cuba behind an imminent American blockade – to restore the liberal republic. The rebellion was put down, but liberal-federalist sentiments would be waiting to resurface at the first sign of military defeat.

[3] Mexican officers had much more battlefield experience than their American counterparts. It is not clear whether the same could be said of rank-and-file soldiers. Due to the generalized levy in Mexico, the army was full of *vagos*men thought unproductive to society by local authorities and priests – who had to fill draft quotas for the central government. If anything, the spiral of conscription and desertion during those years shows a major effect of mobilization that affected even the smallest locality in Mexico, but it did not result in a very high-quality army. The point, however, is that the Americans seemed no better. Zachary Taylor himself "doubted these regiments were ready for battle when he began the campaign" (Guardino, 2016, 121).

studies, I pay attention to the assessment of British diplomacy, given its superior resources, access to information, and high stakes in predicting the outcome. Assessing the situation for the Foreign Office, the British Plenipotentiary in Mexico saw the determination of General Arista and the superiority of the Mexican cavalry and infantry as factors that could give Mexico a sound victory:

> General Arista, to whom the command of the Mexican Army of the North (8,000 men) is given, is a man of prudence; he has long been accustomed to that part of the country, possesses large property in the neighborhood, and his enemies have reproached him with attempting to create a separate Republic out of the State bordering on the Rio Bravo. The army desired his presence and it is whispered that on presenting his name to General Paredes it was urged in recommendation that if the command was not given to him, it might be assumed by him under less favorable auspices ... if, as is feared, the Mexicans should cross the Rio Bravo, I do not see how General Taylor can avoid hostilities. His artillery is far superior to any that the Mexicans can bring into the field, the cavalry is chiefly composed of Poles and probably good, but not nearly as numerous as that under General Arista. The latter possesses also a body of Rancheros or irregular cavalry, an excellent force for support duty. With regards to the United States infantry, it is composed of so many nations that it is difficult to say in what state of efficiency it is. The officers, I believe, are very good. The Mexican infantry is composed of Indians and half-breeds, and would, if properly officered, become excellent soldiers. They are enduring and patient under privations beyond example, and are capable of making the most astonishing marches.... These, My Lord, are the elements opposed to each other on the northern frontiers of the Republic. The government expects intelligence daily from Matamoros, and, as usual, has already announced the certainty of victory and annihilation of the United States troops.[4]

Hostilities finally broke out when the Mexicans, concentrated in Matamoros, sent a cavalry detachment to raid a few villages north of the Rio Grande and proceeded to shell and besiege Fort Texas on May 3, 1846. The Battle of Palo Alto on May 8, 1846, resulted in a draw between the forces of General Mariano Arista and Taylor, who was trying to open a way to reach his troops behind the siege. Arista then took hold of Resaca de la Palma and waited for the Americans to attack. After an unlikely victory, 1,700 men led by Taylor were able to relieve Fort Texas. One Mexican official said after the battle, "If I had had with me yesterday $100,000 in silver, I would have bet the whole of it that no 10,000 on earth could drive us from our position" (Bauer, 1974, 63). Historians seem to agree that if it were not for the coup of Paredes against Herrera, which took 3,000 Mexican troops away from Matamoros and into Mexico City, "it is possible that a Mexican victory against Taylor would have made it harder for [President James K.] Polk to continue an offensive war" (Guardino, 2016, 84).

4 Letter from Charles Bankhead, Minister Plenipotentiary of Her Majesty in Mexico, to Earl Aberdeen, Foreign Secretary, Mexico City. March 1, 1846. British National Archives FO/204/91, Part 2, p. 209.

As soon as May 10, news of the victorious battles arrived at Washington. Polk composed a message asking Congress to appropriate 10 million USD and levy an army of 50,000, the largest ever assembled in the United States. Encouraged by the prospect of a quick and decisive victory, Congress officially declared war on May 13. The size of the Mexican army on the other side of the Rio Grande totaled 18,882 permanent troops (Santoni, 1997, 96), so the Mexican Congress passed a battery of taxes as well. It was announced that the clergy would contribute 1 million Mexican pesos to the cause. Taking from the elites was made necessary by the lack of credit and the drop in tariffs. Since independence, Mexico's yearly expenditure had doubled its revenues, which meant that the treasury was depleted. Foreign debt had been the usual resource for financing such deficits, but after defaulting on this debt, Mexico was virtually excluded from credit markets. After the declaration of war, the American navy deployed a full blockade of the main ports in Mexico, which would effectively prevent the collection of customs duties during the rest of the conflict. With major ports like Veracruz and Tampico blocked, Mexico opened new ports in Tecaluto, Tuxpan, and Soto la Marina, exempting commercial vessels from port taxes and reducing import taxes to a quarter of their former value, but raids by the American navy and the high risks involved reduced foreign trade by at least half. The only exception made by the US navy was Yucatán, because secessionist elites there had taken control of all ports (Bauer, 1974, 111). Beyond Yucatán, the initial defeat of the Mexican army also had the expected effect of bolstering rebellion in the present states of Colima, Michoacán, Oaxaca, Puebla, and Tabasco (Levinson, 2005, 49), making the levy of local taxes and conscription much more difficult.

Thus as the American army crossed the Rio Grande, the situation in Mexico City was one of disaffection. Diplomats reported a widespread "willingness to receive an American proposal for negotiation" (Bauer, 1974, 76) among the elites. The upper classes knew that they would have to bear all the financial weight of the war. Yet once the nationalist sentiment had been fired up, all those who suggested this exit option – such as Herrera some months before – were deemed traitors and viciously attacked. The war had to be fought, but the government could change, so "in the late spring and early summer of 1846 a great alliance coalesced against Paredes" (Guardino, 2016, 86), including mostly federalists and liberals of different persuasions. The trigger was the withdrawal of the remaining 2,638 Mexican troops, which were deemed insufficient to defend Matamoros and turned to Monterrey to establish a new line of defense to the south, while Taylor and some 2,300 troops occupied the surrendered city (Bauer, 1974, 82). News of the breach of the border had turned the political tide in Mexico City in favor of the federalist *liberales puros*, who organized a revolt against the Paredes government, now represented by his vice-president, Nicolas Bravo. "Paredes' inability to defend the country and his monarchist sympathies swayed the public opinion to the other extreme" (Bazant, 1991, 20), and "the country, horrified by the defeats, now burst into flames" (Sierra, 1982, 112). The revolt was led by Gómez Farías, who appointed General José Mariano Salas president on August 6, 1846. Their first measure was to reinstitute the Constitution of 1824.

In this way, before Mexico had even lost the war, a single military defeat against Taylor had already caused the rise of the traditional anti-state party to government and the repeal of Mexico's centralist constitution, which had been in place since 1835. Ten years of colossal efforts to centralize the country and build the state were thus redressed abruptly by the initial defeat in the Rio Grande and the progress of the invasion. Yet, paradoxically, decentralization also legitimized the national state, appeased some revolts, and "dramatically increased mobilization for the war effort" (Guardino, 2016, 90). "Federalism aided Mexico's war effort in this way, and frankly it is impossible to imagine Mexico resisting its wealthier neighbor as well as it did without having rejected centralism. Thus, the turn toward federalism both hampered and aided Mexico during the war" (Guardino, 2016, 91), and the liberals were eventually forced to begin the process of centralization.

Because the liberals were now in power and needed to strengthen the national army, they shifted from a view of federalism as opposed to the national state to a more functional view of federalism as a way to secure the allegiance of subnational states while consolidating the national state (Santoni, 1996, 6). The *puros* quickly abandoned the idea of lowering taxation and forming civil militias. Despite their former anti-statist beliefs, Salas and the head of cabinet, Gómez Farías, introduced emergency taxes to rebuild the Army of the North. They also strengthened the central bureaucracy by increasing the salaries and responsibilities of public employees and establishing the ineligibility of those who failed certain exams (Santoni, 1996, 138). Of course, this put pressure on public officials, local elites, and the Church, thus generating great tension.

The pressure on the government would increase further as a product of the developments on the front. In search of a more defensible position, Mexican troops withdrew from Monterrey to San Luis Potosí on September 24, surrendering yet another city to Taylor (Bauer, 1974, 100). Although a pyrrhic victory for Taylor, the defeat forced the liberal government to turn to Santa Anna – who had recently returned from Cuba, avoiding the American blockade – and make him commander of the Army of the North.[5] President Salas was struggling to govern. His new property tax – which established the imprisonment of real estate owners who did not pay the equivalent of one

5 Apparently Santa Anna had promised Polk that where he allowed United States naval forces to sail through the blockade of Veracruz, he would concede territories beyond the Rio Grande, and thus he had returned and communicated his intention to lead the army to the new liberal government. Initially Santa Anna's return was viewed with suspicion, as he had suggested that defending Monterrey was not a good idea. Yet after Monterrey fell, his prediction showed him to be a knowledgeable strategist, and liberals had no one else to resort to with the charisma to raise and lead an army to victory under the most stringent financial circumstances.

month's rent to the state – put him at odds with Mexico City's elite, and he had no authority over the military.

Santa Anna knew that the only way to restore (his) authority was to achieve victory on the battlefield, and thus he started the herculean task of building a massive army of 20,000 men in San Luis Potosí, where he had a mere 10,000. The idea required an unparalleled mobilization effort, something of the likes of that of Bolívar and San Martín during the South American independence wars. "The gathering, arming and clothing of an army nearing twenty thousand men in San Luis Potosí between October 1846 and January 1847 was a prodigious feat, probably one of the greatest accomplishments of the nineteenth-century nation-state in Mexico" (Guardino, 2016, 142). The process of mobilization started with a forced contribution from real estate owners and a forced loan imposed upon the Church, both of which were implemented through "the whole gamut of methods, even violence" (Smith, 1919, 8). Soon Santa Anna was able to assemble a large force, which, if not able to secure victory in the next battle, did at least have the effect of deterring Taylor. Thus, with the situation in the north relatively stabilized, elections were organized, which took place in December and resulted in the election of Santa Anna, with Gómez Farías once again as his vice-president.

Formerly a staunch anti-statist, Gómez Farías had already transformed into the most fervent defender of strengthening the central army. With Santa Anna in the north, he was left in charge of the administration and gathering funds for the war effort. Since domestic sources were the only ones available to finance the war, and drafts issued for 2 million pesos MXN had rendered meager returns in November (Smith, 1919, 254), his first measure was to pass a series of laws that taxed and confiscated ecclesiastical property for a total of 15 million pesos MXN on January 11. The Church and other conservative elites were baffled but could not refuse to make this contribution in a context where even the poorest Mexicans were donating across the country and local priests were melting down church bells to produce ammunition. The tables had now turned, and it was the conservatives who, unable to express their discontent with the war, kept a keen eye on the progress on the battlefield, perhaps even secretly hoping for a defeat that would bring them back to power.

In January 1847, Taylor took the small town of Saltillo with 4,000 men. Almost concurrently, Santa Anna received intelligence that General Winfield Scott was preparing for an invasion of Veracruz and a march from there toward central Mexico. Santa Anna, forced to take the offensive in the north, decided to attack Monterrey during the winter. A new law allowed the government to confiscate another 5 million pesos in Church lands to pay for the mobilization of Santa Anna's massive army, which was now four times the size of the American forces (Smith, 1919, 12, 254).

The Mexican offensive, which seemed destined for victory, ran across all sorts of problems. Among other things, it was hit unexpectedly by "the worst winter weather northern Mexico had seen for several decades" (Guardino,

2016, 146). This affected the logistics of the campaign, rendering food and water supplies scarce and forcing Santa Anna to attack undersupplied and unprepared.

The two generals finally faced each other in the Battle of Buena Vista on February 22, 1847. The battle produced heavy losses on both sides and exhausted both armies. After the first day "many Americans ... believed that the American army would soon collapse when the fighting began the next day" (Guardino, 2016, 152). Yet the cold had severely worn out the Mexican troops, allowing Taylor to maintain his position. In practice, the retreat of Santa Anna led to a stalemate in the north, but Buena Vista looked very much like an American victory, and thus it unraveled domestic politics in Mexico (Spahr, 2015, 260).

Right after the defeat, on February 24, the state of Oaxaca refused to implement the January 11 laws (Levinson, 2005, 54). This rebellion extended to Zacatecas, Durango, San Luis Potosí, Sinaloa, and Tabasco (Henderson, 2007, 162), and when news of the defeat and the subsequent revolts reached Mexico City on February 27, the clerical and conservative elites organized a general revolt against the confiscatory laws of the liberals. This revolt was known as the Rebelión de los Polkos and was led by young members of the National Guard drawn from Mexico City – the urban youth would dance the polka at the time, but the name could also be due to how the rebellion played out at the hands of President Polk. It included some 3,000 men at arms, and although they did not try to overturn the new federalist constitution, they were fundamentally supported by conservative elements in the Church and property owners in Mexico City, who had a lot to lose if the liberals continued to make them the focus of their confiscatory policies. Thus they asked for the January laws to be repealed immediately, which divided the country and led to a long month of violence in the streets of the capital. Only by late March would Santa Anna be able to return with a 4,000-strong detachment and quell the rebellion.

The leaders of the revolt accepted a truce in exchange for the derogation of the confiscatory laws and the resignation of Gómez Farías. Applying his usual pragmatism, Santa Anna repealed the decrees and promised to protect ecclesiastical property, receiving a generous loan from the Church in return. After all, the American threat was not gone, and as long as he commanded the largest contingent of troops, neither the liberals nor the conservatives could sack him.

General Winfield Scott had now managed to capture Veracruz on March 29 and started his march toward the capital, forcing Santa Anna to hurriedly gather an army of 12,000 and march to Cerro Gordo. Here the 8,500 American troops were once again outnumbered by the Mexican forces. Santa Anna was able to force a fight in his own native state, where he could call favors, have locals help with the logistics and supplies, and pick a position that could negate the advantages of the American artillery (Guardino, 2016, 196). Santa Anna had always defended Veracruz successfully.

The victory of Scott at Cerro Gordo is quite difficult to explain. Historians sometimes resort to a legend about the scouting abilities of a young Robert E. Lee, who led the victorious surprise attack. This victory was so legendary that it contributed to both his fame and that of two future American presidents, Ulysses S. Grant and Franklin Pierce, who were also under the command of Scott. Famously, Lord Wellington praised Scott as the greatest living general for overcoming the difficulties of fighting with a much smaller force deep inside enemy territory and with all strategic positions negated by the enemy.

Meanwhile, Mexicans suspected that this unlikely defeat was part of a deal Santa Anna must have struck with the Americans when he was allowed to bypass their blockade and return from Cuba. Thus the Mexican Congress passed a law making it treason to negotiate a peace treaty with the enemy. After Scott continued to take Puebla on May 15, 1847, Santa Anna offered a truce start negotiations against a down payment of 10,000 USD, but after taking the money, he never entered negotiations (Brill, 2015, 279). By tricking the Americans in this way, he might have tried to show his compatriots where his allegiance lay, but suspicion never faded. In the twentieth century the legend of Santa Anna's treason made it into one of Diego Rivera's murals in the Palace of Government of Mexico City, where he is shown handing the keys of the city to Scott.

As Scott approached the capital, the whole of Mexico descended into chaos. The government passed yet another domestic tax of 1 million pesos in June, and in a situation of complete desperation, confiscatory measures were adopted unconstitutionally against elites both in Mexico City and across the country, taking horses, cattle, grain, forage, lead, and anything the government could lay its hands on (Smith, 1919, 254). This created enormous dissatisfaction among the peripheral elites. The state of Guanajuato suspended the levy, and a similar apathy was noted in the states of Tamaulipas, Nuevo León, and Coahuila (Levinson, 2005, 54). As we will see, in Yucatán the situation spiraled into a veritable social revolution that would continue after the war (Gabbert, 2019).

However, like on the eve of the fall of Asunción in 1869 and Lima in 1881, the presence of the invading army at the doors of Mexico City was met by notable cohesion and sacrifice. "The army that Santa Anna put together with the help of Mexicans from just about every social group and political faction in Mexico was the most diverse force that Mexico fielded in the war" (Guardino, 2016, 233). In that sense, those weeks were perhaps the most defining moments in the building of the Mexican nation. At the height of mobilization, the forces defending the capital amounted to 20,000 – partly drawn from the National Guard coming from central states like Hidalgo, Michoacan, and Oaxaca – and a large number of partisans scattered across the city limits. Mexico City, however, was one of the largest cities in the world with 150,000 inhabitants, which made it very difficult to defend even with those numbers.

After a new collapse of negotiations, Scott was able to score a new victory at Molino del Rey on September 8. Searching for any source of finance, Santa

Anna organized a meeting with the bakers of the capital to levy donations from the guilds (Smith, 1919, 254). These efforts made little difference, as the Americans hastened to take the Castle of Chapultepec on September 13. The next day, Scott entered Mexico City and announced victory in the National Palace, but Mexicans in the city continued to fire muskets and throw stones at the invaders, who responded by firing cannons at hostile buildings and executing civilians. The Mexican elite quickly started to fear riots and saw the need to collaborate with the Americans to safeguard their property, so the city council eventually asked Mexicans to lay down their arms. Scott also threatened to confiscate Church property if priests continued to rally the people against him, eventually securing the collaboration of the ecclesiastical authorities as well. Chased by Scott's troops and a mob that requested "death to Santa Anna" (Guardino, 2016, 283), the Mexican general went into exile once again.

Figure 9.1 shows very clearly how the ebbs and flows on the battlefield corresponded in constant conjunction with the strengthening and weakening of coalitions in the domestic realm. Invariably, every time there was preparation for war, the central government in Mexico, no matter its political orientation, pushed for more extraction and mobilization. Also invariably after defeat on the battlefield, governments collapsed, coalitions were shattered, and rebellions sprang up across the country. In this way, a closer look at the micro-dynamics of war reveals much about the effect of its outcomes on the state formation process. Of course, the final defeat of Mexico meant the collapse of the project – at least until the rise of the next foreign enemy.

Although overshadowed by the American Civil War and willingly forgotten by Americans and Mexicans due to the shame it evokes, the Mexican–American War was the deadliest interstate war in all of the Americas during the first half of the nineteenth century, with 19,283 battle deaths. The United States lost 12 percent of its 104,556-strong army in this war, "the highest death rate of any war in our history" according to John S. D. Eisenhower (1989, 18), son of President Dwight D. Eisenhower. It was also the deadliest international war in Mexico's history, with casualties amounting to some 10,000 (Clodfelter, 2017, 249) to 25,000 men (Henderson, 2007, 179) – the size of the army is estimated at 20,000 before the war (Singer, 1988).[6] It would be unreasonable to assume that such an impactful experience would only have territorial consequences. Indeed, the consequence was a complete collapse of the Mexican state and armed forces, partisan polarization, and the long-term reproduction of state-weakening dynamics. Historians have even registered how elites questioned the very existence of Mexico as a nation after the defeat (Hale, 1957; Craib, 2002).

[6] Even though estimates vary greatly, it is clear that Mexican casualties were at the very least 50 percent of its standing army of 20,000 at the outset of hostilities. For historian Timothy Henderson (2007, 179), "One common estimate says that some 25,000 died, though other estimates place the toll at twice that number."

Mexico		Battlefield
Herrera attempts negotiations; having failed, his liberal coalition obstructs mobilization		Texas accepts annexation to the United States; concentration of troops around Matamoros
Paredes performs a coup; his new conservative-centralist government mobilizes fully	1846	Mexico initiates the hostilities Palo Alto (Mexican defeat)
Widespread rebellion; a new coup by Gomez Farías brings the liberals back to power and the 1824 Federalist Constitution is reinstated		United States formally declares war Fall of Monterrey (Mexican defeat)
New rebellions and mutinies; weakened, the liberal government appoints Santa Anna Renewed mobilization to San Luis Potosí	1847	Buena Vista (Mexican defeat)
"Polk's Rebellion" in Mexico City is followed by many local revolts Caste War in Yucatan		Cerro Gordo (Mexican defeat) Full of Mexico City (Mexican defeat)
Santa Anna goes into exile; liberal interim governments face anarchy and struggle to secure territorial integrity	1848	Treaty of Guadalupe Hidalgo
Herera returns to office Rebellions along liberal-conservative fault lines continue		

FIGURE 9.1 Mexican–American War timeline

In the figure of interim president Manuel de la Peña y Peña, the *moderado* liberals assumed power in the government under occupation. He would be succeeded by Herrera, another liberal ousted in the early stages of the war for his willingness to negotiate territorial concessions in what, in hindsight, would have been an intelligent bargain. However, the authorities in Mexico City were contested all over the country. The period from September 1847 to February 1848 is properly characterized as one of "perfect anarchy" (Levinson, 2005, 57) or "systematic anarchy" (Gonzalez Navarro, 1977, 378). Groups of completely disorganized Mexican partisans attacked Scott's supply lines and occupation forces. Generals Alvarez and Paredes, among others, became the leaders of revolts against the occupation and roamed the countryside. State governments where American occupying forces were not present basically did not recognize the authorities in Mexico City, conducted their own elections, and refused to send tribute to the capital. Only when popular uprisings erupted against local authorities did they resort to the provisional national authorities for help, which usually never came.

Because of this situation, the Mexican Congress had little choice but to ratify the Treaty of Guadalupe Hidalgo of February 2, 1848. By its terms, Mexico lost the states of California, New Mexico, Texas, and a portion of Tamaulipas beyond the Rio Grande. In compensation, the United States army would withdraw from the rest of the territory and pay an indemnification of 15 million pesos. The Americans did not pay this to buy territories but to pay for the damages caused by the war and, more importantly, because "without it the consequences would have been chaos, dismemberment, and annexation" (Sierra, 1982, 121). In fact, the liberal government "no doubt would have collapsed had it not received at the outset the 3 million pesos of the indemnity account" (Bazant, 1991, 26). The indemnity payments continued until the agreed total of 15 million pesos was disbursed in 1850; in the meantime, it helped levy just enough troops to get the country under control.

Yet while the treaty and a subsequent armistice intended to end hostilities against the American occupation, "during the remainder of that year, campesino and indigenous alienation continued to explode into geographically diffuse rebellions against the Mexican government" (Levinson, 2005, 85). A rebellion in Yucatán in particular, known as the Caste War, had spiraled out of control. Some 30,000 Mayans under the command of leaders Cecilio Chi and Jacinto Pat had become uncontrollable. Indigenous rebels had taken control of almost the entire province and massacred large creole populations (Reed, 1964; Katz, 2014). The state of anarchy was such that it forced the elites of Yucatán to renounce their independent status – declared back in 1841 and having resulted in de facto autonomy ever since – in exchange for help from the Mexican army. Yucatán would be reannexed on August 17, 1848. A similarly violent popular uprising had started in Sierra Gorda. Thus although the American "occupation forces left shortly afterwards," they did so "to the mixed joy of the Mexican landed class which was by this time threatened by a social revolution" (Bazant, 1991, 444) across the country.

Also before the final withdrawal of US troops began on September 6, 1848, a *cuartelazo* by Paredes in June, proclaimed as the Plan de Aguascalientes, attempted the dissolution of the central government and the election of militia commanders at the state level as provisional authorities. "Devastated and near leaderless, the country's entire postwar army had been reduced to 7,413 officers and men, of whom only about 6,000 were fit for duty" (Santoni, 1997, 146). This drastic shrinking of the national army made the rebellions feasible and threatened to dismember Mexico (Vázquez and Meyer, 1985, 69). It was precisely the fear of a complete collapse of the Mexican state that prompted erstwhile enemies like the Yucatán elites to reevaluate their position and exchange their secessionist dream for support against the Mayan uprisings. Thus while this war stripped Mexico of half its territory, it consolidated the other half (Mazzuca, 2021, 270).

In the following months the United States actively supported the Mexican government, even with the transfer of weapons, to keep the domestic situation afloat. The United States had long sided with peripheral elites aiming to debilitate the central government, but now even the elites of Yucatán supported – and even requested the local presence of – a larger army under the authority of Mexico City. Before the war "the United States was identified as the root cause of Mexico's endemic instability, which the US had deliberately fomented in order to weaken Mexico and thus make its conquest and eventual absorption easier" (Shawcross, 2018, 10). Yet "future US interventions in Mexico would follow the 1848 practice of aiding national elites to achieve desired objectives rather than the 1847 tactic of overt invasion. In the latter year, the rulers of Mexico stood ready to cede territory to the United States in return for various types of assistance that would facilitate the reestablishment of their own hegemony" (Levinson, 2005, 119). Strangely enough, Washington would become an important ally to achieve centralization, now supported even by the liberals, while American freebooters and popular uprisings threatened to tear Mexico apart (Vázquez and Meyer, 1985, 69–74).

"By the end of 1848, the depth and ferocity of these rebellions proved so intense that 21,278 federal troops fought guerrillas in the Huasteca, the Sierra Gorda, Puebla, México state, and the Yucatan" (Levinson, 2005, 88). The number exceeded even that of the troops that fought against the United States in major battles during the war. But this would be a contingent army, oriented toward the repression of local peasants, instead of the permanent and professional army that the central state required in the long term. Thus when revolts in Sierra Gorda, Yucatán, and the north started to ebb, as of 1851 the government reduced the war budget and reduced the size of the army to 10,000.

Herrera, the erstwhile traitor who had tried to negotiate with the United States before the war, governed between 1848 and 1851. These years were characterized by some elite cohesion, given the pressing threats from below and the financial support from Washington. Yet the fact that Herrera had sixteen ministers of finance shows that the foundations of this apparent stability were shaky. When he left power in the hands of General Mariano Arista, the pacification of the country had been achieved, which meant the return of great polarization between liberals and conservatives, which would eventually lead to a brief civil war between them in the summer of 1852 and, in the longer run, to the War of the Reform.

Chronic civil war became possible, given the extreme weakness of the national military. Within the army, the postwar situation was one of lack of discipline and morale (Santoni, 1997, 153). If the Mexican army had traditionally been one of *caudillos*, the level of partisanship and the lack of professionalism were now far more evident. The size of the military was drastically reduced, and almost all of the budget was used to pay for salaries and raids against indigenous peoples in the north and in Yucatán. The military were weakened and "the prestige of the army," according to historian Roswell Ripley (1970, 645), "has been entirely swept away."

In the United States, victory strengthened the bureaucrats and the army and arguably led Taylor and Pierce to the presidency, triggered the partisan convergence and realignment that led to the creation of the Republican Party (Gienapp, 1987), and initiated a process of centralization that would lead to the Civil War and the building of the American Leviathan (Bensel, 1991). "The Mexican ruling class [in contrast, was] demoralized, embittered, and divided" (Bazant, 1991, 26). The parties in Mexico fragmented along different lines. In the months after Guadalupe Hidalgo, "highly partisan newspapers, broadsides, and pamphlets also continued to proliferate, and their tone became ever more strident, the positions more rigid, as both liberals and conservatives interpreted Mexico's defeat as the final confirmation of the positions they had long maintained" (Henderson, 2007, 183). The Conservative Party was founded in 1849 with the sole purpose of undermining the liberal postwar government. While the liberals intended to accommodate these positions, divisions among *moderados* and *puros* became irreconcilable. The more extreme positions eventually prevailed, and as the threats of popular rebellion and secessionism receded, liberals and conservatives started to consider resolving their differences through violence (Bazant, 1985, 449). "The period 1848 to 1861, bookended by the US–Mexican War and the French intervention, has seen historians focus on domestic Mexican politics, particularly the struggle between reactionary conservatives and progressive liberals culminating in the War of the Reform" (Shawcross, 2018, 21).

These fears became real in 1852, when a conservative military revolt in Guadalajara deposed a liberal governor by force. Revolts spread to other provinces and lasted for months, escalating into a civil war of national proportions. "Partisan polarization had become the master force in Mexican politics" (Mazzuca, 2021, 298). The situation led to the resignation of President Arista. Facing a power vacuum and unable to compromise, the liberals and the conservative *caudillos* agreed to bring back a figure who had mastered the art of walking the tightrope of Mexican politics in the last thirty years: Santa Anna.

Santa Anna took office on March 17, 1853, and for the last time in his fascinating career. Given the situation of civil war he was facing, he requested and was granted the powers of a dictator. The chaos was such that "both conservatives and liberals were bowing to his leadership, each convinced they could bring him to their side" (Bazant, 1991, 28). Using money from new taxes and selling new territory to the United States in Arizona, Santa Anna was able to increase the number of soldiers in the standing army and stabilize the country, but only for a very short time. The liberals would not tolerate a permanent suspension of the Constitution of 1824, and as early as March 1, 1854, they announced the Plan de Ayutla. The rebellion spread throughout the country and became unstoppable, forcing Santa Anna to resign on August 12, 1855, and leave the country once and for all. "The upshot was the bloodiest civil war Mexico had yet seen, the so-called War of the Reform, which raged from 1858 to 1861" (Henderson, 2007, 186).

9.3 CENTRAL AMERICA AND COSTA RICAN EXCEPTIONALISM

Central America provides a small-scale confirmation of the dynamics reviewed in South America. Guatemala, the regional seat of Spanish officials in colonial times, rapidly declined in the state capacity hierarchy during the nineteenth century, succumbing to the Salvadoran and Honduran liberals led by Francisco Morazán in the first half of the century and still unable to regain its position after the failed late-century adventures of Rufino Barrios. Costa Rica, the country that now sits atop the state capacity ranking in the isthmus, was a peripheral territory thinly populated in colonial times. According to the testimony of an English traveler, by 1825 San José had contact with the outside world only through a weekly magazine arriving from Guatemala (Stone, 1975, 111). Historians agree that the Costa Rican state was "rachitic" at the time and financially dependent on Guatemala and León. Tax revenue was so low it could not afford the salaries of a bureaucracy of dozens (Vega Carballo, 1981, 13–18, in Somma, 2011, 298). The colonial army in Costa Rica "did not have permanent units and was numerically small ... did not have weaponry, disciplined troops, nor military chiefs" (Cerdas and Vargas, 1988, 15, in Somma, 2011, 299).

Explanations of Costa Rican exceptionalism often idealize the character of the elites and resource endowment at the time of independence, but previous studies have shown that most countries in Central America entered the independence period with roughly similar conditions in this regard (Mahoney, 2001, 194). Other literature has highlighted ethnic homogeneity (Acuña and Molina Jiménez, 1986) and the small size of estates (Monge Alfaro, 1980; Gudmundson, 1983; Cardoso, 1987) as potential advantages, but as one author correctly notes, while these factors remained constant, Costa Rica endured significant political instability from 1820 to 1850 and showed signs of state formation only afterward (Somma, 2011, 297).

The absence of a dominant urban hub posed a real problem for Costa Rican state formation after independence. The problem of the capital city was recurrent during the first decades of Costa Rican history. After the collapse of the First Mexican Empire, the republican cities of San José and Alajuela fought the royalist forces of Cartago and Heredia for preeminence in the Battle of Ochomogo of 1823. At the time, the four cities were roughly equal in strength, which prevented the clear dominance of one central elite (Molina Jiménez, 2005), but the victory in Ochomogo strengthened the liberal elites in San José and spearheaded an incipient Costa Rican nationalist project.

The separation from the Mexican Empire, however, resulted in Costa Rica forming part of a larger Federal Republic of Central America (1824–1839). The federation was ruled by a central elite of liberals and opposed by a peripheral elite of conservative landowners and priests who intended to preserve their traditional autonomy and privileges. The first president of the Federation, Manuel José Arce (1825–1829), had to walk a fine line between these two parties and was deposed by a liberal revolt. His successor, Francisco Morazán, moved the capital to San Salvador – away from the conservative Guatemala City – while peripheral elites continued to seek the collapse of the federation. Although liberal ideology tended to favor decentralization, low taxes, and free trade, the continued opposition compelled Morazán to develop a strong central bureaucracy and army to raise taxes and centralize authority in San Salvador – mostly at the expense of conservative opposition in Guatemala and the Catholic Church (Woodward, 1993).

Finally, absent any strong external threat that justified the subordination to San Salvador or the maintenance of a strong liberal army, conservative elites took advantage of a brutal cholera epidemic and rallied the population around Rafael Carrera in a revolt that ended the federalist experiment in 1839.

While liberals in San Salvador were struggling to prevent centrifugal tendencies, their peers in San José were also wrestling power from their local peripheral elites. Still agitated by the problem of the local capital, the Costa Rican Congress passed the Ley de la Ambulancia in 1834, which established the rotation of the capital between Alajuela, Cartago, Heredia, and San José. The bill was initially applied, but President Braulio Carrillo soon rejected the plan, provoking the War of the League of 1835. San José mobilized 10,000 soldiers to fight an equivalent force raised by the other three cities and upon victory could finally impose its hegemony over Costa Rica. As one author puts it, "If we assume that the adult male population was one fourth of the total population of the country – which was estimated to be 78,365 by 1836 – we get that about half of it participated of this conflict" (Somma, 2011, 275). If Montevideo was the Troy of South America as per Dumas's analogy, San José was already becoming the Sparta of Central America during the first years of independence.

After this civil war, Carrillo implemented a series of centralizing reforms, including the foundation of a military academy and the introduction of a civil code and police regulations, among others. As everywhere else, this led to the opposition of the peripheral elites (Diaz Arias, 2012, 28), who "sabotaged over and over the centralizing and legitimizing public policies emanating from the central state" (Vega Carballo, 1981, 39), and four coups took place in the following decade, in 1838, 1842, 1845, and 1849, holding back nation and state building. For example, although the number of salaried soldiers grew from a mere 153 men in 1825 (Solis and Gonzalez Pacheco, 1992, 45) to 2,812 men in 1830, "the army, composed of campesinos and artisans, did not achieve important institutional development between 1821 and 1849" (Molina Jiménez, 2000, 26).

The growth of a central army was more notable after tensions with Nicaragua over possession of the Nicosia territories in 1850. By then the project of a Federal Republic of Central America was long dead and Costa Rica had acquired a flag, a state emblem, and a national currency (Diaz Arias, 2012, 28). President Juan Rafael Mora announced a *Reglamento de Milicias* in 1850 and established the Military School in San José in 1852 (Fallas Santana, 1982, 37–58). According to one cabinet member, the government was "adopting the wise and well known maxim *si vis pacis para bellum* [if you seek peace, prepare for war]" (Fallas Santana, 2007, 15), using the external threat to cement San José's dominance once and for all. The ranks of the army had expanded from 5,000 in 1850 to 7,187 in 1854 (Molina Jiménez, 2000, 60) when an unexpected external threat made San José the Sparta of Central America once again.

The Filibuster War, remembered in Costa Rica as the *Campaña Nacional*, was a major event in the formation of the Costa Rican state. The war was prompted by the arrival of the American filibuster William Walker in Nicaragua in 1855. Walker had acquired fame immediately after the Mexican–American War, when he and thirty-four other mercenaries founded the Republic of Sonora and asked for annexation to the United States. This request was rejected by Washington and the secessionist attempt was suffocated by the Mexican army, but Walker became a well-known *condottiero* – or rather, *filibustero* – in the region.

In 1855 Nicaraguan liberals based in the city of León called Walker to help them in their fight against the conservatives based in Granada, but after becoming the commander in chief of the armies of Nicaragua, Walker was soon regarded as planning an invasion of all Central American states (Obregón Loria, 1991, 8). His more moderate plans might have been to take control of a precarious but much-used interoceanic route across the San Juan River and the Lake of Nicaragua, which preceded the Panama Canal. Nicaraguan claims over this route stepped on Costa Rican ones, and this territorial issue, together with the fear of an all-out invasion of the region, led to war between both countries.

The *Campaña Nacional* would be a completely new experience for Costa Ricans due to the prolonged duration of the campaign, the travails of mobilizing into Nicaragua, and the costs this imposed on its elites. A Costa Rican army of 10,000 men was levied (Obregón Loria, 1991, 84; Molina Jiménez, 2000, 32). As in the Battle of Ochomongo, the army amounted to roughly 10 percent of the Costa Rican population at the time (Solis and Gonzalez Pacheco, 1992, 41), but this time mass mobilization would last two years instead of one month. These numbers are impressive. Consider that the army of Napoleon that marched to Moscow in 1812 – the largest ever assembled in European history at that point – was equivalent to 2.7 percent of the French population. Of course, such mass mobilization required Mora to severely tax his people in a context of plummeting exports and the absence of international credit (Molina Jiménez, 2000, 49). He did this right at the beginning of the war through an exceptional war tax directed at coffee growers (Cabrera Geserick, 2013, 134). Some cities, like Alajuela and Heredia, which had to pay hefty taxes, were less affected by the levy and were able to keep their men working in the plantations.

On the other side of the border, Walker also developed the Nicaraguan state in critical ways. Some of the best recent work on the subject has noted that Walker was able to expand the bureaucracy and extend taxation considerably (Gobat, 2018, 165–170). Facing war with Costa Rica, "Walker's regime carried out an assault of elite power that would not be replicated until the Sandinista Revolution of 1979–1990. Ultimately 132 estates and over 82 houses were confiscated" (Gobat, 2018, 232). According to Walker's correspondence, he also shipped in 1,200 American mercenaries to become part of his army (Obregón Loria, 1991, 65), although scholars agree he had a tendency to underestimate his numbers for dramatic effect, and serious estimates vary between 5,200 (Bolaños Geyer, 2003, 433) and 12,000 (Scott, 1975, 141; see Cabrera Geserick, 2013, 125).

After the declaration of war was issued, a Costa Rican vanguard of 2,500 left San José on March 4, 1856, obtaining a first victory in the Battle of Santa Rosa on March 25. In this first international engagement, "the military victory proved to the Costa Ricans that the state could field a military capable of defending them, a basic responsibility of a government" (Cabrera Geserick, 2013, 138). The army of Mora succeeded again in the Battle of Rivas of April 11, but before leaving Rivas, Walker threw his dead men into the wells of the town to poison the water, causing cholera to spread among Costa Rican troops and forcing Mora to order a retreat. According to Michael Gobat (2018, 73), the retreat of the Costa Ricans was pictured in Nicaragua as a victory, which boosted the prospects of the filibuster state.

Meanwhile, the cholera epidemic spread in Costa Rica with the returning troops, causing the death of 8 to 10 percent of the population in what amounts to the worst demographic disaster ever recorded in the country's history

(Molina Jiménez, 2000, 42; Fallas Santana, 2007, 20). People died at a rate of more than 100 per day. The elites and the general populace were equally affected. Mora's vice-president and several cabinet members died (Calvo Mora, 1909, 36). Costa Ricans were outraged. In late 1856, Mora started negotiations with local elites and other parties in order to resume the campaign and avenge their dead.

Predicting the course of the war had proven impossible for contemporary observers. Right before Rivas the American Consul in San José had reported:

> A force of three thousand Costa Ricans, commanded by the President in person is now on the front, acting thus far upon the defensive. The men are well armed and not wanting in spirit but have had little experience in war. A body of three to five thousand is also supposed to be marching from Guatemala. With these forces and the public sentiment aroused against him in Nicaragua, it is scarcely feasible that Walker will be able to sustain himself.[7]

Yet, as we have seen, Walker won and sustained himself. Not just that, he had now become president of Nicaragua. This did not discourage the consul, however, who now hastened to predict a rapid collapse of the Mora government and a Costa Rican defeat. In his words:

> The present condition of Costa Rica is disastrous. The object sought to be accomplished by the expedition to Nicaragua was unattained. The cholera, which broke out among the troops in Rivas causing their precipitous retreat, accompanied them on the return, and has swept over the entire country with fearful effect. Probably fifteen per cent of the population has perished and the crisis still continues ... there will probably be a change in the administration which should it come, I hope may be accomplished peaceably.[8]

Despite his impartiality in the matter and his preferential access to information, and despite being under considerable pressure to predict these events, the guesses of the American diplomat turned out to be wrong for a second time. Although facing the opposition of his new vice-president, Vicente Aguilar, Mora did send his resignation to Congress, but legislators rejected it. Popular support for the war effort remained high, and many *patricios* and members of the clergy contributed voluntarily to the cause (Fallas Santana, 2007, 21).[9]

7 Letter of the consul in San Jose [illegible] to Secretary of State William L. Marcy. March 9, 1856, US National Archives. T-35/1.

8 Letter of the consul in San Jose [illegible] to Secretary of State William L. Marcy. August 6, 1856, US National Archives. T-35/5.

9 One ordinary citizen participating in the congressional debates expressed: "Each needs to contribute, we will do so with our blood, let the rich contribute with their money" (Obregón Loria, 1991, 182). A similar level of commitment took place at the level of the elites. In one of those debates, Aguilar asked Mora, "What do you count with for this war?" to which he responded, "I count with my capital, and with yours" (Obregón Loria, 1991, 182).

Moreover, the prospect of other Central American countries now effectively joining the war effort[10] had convinced the population of the possibility of victory and generated a rally round the flag effect. Thus mobilization was resumed, and in October 1856 a contingent of yet another 10,000 troops – now better equipped – marched to the border.

The second campaign was fought mostly along the San Juan River in an attempt to block the transit route for the filibusters. It ended once again with the capture of Rivas, this time after a long siege and with the assistance of Salvadoran, Honduran, and Guatemalan forces. In total the *Campaña Nacional* took some 2,100 Costa Rican lives in battle and around 10,000 due to the cholera epidemic. Costa Rica, in sum, lost 10 percent of its population to the most severe international war in Central American history.[11]

After the war, the idea of a Costa Rican nation spread widely: "Effectively, the 1856 National Campaign served to create and strengthen ideological elements that either were absent in Costa Rican society or manifested weakly and had not been appropriated by the dominant classes. We refer concretely to concepts such as sovereignty, territorial integrity, independence, national defense, etc." (Solis and Gonzalez Pacheco, 1992, 40). Mora took serious steps to compensate veterans and enshrine martyrs. As one author puts it, by "welcoming as heroes the victorious soldiers returning from the battles of Santa Rosa, Rivas, and the river San Juan, nationalism was fomented, increasing the prestige of the military chiefs and the image of the army as representative of the interests of the whole society" (Fallas Santana, 2007, 14). This was "a substitute independence war, with its pantheon of heroes, chronology of prowesses, and patriotic ritual" (Molina Jiménez, 2000, 83).

Victory in the Filibuster War resulted in the incorporation of the Guanacaste province to Costa Rica, then known as Moracia, after Mora. This was soon followed by the foundation of the Costa Rican National Bank and the erection of a fine National Palace in San José (Bancroft, 1887, 373). Both institutions epitomized a new consensus among centralist liberal elites that secured Costa Rican economic growth in the late nineteenth century. Although political conflict would not disappear automatically, the convergence between the

10 Guatemala and El Salvador dispatched thousands of soldiers, although their contribution continued to be trivial in comparison with Costa Rica's, by far the least populated of all Central American countries in the 1850s. With 101,000 inhabitants, the population of Costa Rica amounted to one-eighth of the population of Guatemala (850,000) and roughly one-third of the population of El Salvador (366,000), Honduras (350,000), and Nicaragua (300,000). These population estimates also show that Costa Rica was, like Chile and Uruguay in the Southern Cone, in a situation of relative weakness, where conscription and mobilization for war imposed a relatively higher cost on its population (Soto Valenzuela, 1957, 74).

11 All other Central American forces combined, including Nicaragua, lost approximately 3,000 men (Obregón Loria, 1991, 261). The disproportionate contribution of Costa Rica to the war effort immediately stands out in relative terms if one considers these countries' populations. Sarkees and Wayman (2010) calculate 7,700 battle deaths associated with this interstate war, which makes it the most severe in Central American history.

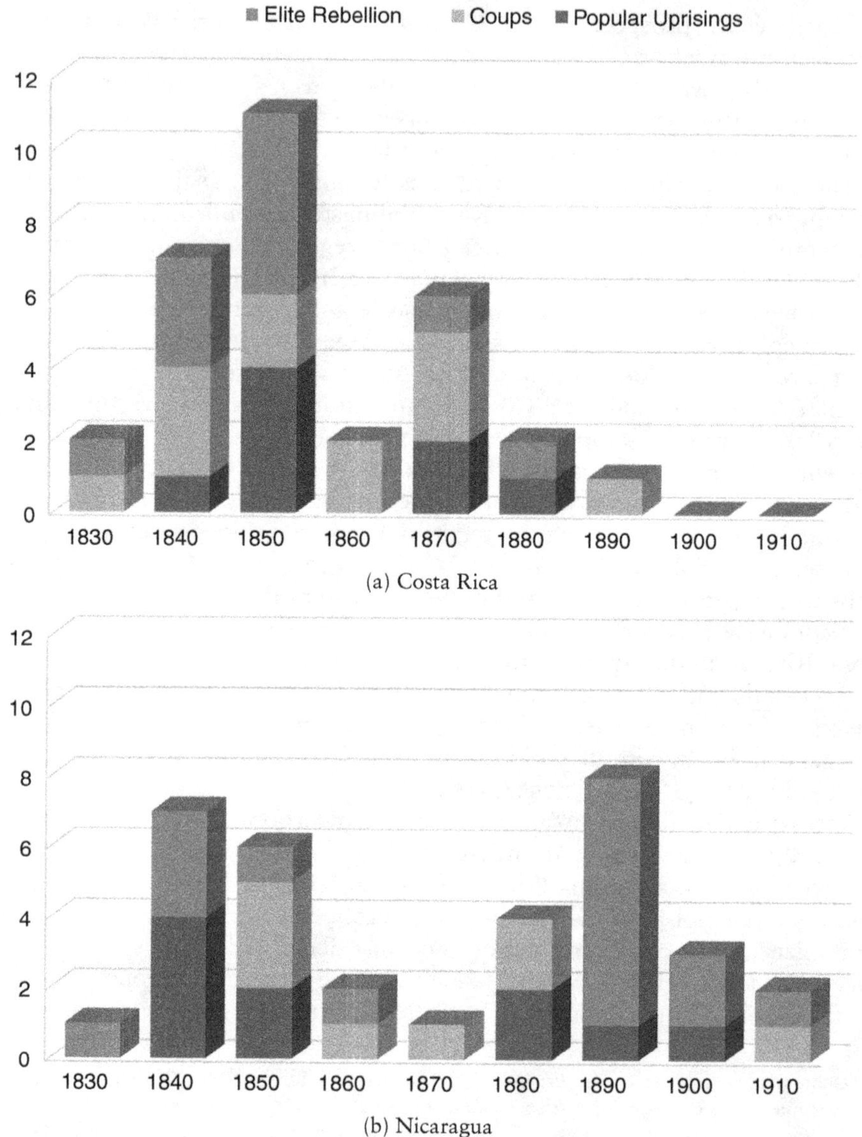

FIGURE 9.2 Rebellions per decade in Costa Rica and Nicaragua

major parties became evident in the declining frequency and milder nature of revolts after the National Campaign. Figure 9.2 shows how "Costa Rica was no exception to the kind of civil conflict that tore the isthmus apart after independence from Spain in 1821" (Molina Jiménez, 2000, 23) but became an exception after this war. Compared to Nicaragua, a country that – together with all its other Central American neighbors – saw rebellions increase in the last decades of the nineteenth century, it is clear how the Costa Rican trajectory changed thereafter.

In line with bellicist expectations, the military became a decisive actor in Costa Rican politics, and coups were still frequent after the war. Mora was ousted by a coup in 1859 for reasons similar to those for the ousting of Balmaceda in Chile and Flores in Uruguay: "With the National Campaign the authority exercised by the president was strengthened and legitimized by association to the defense of sovereignty" (Fallas Santana, 2007, 14), and elites conspired with a praetorian military to limit personalism (Bancroft, 1887, 378). Máximo Blanco and Lorenzo Salazar, two veterans of the National Campaign, basically "decided the time a president should remain as chief of government and when it had to be replaced" (Solis and Gonzalez Pacheco, 1992, 54) during the following decade. Colonel Tomás Guardia, another veteran of the Filibuster War, then presided over the country from 1870 to 1882 – "a period when the military were the ones to truly exercise power, even if not always directly" (Solis and Gonzalez Pacheco, 1992, 45). Guardia "built up the army and the bureaucracy" (Lentner, 1993, 40), expanding military personnel from 12,000 men in 1873 to 15,300 in 1877 and 25,000 in 1882.

Finally, while elites in Managua, Tegucigalpa, San Salvador, and Guatemala City constantly fought among and against each other in the last decades of the nineteenth century, Costa Ricans prepared for war but sought peace and prosperity, quickly becoming the most developed country in the isthmus. As one author puts it, Costa Ricans "were able to accomplish this feat only because they did not become embroiled in the warfare that wreaked havoc in the rest of the region" (Mahoney, 2010, 195). In the Central American wars of the late nineteenth century, such as Barrio's War of Reunification, bellicist dynamics play out, but no Central American state besides Costa Rica was lucky enough to stay on the winning side consistently.

Although historians have been long aware of the role that the 1856–1857 National Campaign played in the process of Costa Rican state formation (Bancroft, 1887; Vega Carballo, 1981; Muñoz Guillén, 1989; Solis and Gonzalez Pacheco, 1992; Fallas Santana, 2007; Gobat, 2018), few consider this war the source of Costa Rican exceptionalism. In part, this could be due to a contemporary image of Costa Rica as a demilitarized country. This 'Switzerland of Latin America' seems to have forgotten its military origins. It is thus important to keep in mind that "despite the absence of an army since 1949, Costa Rica's character to some extent has been shaped by military events and military men. The country's nationalism was consolidated through its military victory over Walker in 1856, and the young self-sacrificing soldier, Juan Santamaría, became a symbol of the nation. Establishment of political stability is attributed to General Tomás Guardia who, after a coup, ruled from 1870 to 1886" (Lentner, 1993, 108).

9.4 AFTER VICTORY: THE FRANCO-MEXICAN WAR

Walker's attempts to chip away Mexican territory and create his own fiefdom in Central America had been made possible by the complete disintegration of Mexico after the Mexican–American War. With Santa Anna heading once more into exile, General Juan Alvarez appointed a liberal cabinet featuring two young radicals, Benito Juárez, minister of justice, and Miguel Lerdo de Tejada, minister of development. Although still federalists, this new generation had suffered under Santa Anna's tyranny and thus supported the rule of law vis-à-vis the whims of *caudillos* and priests. In the years after the defeat against the United States, federalism "lost favor amongst the liberals when they realized that only a strong central authority could build the national economic, social and political system that they desired" (Schoonover, 1978, 10). "Liberals, therefore, became just as centralist as their conservative rivals" (Bazant, 1991, 35).[12]

In line with this transformation, a series of Reform Laws was enacted, starting in 1855. The first of them, known as the Juárez Law, restricted the jurisdiction of ecclesiastical courts strictly to priestly matters and severely reduced privileges like clerical immunity, leading to a conservative revolt of army officers and priests that soon forced Alvarez's resignation. Only the more moderate Ignacio Comonfort, his minister of war, could gather enough support within the army to take back Puebla and reestablish some semblance of order (Bazant, 1991, 33). Yet the liberals continued with the offensive. The Lerdo Law, which confiscated Church property worth some 300 million pesos, was passed in 1856. So much land was taken from the Catholic Church that "a class of landowners would be created by this legislation, in cities and rural regions alike, and their taxes would augment the national income" (Alba, 1982, 141). Finally, in 1857, the Iglesias Law – after the new minister of justice, José María Iglesias – proscribed the practice of charging common people for the administration of parochial services like the officiation of marriages, baptisms, and the like. To resolve what Melchor Ocampo, minister of foreign affairs, called the "systematic anarchy" in which the country had been left since the Mexican–American War (Gonzalez Navarro, 1977, 378), a new 1857 Constitution incorporated the Reform Laws and enshrined individual rights and freedoms against the power of peripheral elites. While the liberals kept the federalist system in place, its spirit was far more centralist than that of the 1824 Federal Constitution of the United Mexican States. The 1857 Magna Carta was

[12] The Mexican–American War was also a prominent trigger of this transformation. "The war with the United States had inevitably left a mark on the minds of most liberals ... the federation, as it had existed in Mexico since the adoption of the 1824 constitution, had made easier the separation of Texas and the temporary secession of Yucatán, and had subsequently been the cause of the defeat and dismemberment of the country.... Perhaps centralism was the right course after all, though not if it meant the domination of the army and the Church. Now that the government was a liberal one, it was advisable to strengthen it, especially since the proximity of the American border weakened the hold of central Mexico on the states of the north, making further dismemberment of the country possible in the future" (Bazant, 1991, 35).

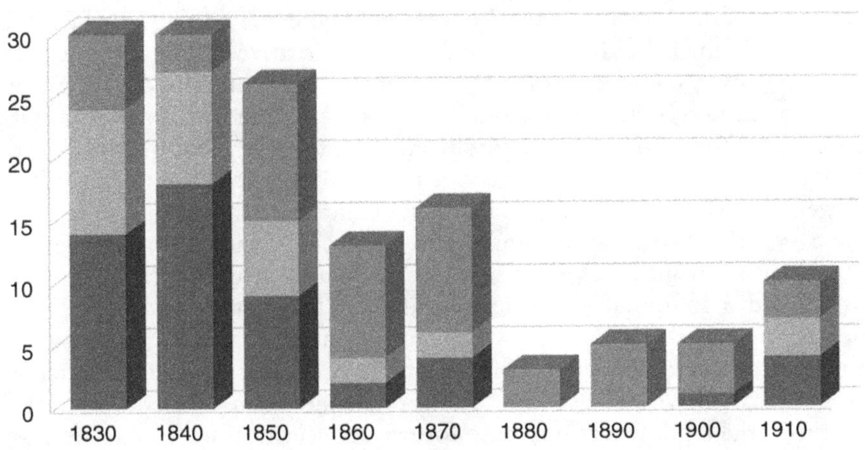

FIGURE 9.3 Rebellions per decade in Mexico

tellingly titled the Political Constitution of the Mexican Republic, and it gave the central government considerable power to tax and intervene in subnational states (Bazant, 1985, 457).

In the context of state weakness following the Mexican–American War, however, it was implausible for the government to succeed at power centralization without facing resistance. Mexico was trapped in a virtual stalemate between central and peripheral elites – the former now closer to the liberal party and the latter aligned with the conservatives. Predictably, the conservatives rebelled. General Félix Zuloaga pronounced the Plan de Tacubaya, which envisioned the redress of the Reform Laws and the suspension of the constitution. Comonfort intended a compromise once again, but he was deposed by Zuloaga in a coup on December 11, 1857.

Figure 9.3 shows the distribution of rebellions in Mexican history – that is, every recorded instance of the use or the credible threat of violence to achieve political goals by an identifiable domestic political group that defies the authority of the state (Madrid and Schenoni, 2024) – according to three main categories. As can be clearly seen, elite rebellions – a category that includes secessionist attempts and major revolts by opposition parties – were notably prominent under the federalist–liberal Constitution of 1824 and under the centralist–conservative Constitution of 1836 and would continue to be so after the defeat against the United States. As we will see, only victory over the French would bring an end to this endemic, systematic anarchy. Yet because Figure 9.3 focuses on the onset of rebellion, the apparent decline in the 1860s does not do justice to the intensity of the conservative–liberal confrontation that started with the Zuloaga rebellion. Defeated in Mexico City, the liberals formed a parallel government in Guanajuato under the leadership of Benito Juárez. Half of the Mexican states – in the Gulf and in the north – sided with the liberals, while the other half sided with the conservatives. "In earlier decades, when faced by a counter-revolution, the liberals had submitted to the army virtually without resistance" (Bazant, 1985, 460), but in this case the country was divided into two de facto states with effective territorial control, making the War of the Reform (1857–1860) a serious threat to Mexico's integrity. Similarly to Argentina, Mexico would spend almost an entire decade in this situation.

In 1858 the liberal government moved from Guanajuato to Veracruz and, benefiting from access to the arms trade and tariffs through the port, consolidated a marginal strategic advantage. The expropriation of Church property in central Mexico allowed Juárez to access foreign credit, pay for imports, and keep a new class of local landowners closer to the liberal cause. Juárez tried to "drive a wedge into the hitherto solidly conservative countryside by letting large landowners purchase former ecclesiastical haciendas" (Bazant, 1991, 37) while "trying to affirm the supremacy of the state over the church" (Alba, 1982, 141) and attracting foreign investment and loans guaranteed by former ecclesiastical property. On July 7, 1859, Juárez took all these measures to their logical extreme, declaring the confiscation of all Church wealth, which attracted another wave of capital to Veracruz in the form of land and property purchases. The conservative government tried to take Veracruz twice in 1858 and 1860 but failed. The liberals, on the other hand, were luckier and took the capital on their first attempt in December 1860. In June 1861 Juárez was elected president in Mexico City.

Conservative guerrillas, however, were still widespread, and the smart financial strategy that had allowed Juárez to win almost immediately doomed his government. After the confiscations, Juárez was left with no assets to pay for his own debt, much less the one that the conservatives had left behind. He was thus forced to declare a default on Mexico's sovereign debt in July. Creditors in Europe were furious and resorted to their governments for a forceful collection of the debt. The scenario was set for the Second French Intervention of Mexico, also known as the Franco-Mexican War (1861–1867).

On October 31, 1861, Great Britain, France, and Spain signed a convention to intervene in Mexico to support the conservatives and collect their debt. Spanish troops landed in Veracruz shortly afterward, followed by the other forces. Yet it soon became clear that the French government had greater ambitions. In April 1862 the Spanish and British withdrew, and on July 3, Napoleon III instructed General Charles de Lorencez to establish a stable government in Mexico. His French army of around 6,500 men started a march to Mexico City, hoping to recreate the military feats that had given worldwide fame to General Winfield Scott.

Because Napoleon III was intervening in support of the conservative elites, the Second French Intervention could be seen as a continuation of the War of Reform. However, this international war was radically different in its implications. The fight was now against a foreign enemy, and although some recalcitrant conservatives believed the French would be instrumental to their cause, most Mexicans were wary of losing their sovereignty. It is thus unsurprising that several conservative generals switched sides and offered their services to Juárez. Because the war was felt by most Mexicans to be a war against an external invader that threatened the existence of Mexico, "the issue was not liberalism against conservatism, as it had been in 1858–60, but Mexican independence against conquest by a foreign power" (Bazant, 1985, 466).

The march toward the capital was therefore not easy for the French. The Mexican army faced them in the First Battle of Puebla on May 5, 1862, in which a 5,000-strong Mexican army confronted French forces of around 6,000 men. The larger and better-equipped French army tried to take the strategic Cerro de Guadalupe, but the fierce resistance of the locals stopped the attack. In the greatest feat of the battle, the second brigade, led by the young General Porfirio Díaz, pushed back, causing a large number of casualties to the enemy – some 476 French died, compared to 227 Mexicans. It was a costly battle for Mexico, but it strengthened Juárez's position considerably, attracting more conservatives to his side and stirring Mexican nationalism.

The effects of the *Cinco de Mayo* would be prolonged. General Porfirio Díaz, much like Santa Anna before him, would cement his public image as the defender of Puebla and become the most important figure in Mexican politics after Juárez's death.

In the short term, the victory attracted the support of militias from across the country, who now rallied around Juárez to expel the invaders from their camp in Orizaba and ultimately from Veracruz. For a moment it appeared as if the French adventure was near its end. In the views of a British naval officer:

> The French have very little provisions left in Orizaba and as their supplies from the surrounding country are cut off, they must of necessity draw supplies from Veracruz or, failing in that, be reduced to the necessity of withdrawing their force nearer the coast or entering into negotiations with the Government. The last accounts from Mexico (received this day) state that General Gonzalez Ortega with 7,000 was about to join the army under Zaragoza. This reinforcement would increase that army to about 18,000 men, with which it is said to be Zaragoza's intention to surround Orizaba, with a view to reduce the French to extremities. General Douay, with a small force of about 400 men, arrived here from France some weeks ago.... The small force that landed with General Douay has suffered severe loss from yellow fever, which is raging amongst the French in Veracruz.[13]

For a moment, pressure from Washington and London suggested that political forces in Paris would abandon the adventure and retreat, but the

[13] Commodore Hugh Dunlop to the Secretary of the Admiralty, HMS *Ariadne* at Veracruz. May 31, 1862. British National Archives FO/414/25, p. 30.

French legislature hesitated and left the decision in the hands of the executive. After news of the defeat reached Napoleon III, the French emperor took the conquest of Mexico as a personal challenge. Determined to restore the prestige of his army, he sacked Lorencez and replaced him with General Élie Forey, who would be supported by a contingent of 24,000 new soldiers. After the defeat, Forey struggled to secure the cooperation of the merchants in Veracruz and had to tax them more leniently, but in the end he was able to hold the port.

French insistence forced Mexico to conscript and train 30,000 men – an effort similar to that of Santa Anna in Monterrey, requiring the personal sacrifice of citizens all over the country. Mexicans contributed with their lives and possessions to fend off the largest invading force in history. Deprived of foreign loans and the foreign taxes from Veracruz, Juárez imposed new direct taxes on elites, such as a tax on urban property, and declared a *levée en masse*, conscripting every able-bodied male above fourteen years old (Scheina, 2003). The mobilization for a second defense of Puebla, which should count as one of the greatest war efforts in Mexican history, left nobody untouched. The British foreign secretary, Earl Russell, rushed to sign a treaty to exempt British citizens from forced loans that suddenly became ubiquitous, but the Mexican government only committed to avoid legislation targeted specifically against them. As much as Mexico depended on British diplomatic support, the necessities of the war required Juárez to tax elites heavily and across the board, including foreign workers and investors.[14]

Delayed by the winter season, the second siege of Puebla started on March 26, 1863, and provides a great example of the contingency of warfare, with several key French victories resulting from a melee. In the Battle of Camarón, considered a founding event of the *légion étrangère*, 65 French soldiers fought 3,000 Mexicans, causing them 800 casualties. This event served as a turning point in the fight, and Puebla fell into French hands on May 17, 1863.

Aware of the difficulties of defending Mexico City, Juárez and his cabinet fled to San Luis Potosí. The defeat in the Second Battle of Puebla led to several defections, particularly among the conservatives, who had flocked toward him before. Now those peripheral elites found a more convenient partner in the French – already aided by a considerable number of conservatives – and changed sides, diminishing the size of Juárez's coalition.

On June 7, 1863, the capital surrendered to the French army and a commission of notables was appointed by the occupation forces, which implemented a fiscal reform. In practice, war forced Forey and his successor, General Achille Bazaine, to centralize power even further and postpone any conservative measures besides the establishment of a monarchy. The crown of

14 Foreign Secretary Earl Russell to Sir Charles L. Wyke, Plenipotentiary of Her Majesty in Mexico. Foreign Office. June 27, 1862. British National Archives FO/414/25, p. 21.

a new Mexican Empire was offered to the Austrian archduke Maximilian who delayed his response, keeping everyone in suspense.

Weighing on the mind of Maximilian was a key fact: The war was far from won. The French had conquered Veracruz, Puebla, and Mexico City, but their control extended to three states while Juárez still controlled eighteen others. Furthermore, the successful invasion had resulted in strengthening the support of the United States for the Mexican liberals, who feared a conspiracy between the Confederation and the French. The US Plenipotentiary in Mexico City put it like this:

> I have always believed that the invasion of Mexico and the overthrow of its government by France was to be connected in some way with the rebellion in the United States. If the French power is extended over the whole Mexican territory, will not the Emperor find some reason for connecting Arizona and Texas with his Mexican colony. Will not the South make terms with him in such case. A guarantee of Southern independence might be considered worth the transfer of Arizona and Texas to the French colony of Mexico.[15]

The fate of the two wars now seemed intertwined, each uncertain and each partly dependent on the fate of the other. The stability of all of North America was hanging by a thread.

By Christmas 1863, however, it seemed that the French military control of Mexico City was consolidated, and Maximilian decided to accept the offer. During his regency period, the emperor realized that with Juárez well entrenched in San Luis Potosí and in control of the north, he would require the support of French troops. Still in Europe, he secured the support of Napoleon III and decided not to redress the liberal laws – in particular the confiscation of Church property – that were necessary for Mexico to honor its debts, thus retaining the support of European capitals (Hanna and Hanna, 1971, 115).

The following months were tragic for the liberals, who were defeated every single time they faced the French army – in Querétaro, Guanajuato, Oaxaca, and Chihuahua. While watching his commanders getting defeated and sometimes killed, Juárez was forced to move the capital further north, to Saltillo and then to Monterrey. After Guadalajara fell to Bazaine, even the *moderado* liberals – like Santiago Vidaurri, a prominent liberal leader in the north who refused to continue the collection of taxes – started to defect.

Once he arrived in Mexico in June 1864, like any ruler facing a war, Emperor Maximilian I completed his move to the state-building camp and sided with the central elites of Mexico City conservatives. He expanded public infrastructure and national bureaucracy considerably, extended rights to all Mexican subjects, abolished debt peonage and other forms of servitude, and even developed nationalist rituals and symbols aimed at creating a new Mexican imperial identity (Bazant, 1985; Ibsen, 2010; McAllen, 2014). Most of these measures

15 Letter from Minister Thomas Corwin to Secretary of State William H. Seward. Mexico City. June 26, 1863. US National Archives M97/30.

were clearly oriented toward gaining the support of peasants and the lower classes. Some were perhaps attempts to appeal to Juárez himself. But Mexican nationalism, forged in similar wars against foreign invaders, already ran deep in Mexican blood, and particularly in that of the masses. No matter what the emperor did, most people continued to see Juárez, a Zapotec native himself, as a natural leader and Maximilian as an illegitimate foreign-imposed tyrant.

Three years into the invasion, the fog of war was still thick enough that those best connected, resourced, and informed, such as the US Plenipotentiary in Mexico, even when they had high stakes in predicting the outcome, felt completely in the dark:

> From all the conflicting reports brought to the city from different parts of the country it is almost impossible to form an opinion as to the true state of affairs in what is now called the Empire. The liberals seem to be hopeful and confidently predict that Maximilian will not remain in the country three years. The friends of the new government, on the other hand, are equally confident that the days of republicanism in Mexico are ended. The events which have transpired within the past months are of a nature to encourage both parties.[16]

However, it also seemed clear that the trend favored the French, as more and more states fell under their power. By 1865 the army under Bazaine had swelled to some 64,000 men, which provided a significant numerical advantage but was also draining the resources of France. A convention was therefore signed between Napoleon III and the Mexican government in Miramar, which outlined the roadmap for the creation of a Mexican army that would allow for the progressive withdrawal of French troops. As victory continued to bless Bazaine – who was soon named Maréchal d'Empire – the withdrawal of the French army was seen as a first step toward the normalization of the new order. Systematically defeated, Juárez had to move further north to Paso del Norte – today's Ciudad Juárez. His final defeat must have seemed inevitable then.

Yet an exogenous development changed everything for the Mexican liberals: the end of the American Civil War. While the conflict between the Union and the Confederation had kept Washington's hands tied for most of the conflict – trying to prevent, for example, an explicit alliance of Maximilian with the South – the American allies were now free to offer Juárez weapons and financial support to expel the French from the Americas and return Mexico to their sphere of influence. Since April 1865, liberal forces had started to push back, and with each liberal victory the coalition around Juárez grew in size (Schoonover, 1978).

Figure 9.4 shows the timeline of the main events on the battlefield and how they correlate with the internal dynamics within the Juárez coalition and the Intervention. This snapshot of the events of the Franco-Mexican War shows very clearly how the centralist coalitions were weakened by defeat

[16] Letter from the Plenipotentiary of the US in Mexico, Minister Thomas Corwin, to Secretary of State William H. Seward. Mexico City. August 29, 1864. US National Archives M97/30.

Intervention	Mexico (Juàrez)		Battlefield
	Mobilization against the European blockade	1862	Blockade of Veracruz First Battle of Puebla (French defeat)
French struggle to remain on hold of Veracruz and enforce the blockade Lorencez is sacked and replaced by Foray	Conservatives join Juárez coalition Cinco de Mayo myth and increased patriotism Successful recruitment of 30,000	1863	Second Battle of Puebla (French victory)
After taking the capital the Intervention accepts liberal laws and builds a broad coalition	Juárez leaves Mexico City and both conservatives and moderate liberals abandon Juárez's coalition	1864	Battle of Guadalajara (French victory)
Emperor Maximilian I arrives French occupation troops continue to grow, reaching over 50,000 Attempts at a new imperial nationalism	More liberals leave Juárez's coalition Juárez is forced to move the capital to the north until Paso del Norte (Ciudad Juárez)	1865	End of the American Civil War
Increased repression (Black Decree) Napoleon III announces partial troop withdrawal Empress Charlotte leaves Mexico	Juárez decides to go on the offensive The coalition strengthens with the return of liberals and incorporates local leaders	1866	Fall of Monterrey (French defeat) Battle of La Carbonara (French defeat)
Napoleon III announces complete withdrawal Bazaine leaves and conservatives abandon the government	Porfirio Díaz and liberal military gain great prominence Most conservatives bandwagon with Juárez	1867	Battle of Queretaro (French defeat)
Execution of Maximilian	Liberal hegemony consolidates		

FIGURE 9.4 Second French Intervention timeline

and strengthened by victory, how even the conservatives were compelled to centralize power in the context of war, and the turning point that the end of the American Civil War meant for the Second French Intervention. The impact of each of these events on domestic equilibria was almost immediate.

Foreseeing the change of tide, Maximilian issued a decree – known as the Black Decree – that ordered the execution of those who bore arms against the imperial regime. The measure backfired, martyring liberal leaders and reinforcing local support for the liberal cause. Napoleon III, heavily indebted due to this Mexican adventure and unwilling to confront the United States, announced the withdrawal of his troops in 1866 (Bushnell, 1994, 202). The first major military defeats of the Mexican Empire in the north followed, bringing about the expected domestic dynamics: Cabinet reshuffles started to take place as Maximilian's position grew weaker, and peripheral elites of the conservatives became more influential. Throughout the war, moderate conservatives and liberals had been flocking toward the potential winner. Both Maximilian and Juárez needed to foster mobilization, and they surrounded themselves with central elites, but they were easy prey to the peripheral elites of dissidents every time mobilization failed to pay out. Now the tables had turned against the French, which strengthened the centralists on Juárez's side but seriously impaired Maximilian (Pani, 2001). His subsequent inability to consolidate domestic support ended up securing the victory for the Mexican republicans (Bazant, 1985, 468). In June 1867, Maximilian and his generals were executed by firing squad, and one month later, Juárez entered, victorious, to take possession of Mexico City.

Victory in the Franco-Mexican War meant, first and foremost, the end of the Conservative Party – then the party of the peripheral elites. In the light of the Second French Intervention, conservatives became "traitors" (Krauze, 1994, 20) *tout court*. Despite the importance of the role that conservative elites like Alamán played in the first stage of the state-building process, their ideas and feats were wiped from the official history, sometimes referred to as the *historia de bronce* (Van Young, 2020, 160). Only more recently have the conservatives been rescued from oblivion (O'Gorman, 1986).

Naturally, the crushing defeat of the conservative party allied to the French meant that the postwar period was one of liberal hegemony. In this way, the central elites, now incarnated in the liberal party, imposed the state-building project on the peripheral elites. As Mazzuca (2021, 272) notes, "The consensus vision among historians is that before 1867 Mexico was a failed state" until "the Liberal triumph (1867) paved the way to violence monopolization." Anointed with victory, liberalism was not so much a party anymore as a "unifying myth that was consecrated as the symbol of resistance to foreign invasion, the grammar of patriotism, the language of consensus, and the key to progress" (Pani, 2017, 571).

Consequently, Juárez, who had already been the republican president for three periods (1858–1867), remained in charge until his death in 1872.

A veritable "myth" of Juárez was created by this international victory (Weeks, 1987; Galeana, 2007), which led to further centralization of power in his hands. During his tenure, "Mexico's survival as an independent nation seemed assured. The church had lost most of its economic and political hold on the country; church inspired coups were a thing of the past." As Katz (1986, 5) notes, "The old Conservative army, so prone to indiscipline and revolt, had been dissolved for good. Regional government was firmly in Liberal hands." By the end of his life, Juárez had been able "to set up a strong centralized state which would have immeasurably increased his independence from an increasingly divided social and political constituency" (Katz, 1986, 8). The faculties and relative power of Congress were limited, and the president was granted the power to veto any bill, which could only be overridden by a two-thirds majority.

Juárez also greatly expanded the size of the state bureaucracy, and in 1870 he issued a broad amnesty securing the return of property and offices to central elites. The number of schools skyrocketed from 2,424 in 1857 to 8,103 in 1874. The Church was the great loser, and it never regained its previous role as educator, service provider, tax collector, and source of credit. Consolidating the role of the state in these matters, Juárez issued a modern civil code in 1870, replicating the best features of the French-inspired one implemented by Maximilian. Finally, and against the old liberal tradition, Juárez gave the army an increased budget and political role, recognizing its newly acquired prestige and influence as well as creating a new awareness in the military of being an integral part of the state-building project (Katz, 1986, 8–11).

Juárez was even able to secure foreign credit and investment for the development of a railroad network. This case – together with those of Chile and Argentina, among others – exemplifies how victory in international war could change the expectations of lenders, making credit extremely cheap and beneficial in the long term, even in situations of extreme conditionality (Queralt, 2022). Although Juárez had famously defaulted on the Mexican debt in 1861, with the conservatives completely defeated, he now had sufficient political clout to service his debts and guarantee property rights.

These policies paid off handsomely, and by 1873 the country had a railway line connecting Mexico City with Veracruz (Bushnell, 1994, 203). The formula was easy: The protection of private property and domestic order by an ever-stronger state would attract foreign capital, which would in turn expand foreign trade and generate enough revenue to make all debts payable. From 1870 "until about 1900, the application of these policies strengthened the Mexican state" (Katz, 1986, 24). As Edward Beatty (2001, 27) notes, while Mexican public spending had been consistently shrinking since independence, this tendency changed thereafter.

The Restored Republic was not completely free from violence and instability, which were endemic to nineteenth-century Mexico, but tamed them considerably by developing "a perfect police state" (Sinkin, 1979, 89). To enhance law and order in the countryside, Juárez staffed his new rural police with demobilized soldiers. He also used federal troops to intervene at any sight of trouble, deterring rebellion by political groups, bandits, and governors themselves. Juárez's successor, Sebastián Lerdo de Tejada, followed the playbook and thus "was able to strengthen the role of the state considerably" (Katz, 1986, 17). State reach extended to the outermost territories still controlled by local *caudillos*. This pacification of the countryside was facilitated by the modernization of the army and the extension of the railroad beyond the 1873 line from Mexico City to Veracruz and in other directions from the capital.

The Lerdo administration fell victim to a coup led by Porfirio Díaz in 1876. Díaz and a group of acolytes had been revolting against Juárez since 1868 – most prominently after losing the national elections against him and Lerdo, which led to the Plan de la Noria of November 1871. Although his revolts were against extreme power centralization, once in power Díaz strengthened the central state further, so much so that the probability of a coup or a factional rebellion like his decreased markedly thereafter. In fact, the 1876 Díaz uprising was virtually the last of its kind in the nineteenth century and put an end to the era of the *pronunciamientos*. From 1821 to 1876, more than 1,500 *pronunciamientos* had taken place all over Mexico, calling for or supporting a revolt, usually against the national government. The practice faded away thereafter (Fowler, 2011, 246).

A hero of the war against France, Díaz accelerated the state-building process even further. Although initially a member of the national guard, Díaz "subordinated the institution to his now favorite military force, the standing army" (Sabato, 2018, 158), which was virtually incorporated into the governing coalition in a corporatist fashion. He also included in his coalition a middle-class contingent from small townships that contested vestigial oligarchies, further consolidating the power of the national state over governors and peripheral elites. Moreover, he benefited from tensions with the Hayes administration in the United States – which initially refused to recognize the new government – to regain territorial control over the border and increase the overall size and payroll of the military. Eventually Washington granted his government recognition, opening a new era of major American investment in Mexico. It was the beginning of the *Porfiriato*, the longest period of political stability and economic growth Mexico had ever experienced.

After his first term ended in 1880, and relying on a strong, cohesive, and hegemonic liberal party, Díaz stepped down. His successor, General Manuel González, further strengthened the alliance between party and armed forces that was at the core of the state-building project. He also signed a series of contracts to develop the Central Mexican Railway, connecting the Mexican capital to virtually all states in the south of the United States and connecting all major cities to the north of the country (Bushnell, 1994, 207).[17] By the end of González's tenure in 1884, Mexico was clearly on a steep state-building trajectory.

Mexico was the only country in Latin America to undergo two episodes of major international war in the nineteenth century, one a defeat, the other a victory. This can be seen in the longitudinal analysis of some indicators in Figure 9.5. The most telling of these is clearly the evolution of per capita GDP, according to figures from Jutta Bolt et al. (2018). Levels in 1820 remain relatively stable until the Mexican–American War, a severe defeat after high mobilization that sends this proxy of state capacity on a downward trajectory for a decade. The change to a new positive trajectory is surprisingly concurrent with Mexico's greatest victory of the nineteenth century against France. The integration of Mexico into the global economy in the 1870s might explain the booming rates of growth too, but the outcomes of war seem to provide an explanation for both the upward and the downward changes.

The negative effect that the anarchy triggered by the defeat against the United States had on Mexico is evident too in the Composite Index of National Capabilities (CINC) (Singer, 1988), and this indicator stabilizes after victory. We see a similar trend in diplomatic representation (Singer and Small, 1966; Bayer, 2006), although the effects are more subdued due to the severed relations with former contenders.

The fact that changes in these trajectories correspond to the timing of war outcomes – while country-specific confounders remain unchanged – provides strong support for bellicist theory. This chapter provides a qualitative narrative that fleshes out this relationship in more detail. The destiny of the Centralist Republic of Mexico (1835–1846) became tied to the military fortunes of its most prominent *caudillo*, Santa Anna. The Mexican–American War (1846–1848) shattered the project. The following years were marked by a return to extreme decentralization – with the reenactment of the 1824 Federal Constitution – and a virtual collapse of the state, ending in the War of Reform (1858–1861). Only victory against the French invaders (1861–1867) helped rebuild the elite consensus on the necessity of a strong central state based on a hegemonic liberal party.

17 "The first railway line between the US and Mexico was inaugurated in 1884. US investments in Mexico were increasing at a breathtaking pace. For the first time since Maximilian's defeat Mexico had diplomatic relations with all major European countries. Railway construction and the final defeat of the Apaches, which occurred in the years between 1880 and 1884, opened up vast expanses of Mexico's northern frontier, much of which had been hitherto inaccessible. Then under Porfirio Díaz, who was elected president again in 1884 and remained president until 1911, Mexico underwent its most profound economic, political, and social transformation since the advent of independence in 1821" (Katz, 1986, 28).

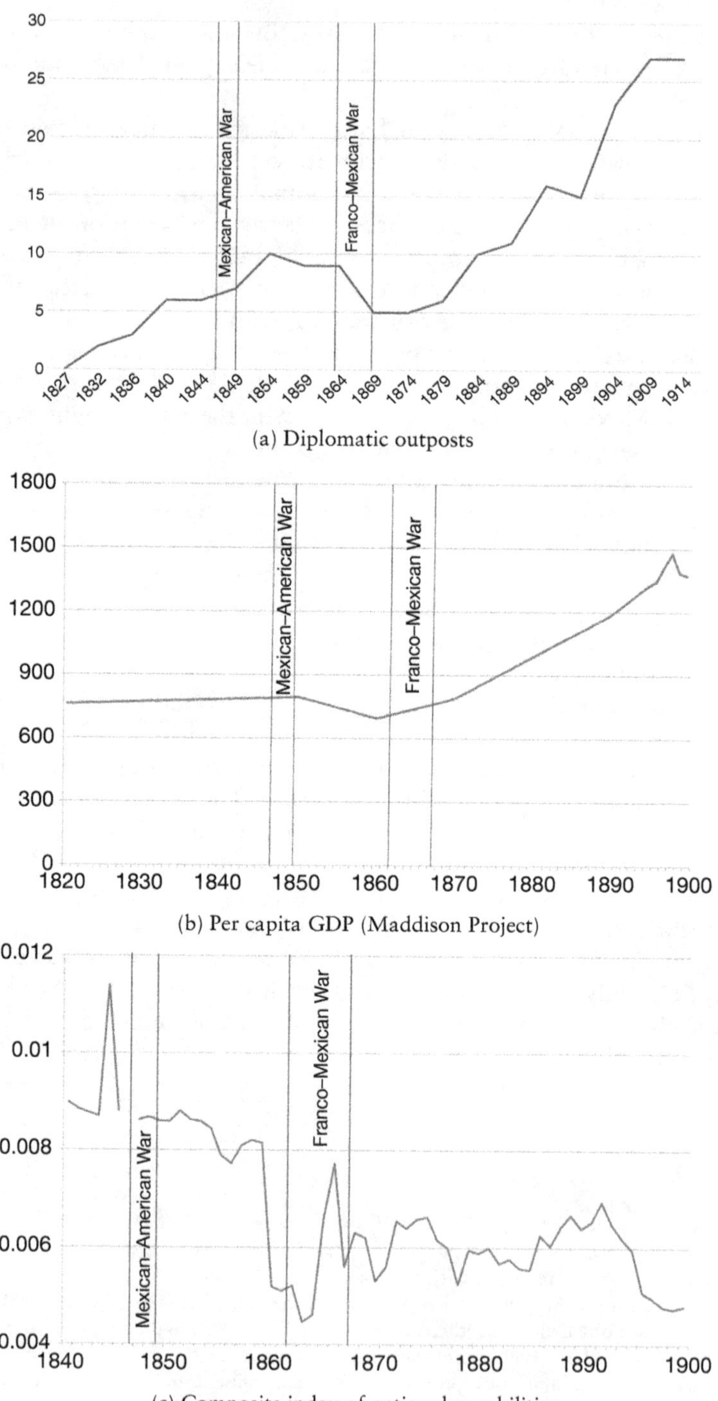

(a) Diplomatic outposts

(b) Per capita GDP (Maddison Project)

(c) Composite index of national capabilities

FIGURE 9.5 Postwar trajectories in Mexico

10

Conclusion

As the reader reaches these last pages, hopefully a sufficiently persuasive case has been made that war did make the state in Latin America and that a more complete version of bellicist theory that incorporates the contingency of war outcomes and considers their postwar institutional effects can go to great lengths in explaining variation in state capacity and development today.

This book contributes to a heated debate about state formation in nineteenth-century Latin America and the enduring importance of dynamics that took place back then. In this regard, it set out to show that the relative levels of state capacity that characterize the region today can be traced to the outcomes of wars in that era. Throughout the book, I have inferred this relationship in several complementary ways.

In the first part, I showed the illustrious intellectual history of this hypothesis and the fact that wars were prominent during the nineteenth century, when Latin American states formed. In the twentieth century the starkness of the state capacity ranking and the paucity of state formation confirm the bellicist expectation that without war, little state formation takes place.

In the second part I performed a series of region-wide studies of intra-regional variation on indicators of wartime mobilization and state capacity. In Chapter 4 I showed that the coercion–extraction cycle – that is, domestically oriented taxation followed by domestic unrest – was triggered by militarized interstate disputes that could seldom be financed by resorting to foreign loans or tariffs. In Chapter 5 I found a statistically significant effect of losing – vis-à-vis winning – a war on indicators of state capacity such as per capita revenue and railroad mileage, generating a gap between winners and losers that increased over the long term. In Chapter 6 I demonstrated that winners of nineteenth-century wars were at the top of the hierarchy of state capacity in Latin America c. 1900, while losers were at the bottom.

In the third part I looked at the precise mechanisms and sequences predicted by classical bellicist theory, zooming into cases of severe warfare. In each and every one of these wars, theory and history match. First, state capacity levels are relatively constant before war, due to an underlying stalemate between pro-state central elites and anti-state peripheral elites. Second, preparation for war against an external threat weakens the constraint posed by peripheral elites, allowing for the formation of wartime institutions and the initiation of the extraction–coercion cycle in every contender. Third, the fortuitous results of key battles embolden and strengthen state-building coalitions on the winning side, while state builders on the other side suffer a concurrent blow. Fourth and finally, state institutions born out of victory or defeat consolidate postwar trajectories, with two state institutions being key in this regard: the military and nationalist parties.

The case studies contain a wealth of information and are worth considering in detail. For each contender in a war, the complex mechanism described above renders multiple concrete observational implications. Wars themselves have at least two contenders. Therefore the fact that the predictions of the theory match every case analyzed without exception should be taken as a very strong indication that the micro-level logic underpinning the macro-level correlations in previous chapters is very solid.

Moreover, while the major wars initially listed in Table 3.4 – the La Plata War, the Mexican–American War, the Filibuster War, the Franco-Mexican War, the Paraguayan War, and the War of the Pacific – were covered in detail, I also briefly noted that the mechanisms fit almost every other war in nineteenth-century Latin America. Wars in the River Plate region – like the Argentina–Brazil War and the Siege of Montevideo – were also summarily discussed in Chapter 7, while minor wars on the Pacific coast and in the Andes – like the Peru–Great Colombia War, the War of the Confederation, the Peru–Bolivia War, and the Chincha Islands War – were covered in Chapter 8, and minor wars in Mexico and Central America – such as the Battle of Tampico and the Pastry War – were discussed in Chapter 9. Other interstate conflicts like the Colombia–Ecuador War, the Dominican Restoration War, and three Central American wars were also summarily discussed in Chapter 4. Although many of these discussions are admittedly too short to provide conclusive proof, the vignettes provided show that the logic of classical bellicist theory applies to them as well. The case studies in Part III should therefore reassure us that the findings in the cross-national analyses presented in Part II are due to the mechanisms detailed in the theory.

This book also elaborates on an understanding of bellicist theory that is more in line with the ideas of Max Weber and Otto Hintze and was still reflected in the early scholarship of Charles Tilly. More recent research on this paradigm has adopted the view that war outcomes affect state capacity trends via a selection mechanism – that is, by killing the losers – or disregard war outcomes to focus on the prewar phase, with state capacity simply plateauing after the ends of wars. Both views pay little attention to the inherent contingency of warfare and its reverberations into the postwar period. Irrespective of the merits of such works, this book demonstrates that wars of the past have an effect that lingers on, and that the classics of bellicist theory put especial emphasis on this mechanism.

While more recent understandings of bellicist theory do not fit the dynamics at work in nineteenth-century Latin America, this original specification works particularly well. Fitting the history of seventeen national states throughout a century means that the theory explains a big portion of the observable universe. Not only did Latin America contain almost half of the states in the world by the turn of the twentieth century, but, being characterized by the survival of all contenders, it is perhaps the only region in which the theory could be tested in full – that is, including information on all the defeated states in the postwar period. This feature has allowed us to zoom in on losers like Paraguay and Peru – a specimen that remains unseen in other regions – and test our predictions on them.

Moreover, because Latin America has been the poster child of those who argue against bellicist theory across the social sciences, the fact that classical bellicist theory explains state formation in the region better than any alternative and almost to the smallest detail should give renewed credit to Weber, Hintze, and others in this tradition.

The analyses provided, however, do not exhaust the many implications of this theory that could still be tested in nineteenth-century Latin America. One important aspect that remains under-explored in my analyses are the subnational implications of the classical bellicist argument. Although previous scholarship has explored bellicist implications at the subnational level in the context of civil wars (see Rodríguez-Franco, 2016; Sanchez Talanquer, 2017; Flores Macías, 2018; Garfias, 2018; Arias and de la Calle, 2021; Paglayan, 2022), very few studies have so far explored the subnational variation in state capacity that takes place due to international war. Because border areas are usually mobilization hotspots and theaters of combat, war outcomes should produce clear long-term contrasts between winners and losers alongside borders. This intuition seems to be corroborated in Latin America if we look at the borders of Brazil and Paraguay, Chile and Peru, and Costa Rica and Nicaragua, to mention some examples, but could by looking at geographic discontinuities.

The theory should also generalize to Latin America beyond the nineteenth century. Although twentieth-century wars were few and far between and ended in stalemates – like the Chaco War (1932–1935), the last proper war in the region (Schenoni et al., 2023) – the case could be made that defeat in some prominent militarized disputes can explain marginal changes in state-building trajectories. Joel S. Migdal (1988, 274) notes that Cuba, a paradigmatic case of a strong state in Latin America, benefited from having successfully withstood a permanent threat of invasion – during the Cold War. Marcus Kurtz (2013, 7) noted that Argentina, being at the top of the hierarchy during the first decades of the twentieth century, began a steady decline benefited from having successfully withstood a permanent threat of invasion its failure to jump on the bandwagon with the allies in World War II (Escudé, 1981). Later on, Argentina endured a defeat in the Malvinas/Falklands War, which arguably affected the authority of the military and the state. Similarly, it is said about the 1941 Zarumilla War that "while Peru's victory allowed it to consolidate national unity, Ecuador's defeat only burdened the state with huge military budgets and the growing political influence of the military" (Downes, 2005, 366). Peru and Ecuador endured other confrontations – the Paquisha War and the Cenepa War – the effects of which could be gauged. This focus on victory and defeat could complement the effects of rivalries – a form of preparation for war – on state capacity, which previous research has already corroborated (Thies, 2004).

Because twentieth-century Latin America tells a tale of state stagnation due to chronic peace – and absent the cause, absent the effect – looking back at Europe could open even more promising paths for future researchers. Tilly himself suggested that Europe's modern history not only is important for theorizing state formation but "conversely, ostensibly general formulations which can already be proposed to account for the contemporary world deserve checking against the vast, well-documented European experience" (Tilly, 1975, 14). Following his advice, then, we might look back at the cases where European states survived after defeat and see whether the insights drawn from Latin America offer a better representation of the European experience.

One intuitive way to do this is via speculations and counterfactual thought experiments based on the theory as now reformulated. For example, we could imagine what Europe would have looked like if all losers of war had survived and interstate competition had been halted in the twentieth century. According to classical bellicist theory, such a region might have looked like a geography littered with what Guillermo O'Donnell called "brown areas" of low state capacity. In other words, that counterfactual Europe would look like Latin America today.

In a way, one need not go beyond the classical work of Theda Skocpol (1979) to start noting how defeat in war might have led to state weakening and collapse in Europe, just as classical bellicist theory proposed. Let us take some of her paradigmatic cases for the purposes of illustrating the argument.

France is a case in point of a state that climbed down the ladder of state capacity from "near-dominance over Europe to the humiliation of martial defeats and royal bankruptcy" (Skocpol, 1979, 52). Since the Fronde (1648–1653) in the early reign of Louis XIV, France experienced state formation at a rapid pace. Reforms like the deployment of the intendants and the administrative, financial, and fiscal institutions introduced by Colbert were accompanied by victory in the War of Devolution (1667–1668) and the Dutch War (1672–1678). Defeat in the War of the League of Augsburg (1688–1697) and the War of Spanish Succession (1701–1714) coincide with the weariness of absolutism and state weakening. Later on, stalemate in the War of Austrian Succession (1740–1748) – where bitterness about the result was immortalized in the phrase *bête comme la paix* – and defeat in the Seven Years' War (1756–1763) led, as is well known, to the collapse of the French state. Prisons like La Bastille, once symbols of the mighty French state, became symbols of revolution and chaos.

Notably, the monopoly over violence and the legitimacy of the French state would have to be rebuilt by war, and following the rhythm of victories and defeats on the battlefield. It is telling that the stalemate between republicans and monarchists from 1789 to 1792 would only be broken after war with Austria and Prussia was declared, leading to the second phase of the revolution. The invasion of these powers led to the massacre of the six hundred Swiss Guards in the insurrection of August 10 and the September Massacres. After victory in the Battle of Valmy on September 20, the First Republic was declared, and stability reigned again as the French occupied Savoy, Nantes, and Frankfurt. But then Britain began military preparations in late 1792 and Spain and Portugal entered the anti-French coalition in January 1793, leading to French defeats on several fronts. This turn of events was followed by domestic uprisings in the form of the war in the Vendée and the federalist revolts in Bordeaux, Marseille, and other major cities. After Louis XVI was guillotined, his executors, the Girondins, were also beheaded for their federalist sympathies, and the Reign of Terror began. When the tide turned in 1794 and the French armies drove the Austrians, British, Dutch, and Spanish beyond the Rhine and the Pyrenees, Robespierre became a tyrant – as victorious executives often do. After the single coup of Thermidor ended the dictatorship, relative stability followed. Due to space constraints it is impossible to continue pointing here to the constant conjunction of battle outcomes and domestic events, but it is also well known how Napoleon's victories during the Revolutionary Wars and the Napoleonic Wars led to the consolidation of a new order.

Of course, the final defeat of France after the Napoleonic Wars brought state weakening and chronic regime instability. Yet the demise of France explains, in a way, state building in the United Kingdom. Some authors have tried to explain the contrast between how wars affected these two countries by reference to the comparative strength of capitalism in each of them (Teschke, 2017, 44), but war outcomes provide a straightforward and convincing alternative story for why England consolidated its fiscal–military state after 1688 (Brewer, 1990) and Great Britain became the most advanced fiscal state by 1815 (Bonney, 1999, 14). Of course, it is beyond the capacity of these conclusions to demonstrate a correlation between outcomes and state strengthening at the level of individual wars – much less battles – but dynamics in the United Kingdom seem to mirror the French example above also in the nineteenth and twentieth centuries.

Prussia is also a great example – and one worth being briefly discussed, given its prominence in the literature. The famous reforms of Frederick the Great seem to coincide with his victory in the Seven Years' War, which had already made Prussia one of the most capable states in Europe by the time of the Napoleonic Wars. Although it is often thought that the origins of the strong Prussian state are to be found in the reforms subsequent to the defeat in the Battle of Jena-Auerstedt of October 14, 1806, history seems to be more in line with classical bellicist theory. Reforms undertaken immediately after the defeat were anti-absolutist and anti-statist and weakened the central government considerably. Although some of the reforms introduced – like meritocracy in the army – would prove state-strengthening in the long term, the deleterious effects of the reforms led to the dismissal of the reformist Karl Freiherr vom Stein in 1808 and a fiscal crisis in 1810. The real turn of events seems to take place during the War of the Sixth Coalition (1812–1814). It was then that Prussia was finally able to develop a whole new strand of centralist reforms, ending in the institution of compulsory military service in 1814. After a prominent Prussian role in Waterloo, the consolidation of the German state was clearly accompanied by systematic victories in the Austro-Prussian War of 1866 and the Franco-Prussian War of 1870, which set up the Second German Empire as an example of statehood and military might.[1] Defeat in World War I, however, was followed by a weakening of the state, epitomized by hyperinflation and a constant state of rebellion that was only quelled once militarism and mobilization against an external threat kicked in once again and consolidated the Nazi Party. After World War II, while the complete demise of the German state was contemplated in the Morgenthau Plan, mobilization in the context of the Cold War conspired to save it again as a bastion against communism.

Russia seems to provide a similar example. Peter the Great consolidated the administrative service and the professional army roughly at the same time as he obtained victory in the Great Northern War (1700–1721) against Sweden, and the course of state strengthening continued under Catherine the Great, emboldened by victory in the Russo-Turkish War (1768–1774). After victory against Napoleon in 1812, Russia consolidated as the greatest power in the continent. Its domestic might became evident in its invulnerability to the liberal revolutions that affected all other European states during the first half of the nineteenth century. Defeat in the Crimean War (1854–1855), however, seems to have reversed the course of Russian consolidation, initiating a cycle of domestic unrest and failure to effectively monopolize violence. The Russo-Japanese War of 1905 and World War I are clearly at the heart of the demise of the Russian Empire. It seems fair to conclude that "in Tsarist Russia revolutionary crises developed only under the direct impact of defeats in war" (Skocpol, 1979, 81) and that Soviet Russia, after some fairly troublesome decades, consolidated after victory in World War II.

1 Of course, the same pattern followed by Germany in the formation of its national state was mimicked by Italy, where Piedmont was emboldened by a series of victories and conquests of other, until-then-independent Italian states (Lemke and Carter, 2016, 497).

There are many other instances in European history that could fit the classical bellicist narrative, ranging from the Crusades (Blaydes and Paik, 2016) to the demise of the Soviet Union. It is beyond the capacity of this concluding chapter to cover more, but I hope the illustrations provided here do offer a glimpse of the potential explanatory power of classical bellicist theory.

Of course, classical bellicist theory is a universal theory and thus there is no reason to limit these insights to Europe. In China, for example, defeat in external war also seems closely related to state weakening (Skocpol, 1979, 77). The First Opium War (1839–1842), the Second Opium War (1856–1860), and the Sino-Japanese War (1894–1895) all led to a path of state weakening that ended in the Boxer Rebellion (1899–1901) and yet another defeat. Attempts to rebuild the state without victory, like the centralization of the railway administration, ended up provoking the 1911 Revolution and the end of the empire. It would take victory against the Japanese in World War II – and subsequent victories against Tibet, India, and Vietnam – for a new Chinese state to emerge from the ashes and consolidate. It has been already noted that the strength of states in Asia after World War II can be explained by bellicist theory, with the Koreas and Vietnam being the only states to suffer an invasion in the postwar era and China, Japan, and Taiwan being clear cases of state building driven by external threat (Migdal, 1988, 274).

In American history it seems even clearer how a direct path toward state building was cemented by serial victory. While the Constitution endorsed extreme decentralization – allowing a dual military system consisting of a relatively small federal army and strong militias maintained by the states – the victories in the War of 1812 and the Mexican–American War started to consolidate the position of the federal state, arguably leading to the Civil War, where the central elites of the Union defeated the peripheral elites of the Confederation. Subsequent victories in the Spanish–American War, World War I, and World War II clearly led to the expansion of the federal government and the consolidation of one of the strongest states in history. The withdrawal of troops from Vietnam, Afghanistan, and Iraq would be portrayed as small defeats of the sort that could have marginally undermined state authority (Stein and Russett, 1980, 88) but were by no means comparable in scale to the victories that built the American state.

The theory should also generalize to the rest of the world in a contemporary setting. Given the recent absence of great power war and the relative paucity of interstate warfare altogether, it will probably prove more challenging to find cases of clear victory and defeat in this context. However, the apparently contradictory effects of war in the developing world (Sorensen, 2001) and after World War II (Van Creveld, 1999; Chin, 2019) seem to be in principle amenable to an explanation based on war outcomes.

In the Middle East, for example, Israel has clearly become the strongest state in the region after accumulating a series of military victories since its birth – just like Chile and Uruguay in nineteenth-century Latin America (Migdal,

1988, 274). It has also been proposed that the Iraq–Iran War strengthened the Iranian state considerably after victory (Harris, 2017). In South Asia, Pakistan seems to provide an example of a state – akin to Peru in this book – that has suffered repeated defeat, resulting in progressive state weakening (Paul, 2014). Overall, empirical puzzles such as why war weakened Afghanistan while it strengthened Vietnam (Taylor and Botea, 2008) could be answered with a focus on war outcomes – in that case the systematic defeat of governments in Kabul compared to the sequence of victories that emboldened Hanoi seems to prove the point. As with Kandinsky's painting on the cover, once one puts on the glasses of classical bellicist theory, it becomes difficult not to see this pattern.

Finally, this book reaches out to some related literatures in political science, encouraging new avenues of research.

While classical bellicist theory is chiefly concerned with international wars, some insights provided in this book could inform the study of how civil warfare affects rebel orders and state institutions in the long term (Arjona, 2014; Schwartz, 2023). Violent dynamics including groups such as insurgencies and criminal organizations are similarly likely to be affected by conflict outcomes, although through different mechanisms.

A particularly promising area for the study of subnational effects lies in the interstices of international and domestic politics. For example, classical bellicist theory seems to generate a set of interesting predictions for dynamics of foreign subversion (Lee, 2020): While in contexts of mild competition rival states are likely to weaken each other in border areas, it is equally likely that preparation for war will force states to strengthen and increase their presence in border areas and that after wars have been fought, winners and losers will show contrasting strength precisely in those areas.

This book also illuminates the reasons why externally forced state building does not work: If victory makes the state, defeating states to build them up again becomes a contradiction (Downes, 2021). A literature on foreign-imposed regime change has long been faced with this puzzle. From a classical bellicist perspective, the exceptionality of Germany and Japan – virtually the only two successful cases in this literature – probably lies in the speed and extent of postwar mobilization against a new external threat after these states were defeated, which allowed them to stop the process of state institutional bleeding.

For scholars of international relations, this book also underscores the importance of exploring the causes and consequences of war outcomes. Curiously, the literature on the causes of battlefield success has remained rather secluded in the subfield of security studies to the point that some of its key insights – for example, about the contingency of warfare – are usually disregarded in other subfields. Similarly, the effects of war outcomes have remained widely understudied despite the general appeal of the topic in political theory and other disciplines (Giustozzi, 2011, 23–25). More than three decades ago, Van Raemdonck and Diehl (1989, 259) said war outcomes were "an important but underdeveloped segment of peace research. Because of the limited number of empirical works and the lack of consensus on a number of key questions, there is a crowded agenda for future research in this area." Yet, despite some exceptions (Jaggers, 1992, 38; Hoffman, 2015, 24), the situation has not changed.

Luckily, there seems to be some interest in amending these shortcomings. Debates on civil wars (Walter, 1997; Wallensteen, 2015) and regime survival (de Mesquita et al., 1992; Lachapelle et al., 2020; Levitsky and Way, 2022) and at the intersection of both (Lyons, 2016; Martin, 2022) have expressed renewed interest in the effects of war outcomes. Here the link between military victory and postwar stability has been discussed along the lines of the classical bellicist argument, opening promising lines of enquiry. This book should reinforce those intuitions and agendas.

Last but not least, the review of classical bellicist theory that I offer in this book may generate renewed interest in the ideas of Max Weber, Otto Hintze, and others. Rescuing some of their ideas has been greatly rewarding, and I hope that others will follow me in coming back to them for lessons. It is a humbling thought, which this book tries to transmit, that much of what we need in order to understand politics today might have happened a long time ago and might have been already figured out by old authors that we unduly forget. Paraphrasing Borges one last time, the certainty that everything has already been written can annul us, but we can always try to keep alive those ideas we deem to be right.

References

Abad, Leticia. 2013. Persistent Inequality? Trade, Factor Endowments, and Inequality in Republican Latin America. *Journal of Economic History*, 73(1), 38–78.

Abadie, Alberto, Diamond, Alexis, and Hainmueller, Jens. 2015. Comparative Politics and the Synthetic Control Method. *American Journal of Political Science*, **59**(2), 495–510.

Abente, Diego. 1987. The War of the Triple Alliance: Three Explanatory Models. *Latin American Research Review*, **22**(2), 47–69.

Abramson, Scott F. 2017. The Economic Origins of the Territorial State. *International Organization*, 71(1), 97–130.

Acemoglu, Daron. 2012. *Why Nations Fail: The Origins of Power, Prosperity and Poverty*. New York: Crown.

Acemoglu, Daron, Moscona, Jacob, and Robinson, James. 2016. State Capacity and American Technology: Evidence from the Nineteenth Century. *American Economic Review*, **106**(5), 61–67.

Acevedo, Eduardo. 1934. *Anales Históricos del Uruguay*, vol. 5. Montevideo: Casa A. Barreiro y Ramos.

Acuña, Victor, and Molina Jiménez, Ivan. 1986. *El Desarrollo Económico y Social de Costa Rica: De la Colonia a la Crisis de 1930*. San José: Alma Mater.

Adelman, Jeremy. 1998. Spanish–American Leviathan? State Formation in Nineteenth-Century Spanish America: A Review Article. *Comparative Studies in Society and History*, **40**(1), 391–408.

Agamben, Giorgio. 2005. *State of Exception*. Chicago: University of Chicago Press.

Alaman, Lucas. 1985. *[1852] Historia de Méjico desde los primeros movimientos que prepararon su independencia en el año de 1808, hasta la época presente*, vol. 5. Mexico City: J. M. Lara.

Alba, Victor. 1982. Mexico's Several Independences. Pages 6–16 of: Raat, Dirk (ed.), *Mexico from Independence to Revolution 1810–1910*. Lincoln: University of Nebraska Press.

Alliende, María. 1993. *Historia del Ferrocarril en Chile*. Santiago: Pehuen.

Almeida, Paulo Roberto. 2017. *Formação da Diplomacia Económica no Brasil*. Brasília: Fundação Alexandre de Gusmão.

Amaral, Samuel. 2002. *The Rise of Capitalism on the Pampas*. New York: Cambridge University Press.

Andersson, Per. 2018. Democracy, Urbanization, and Tax Revenue. *Studies in Comparative International Development*, 53(1), 111–150.

Andrada e Silva, Raúl. 1978. *Ensaio sobre a ditadura do Paraguai: 1814–1840*. São Paulo: Coleção Museu Paulista.

Angrist, Joshua, and Pischke, Jörn-Steffen. 2008. *Mostly Harmless Econometrics: An Empiricist's Companion*. Princeton: Princeton University Press.

Anna, Timothy E. 1998. *Forging Mexico: 1821–1835*. Lincoln: University of Nebraska Press.

Arancibia Clavel, Patricia. 2007. *El Ejército de los Chilenos, 1540–1920*. Santiago: Editorial Biblioteca Americana.

Archer, Christon I. 2000. *The Wars of Independence in Spanish America*. Jaguar Books on Latin America, 20. Wilmington: Scholarly Resources.

Arias, Luz Marina, and de la Calle, Luis. 2021. The Legacy of Civil War Dynamics: State Building in Mexico, 1810–1910. *Latin American Research Review*, 56(4), 814–830.

Arjona, Ana. 2014. Wartime Institutions: A Research Agenda. *Journal of Conflict Resolution*, 58(8), 1360–1389.

Arozteguy, Abdon. 1889. *La Revolución Oriental de 1870*. Buenos Aires: Editor Félix Lajouane.

Arraíz, Antonio. 1991. *Los Días de la Ira: Las Guerras Civiles en Venezuela, 1830–1903*. Valencia: Vadell Hermanos Editores.

Arreguin-Toft, Ivan. 2005. *How the Weak Win Wars: A Theory of Asymmetric Conflict*. New York: Cambridge University Press.

Arrom, Silvia M. 1988. Popular Politics in Mexico City: The Parian Riot, 1828. *Hispanic American Historical Review*, 68(2), 245.

Atzili, Boaz. 2011. *Good Fences, Bad Neighbors*. Chicago: University of Chicago Press.

Autor, David H. 2003. Outsourcing at Will: The Contribution of Unjust Dismissal Doctrine to the Growth of Employment Outsourcing. *Journal of Labor Economics*, 21(1), 1–41.

Bancroft, Hubert. 1887. *History of Central America*, vol. 8. San Francisco: The History Company.

Banks, Arthur S., and Wilson, Kenneth A. 2015. Cross-National Time-Series Data Archive. Online access: www.databanksinternational.com.

Baratta, Maria Victoria. 2019. *La Guerra del Paraguay y la Construcción de la Identidad Nacional*. Buenos Aires: Editorial SB.

Barnhart, Joslyn. 2021. The Consequences of Defeat: The Quest for Status and Morale in the Aftermath of War. *Journal of Conflict Resolution*, 65(1), 195–222.

Barran, José, and Nahum, Benjamin. 1978. *Historia Rural del Uruguay Moderno*. Montevideo: Banda Oriental.

Barrientos, Alfonso E. 1948. Ramón Rosa y Guatemala. *Revista del Archivo y Bibliotecas Nacionales de Honduras*, 27(1), 2–19.

Barros Arana, Diego. 1979. *Historia de la Guerra del Pacífico*. Santiago: Editorial Andres Bello.

Bas, Muhammet A., and Schub, Robert J. 2016. How Uncertainty about War Outcomes Affects War Onset. *Journal of Conflict Resolution*, 60(6), 1099–1128.

Basadre, Jorge. 1931. *Perú: Problema y Posibilidad*. Lima: Banco Internacional del Peru.

2005. *Historia de la República del Perú*. Lima: El Comercio.

Bates, Robert H. 2014. The Imperial Peace. Pages 424–444 of: Akyeampong, Emmanuel, Bates, Robert H., Nunn, Nathan, and Robinson, James (eds.), *Africa's Development in Historical Perspective*. New York: Cambridge University Press.

Bauer, Karl Jack. 1974. *The Mexican War, 1846–1848*. New York: Macmillan.

Bayer, Reşat. 2006. Diplomatic Exchange Dataset. Online access: http://correlatesofwar.org.

Bazant, Jan. 1985. Mexico: From Independence to 1867. Pages 423–449 of: Bethell, Leslie (ed.), *The Cambridge History of Latin America*, vol. 5. New York: Cambridge University Press.

1991. From Independence to the Liberal Republic 1821–1867. Pages 1–48 of: Bethell, Leslie (ed.), *Mexico since Independence*. New York: Cambridge University Press.

Beatty, Edward. 2001. *Institutions and Investment: The Political Basis of Industrialization in Mexico before 1911*. Stanford: Stanford University Press.

Benard, Stephen. 2012. Cohesion from Conflict: Does Intergroup Conflict Motivate Intragroup Norm Enforcement and Support for Centralized Leadership? *Social Psychology Quarterly*, 75(2), 107–130.

Benavides Santos, Arturo. 1972. *Historia Compendiada de la Guerra del Pacífico*. Santiago: Editorial Francisco de Aguirre.

Bendor, Jonathan, and Shapiro, Jacob N. 2019. Historical Contingencies in the Evolution of States and Their Militaries. *World Politics*, 71(1), 126–160.

Bensel, Richard Franklin. 1991. *Yankee Leviathan: The Origins of Central State Authority in America, 1859–1877*. Cambridge: Cambridge University Press.

Bernhard, Michael. 2015. Chronic Instability and the Limits of Path Dependence. *Perspectives on Politics*, 13(4), 976–991.

Besley, Timothy, and Persson, Torsten. 2009. The Origins of State Capacity: Property Rights, Taxation, and Politics. *American Economic Review*, 99(4), 1218–1244.

Besley, Timothy, and Torsten, Persson. 2011. *Pillars of Prosperity: The Political Economy of Development Clusters*. Princeton: Princeton University Press.

Bethell, Leslie. 1989. *Brazil: Empire and Republic, 1822–1930*. Cambridge: Cambridge University Press.

1996. *The Paraguayan War (1864–1870)*. London: Institute of Latin American Studies.

Beyerchen, Alan. 1992. Clausewitz, Nonlinearity, and the Unpredictability of War. *International Security*, 17(3), 59–90.

Biddle, Stephen. 2006. *Military Power: Explaining Victory and Defeat in Modern Battle*. Princeton: Princeton University Press.

Biddle, Stephen, and Long, Stephen. 2004. Democracy and Military Effectiveness: A Deeper Look. *Journal of Conflict Resolution*, 48(4), 525–546.

Bignon, Vincent, Esteves, Rui, and Herranz-Loncán, Alfonso. 2015. Big Push or Big Grab? Railways, Government Activism, and Export Growth in Latin America, 1865–1913. *Economic History Review*, 68(4), 1277–1305.

Blakemore, Harold. 1993. From the War of the Pacific to 1930. Pages 146–162 of: Bethell, Leslie (ed.), *Chile since Independence*. New York: Cambridge University Press.

Blanchard, Peter. 2008. *Under the Flags of Freedom: Slave Soldiers and the Wars of Independence in Spanish South America*. Pitt Latin American Series. Namur: University of Pittsburgh Press.

Blanton, Richard, and Fargher, Lane. 2007. *Collective Action in the Formation of Pre-modern States*. New York: Springer.

Blaydes, Lisa, and Paik, Christopher. 2016. The Impact of Holy Land Crusades on State Formation: War Mobilization, Trade Integration, and Political Development in Medieval Europe. *International Organization*, 70(3), 551–586.

Blumenthal, Edward. 2019. *Exile and Nation-State Formation in Argentina and Chile, 1810–1862*. London: Palgrave Macmillan.

Boix, Carles. 2015. *Political Order and Inequality*. New York: Cambridge University Press.

Bolaños Geyer, Alejandro. 2003. *William Walker: El Predestinado*. Alajuela: Museo Histórico Cultural Santamaría.

Bolt, Jutta, Inklaar, Robert, de Jong, Herman, and van Zanden, Jan Luiten. 2018. Rebasing Maddison: New Income Comparisons and the Shape of Long-Run Economic Development. *GGDC Research Memorandum*, 174(1), 1–21.

Bonilla, Heraclio. 1980. *Un Siglo a la Deriva: Ensayos sobre el Peru, Bolivia y la Guerra*. Lima: Instituto de Estudios Peruanos.

Bonney, Richard. 1999. *The Rise of the Fiscal State in Europe c.1200–1815*. OUP Catalogue. Oxford: Oxford University Press.

Bornstein, Gary. 2003. Intergroup Conflict: Individual, Group, and Collective Interests. *Personality and Social Psychology Review*, 7(2), 129–145.

Bouchard, Michel. 2011. The State of the Study of the State in Anthropology. *Reviews in Anthropology*, 40(3), 183–209.

Boyd, Melisa. 2010. A Reluctant Advocate: Mariano Otero and the Revolucion de Jalisco. Pages 162–179 of: Fowler, Will (ed.), *Forceful Negotiations: The Origins of the Pronunciamiento in Nineteenth-Century Mexico*. Lincoln: University of Nebraska Press.

Brading, David. 1985. *The Origins of Mexican Nationalism*. Cambridge: Cambridge University Press.

Brading, David A. 1991. *The First America: The Spanish Monarchy, Creole Patriots and the Liberal State 1492–1867*. Cambridge; New York: Cambridge University Press.

Bragoni, Beatriz. 2010. *Un Nuevo Orden Político: Provincias y Estado Nacional, 1852–1880*. Buenos Aires: Biblos.

Brecke, Peter. 1999. Violent Conflicts 1400 AD to the Present in Different Regions of the World. In: *1999 Meeting of the Peace Science Society*.

Brewer, John. 1989. *The Sinews of Power: War, Money, and the English State, 1688–1783*. New York: Alfred A. Knopf.

1990. *The Sinews of Power: War, Money, and the English State, 1688–1783*, 1st Harvard University pbk. ed. Cambridge, MA: Harvard University Press.

Brill, Kristen. 2015. Winfried Scott in Central Mexico. Pages 259–266 of: Thompson, Antonio, and Frentzos, Christos (eds.), *The Routledge Handbook of American Military and Diplomatic History*. London: Routledge.

Buarque de Holanda, Sergio. 1972. *História Geral da Civilização Brasileira*. São Paulo: Difuşão Europeia do Livro.

Bulnes, Gonzalo. 1976. *Resumen de la Guerra del Pacífico*. Santiago: Editorial del Pacífico.

Burr, Robert N. 1974. *By Reason or Force: Chile and the Balancing of Power in South America 1830–1905*. Berkeley: University of California Press.

Bushnell, David. 1994. *The Emergence of Latin America in the Nineteenth Century*, 2nd ed. New York: Oxford University Press.

Bustamante, Gregorio. 1935. *Historia Militar de El Salvador de la Independencia a Nuestros Días*. San Salvador: Talleres Gráficos Cisneros.

Butt, Ahsan I. 2013. Anarchy and Hierarchy in International Relations: Examining South America's War-Prone Decade, 1932–41. *International Organization*, **67**(3), 575–607.

Buzan, Barry, Waever, Ole, and de Wilde, Jaap. 1998. *Security: A New Framework for Analysis*. Boulder: Lynne Rienner.

Byrd Simpson, Leslie. 1982. Santa Anna's Leg. Pages 121–135 of: Raat, Dirk (ed.), *Mexico from Independence to Revolution 1810–1910*. Lincoln: University of Nebraska Press.

Cabal, Manuel. 2022. Regionalism against Centralization: Resistance to Federal Education after the Mexican Revolution. *Publius*, 53(1), 28–54.

Caballero Campos, Herb. 2013. *El país ocupado*. Asunción: Editorial el Lector.

Cabrera Geserick, Marco Antonio. 2013. *The Legacy of the Filibuster War: National Identity, Collective Memory, and Cultural Anti-Imperialism*. Ph.D. thesis, Arizona State University.

Callen, Zachary. 2016. *Railroads and American Political Development: Infrastructure, Federalism, and State Building*. Lawrence: University Press of Kansas.

Calvo Mora, Joaquin. 1909. *La Campaña Nacional contra los Filibusteros en 1856–1857*. San José: Tipográfica Nacional.

Campbell, John. 1993. The State and Fiscal Sociology. *Annual Review of Sociology*, **19**, 163–185.

Campobassi, José Salvador. 1962. *Sarmiento y Mitre: Hombres de Mayo y Caseros*. Buenos Aires: Editorial Losada.

Capdevila, Luc. 2012. El Recuerdo de la Guerra de la Triple Alianza como Sustrato de la Identidad Paraguaya. Pages 31–49 of: Crespo, Horacio, Palacio, Juan Manuel, and Palacios, Guillermo (eds.), *La Guerra del Paraguay: Historiografías, Representaciones, Contextos*. Mexico City: El Colegio de Mexico.

Capdevila, Luc. 2014. Guerra, Estado y Nación en América Austral en la década de 1860: la Contienda de la Triple Alianza. Pages 199–218 of: Palacios, Guillermo, and Pani, Erika (eds.), *Guerra, Estado y Nación en la década de 1860*. Mexico City: Colegio de Mexico.

Capoccia, Giovanni, and Kelemen, R. Daniel. 2007. The Study of Critical Junctures: Theory, Narrative, and Counterfactuals in Historical Institutionalism. *World Politics*, **59**(3), 341–369.

Carcano, Ramón. 1941. *Guerra del Paraguay: Acción y Reacción de la Triple Alianza*. Buenos Aires: Domingo Viau y Cia.

Cardenas, Mauricio. 2010. State Capacity in Latin America. *Economía*, 10(2), 1–45.

Cardoso, Ciro. 1987. La Formación de la Propiedad Cafetalera en la Costa Rica del Siglo XIX. Pages 185–224 of: Duncan, Kenneth, and Rutledge, Ian (eds.), *Tierra y Mano de Obra e América Latina. Ensayos sobre el Desarrollo del Capitalismo Agrario en los Siglos XIX y XX*. Mexico City: Fondo de Cultura Económica.

Carneiro, Robert L. 1970. A Theory of the Origin of the State. *Science*, **169**(3947), 733–738.

Carter, Christopher L. 2023. Extraction, Assimilation, and Accommodation: The Historical Foundations of Indigenous–State Relations in Latin America. *American Political Science Review*, 1–16.

Carvalho, José Murilo de. 2007. *A Construção da Ordem–Teatro das Sombras*. Rio de Janeiro: Civilização Brasileira.

2009. Radicalismo e Republicanismo. Pages 21–48 of: Carvalho, José Murilo de, and Bastos das Neves, Lucia (eds.), *Repensando o Brasil do Oitocentos: Cidadania, Política e Liberdade*. Rio de Janeiro: Civilização Brasileira.

Castro, Celso, Izecksohn, Victor, and Kraay, Hendrik. 2004. Da História Militar à Nova História Militar. Pages 11–42 of: Castro, Celso, Izecksohn, Victor, and Kraay, Hendrik (eds.), *Nova Historia Militar Brasileira*. São Paulo: FVG Editora.

Cavieres, Eduardo, and Aljivín de Lozada, Cristobal. 2005. *Chile–Peru, Peru–Chile: 1820–1920*. Valparaiso: Ediciones Universitarias.

Cederman, Lars-Erik, Galano Toro, Paola, Girardin, Luc, and Schvitz, Guy. 2023. War Did Make States: Revisiting the Bellicist Paradigm in Early Modern Europe. *International Organization*, **77**, 324–362.

Centeno, Miguel Angel. 1997. Blood and Debt: War and Taxation in Nineteenth-Century Latin America. *American Journal of Sociology*, **102**(6), 1565–1605.

2002. *Blood and Debt: War and the Nation-State in Latin America*. University Park: Penn State University Press.

Centeno, Miguel Angel, and López-Alves, Fernando. 2001. *The Other Mirror: Grand Theory through the Lens of Latin America*. Princeton: Princeton University Press.

Cerdas, Ana, and Vargas, Gerardo. 1988. *La Abolición del Ejército en Costa Rica: Hito de un Camino de Democracia y Paz*. San José: Ministerio de Cultura.

Cervo, Amado, and Bueno, Clodoaldo. 2011. *História da Politica Exterior do Brasil*. Brasília: Universidade de Brasília.

Chacon, Vamireh. 1981. *História dos Partidos Brasileiros*. Brasília: Universidade de Brasília.

Chaves, Julio. 1985. *El Supremo Dictador: Biografía de José Gaspar de Francia*. Asunción: Carlos Schauman.

Chiaramonte, José Carlos. 1971. *Nacionalismo y Liberalismo Económicos en Argentina 1860–1880*. Buenos Aires: Solar.

Chiavenatto, Julio José. 1979. *Genocidio Americano: A Guerra do Paraguai*. São Paulo: Editora Brasiliense.

Child, Jack. 1985. *Geopolitics and Conflict in South America: Quarrels among Neighbors*. New York: Praeger.

Chin, Warren. 2019. Technology, War and the State: Past, Present and Future. *International Affairs*, **95**(4), 765–783.

Chowdhury, Arjun. 2018. *The Myth of International Order: Why Weak States Persist and Alternatives to the State Fade Away*. New York: Oxford University Press.

Cid, Gabriel R. 2011. *La Guerra contra la Confederación*. Santiago: Universidad Diego Portales.

2013. La Guerra Contra la Confederación y la Nación Chilena. *Tradición y Saber*, 10(1), 126–150.

Clare, Joe, and Danilovic, Vesna. 2010. Multiple Audiences and Reputation Building in International Conflicts. *Journal of Conflict Resolution*, 54(6), 860–882.

Clark, Gregory. 2001. Debt, Deficits, and Crowding Out: England, 1727–1840. *European Review of Economic History*, 5(3), 403–436.

Clausewitz, Carl von. 1984. *On War*. Princeton: Princeton University Press.

Clemens, Michael A., and Williamson, Jeffrey G. 2004. Why Did the Tariff-Growth Correlation Change after 1950? *Journal of Economic Growth*, 9(1), 5–46.

Clodfelter, Micheal. 2017. *Warfare and Armed Conflicts: A Statistical Encyclopedia of Casualty and Other Figures, 1492–2015*. Jefferson: McFarland.

Coatsworth, John H., and Williamson, Jeffrey G. 2002. The Roots of Latin American Protectionism: Looking before the Great Depression. NBER Working Paper, 1(8999), 1–30.

Cohen, Youssef, Brown, Brian, and Organski, Abramo F. K. 1981. The Paradoxical Nature of State Making: The Violent Creation of Order. *American Political Science Review*, 75(4), 901–910.

Collier, David, Brady, Henry E., and Seawright, Jason. 2004. Sources of Leverage in Causal Inference: Toward an Alternative View of Methodology. Pages 229–266 of: Brady, Henry E., and Collier, David (eds.), *Rethinking Social Inquiry: Diverse Tools, Shared Standards*. Lanham: Rowman & Littlefield.

Collier, Ruth Berins, and Collier, David. 1991. *Shaping the Political Arena: Critical Junctures, the Labor Movement, and Regime Dynamics in Latin America*. Princeton: Princeton University Press.

Collier, Simon. 1993. From Independence to the War of the Pacific. Pages 123–146 of: Bethell, Leslie (ed.), *Chile since Independence*. New York: Cambridge University Press.

Collier, Simon, and Sater, William. 2004. *A History of Chile, 1808–2002*. Cambridge: Cambridge University Press.

Contreras, Carlos. 2005. El Impuesto de la Contribución Personal en el Perú del Siglo XIX. *Historica*, 29(2), 67–106.

Contreras, Carlos, and Cavieres, Eduardo. 2005. Politicas Fiscales, Economia y Crecimiento. Pages 169–219 of: Cavieres, Eduardo, and Aljivín de Lozada, Cristobal (eds.), *Chile–Peru, Peru–Chile: 1820–1920*. Valparaiso: Ediciones Universitarias.

Contreras, Carlos, and Cueto, Marcos. 2004. *Historia del Perú contemporáneo: Desde las luchas por la independencia hasta el presente*, vol. 27. Lima: Instituto de Estudios Peruanos.

Cornblit, Oscar. 1978. Levantamientos de Masas en Peru y Bolivia durante el Siglo Dieciocho. Pages 58–119 of: Donghi, Halperin (ed.), *El Ocaso del orden colonial en Hispanoamérica*. Buenos Aires: Editorial Sudamericana.

Cortes Conde, Roberto. 1989. *Dinero, Deuda y Crisis (1862–1890)*. Buenos Aires: Sudamericana–Instituto Di Tella.

Costeloe, Michael P. 1981. Spain and the Spanish American Wars of Independence: The *Comisión de Reemplazos*, 1811–1820. *Journal of Latin American Studies*, 13(2), 223–237.

1993. *The Central Republic in Mexico, 1835–1846: Hombres de bien in the Age of Santa Anna*. Cambridge Latin American Studies, 73. Cambridge; New York: Cambridge University Press.

Cotler, Julio. 1978. *Clases, Estado y Nación en el Perú*. Mexico City: Universidad Nacional Autónoma de Mexico.

Cox, Gary W., Dincecco, Mark, and Onorato, Massimiliano G. 2023. Window of Opportunity: War and the Origins of Parliament. *British Journal of Political Science*, 1–17.

Craib, Raymond B. 2002. A National Metaphysics: State Fixations, National Maps, and the Geo-historical Imagination in Nineteenth-Century Mexico. *Hispanic American Historical Review*, **82**(1), 33–68.

Crespo, Horacio, Palacio, Juan Manuel, and Palacios, Guillermo. 2012. Introduccion. Pages 1–42 of: Crespo, Horacio, Palacio, Juan Manuel, and Palacios, Guillermo (eds.), *La Guerra del Paraguay: Historiografías, Representaciones, Contextos*. Mexico City: El Colegio de Mexico.

Crowther, Win. 1973. *Technological Change as Political Choice: The Engineers and the Modernization of the Chilean State Railways*. Ph.D. thesis, University of California.

Cruz, Ernesto, and Feliú Cruz, Guillermo. 1936. *Epistolario de Don Diego Portales, 1821–1837*. Santiago: Direccion General de Prisiones.

Cruz, Juan de la. 2018. *La Guerra de la Restauración: Triunfo del Pueblo Dominicano en Armas*. Santo Domingo: Editora Nacional.

D'Altroy, Terence N. 2002. *The Incas*. Peoples of America. Malden, MA: Blackwell.

Darden, Keith, and Mylonas, Harris. 2016. Threats to Territorial Integrity, National Mass Schooling, and Linguistic Commonality. *Comparative Political Studies*, **49**(11), 1446–1479.

Davies, Norman. 2011. *Vanished Kingdoms: The Rise and Fall of States and Nations*. New York: Viking.

Davis, Roger. 1983. *Ecuador under Gran Colombia, 1820–1830: Regionalism, Localism, and Legitimacy in the Emergence of an Andean Republic (Simon Bolivar, Juan Jose Flores, Jose Joaquin de Olmedo)*. Tucson: University of Arizona.

de Chaisemartin, Clement, and D'Haultfoeuille, Xavier. 2018. Fuzzy Differences-in-Differences. *Review of Economic Studies*, **85**(2), 999–1028.

2020. Two-Way Fixed Effects Estimators with Heterogeneous Treatment Effects. *American Economic Review*, 110(9), 2964–2996.

de la Escosura, Leandro Prados. 2009. Lost Decades? Economic Performance in Post-independence Latin America. *Journal of Latin American Studies*, 41(2), 279–307.

De Marco, Miguel Angel. 2003. *La Guerra del Paraguay*. Buenos Aires: Planeta.

de Mesquita, Bruce B., Siverson, Randolph M., and Woller, Gary. 1992. War and the Fate of Regimes: A Comparative Analysis. *American Political Science Review*, **86**(3), 638–646.

Delay, Brian. 2008. *War of a Thousand Deserts: Indian Raids and the US–Mexican War*. New Haven: Yale University Press.

della Paolera, Gerardo, and Taylor, Alan. 2001. *Straining at the Anchor: The Argentine Currency Board and the Search for Macroeconomic Stability, 1880–1935*. Chicago: University of Chicago Press.

della Paolera, Gerardo, and Taylor, Alan M. 2013. Sovereign Debt in Latin America, 1820–1913. *Revista de historia económica*, 31(2), 173–217.

Desch, Michael C. 1996. War and Strong States, Peace and Weak States? *International Organization*, 50(2), 237–268.

1999. *Civilian Control of the Military: The Changing Security Environment*. Baltimore: Johns Hopkins University Press.

2002. Democracy and Victory: Why Regime Type Hardly Matters. *International Security*, 27(2), 5–47.

Di Meglio, Gabriel Marco. 2018. Un Ejército de Muchos Nombres: La Difícil Formación de las Fuerzas Militares Rioplatenses en la Guerra entre las Provincias Unidas y el Imperio del Brasil. *Claves, Revista de Historia*, 4(7), 127–162.

Di Privitellio, Luciano. 2016. Sarmiento y la Invención de la Argentina. Pages 1–9 of: Meglioli, Mauricio, and De Titto, Ricardo (eds.), *Una y Otra Vez Sarmiento*. Buenos Aires: Prometeo.

Díaz, José, Luders Schwarzenberg, Rolf, and Wagner, Gert. 2016. *Chile 1810–2010: La República en Cifras*. Santiago: Ediciones Universidad Católica.

Díaz Arias, David. 2012. *Construcción de un Estado Moderno: Política, Estado, e Identidad Nacional en Costa Rica 1821–1914*. San José: Editorial Universidad de Costa Rica.

Dincecco, Mark, and Prado, Mauricio. 2012. Warfare, Fiscal Capacity, and Performance. *Journal of Economic Growth*, 17(3), 171–203.

Dincecco, Mark, and Wang, Yuhua. 2018. Violent Conflict and Political Development over the Long Run: China versus Europe. *Annual Review of Political Science*, 21(1), 341–358.

Doratioto, Francisco. 2002. *Maldita Guerra: Nova História da Guerra do Paraguai*. São Paulo: Companhia das Letras.

Downes, Alexander B. 2021. *Catastrophic Success: Why Foreign-Imposed Regime Change Goes Wrong*. Ithaca: Cornell University Press.

Downes, Richard. 2005. La Guerra de 1941 entre Ecuador y Peru: Una reinterpretacion. *Hispanic American Historical Review*, 85(2), 366–367.

Downing, Brian. 1993. *The Military Revolution and Political Change: Origins of Democracy and Autocracy in Early Modern Europe*. New York: Princeton University Press.

Duşa, Adrian. 2018. *QCA with R: A Comprehensive Resource*. London: Springer.

Dyson, Kenneth. 2014. *States, Debt, and Power: "Saints" and "Sinners" in European History and Integration*. Oxford: Oxford University Press.

Earle, Rebecca. 2000. *Spain and the Independence of Colombia: 1810–1825*. Exeter: University of Exeter Press.

Edwards, Alberto. 1932. *El Gobierno de Don Manuel Montt, 1851–1861*. Santiago: Nascimiento.

Eichengreen, Barry, El-Ganainy, Asmaa, Esteves, Rui, and Mitchener, Kris James. 2019. *Public Debt through the Ages*. Tech. rept. National Bureau of Economic Research.

Eisenhower, John S. D. 1989. *So Far from God: The US War with Mexico, 1846–1848*. Norman: University of Oklahoma Press.

Elias, Norbert. 2000. *The Civilizing Process*. Oxford: Blackwell.

Eller, Anne. 2015. Las Ramas del Árbol de la Libertad: La Guerra de la Restauración en la República Dominicana y en Haiti. *Caribbean Studies*, 43(1), 113–144.

Ertman, Thomas. 1997. *Birth of the Leviathan: Building States and Regimes in Medieval and Early Modern Europe*. Cambridge: Cambridge University Press.

Ertman, Thomas. 2017. Otto Hintze, Stein Rokkan and Charles Tilly's Theory of European State-Building. Pages 52–70 of: Kaspersen, Lars Bo, and Strandsbjerg, Jeppe (eds.), *Does War Make States? Investigations of Charles Tilly's Historical Sociology*. New York: Cambridge University Press.

Escudé, Carlos. 1981. *The Argentine Eclipse: The International Factor in Argentina's Post-WWII Decline*. Ph.D. thesis, Yale University.

Espinosa, Aurelio. 2006. The Spanish Reformation: Institutional Reform, Taxation, and the Secularization of Ecclesiastical Properties under Charles V. *Sixteenth Century Journal*, 37(1), 3–24.

Eyzaguirre, Jaime. 1977. *Historia de las Instituciones Políticas y Sociales de Chile*. Santiago: Editorial Universitaria.

Fairfield, Tasha. 2015. *Private Wealth and Public Revenue in Latin America*. New York: Cambridge University Press.

Fallas Santana, Carmen. 1982. *El Fortalecimiento del Estado en Costa Rica en la Década de 1850*. Ph.D. thesis, Universidad de Costa Rica.

Fallas Santana, Carmen. 2007. La Campaña Nacional 1856–1857 y la Construcción del Estado Nación. *Revista Estudios*, 20(1), 13–25.

Farcau, Bruce W. 2000. *The Ten Cents War: Chile, Peru, and Bolivia in the War of the Pacific, 1879–1884*. Westport: Greenwood.

Fazal, Tanisha M. 2004. State Death in the International System. *International Organization*, 58(2), 311–344.

2011. *State Death: The Politics and Geography of Conquest, Occupation, and Annexation*. Princeton: Princeton University Press.

Fearon, James D. 1995. Rationalist Explanations for War. *International Organization*, 49(3), 379–414.

Federico, Giovanni, and Tena, Antonio. 2019. World Trade, 1800–1938: A New Synthesis. *Revista de historia económica*, 37(1), 9–41.

Feinstein, Yuval, and Wimmer, Andreas. 2023. Consent and Legitimacy: A Revised Bellicose Theory of State-Building with Evidence from around the World, 1500–2000. *World Politics*, 75(1), 188–232.

Feltham, Janet, Haas, Jonathan, Pozorski, Sheila, and Pozorski, Thomas. 2009. The Origins and Development of the Andean State. *Bulletin of Latin American Research*, 8(1), 124.

Ferreres, Orlando. 2005. *Dos Siglos de Economía Argentina (1810–2004)*. Buenos Aires: Fundación Norte y Sur.

Figueroa, Valentin. 2023. The Protestant Road to Bureaucracy. *World Politics*, 75(2), 390–437.

Finch, Martin. 1981. *The Political Economy of Uruguay since 1870*. London: Macmillan.

Flores Macías, Gustavo. 2018. The Consequences of Militarizing Anti-Drug Efforts for State Capacity in Latin America: Evidence from Mexico. *Comparative Politics*, 51(1), 1–20.

Flores Zendejas, Juan. 2020. Explaining Latin America's Persistent Defaults: An Analysis of the Debtor–Creditor Relations in London, 1822–1914. *Financial History Review*, 27(3), 319–339.

Fowler, Will. 1998. *Mexico in the Age of Proposals, 1821–1853*. Contributions in Latin American Studies, no. 12. Westport: Greenwood Press.

Fowler, Will. 2011. "I Pronounce Thus I Exist": Redefining the Pronunciamiento in Independent Mexico, 1821–1876. Pages 246–266 of: *Forceful Negotiations: The Origins of the Pronunciamiento in Nineteenth-Century Mexico*. Lincoln: University of Nebraska Press.

Fukuyama, Francis. 2004. The Imperative of State-Building. *Journal of Democracy*, 15(2), 17–31.

Fukuyama, Francis. 2011. *The Origins of Political Order: From Prehuman Times to the French Revolution*. New York: Farrar, Straus and Giroux.

Gabbert, Wolfgang. 2019. *Violence and the Caste War of Yucatan*. Cambridge: Cambridge University Press.

Galeana, Patricia. 2007. *Juárez en la História de Mexico*. Mexico City: Porrúa.

Galvez, Manuel. 1950. *Vida de Sarmiento: El Hombre de Autoridad*. Buenos Aires: Editorial TOR.

Garavaglia, Juan Carlos. 2003. La Apoteósis del Leviathán: El Estado en Buenos Aires durante la primera mitad del Siglo XIX. *Latin American Research Review*, 38(1), 135–168.

2014. La Disputa por la Nación: Rentas y Aduanas en la Construcción Estatal Argentina 1850–1865. *Economic History Research*, 10(1), 34–45.

2016. Las Fuerzas de Guerra Argentinas durante el Conflicto de la Triple Alianza 1865–1870. Pages 110–123 of: Garavaglia, Juan Carlos, and Fradkin, Raul (eds.), *A 150 Años de la Guerra de la Triple Alianza con el Paraguay*. Buenos Aires: Prometeo.

Garcia, Laura, and Mahoney, James. 2023. Critical Event Analysis in Case Study Research. *Sociological Methods and Research*, 52(1), 480–524.

Garfias, Francisco. 2018. Elite Competition and State Capacity Development: Theory and Evidence from Post-revolutionary Mexico. *American Political Science Review*, 112(2), 339–357.

Garfias, Francisco, and Sellars, Emily. 2022. When State Building Backfires: Elite Coordination and Popular Grievance in Rebellion. *American Journal of Political Science*, 65(4), 977–992.

Gelman, Andrew, and Hill, Jennifer. 2006. *Data Analysis Using Regression and Multilevel/Hierarchical Models*. New York: Cambridge University Press.

Gerring, John, and Cojocaru, Lee. 2016. Selecting Cases for Intensive Analysis: A Diversity of Goals and Methods. *Sociological Methods & Research*, 45(3), 392–423.

Gibler, Douglas. 2018. *International Conflicts 1816–2010*. London: Rowman & Littlefield.

Gibler, Douglas M., Miller, Steven V., and Little, Erin K. 2016. An Analysis of the Militarized Interstate Dispute (MID) Dataset, 1816–2001. *International Studies Quarterly*, 60(4), 719–730.

Gienapp, William E. 1987. *The Origins of the Republican Party, 1852–1856*. New York: Oxford University Press.

Gilbert, Dennis. 1977. *The Oligarchy and the Old Regime in Peru*. Ph.D. thesis, Cornell University.

Giraudi, Agustina. 2012. Conceptualizing State Strength: Moving beyond Strong and Weak States. *Revista de Ciencia Política*, 32(3), 599–611.

Giustozzi, Antonio. 2011. *The Art of Coercion*. New York: Columbia University Press.

Gobat, Michael. 2018. *Empire by Invitation: William Walker and Manifest Destiny in Central America*. Cambridge, MA: Harvard University Press.

Goenaga, Agustín, Sabaté, Oriol, and Teorell, Jan. 2023. The State Does Not Live by Warfare Alone: War and State Capacity in the Long Nineteenth Century. *Review of International Organizations*, 1(18), 393–418.
Goertz, Gary. 2017. *Multimethod Research, Causal Mechanisms, and Case Studies: An Integrated Approach*. Princeton: Princeton University Press.
2020. *Social Science Concepts: A User's Guide*. Princeton: Princeton University Press.
Goertz, Gary, and Levy, Jack. 2007. *Explaining War and Peace: Case Studies and Necessary Condition Counterfactuals*. London: Routledge.
Goertz, Gary, and Mahoney, James. 2012. *A Tale of Two Cultures: Qualitative and Quantitative Research in the Social Sciences*. Princeton: Princeton University Press.
Goertz, Gary, Diehl, Paul, and Balan, Alexandru. 2016. *The Puzzle of Peace: The Evolution of Peace in the International System*. New York: Oxford University Press.
Goldsmith, Raymond. 1986. *Brasil 1850–1984: Desenvolvimento Financeiro sob um Século de Inflação*. São Paulo: Harper & Row.
Góngora, Mario. 1994. *Ensayo Histórico sobre la Noción de Estado en Chile en los Siglos XIX y XX*. Santiago: Editorial Universitaria.
Gonzalez Navarro, Moisés. 1977. *Anatomía del Poder en Mexico (1848–1853)*. Mexico City: El Colegio de Mexico.
Gould, Roger V. 2003. *Collision of Wills: How Ambiguity about Social Rank Breeds Conflict*. Chicago: University of Chicago Press.
Graham, Richard. 2013. *Independence in Latin America: Contrasts and Comparisons*, 3rd rev. ed. Austin: University of Texas Press.
Griffin, Charles. 1962. The States of Latin America. Pages 516–541 of: Hinsley, Francis (ed.), *The New Cambridge Modern History*, vol. 11. New York: Cambridge University Press.
Grosjean, Pauline. 2014. Conflict and Social and Political Preferences: Evidence from World War II and Civil Conflict in 35 European Countries. *Comparative Economic Studies*, 56(3), 424–451.
Grotius, Hugo. 1901. *Rights of War and Peace Including the Law of Nature and of Nations*. London: Walter Dunne.
Grzymala-Busse, Anna. 2023. Tilly Goes to Church: The Religious and Medieval Roots of European State Fragmentation. *American Political Science Review*, 1–20.
Guajardo, Guillermo. 2007. *Tecnología, Estado y ferrocarriles en Chile, 1850–1950*. Mexico City: Universidad Nacional Autonoma de Mexico.
Guardino, Peter. 2016. *The Dead March*. Cambridge, MA: Harvard University Press.
Gudmundson, Lowell. 1983. Costa Rica before Coffee: Occupational Distribution, Wealth Inequality, and Elite Society in the Village Economy of the 1840s. *Journal of Latin American Studies*, 15(1), 427–452.
Hahner, June E. 1969. *Civilian–Military Relations in Brazil 1889–1898*. Columbia: University of South Carolina Press.
Hale, Charles A. 1957. The War With the United States and the Crisis in Mexican Thought. *The Americas*, 14(2), 153–173.
Halperín Donghi, Tulio. 1982. *Guerra y finanzas en los orígenes del Estado argentino (1791–1850)*. Buenos Aires: Editorial de Belgrano.
1993. *The Contemporary History of Latin America*. Latin America in Translation. Durham, NC: Duke University Press.
2002. *Revolución y guerra: Formación de una elite dirigente en la Argentina criolla*, 2nd ed. Historia y cultura. Buenos Aires: Siglo Veintiuno.

2005. *Una nación para el desierto argentino*. Buenos Aires: Prometeo.

Hamnett, Brian R. 1999. *A Concise History of Mexico*. Cambridge Concise Histories. Cambridge; New York: Cambridge University Press.

Hampe, Karl. 1894. *Geschichte Konradins von Hohenstaufen*. Innsbruck: Wagner.

Hanna, Alfred, and Hanna, Kathrin. 1971. *Napoleon III and Mexico: American Triumph over Monarchy*. Chapel Hill: University of North Carolina Press.

Harris, Kevan. 2017. *A Social Revolution: Politics and the Welfare State in Iran*. Berkeley: University of California Press.

Heise, Julio. 1978. *Años de Formación y Aprendizaje Político, 1810–1833*. Santiago: Editorial Universitaria.

Helg, Aline, and Vergnaud, Lara. 2019. The Wars of Independence in Continental Iberian America: New Opportunities for Liberation. Pages 197–119 of: Berlin, Ira, Fields, Barbara J., Miller, Steven F., Reidy, Joseph P., and Rowland, Leslie S. (eds.), *Slave No More: Self-Liberation before Abolitionism in the Americas*. Chapel Hill: University of North Carolina Press.

Helmke, Gretchen, and Levitsky, Steven. 2004. Informal Institutions and Comparative Politics: A Research Agenda. *Perspectives on Politics*, 2(4), 725–740.

Henderson, Errol A., and Bayer, Reşat. 2013. Wallets, Ballots, or Bullets: Does Wealth, Democracy, or Military Capabilities Determine War Outcomes? *International Studies Quarterly*, 57(2), 303–317.

Henderson, Peter V. 2008. *Gabriel García Moreno and Conservative State Formation in the Andes*. Austin: University of Texas Press.

Henderson, Timothy J. 2007. *A Glorious Defeat: Mexico and Its War with the United States*. New York: Hill and Wang.

Hensel, Paul R., and Mitchell, Sara McLaughlin. 2017. From Territorial Claims to Identity Claims: The Issue Correlates of War (ICOW) Project. *Conflict Management and Peace Science*, 34(2), 126–140.

Herbst, Jeffrey. 2004. Let Them Fail: State Failure in Theory and Practice. Pages 302–318 of: Rotberg, Robert (ed.), *When States Fail: Causes and Consequences*. Princeton: Princeton University Press.

2014. *States and Power in Africa: Comparative Lessons in Authority and Control*. New York: Princeton University Press.

Herranz-Loncán, Alfonso. 2014. Transport Technology and Economic Expansion: The Growth Contribution of Railways in Latin America before 1914. *Journal of Iberian and Latin American Economic History*, 32(1), 13–45.

Hintze, Otto. 1961a. Verfassungsgeschichte polens vom 16. bis 18. jahrhundert. Pages 511–562 of: Oestreich, Gerhard (ed.), *Gesammelte Abhandlungen*, vol. Staat und Verfassung: Gesammelte Abhandlungen zur allgemeinen Verfassungsgeschichte. Göttingen: Vandenhoeck & Ruprecht.

1961b. Der Durchbruch des demokratischen Nationalstaates in der amerikanischen und französischen Revolution. Pages 503–510 of: Oestreich, Gerhard (ed.), *Gesammelte Abhandlungen*, vol. Staat und Verfassung: Gesammelte Abhandlungen zur allgemeinen Verfassungsgeschichte. Göttingen: Vandenhoeck & Ruprecht.

1961c. Die Entstehung des modernen Staatlebens. Pages 497–503 of: Oestreich, Gerhard (ed.), *Gesammelte Abhandlungen*, vol. Staat und Verfassung: Gesammelte Abhandlungen zur allgemeinen Verfassungsgeschichte. Göttingen: Vandenhoeck & Ruprecht.

1961d. Staatenbildung und Kommunalverwaltung. Pages 216–241 of: Oestreich, Gerhard (ed.), *Gesammelte Abhandlungen*, vol. Staat und Verfassung: Gesammelte Abhandlungen zur allgemeinen Verfassungsgeschichte. Göttingen: Vandenhoeck & Ruprecht.

1961e. Die Wurzeln der Kreisverfassung in den Ländern des nordöstlichen Deutschland. Pages 186–216 of: Oestreich, Gerhard (ed.), *Gesammelte Abhandlungen*, vol. Staat und Verfassung: Gesammelte Abhandlungen zur allgemeinen Verfassungsgeschichte. Göttingen: Vandenhoeck & Ruprecht.

1961f. Das Verfassungsleben der heutigen Kulturstaaten. Pages 390–423 of: Oestreich, Gerhard (ed.), *Gesammelte Abhandlungen*, vol. Staat und Verfassung: Gesammelte Abhandlungen zur allgemeinen Verfassungsgeschichte. Göttingen: Vandenhoeck & Ruprecht.

1961g. Machtpolitik und Regierungsverfassung. Pages 424–456 of: Oestreich, Gerhard (ed.), *Gesammelte Abhandlungen*, vol. Staat und Verfassung: Gesammelte Abhandlungen zur allgemeinen Verfassungsgeschichte. Göttingen: Vandenhoeck & Ruprecht.

1961h. Der österreichische und der preußische Beamtenstaat im 17. und 18. Jahrhundert. Pages 321–358 of: Oestreich, Gerhard (ed.), *Gesammelte Abhandlungen*, vol. Staat und Verfassung: Gesammelte Abhandlungen zur allgemeinen Verfassungsgeschichte. Göttingen: Vandenhoeck & Ruprecht.

1970. Der moderne Kapitalismus als historisches Individuum. Pages 114–164 of: Oestreich, Gerhard (ed.), *Feudalismus—Kapitalismus*. Göttingen: Vandenhoeck & Ruprecht.

1975. The Formation of States and Constitutional Development: A Study in History and Politics. Pages 157–177 of: Gilbert, Felix (ed.), *The Historical Essays of Otto Hintze*. New York: Oxford University Press.

1981. Der Beamtendstand. Pages 16–77 of: Krüger, Kersten (ed.), *In Beamtentum und Bürokratie*. Göttingen: Vandenhoeck & Ruprecht.

1982a. Föderalistischer Imperialismus. Betrachtungen um den Kelloggpakt. Pages 210–216 of: Oestreich, Gerhard (ed.), *Soziologie und Geschichte: Gesammelte Abhandlungen zur Soziologie, Politik und Theorie der Geschichte*. Göttingen: Vandenhoeck & Ruprecht.

1982b. Soziologische und geschichtliche Staatsauffassung: Zu Franz Oppenheimers System der Soziologie. Pages 239–305 of: Oestreich, Gerhard (ed.), *Soziologie und Geschichte: Gesammelte Abhandlungen zur Soziologie, Politik und Theorie der Geschichte*. Göttingen: Vandenhoeck & Ruprecht.

Hobbes, Thomas. 1914. *Leviathan*. Law Books Recommended for Libraries: International Law, 91. London: J. M. Dent & Sons; E. P. Dutton & Co.

Hoffman, Philip. 2015. *Why Did Europe Conquer the World?* Princeton: Princeton University Press.

Holbein, John B., and Hillygus, D. Sunshine. 2016. Making Young Voters: The Impact of Preregistration on Youth Turnout. *American Journal of Political Science*, 60(2), 364–382.

Holland, Paul W. 1986. Statistics and Causal Inference. *Journal of the American Statistical Association*, 81(396), 945–960.

Holsti, Kalevi J. 1996. *The State, War, and the State of War*. New York: Cambridge University Press.

Hornstein, Katie. 2017. *Picturing War in France, 1792–1856*. New Haven: Yale University Press.

Hui, Victoria. 2005. *War and State Formation in Ancient China and Early Modern Europe*. New York: Cambridge University Press.

2017. How Tilly's State Formation Paradigm is Revolutionizing the Study of Chinese State-Making. Pages 268–295 of: Kaspersen, Lars Bo, and Strandsbjerg, Jeppe (eds.), *Does War Make States? Investigations of Charles Tilly's Historical Sociology*. New York: Cambridge University Press.

Humud, Carlos. 1969. *El Sector Público Chileno entre 1830 y 1930*. Ph.D. thesis, Universidad de Chile.

Hunefeldt, Christine. 2004. *A Brief History of Peru*. New York: Facts on File.

Hunt, Shane. 1984. *Guano y Crecimiento del Perú en el siglo XIX*. Lima: HISLA.

Huntington, Samuel. 1970. Social and Institutional Dynamics of One-Party Systems. Pages 1–34 of: Huntington, Samuel, and Moore, Clement (eds.), *Authoritarian Politics in Modern Society: The Dynamics of Established One-Party Systems*. New York: Basic Books.

Ibsen, Kristine. 2010. *Maximilian, Mexico, and the Invention of Empire*. Nashville: Vanderbilt University Press.

Imai, Kosuke, and Kim, In Song. 2019. When Should We Use Unit Fixed Effects Regression Models for Causal Inference with Longitudinal Data? *American Journal of Political Science*, 63(2), 467–490.

Izecksohn, Victor. 2002. *O Cerne da Discórdia: A Guerra do Paraguai e o Núcleo Profissional do Exército*. Rio de Janeiro: Editora E-Papers.

2009. A Guerra do Paraguai. Pages 275–304 of: Grinberg, Kelia, and Salles, Ricardo (eds.), *O Brasil Imperial*, vol. 2. Rio de Janeiro: Civilização Brasileira.

Jackson, Jay. 1993. Realistic Group Conflict Theory: A Review and Evaluation of the Theoretical and Empirical Literature. *Psychological Record*, 43(3), 395–413.

Jaggers, Keith. 1992. War and the Three Faces of Power: War Making and State Making in Europe and the Americas. *Comparative Political Studies*, 25(1), 26–62.

Jones, Charles. 2013. International Relations in the Americas during the Long Eighteenth Century, 1663–1820. Pages 138–157 of: Suzuki, Shogo, Zhang, Yongjin, and Quirk, Joel (eds.), *International Orders in the Early Modern World: Before the Rise of the West*. London: Routledge.

Jones, Daniel M., Bremer, Stuart A., and Singer, J. David. 1996. Militarized Interstate Disputes, 1816–1992: Rationale, Coding Rules, and Empirical Patterns. *Conflict Management and Peace Science*, 15(2), 163–213.

Jung, Dietrich. 2006. *Democratization and Development: New Political Strategies for the Middle East*. New York: Springer.

Kacowicz, Arie. 2005. *The Impact of Norms in International Society: The Latin American Experience, 1881–2001*. Notre Dame: Notre Dame University Press.

Kallsen, Osvaldo. 1983. *Historia del Paraguay Contemporáneo*. Asunción: Imprenta Modelo.

Kalyvas, Stathis N., and Balcells, Laia. 2010. International System and Technologies of Rebellion: How the End of the Cold War Shaped Internal Conflict. *American Political Science Review*, 104(3), 415–429.

Karaman, Kivanc, and Pamuk, Sevket. 2013. Different Paths to the Modern State in Europe: The Interaction between Warfare, Economic Structure, and Political Regime. *American Political Science Review*, 107(3), 603–626.

Katz, Friedrich. 1986. Mexico: Restored Republic and Porfiriato. Pages 1–78 of: Bethell, Leslie (ed.), *The Cambridge History of Latin America*. New York: Cambridge University Press.

2014. Rural Rebellions after 1810. Pages 521–560 of: *Riot, Rebellion, and Revolution*. Princeton: Princeton University Press.

Kennedy, Ryan. 2014. Fading Colours? A Synthetic Comparative Case Study of the Impact of Colour Revolutions. *Comparative Politics*, **46**(3), 273–292.

Kiser, Edgar, and Linton, April. 2001. Determinants of the Growth of the State: War and Taxation in Early Modern France and England. *Social Forces*, **80**(2), 411–448.

Klein, Herbert S. 1985. La economía de la Nueva España, 1680–1809: Un análisis a partir de las cajas reales. *Historia Mexicana*, **34**(4), 561–609.

Krasner, Stephen D. 1999. *Sovereignty: Organized Hypocrisy*. Princeton: Princeton University Press.

Krauze, Enrique. 1994. *Siglo de caudillos: Biografía política de México (1810–1910)*, 1st ed. Colección Andanzas, 207. Barcelona: Tusquets Editores.

Kurtz, Marcus. 2013. *Latin American State Building in Comparative Perspective: Social Foundations of Institutional Order*. New York: Cambridge University Press.

Kurtz, Marcus, and Schrank, Andrew. 2012. Capturing State Strength: Experimental and Econometric Approaches. *Revista de Ciencia Política*, **32**(3), 613–621.

Lachapelle, Jean, Levitsky, Steven, Way, Lucan A., and Casey, Adam E. 2020. Social Revolution and Authoritarian Durability. *World Politics*, **72**(4), 557–600.

Lake, David, and O'Mahony, Angela. 2004. The Incredible Shrinking State: Explaining Change in the Territorial Size of Countries. *Journal of Conflict Resolution*, **48**(5), 699–722.

Lauderbaugh, George. 2012. *The History of Ecuador*. Santa Barbara: Greenwood.

Lee, Alexander, and Paine, Jack. 2023. The Great Revenue Divergence. *International Organization*, **77**(2), 363–404.

Lee, Melissa M. 2020. *Crippling Leviathan: How Foreign Subversion Weakens the State*. Ithaca: Cornell University Press.

Lemke, Douglas, and Carter, Jeff. 2016. Birth Legacies, State Making, and War. *Journal of Politics*, **78**(2), 497–511.

Lentner, Howard H. 1993. *State Formation in Central America: The Struggle for Autonomy, Development, and Democracy*. Contributions in Latin American Studies. Westport: Greenwood Press.

Levi, Margaret. 1988. *Of Rule and Revenue*. Berkeley: University of California Press.

1997. *Consent, Dissent, and Patriotism*. Cambridge: Cambridge University Press.

1998. Conscription: The Price of Citizenship. Pages 109–147 of: Bates, Robert, Greif, Avner, Rosenthal, Jean Laurent, and Weingast, Barry (eds.), *Analytic Narratives*. Princeton: Princeton University Press.

Levinson, Irvin. 2005. *Wars within Wars: Mexican Guerrillas, Domestic Elites, and the United States of America 1846–1848*. Fort Worth: Texas University Press.

Levitsky, Steven, and Way, Lucan. 2022. *Revolution and Dictatorship: The Violent Origins of Durable Authoritarianism*. Princeton: Princeton University Press.

Levy, Maria B., and Andrade, Ana M. R. 1985. Fundamentos do Sistema Bancário no Brasil, 1834–1860. *Estudos Econômicos*, **15**(1), 17–48.

Lewis, Paul H. 1986. Paraguay from the War of the Triple Alliance to the Chaco War 1870–1932. Pages 475–496 of: Bethell, Leslie (ed.), *The Cambridge History of Latin America*, vol. 5. London: Cambridge University Press.

Lima Neto, Oswaldo. 2001. *Transportes no Brasil: História e Reflexões*. Brasília: Geipot.
López, Jacinto. 1980. *Historia de la Guerra del Guano y el Salitre*. Lima: Editorial Universo.
López, Mario Justo. 1994. *Historia de los Ferrocarriles Nacionales 1866–1886*. Buenos Aires: Lumiere.
López-Alves, Fernando. 2000. *State Formation and Democracy in Latin America, 1810–1900*. Durham, NC: Duke University Press.
2001. The Transatlantic Bridge: Mirrors, Charles Tilly, and State Formation in the River Plate. Pages 150–172 of: Centeno, Miguel, and López-Alves, Fernando (eds.), *The Other Mirror: Grand Theory through the Lens of Latin America*. Princeton: Princeton University Press.
López Taverne, Elvira. 2014. *El Proceso de Construcción Estatal en Chile: Hacienda Pública y Burocracia (1817–1860)*. Santiago: Centro de Investigaciones Diego Barros Arana.
López Taverne, Elvira, and Fernández Abara, Joaquiín. 2018. Regionalismo versus Centralismo: La Formación del Estado en Chile (1810–1850). *Illes i Imperis*, 20(1), 7–17.
Lugones, Leopoldo. 1988. *Historia de Sarmiento*. Buenos Aires: Academia Argentina de Letras.
Lustick, Ian S. 1997. The Absence of Middle Eastern Great Powers: Political "Backwardness" in Historical Perspective. *International Organization*, 51(4), 653–683.
Lynch, Christian E. C. 2014. *Da Monarquia à Oligarquia: História Institucional e Pensamento Político Brasileiro (1822–1930)*. São Paulo: Alameda.
Lynch, John. 1985. The River Plate Republics from Independence to the Paraguayan War. Pages 615–676 of: Bethell, Leslie (ed.), *The Cambridge History of Latin America*, vol. 3. New York: Cambridge University Press.
1993. From Independence to National Organization. Pages 1–46 of: Bethell, Leslie (ed.), *Argentina since Independence*. New York: Cambridge University Press.
Lynch, John M. 1992. The Institutional Framework of Colonial Spanish America. *Journal of Latin American Studies*, 24(1), 69–81.
Lyons, Terrence. 2016. The Importance of Winning: Victorious Insurgent Groups and Authoritarian Politics. *Comparative Politics*, 48(2), 167–184.
MacMillan, Margaret. 2020. *War: How Conflict Shaped Us*. New York: Random House.
Madrid, Raúl. 2019. *The Partisan Origins of Democracy in Latin America*. Notre Dame: Paper presented at the Kellogg Institute for International Studies, October 3.
Madrid, Raúl and Schenoni, Luis. 2024. Reining in Rebellion: The Decline of Political Violence in South America, 1830–1929. *International Security*, 48(3), 129–167.
Maestri, Mario. 2016. *Paraguay: La republica campesina 1810–1865*. Asunción: Intercontinental Editora.
Mahoney, James. 2001. *The Legacies of Liberalism: Path Dependence and Political Regimes in Central America*. Baltimore: Johns Hopkins University Press.
2003. Long-Run Development and the Legacy of Colonialism in Spanish America. *American Journal of Sociology*, 109(1), 50–106.
2010. *Colonialism and Postcolonial Development: Spanish America in Comparative Perspective*. New York: Cambridge University Press.
Mahoney, James, and Rueschemeyer, Dietrich. 2003. *Comparative Historical Analysis in the Social Sciences*. New York: Cambridge University Press.

Mahoney, James, and Thelen, Kathleen. 2010. *Explaining Institutional Change: Ambiguity, Agency, and Power*. New York: Cambridge University Press.

2015. *Advances in Comparative-Historical Analysis*. New York: Cambridge University Press.

Mallon, Florencia E. 2010. Indigenous Peoples and Nation-States in Spanish America, 1780–2000. Pages 281–308 of: Moya, José C. (ed.), *The Oxford Handbook of Latin American History*. Oxford: Oxford University Press.

Mampilly, Zachariah Cherian. 2011. *Rebel Rulers: Insurgent Governance and Civilian Life during War*. Ithaca: Cornell University Press.

Mann, Michael. 1988. *States, War and Capitalism: Studies in Political Sociology*. New York: Basil Blackwell.

1993. *The Sources of Social Power*, vol. 2. New York: Cambridge University Press.

2008. Infrastructural Power Revisited. *Studies in Comparative International Development*, 43(3–4), 355–365.

2012. *The Sources of Social Power*. New York: Cambridge University Press.

Manrique, Nelson. 1988. *Yawar Mayu: Sociedades Terratenientes Serranas, 1879–1910*. Lima: Instituto Francés de Estudios Andinos.

Manson, Theodorus. 1971. *Guerra en el Pacífico Sur*. Santiago: Editorial Francisco de Aguirre.

Mares, David R. 2001. *Violent Peace: Militarized Interstate Bargaining in Latin America*. New York: Columbia University Press.

Mares, Isabela, and Queralt, Didac. 2015. The Non-democratic Origins of Income Taxation. *Comparative Political Studies*, 48(14), 1974–2009.

Mariátegui, José Carlos. 1959. *Siete Ensayos de Interpretación de la Realidad Peruana*. Lima: Empresa Editora Amauta.

Marichal, Carlos. 1989. *A Century of Debt Crises in Latin America: From Independence to the Great Depression, 1820–1930*. Princeton: Princeton University Press.

1999. *La bancarrota del virreinato: Nueva España y las finanzas del imperio español, 1780–1810*. Mexico City: Fondo de Cultura Economica USA.

2006. Money, Taxes, and Finance. Pages 423–460 of: Bulmer-Thomas, Victor, Coatsworth, John, and Cortes-Conde, Roberto (eds.), *The Cambridge Economic History of Latin America*, vol. 1. New York: Cambridge University Press.

Martin, Philip A. 2022. Insurgent Armies: Military Obedience and State Formation after Rebel Victory. *International Security*, 46(3), 87–127.

Martinez, Eduardo. 1982. La Batalla de Cuaspud. *Cartillas de la Divulgación Ecuatoriana*, 3(36), 3–18.

Masterman, George Frederick. 1870. *Seven Eventful Years in Paraguay*. London: Sampson Low, Son, and Marston.

Mazzuca, Sebastián. 2017. Critical Juncture and Legacies: State Formation and Economic Performance in Latin America. *Qualitative and Multi-Method Research*, 1(15), 28–34.

Mazzuca, Sebastián. 2021. *Latecomer State Formation: Political Geography and Capacity Failure in Latin America*. New Haven: Yale University Press.

Mazzuca, Sebastián, and Robinson, James A. 2009. Political Conflict and Power Sharing in the Origins of Modern Colombia. *Hispanic American Historical Review*, 89(2), 285–321.

McAllen, Mary M. 2014. *Maximilian and Carlota: Europe's Last Empire in Mexico*. San Antonio: Trinity University Press.

McEvoy, Carmen. 1994. *Un proyecto nacional en el siglo XIX: Manuel Pardo y su visión del Perú*. Lima: Universidad Católica del Peru.

1997. *La utopía republicana: Ideales y realidades en la formación de la cultura política peruana, 1871–1919*. Lima: Universidad Católica del Peru.

1999. *Forjando La Nación: Ensayos de Historia Republicana*. Lima: Universidad Católica del Peru.

McEvoy, Carmen, and Rabinovich, Alejandro. 2018. *Tiempo de Guerra*. Lima: Instituto de Estudios Peruanos.

McFarlane, Anthony. 1995. Rebellions in Late Colonial Spanish America: A Comparative Perspective. *Bulletin of Latin American Research*, **14**(3), 313–338.

Méndez Vives, Enrique. 2014. *Cinco siglos: Lo esencial de la historia de Uruguay*. Montevideo: Ediciones de la Banda Oriental S.R.L.

Meyer, Eduard. 1989. *Zur Alteren Griechischen Geschichte*. Halle: Max Niemeyer.

Migdal, Joel S. 1988. *Strong Societies and Weak States: State-Society Relations and State Capabilities in the Third World*. New York: Princeton University Press.

Miller, Rory. 1976. The Coastal Elite and Peruvian Politics. *Journal of Latin American Studies*, **14**(1), 97–120.

2011. *Empresas Británicas, Economía, y Política en el Perú: 1850–1934*. Lima: Instituto de Estudios Peruanos.

Mitchener, Kris James, and Weidenmier, Marc D. 2010. Supersanctions and Sovereign Debt Repayment. *Journal of International Money and Finance*, **29**(1), 19–36.

Mitzen, Jennifer, and Schweller, Randall L. 2011. Knowing the Unknown Unknowns: Misplaced Certainty and the Onset of War. *Security Studies*, **20**(1), 2–35.

Molina Jiménez, Ivan. 2000. *La Campaña Nacional (1856–1857): Una Visión desde el Siglo XXI*. Alajuela: Museo Histórico Cultural Santamaría.

2005. Del Legado Colonial al Modelo Agroexportador: Costa Rica (1821–1913). *Cuadernos de Historia de las Instituciones de Costa Rica*, **19**(1), 1–32.

Monge Alfaro, Carlos. 1980. *Historia de Costa Rica*. San José: Librería Trejos.

Mucke, Ulrich. 1998. *Der Partido Civil in Peru 1871–1879*. Stuttgart: Franz Steiner.

Muñoz Guillén, Mercedes. 1989. El Ejército Costarricense y la Conquista de los Atributos de la Estaticidad. Pages 255–273 of: de la Cruz, Vladimir (ed.), *Las Instituciones Costarricenses de las Sociedades Indígenas a la Crisis de la República Liberal*. San José: Editorial de la Universidad de Costa Rica.

Nahum, Benjamin. 1999. *Breve Historia del Uruguay Independiente*. Montevideo: Banda Oriental.

Needell, Jeffrey. 2006. *The Party of Order: The Conservatives, the State, and Slavery in the Brazilian Monarchy*. Stanford: Stanford University Press.

Nieto, Euardo, and Vito, Jaime. 2005. Las Ideas y Los Regimenes Politicos. Pages 139–169 of: Cavieres, Eduardo, and Aljivín de Lozada, Cristobal (eds.), *Chile–Peru, Peru–Chile: 1820–1920*. Valparaiso: Ediciones Universitarias.

North, Douglass C. 1989. Institutions and Economic Growth: An Historical Introduction. *World Development*, **17**(9), 1319–1332.

North, Douglass C., Wallis, John Joseph, and Weingast, Barry. 2009. *Violence and Social Orders: A Conceptual Framework for Interpreting Recorded Human History*. New York: Cambridge University Press.

Nunn, Frederik. 1976. *The Military in Chilean History: Essays on Civil–Military Relations, 1810–1973*. Albuquerque: University of New Mexico Press.

1983. *Yesterday's Soldiers: European Military Professionalism in South America, 1890–1940*. Lincoln: University of Nebraska Press.

Obregón Loria, Rafael. 1991. *Costa Rica y la Guerra contra los Filibusteros*. Alajuela: Museo Histórico Cultural Santamaría.

O'Donnell, Guillermo. 1993. On the State, Democratization and Some Conceptual Problems: A Latin American View with Glances at Some Postcommunist Countries. *World Development*, **21**(8), 1355–1369.

O'Gorman, Edmundo. 1986. *La supervivencia política novo-hispana: Reflexiones sobre el monarquismo mexicano*, 4th ed. Mexico City: Universidad Iberoamericana, Departamento de Historia.

Oliveira Lima, Manuel. 1989. *O Imperio Brasileiro: 1821–1889*. São Paulo: Universidade de São Paulo.

Olson, Mancur. 1965. *The Logic of Collective Action: Public Goods and the Theory of Groups*. Harvard Economic Studies, 124. Cambridge, MA: Harvard University Press.

1993. Dictatorship, Democracy, and Development. *American Political Science Review*, **87**(3), 567–576.

Oppenheimer, Franz. 1926. *Soziologische Streifzüge: Gesammelte Reden und Aufsätze*. Munich: Max Hueber.

1964. *System der Soziologie*. Stuttgart: Gustav Fischer.

1975. *The State*. New York: Free Life Editions.

Ortega, Luis. 1984. Los Empresarios, la Política y la Guerra del Pacífico. *Contribuciones FLASCO*, **1**(24), 5–13.

Osório, Joaquim L. 1915. *Historia do General Osório*. Pelotas: Typografica Diario Popular.

Oszlak, Oscar. 1981. The Historical Formation of the State in Latin America: Some Theoretical and Methodological Guidelines for Its Study. *Latin American Research Review*, **16**(2), 3–32.

1982. *La Formación del Estado Argentino: Orden, Progreso y Organización Nacional*. Buenos Aires: Editorial de Belgrano.

Paglayan, Agustina S. 2022. Education or Indoctrination? The Violent Origins of Public School Systems in an Era of State-Building. *American Political Science Review*, **116**(4), 1242–1257.

Pahre, Robert. 1998. Reactions and Reciprocity: Tariffs and Trade Liberalizations from 1815 to 1914. *Journal of Conflict Resolution*, **42**(4), 467.

Paine, Jack. 2023. A Theory of External Wars and European Parliaments. *International Organization*, **77**(1), 102–143.

Palma, Gabriel. 2000. Trying to Tax and Spend Oneself out of the Dutch Disease: The Chilean Economy from the War of the Pacific to the Great Depression. Pages 217–264 of: Cárdenas, Enrique, Ocampo, José Antonio, and Thorp, Rosemary (eds.), *An Economic History of Twentieth-Century Latin America*. London: Palgrave Macmillan.

Palmer, Glenn, D'Orazio, Vito, Kenwick, Michael R., and McManus, Roseanne W. 2019. Updating the Militarized Interstate Dispute Data: A Response to Gibler, Miller, and Little. *International Studies Quarterly*, **64**(2), 469–475.

Palmer, Glenn, McManus, Roseanne W., D'Orazio, Vito, Kenwick, Michael R., Karstens, Mikaela, Bloch, Chase, Dietrich, Nick, Kahn, Kayla, Ritter, Kellan, and Soules,

Michael J. 2022. The MID5 Dataset, 2011–2014: Procedures, Coding Rules, and Description. *Conflict Management and Peace Science*, 39(4), 470–482.

Pani, Erika. 2001. *Para mexicanizar el Segundo Imperio: El imaginario político de los imperialistas*, 1st ed. Mexico City: Colegio de México, Centro de Estudios Históricos: Instituto de Investigaciones Dr. José María Luis Mora.

2017. Law, Allegiance, and Sovereignty in Civil War Mexico, 1857–1867. *Journal of the Civil War Era*, 7(4), 570–596.

Paniagua, Victoria. 2022. Insuring against Democracy: The Political Economy of Premodern Elites' Asset Portfolio Diversification.

Panizza, Francisco. 1997. Late Institutionalisation and Early Modernisation: The Emergence of Uruguay's Liberal Democratic Political Order. *Journal of Latin American Studies*, 29(3), 667–691.

Paredes, Maritza. 2013. *Shaping State Capacity: A Comparative Historical Analysis of Mining Dependence in the Andes, 1840s–1920s*. Ph.D. thesis, University of Oxford.

Pastore, Mario. 1993. *State-Led Industrialization: The Evidence on Paraguay 1852–1870*. New Orleans: Center for Latin American Studies, Tulane University.

Paul, Thazha. 2014. *The Warrior State: Pakistan in the Contemporary World*. Oxford: Oxford University Press.

Paz, Octavio. 1982. The Meaning of Mexican Independence. Pages 49–54 of: Raat, Dirk (ed.), *Mexico from Independence to Revolution 1810–1910*. Lincoln: University of Nebraska Press.

Peacock, Alan, and Wiseman, Jack. 1967. *The Growth of Public Expenditure in the United Kingdom*. Princeton: Princeton University Press.

Peres Costa, Wilma. 1990. *A Espada de Damocles: O Exército, a Guerra do Paraguai, e a Crise do Império*. Ph.D. thesis, Universidade de São Paulo, São Paulo.

Pereyra Plasencia, Hugo. 2010. *Trabajos sobre la Guerra del Pacífico*. Lima: Instituto Riva-Aguero.

Pérez, Joseph. 1977. *Los movimientos precursores de la emancipación en Hispanoamérica*, vol. 4. Madrid: Alhambra.

Peters, Heinz. 1996. *El Sistema Educativo Paraguayo desde 1811 hasta 1865*. Asunción: Instituto Cultural Paraguayo Aleman.

Peterson, Harold. 1932. Efforts of the United States to Mediate in the Paraguayan War. *Hispanic American Historical Review*, 12(1), 2–17.

Pierson, Paul. 2015. Power and Path Dependence. Pages 123–146 of: Mahoney, James, and Thelen, Kathleen (eds.), *Advances in Comparative Historical Analysis*. Cambridge: Cambridge University Press.

Pike, Fredrick B. 1967. *The Modern History of Peru*. New York: Praeger.

Planas, Pedro. 1998. *La Descentralización en el Peru Republicano*. Lima: Municipalidad Metropolitana de Lima.

Platt, Desmond C. M. 1983. Foreign Finance in Argentina for the First Half-Century of Independence. *Journal of Latin American Studies*, 15(1), 23–47.

Pomer, Leon. 1981. *A Guerra do Paraguai: A Grande Tragédia Rioplatense*. São Paulo: Editora Parma.

Porter, Bruce. 1994. *War and the Rise of the State: The Military Foundations of Modern Politics*. New York: Free Press.

Posen, Barry R. 1993. Nationalism, the Mass Army, and Military Power. *International Security*, 18(2), 80–124.

Powell, Jonathan M., and Thyne, Clayton L. 2011. Global Instances of Coups from 1950 to 2010: A New Dataset. *Journal of Peace Research*, **48**(2), 249–259.

Putnam, Robert D. 1994. *Making Democracy Work: Civic Traditions in Modern Italy*. Princeton: Princeton University Press.

Queralt, Didac. 2019. War, International Finance, and Fiscal Capacity in the Long Run. *International Organization*, **73**(1), 713–753.

2022. *Pawned States: State Building in the Era of International Finance*. Princeton: Princeton University Press.

Rabinovich, Alejandro M., and Sobrevilla Perea, Natalia. 2019. Regular and Irregular Forces in Conflict: Nineteenth Century Insurgencies in South America. *Small Wars and Insurgencies*, **30**(4–5), 775–796.

Rabinovich, Andrés. 2015. Las Guerras Civiles Rioplatenses: Violencia Armada y Configuraciones Identitarias. Pages 137–158 of: Lorenz, Federico (ed.), *Guerras de la Historia Argentina*. Buenos Aires: Ariel.

Ragin, Charles C., and Davey, Sean. 2016. *Fuzzy-Set/Qualitative Comparative Analysis 3.0*. Irvine: Department of Sociology, University of California.

Rapport, Aaron. 2015. Hard Thinking about Hard and Easy Cases in Security Studies. *Security Studies*, **24**(3), 431–465.

Rasler, Karen A., and Thompson, William R. 1985. War Making and State Making: Governmental Expenditures, Tax Revenues, and Global Wars. *American Political Science Review*, **79**(2), 491–507.

Rebuelto, Emilio. 1994. Historia del Desarrollo de los Ferrocarriles Argentinos. Pages 1–23 of: Schickendantz, Emilio, and Rebuelto, Emilio (eds.), *Los Ferrocarriles en Argentina (1857–1910)*. Buenos Aires: Fundación Museo Ferroviario.

Reed, Nelson. 1964. *The Caste War of Yucatan*. Stanford: Stanford University Press.

Reiter, Dan, and Stam, Allan C. 2002. *Democracies at War*. New York: Princeton University Press.

Remmer, Karen. 1984. *Party Competition in Argentina and Chile: Political Recruitment and Public Policy, 1890–1930*. Lincoln: University of Nebraska Press.

Rengger, Johann. 1987. Ensayo histórico sobre la revolución en Paraguay. Pages 15–47: Rengger, Johann, Carlyle, Thomas, and Demersay, Alfred (eds.), *El doctor Francia*. Asunción: El Lector.

Resende-Santos, João. 2007. *Neorealism, States, and the Modern Mass Army*. New York: Cambridge University Press.

Reyes Abadie, Washington, and Vázquez Romero, Andrés. 1998. *Crónica general del Uruguay*. Montevideo: Ediciones de la Banda Oriental.

Rich, Paul, and Stubbs, Richard. 1997. *The Counter-Insurgent State: Guerrilla Warfare and State Building in the Twentieth Century*. New York: St. Martin's Press.

Ripley, Roswell Sabine. 1970. *The War with Mexico*. New York: Harper & Bros.

Rock, David. 1985. *Argentina, 1516–1982: From Spanish Colonization to the Falklands War*. Berkeley: University of California Press.

Rock, David. 2002. *State Building and Political Movements in Argentina, 1860–1916*. Stanford: Stanford University Press.

Rodríguez, Jaime E. 1998. *The Independence of Spanish America*. Cambridge Latin American Studies, 84. Cambridge: Cambridge University Press.

Rodríguez-Franco, Diana. 2016. Internal Wars, Taxation and State Building. *American Sociological Review*, **81**(1), 190–213.

Roel Pineda, Virgilio. 1982. *Conatos, Levantamientos, Campañas e Ideología de la Independencia*, vol. 4. Lima: Editorial Mejia Baca.

Romero, José Luis. 1956. *Historia de las Ideas Políticas en Argentina*. Mexico City: Fondo de Cultura Económica.

Rosa, José María. 1964. *La Guerra del Paraguay y las Montoneras Argentinas*. Buenos Aires: Peña Lillo.

Rosario Pacahuala, Emilio. 2011. Armas, Discurssos y Leyes: La Guerra Contra Chile y el Congreso de la República en 1879. Pages 87–103 of: Fernández, Dino L., Loayza Pérez, Alex, and Garfias Dávila, Marcos (eds.), *Trabajos de Historia: Religión, Cultura y Política en el Perú, Siglos XVII–XX*. Lima: Fondo Editorial de la UNMSM.

Rosenthal, Jean Laurent. 1998. The Political Economy of Absolutism Reconsidered. Pages 64–108 of: Bates, Robert, Greif, Avner, Rosenthal, Jean Laurent, and Weingast, Barry (eds.), *Analytic Narratives*. Princeton: Princeton University Press.

Rouquié, Alain. 1987. *The Military and the State in Latin America*. Berkeley: University of California Press.

Rüstow, Alexander. 1980. *Freedom and Domination: A Historical Critique of Civilization*. Princeton: Princeton University Press.

Sabato, Hilda. 2001. *The Many and the Few*. Stanford: Stanford University Press.

2018. *Republics of the New World: The Revolutionary Political Experiment in Nineteenth-Century Latin America*. Princeton: Princeton University Press.

Sagredo, Rafael. 2001. Balmaceda y los Orígenes del Intervencionismo Estatal. Pages 37–48 of: Ortega, Luis (ed.), *La Guerra Civil de 1891: 100 Años Hoy*. Santiago: Universidad de Santiago de Chile.

Saiegh, Sebastián M. 2013. Political Institutions and Sovereign Borrowing: Evidence from Nineteenth-Century Argentina. *Public Choice*, **156**(1/2), 61–75.

Saint John, Ronald Bruce. 1992. *The Diplomatic History of Peru*. Boulder: Lynne Rienner.

Salles, Ricardo. 1990. *Guerra do Paraguai: Escravidão e cidadania na formacão do exército*. São Paulo: Paz e Terra.

Sambanis, Nicholas, Skaperdas, Stergios, and Wohlforth, William C. 2015. Nation-Building through War. *American Political Science Review*, **109**(2), 279–296.

Sanchez-Albornoz, Nicolás. 1978. *Indios y Tributos en el Alto Peru*. Lima: Instituto de Estudios Peruanos.

Sanchez Quell, Hipólito. 1935. *Política Internacional del Paraguay 1811–1870*. Asunción: Imprenta Nacional.

Sanchez Talanquer, Mariano. 2017. *States Divided: History, Conflict, and State Formation in Mexico and Colombia*. Ph.D. thesis, Cornell University.

Santoni, Pedro. 1996. *Mexicans at Arms: Puro Federalists and the Politics of War 1845–1848*. Fort Worth: Texan Christian University Press.

1997. *The Mexican National Army 1822–1852*. College Station: Texas A&M University Press.

Sanz Fernández, Jesus. 1998. *Historia de los Ferrocarriles de Iberoamérica*. Madrid: Union Fenosa.

Sarkees, Meredith Reid, and Wayman, Frank Whelon. 2010. *Resort to War: A Data Guide to Inter-state, Extra-state, Intra-state, and Non-state Wars, 1816–2007*. Washington, DC: CQ Press.

Sater, William. 1985. *Chile and the War of the Pacific*. Lincoln: University of Nebraska Press.

2007. *Andean Tragedy: Fighting the War of the Pacific, 1879–1884*. Lincoln: University of Nebraska Press.

Saylor, Ryan. 2014. *State Building in Boom Times: Commodities and Coalitions in Latin America and Africa*. New York: Oxford University Press.

Saylor, Ryan, and Wheeler, Nicholas C. 2017. Paying for War and Building States: The Coalitional Politics of Debt Servicing and Tax Institutions. *World Politics*, **69**(2), 366–408.

Scheina, Robert L. 2003. *Latin America's Wars*, 1st ed. Washington, DC: Brassey's.

Schelling, Thomas C. 1966. *Arms and Influence*. New Haven: Yale University Press.

Schenoni, Luis. 2021. Bringing War Back In: Victory and State Formation in Latin America. *American Journal of Political Science*, **65**(2), 405–421.

Schenoni, Luis, Goertz, Gary, Owsiak, Andrew, and Diehl, Paul. 2023. The Saavedra Lamas Peace. Working Paper, 1–34.

Scheve, Kenneth, and Stasavage, David. 2012. Democracy, War, and Wealth: Lessons from Two Centuries of Inheritance Taxation. *American Political Science Review*, **106**(1), 81–102.

Schivelbusch, Wolfgang. 2004. *The Culture of Defeat*. New York: Picador.

Schmitt, Carl. 2005. *Political Theology: Four Chapters on the Concept of Sovereignty*. Chicago: University of Chicago Press.

Schneider, Carsten Q., and Wagemann, Claudius. 2012. *Set-Theoretic Methods for the Social Sciences: A Guide to Qualitative Comparative Analysis*. New York: Cambridge University Press.

Schneider, Louis. 1902. *A Guerra da Triplice Allianca contra o governo da República do Paraguay (1864–1870)*. Rio de Janeiro: Garnier.

Schoonover, Thomas. 1978. *Dollars over Dominion: The Triumph of Liberalism in Mexican–United States Relations, 1861–1867*. Baton Rouge: Louisiana State University Press.

Schremmer, D. Eckart. 1989. Taxation and Public Finance: Britain, France, and Germany. Pages 315–494 of: Mathias, Peter, and Pollard, Sidney (eds.), *The Cambridge Economic History of Europe*, vol. 8. Cambridge: Cambridge University Press.

Schulz, John. 1994. *O Exército na Política: Origens da Intervenção Militar 1850–1894*. São Paulo: EDUSP.

Schumpeter, Joseph. 1991. The Crisis of the Tax States. Pages 99–140 of: Swedberg, Richard (ed.), *The Economics and Sociology of Capitalism*. Princeton: Princeton University Press.

Schurmann, Mauricio, and Coolighan, Maria Luisa. 1956. *Historia del Uruguay*. Montevideo: Monteverde y Cia.

Schvitz, Guy, Girardin, Luc, Rüegger, Seraina, Weidmann, Nils B., Cederman, Lars-Erik, and Gleditsch, Kristian Skrede. 2022. Mapping the International System, 1886–2019: The CShapes 2.0 Dataset. *Journal of Conflict Resolution*, **66**(1), 144–161.

Schwartz, Rachel. 2023. *Undermining the State from Within: The Institutional Legacies of Civil War in Central America*. New York: Cambridge University Press.

Schweller, Randall L. 2008. *Unanswered Threats: Political Constraints on the Balance of Power*. Princeton: Princeton University Press.

Scott, James. 2017. *Against the Grain: A Deep History of the Earliest States*. New Haven: Yale University Press.

Scott, Joseph. 1975. *El Testimonio de Scott*. Managua: Banco de América.

Scully, Timothy R. 1992. *Rethinking the Center: Party Politics in Nineteenth and Twentieth Century Chile*. Stanford: Stanford University Press.

Seeley, John Robert. 1922. *The Growth of British Policy*. Cambridge: Cambridge University Press.

Serrano, Gonzalo. 2017. La construcción de una historia nacional de Chile: El caso de la Guerra contra la Confederacion. Pages 143–157 of: Corti, Paola, Widow, Jose Luis, and Moreno, Rodrigo (eds.), *La Verdad en la Historia*. Santiago: Ril Editores.

Sharman, Jason C. 2015. War, Selection, and Micro-states: Economic and Sociological Perspectives on the International System. *European Journal of International Relations*, 21(1), 194–214.

Sharman, Jason C. 2023. Something New out of Africa: States Made Slaves, Slaves Made States. *International Organization*, 77(3), 497–526.

Shawcross, Edward. 2018. *France, Mexico and Informal Empire in Latin America, 1820–1867*. London: Palgrave.

Sherif, Muzafer. 1966. *In Common Predicament: Social Psychology of Intergroup Conflict and Cooperation*. Boston: Houghton Mifflin.

Sicotte, Richard, and Vizcarra, Catalina. 2009. War and Foreign Debt Settlement in Early Republican Spanish America. *Revista de historia económica*, 27(2), 247–289.

Sierra, Justo. 1982. Mexico's Tragedy. Pages 105–121 of: Raat, Dirk (ed.), *Mexico from Independence to Revolution 1810–1910*. Lincoln: University of Nebraska Press.

Simmel, Georg. 1955. *Conflict*. New York: Free Press.

Singer, J. David. 1988. Reconstructing the Correlates of War Dataset on Material Capabilities of States, 1816–1985. *International Interactions*, 14(2), 115–132.

Singer, J. David, and Small, Melvin. 1966. The Composition and Status Ordering of the International System: 1815–1940. *World Politics*, 18(2), 236–282.

Sinkin, Richard N. 1979. *The Mexican Reform, 1855–1876: A Study in Liberal Nation-Building*. Austin: University of Texas Press.

Skocpol, Theda. 1979. *States and Social Revolutions: A Comparative Analysis of France, Russia and China*. New York: Cambridge University Press.

1985. Strategies of Analysis in Current Research. Pages 3–43 of: Evans, Peter, Rueschemeyer, Dietrich, and Skocpol, Theda (eds.), *Bringing the State Back In*. New York: Cambridge University Press.

Slater, Dan. 2010. *Ordering Power: Contentious Politics and Authoritarian Leviathans in Southeast Asia*. Cambridge: Cambridge University Press.

Smith, Adam. 1976. *An Inquiry into the Nature and Causes of the Wealth of Nations*. Chicago: University of Chicago Press.

Smith, Justin. 1919. *The War with Mexico*. New York: Macmillan.

Soares Alsina, Paulo. 2015. *Rio Branco: Grande Estrategia e o Poder Naval*. São Paulo: FGV Editora.

Soifer, Hillel David. 2012. The Causal Logic of Critical Junctures. *Comparative Political Studies*, 45(12), 1572–1597.

Soifer, Hillel David. 2015. *State Building in Latin America*. New York: Cambridge University Press.

Soifer, Hillel David, and Vom Hau, Matthias. 2008. Unpacking the Strength of the State: The Utility of State Infrastructural Power. *Studies in Comparative International Development*, 43(3–4), 219.

Solis, Edwin, and Gonzalez Pacheco, Carlos. 1992. *El Ejército en Costa Rica: Poder Político y Poder Militar (1821–1890)*. San José: Ediciones Guayacán.

Somma, Nicolás. 2011. *When the Powerful Rebel: Armed Insurgency in Nineteenth-Century Latin America*. Ph.D. thesis, Notre Dame University, IN.

2015. How Do Intergroup Grievances Develop in the Absence of Oppression? Revolutions and Political Parties in Nineteenth-Century Uruguay. *Journal of Historical Sociology*, 28(3), 404–427.

2016. How Do Party Systems Shape Insurgency Levels? A Comparison of Four Nineteenth-Century Latin American Republics. *Social Science History*, 40(2), 219–245.

Sorensen, Georg. 2001. War and State-Making: Why Doesn't It Work in the Third World? *Security Dialogue*, 32(3), 341–354.

Soto Valenzuela, Marco. 1957. *Guerra Nacional de Centroamérica*. Guatemala City: Editorial del Ministério de Educación Pública.

Spahr, Thomas. 2015. The Mexican–American War: A Historiographical Overview. Pages 242–259 of: Thompson, Antonio, and Frentzos, Christos (eds.), *The Routledge Handbook of American Military and Diplomatic History*. London: Routledge.

Spencer, Charles S. 2010. Territorial Expansion and Primary State Formation. *Proceedings of the National Academy of Sciences of the United States*, 107(16), 7119–7126.

Spencer, Charles S., and Redmond, Elsa M. 2004. Primary State Formation in Mesoamerica. *Annual Review of Anthropology*, 33(1), 173–199.

Spruyt, Hendrik. 2001. Diversity or Uniformity in the Modern World? Answers from Evolutionary Theory, Learning, and Social Adaptation. Pages 110–132 of: Thompson, William R. (ed.), *Evolutionary Interpretations of World Politics*. New York: Routledge.

2017. War and State Formation: Amending the Bellicist Theory of State Making. Pages 73–97 of: Kaspersen, Lars Bo, and Strandsbjerg, Jeppe (eds.), *Does War Make States? Investigations of Charles Tilly's Historical Sociology*. New York: Cambridge University Press.

Stasavage, David. 2010. When Distance Mattered: Geographic Scale and the Development of European Representative Assemblies. *American Political Science Review*, 104(4), 625–643.

2011. *States of Credit: Size, Power, and the Development of European Polities*. Princeton: Princeton University Press.

Stein, Arthur A. 1976. Conflict and Cohesion: A Review of the Literature. *Journal of Conflict Resolution*, 20(1), 143–172.

Stein, Arthur A., and Russett, Bruce M. 1980. Evaluating War: Outcomes and Consequences. Pages 399–422 of: Gurr, Ted Robert (ed.), *Handbook of Political Conflict: Theory and Research*. New York: Free Press.

Stern, Steve J. 1987. The Age of Andean Insurrection, 1742–1782: A Reappraisal. Pages 34–93 of: *Resistance, Rebellion, and Consciousness in the Andean Peasant World, 18th to 20th Centuries*. Madison: University of Wisconsin Press.

Stewart, Megan A. 2018. Civil War as State-Making: Strategic Governance in Civil War. *International Organization*, 72(1), 205–226.

Stinnett, Douglas, Tir, Jaroslav, Diehl, Paul F., Schafer, Philip, and Gochman, Charles. 2002. The Correlates of War Project Direct Contiguity Data. *Conflict Management and Peace Science*, 19(2), 59–68.

Stone, Samuel. 1975. *La Dinastía de los Conquistadores: La Crisis del Poder en la Costa Rica Contemporánea*. San José: Editorial Universitaria Centroamericana.

Sumner, William Graham. 1940. *Folkways: A Study of the Sociological Importance of Usages, Manners, Customs, Mores, and Morals*. Boston: Ginn and Co.

Tajfel, Henri, and Turner, John C. 1986. The Social Identity Theory of Intergroup Behavior. Pages 7–24 of: Worchel, Stephen, and Austin, William G. (eds.), *Psychology of Intergroup Relations*. Chicago: Nelson-Hall.

Tarrow, Sidney. 2015. *War, States, and Contention*. Ithaca: Cornell University Press.

Tate, Nicholas. 1979. Britain and Latin America in the Nineteenth Century: The Case of Paraguay 1811–1870. *Ibero-amerikanisches Archiv, Neue Folge*, 5(1), 39–70.

Taylor, Brian D., and Botea, Roxana. 2008. Tilly Tally: War-Making and State-Making in the Contemporary Third World. *International Studies Review*, 10(1), 27–56.

Telles, Pedro Carlos da Silva. 2011. *História da Engenharia Ferroviária no Brasil*. Rio de Janeiro: Noticia e Cia.

Teschke, Benno. 2017. After the Tilly Thesis. Pages 25–51 of: Kaspersen, Lars Bo, and Strandsbjerg, Jeppe (eds.), *Does War Make States? Investigations of Charles Tilly's Historical Sociology*. New York: Cambridge University Press.

Tetlock, Philip, and Belkin, Aaron. 1996. *Counterfactual Thought Experiments in World Politics: Logical, Methodological, and Psychological Perspectives*. Princeton: Princeton University Press.

Thelen, Kathleen. 1999. Historical Institutionalism in Comparative Politics. *Annual Review of Political Science*, 2(1), 369–404.

Thies, Cameron G. 2004. State Building, Interstate and Intrastate Rivalry: A Study of Post-colonial Developing Country Extractive Efforts, 1975–2000. *International Studies Quarterly*, 48(1), 53–72.

2005. War, Rivalry, and State Building in Latin America. *American Journal of Political Science*, 49(3), 451–465.

2022. Domestic Processes, External Threats, and Latin American State-Building: From Comparative Historical Analysis to Comparative Hypothesis Testing. *Journal of Historical Political Economy*, 1(2), 135–157.

Thompson, George. 1869. *The War in Paraguay: With a Historical Sketch of the Country and Its People*. London: Longmans, Green, and Co.

Tilly, Charles. 1975. Reflections on the History of European State-Making. Pages 3–83 of: *The Formation of National States in Western Europe*. Princeton: Princeton University Press.

1985. War-Making and State-Making as Organized Crime. Pages 169–191 of: Evans, Peter, Rueschemeyer, Dietrich, and Skocpol, Theda (eds.), *Bringing the State Back In*. New York: Cambridge University Press.

1988. *From Mobilization to Revolution*. New York: Random House.

1990. *Coercion, Capital, and European States, AD 990*. Cambridge: Basil Blackwell.

Tir, Jaroslav, Schafer, Philip, Diehl, Paul F., and Goertz, Gary. 1998. Territorial Changes, 1816–1996: Procedures and Data. *Conflict Management and Peace Science*, 16(1), 89–97.

Tönnies, Ferdinand. 1957. *Community and Society*. East Lansing: Michigan State University Press.

Torres, João Camilo de Oliveira. 1968. *Os construtores do Império: Ideais e Lutas do Partido Conservador Brasileiro*. São Paulo: Editora Nacional.

Urteaga Quisme, Madai. 2017. La Desigual Capacidad del Estado en América Latina. *Política y Gobierno*, **24**(2), 435–457.

Valenzuela, J. Samuel. 1985. *Democratización vía Reforma: La Expansión del Sufragio en Chile*. Buenos Aires: Ediciones del IDES.

Van Creveld, Martin. 1999. *The Rise and Decline of the State*. Cambridge: Cambridge University Press.

Van Raemdonck, Dirk, and Diehl, Paul. 1989. After the Shooting Stops: Insights on Postwar Economic Growth. *Journal of Peace Research*, **26**(a), 249–264.

Van Young, Eric. 2020. *Writing Mexican History*. Stanford: Stanford University Press.

Vázquez, Josefina Zoraida, and Meyer, Lorenzo. 1985. *The United States and Mexico*. Chicago: University of Chicago Press.

Vázquez, Josefina Zoraida. 1997. The Colonization and Loss of Texas: A Mexican Perspective. Pages 49–54 of: Rodríguez, Jaime, and Vincent, Kathryn (eds.), *Myths, Misdeeds, and Misunderstandings: The Roots of Conflict in US–Mexican Relations*. Wilmington: SR Books.

Vedoveli, Paula. 2019. *Private Capital, Public Credit: Brazil, Argentina, and the Problem of Credibility in International Capital Markets, 1852–1914*. Ph.D. thesis, Princeton University.

Vega Carballo, José Luis. 1981. *Orden y Progreso: La Formación del Estado Nacional en Costa Rica*. San José: Instituto Centroamericano de Administración Pública.

Velasco, Omar. 2018. *El Gran General: Más Allá del Poder y la Gloria*. Bogotá: Editorial Universidad del Cauca.

Villela, André A. 1999. *The Political Economy of Money and Banking in Imperial Brazil 1850–1870*. Ph.D. thesis, London School of Economics and Political Science, London.

Visoni-Alonzo, Gilmar, and Jacob, Frank. 2017. *Latin America's Martial Age: Conflict and Warfare in the Long Nineteenth Century*. Wurzburg: Königshausen & Neumann.

Vom Hau, Matthias. 2012. Nationalism and War Commemoration: A Latin American Exceptionalism? *Nations and Nationalism*, **19**(1), 146–166.

Vu, Tuong. 2010. *Paths to Development in Asia: South Korea, Vietnam, China, and Indonesia*. New York: Cambridge University Press.

Wallensteen, Peter. 2015. *Quality Peace: Strategic Peacebuilding and World Order*. Oxford: Oxford University Press.

Walter, Barbara F. 1997. The Critical Barrier to Civil War Settlement. *International Organization*, **51**(3), 335–364.

Waltz, Kenneth. 1979. *Theory of International Politics*. Boston: Addison Wesley.

1981. The Spread of Nuclear Weapons: More May Be Better. *Adelphi Papers*, **171**, 2–34.

Warren, Harris. 1949. *Paraguay: An Informal History*. Norman: University of Oklahoma Press.

1985. *Rebirth of the Paraguayan Republic: The First Colorado Era, 1878–1904*. Pittsburgh: University of Pittsburgh Press.

Wayman, Frank W., Singer, J. David, and Goertz, Gary. 1983. Capabilities, Allocations, and Success in Militarized Disputes and Wars, 1816–1976. *International Studies Quarterly*, **27**(4), 497–515.

Weber, Max. 1949. *The Methodology of the Social Sciences*. New York: Free Press.
1958. *From Max Weber: Essays in Sociology*. New York: Oxford University Press.
1978. *Economy and Society: An Outline of Interpretive Sociology*, vol. 1. Berkeley: University of California Press.
1994. *Political Writings*. New York: Cambridge University Press.
Weeks, Charles A. 1987. *The Juárez Myth in Mexico*. Tuscaloosa: University of Alabama Press.
Werlich, Peter. 1978. *Peru: A Short History*. Carbondale: Southern Illinois University.
Werneck Sodre, Nelson. 1968. *Formação Histórica do Brasil*. Brasília: Editora Brasiliense.
1979. *História militar do Brasil*. Rio de Janeiro: Civilização Brasileira.
Whigham, Thomas L. 2002. *The Paraguayan War: Causes and Early Conduct*, vol. 1. Lincoln: University of Nebraska Press.
2016. Aspectos Clave de la Larga Resistencia del Paraguay: Disciplina Militar, Cohesión Burocrática y Egomanía Indomada del Mariscal López. Pages 10–36 of: Garavaglia, Juan Carlos, and Fradkin, Raul (eds.), *A 150 Años de la Guerra de la Triple Alianza con el Paraguay*. Buenos Aires: Prometeo.
Whigham, Thomas L., and Potthast, Barbara. 1999. The Paraguayan Rosetta Stone: New Insights into the Demographics of the Paraguayan War, 1864–1870. *Latin American Research Review*, 34(1), 174–186.
White, Richard Alan. 1989. *La primera revolución popular en América: Paraguay (1810–1840)*. Asunción: Carlos Schauman.
Williams, John Hoyt. 1979. *The Rise and Fall of the Paraguayan Republic, 1800–1870*. Austin: University of Texas Press.
Wilson, Peter. 2004. Latin America's Total War. *History Today*, 54(5), 2–12.
Wimmer, Andreas, and Min, Brian. 2009. The Location and Purpose of Wars around the World: A New Global Dataset, 1816–2001. *International Interactions*, 35(4), 390–417.
Wood, James. 2011. *The Society of Equality: Popular Republicanism and Democracy in Santiago de Chile, 1818–1851*. Albuquerque: University of New Mexico Press.
Woodward, Ralph Lee. 1993. *Rafael Carrera and the Emergence of the Republic of Guatemala, 1821–1871*. Athens: University of Georgia Press.
Wright, Henry T. 1977. Recent Research on the Origin of the State. *Annual Review of Anthropology*, 6(1), 379–397.
Young, Eric. 1988. Islands in the Storm: Quiet Cities and Violent Countrysides in the Mexican Independence Era. *Past and Present*, 1(118), 130–155.
Zacher, Mark W. 2001. The Territorial Integrity Norm: International Boundaries and the Use of Force. *International Organization*, 55(2), 215–250.
Zepeda, Beatriz. 2009. *Ecuador: Relaciones exteriores a la luz del bicentenario*. Quito: Flacso.
Ziblatt, Daniel. 2008. *Structuring the State: The Formation of Italy and Germany and the Puzzle of Federalism*. Princeton: Princeton University Press.
Zum Felde, Alberto. 1967. *Proceso Histórico del Uruguay*. Montevideo: Arca.

Index

For EU product safety concerns, contact us at Calle de José Abascal, 56–1°, 28003 Madrid, Spain or eugpsr@cambridge.org.

www.ingramcontent.com/pod-product-compliance
Lightning Source LLC
Chambersburg PA
CBHW032223180525
26900CB00002B/28

* 9 7 8 1 0 0 9 4 4 2 1 3 8 *